Organizational Behavior

BUAD 304

| PEARSON COLLECTIONS |

PEARSON

Cover Art: Courtesy of Getty Images

2   16

Attention bookstores: For permission to return any unsold stock, contact us at pe-uscustomreturns@pearson.com

Pearson Learning Solutions, 501 Boylston Street, Suite 900, Boston, MA 02116

A Pearson Education Company
www.pearsoned.com

ISBN 10: 1269496344

ISBN 13: 9781269496346

Printed in the USA

Table of Contents

Module 5: Organizational Structure and Culture

Module 6: Organizational Change

Copyright Acknowledgements

On the Folly of Rewarding A, While Hoping for B

STEVEN KERR
Ohio State University

Illustrations are presented from society in general, and from organizations in particular, of reward systems that "pay off" for one behavior even though the rewarder hopes dearly for another. Portions of the reward systems of a manufacturing company and an insurance firm are examined and the consequences discussed.

Whether dealing with monkeys, rats, or human beings, it is hardly controversial to state that most organisms seek information concerning what activities are rewarded, and then seek to do (or at least pretend to do) those things, often to the virtual exclusion of activities not rewarded. The extent to which this occurs of course will depend on the perceived attractiveness of the rewards offered, but neither operant nor expectancy theorists would quarrel with the essence of this notion.

Nevertheless, numerous examples exist of reward systems that are fouled up in that behaviors which are rewarded are those which the rewarder is trying to *discourage*, while the behavior he desires is not being rewarded at all.

In an effort to understand and explain this phenomenon, this paper presents examples from society, from organizations in general, and from profit making firms in particular. Data from a manufacturing company and information from an insurance firm are examined to demonstrate the consequences of such reward systems for the organizations involved, and possible reasons why such reward systems continue to exist are considered.

SOCIETAL EXAMPLES

Politics

Official goals are "purposely vague and general and do not indicate . . . the host of decisions that must be made among alternative ways of achieving official goals and the priority of multiple goals . . ." (8, p. 66). They

Steven Kerr (Ph.D.—City University of New York) is Associate Professor of Organizational Behavior, College of Administrative Science, The Ohio State University, Columbus, Ohio.

usually may be relied on to offend absolutely no one, and in this sense can be considered high acceptance, low quality goals. An example might be "build better schools." Operative goals are higher in quality but lower in acceptance, since they specify where the money will come from, what alternative goals will be ignored, etc.

The American citizenry supposedly wants its candidates for public office to set forth operative goals, making their proposed programs "perfectly clear," specifying sources and uses of funds, etc. However, since operative goals are lower in acceptance, and since aspirants to public office need acceptance (from at least 50.1 percent of the people), most politicians prefer to speak only of official goals, at least until after the election. They of course would agree to speak at the operative level if "punished" for not doing so. The electorate could do this by refusing to support candidates who do not speak at the operative level.

Instead, however, the American voter typically punishes (withholds support from) candidates who frankly discuss where the money will come from, rewards politicians who speak only of official goals, but hopes that candidates (despite the reward system) will discuss the issues operatively. It is academic whether it was moral for Nixon, for example, to refuse to discuss his 1968 "secret plan" to end the Vietnam war, his 1972 operative goals concerning the lifting of price controls, the reshuffling of his cabinet, etc. The point is that the reward system made such refusal rational.

It seems worth mentioning that no manuscript can adequately define what is "moral" and what is not. However, examination of costs and benefits, combined with knowledge of what motivates a particular individual, often will suffice to determine what for him is "rational."[1] If the reward system is so designed that it is irrational to be moral, this does not necessarily mean that immortality will result. But is this not asking for trouble?

War

If some oversimplification may be permitted, let it be assumed that the primary goal of the organization (Pentagon, Luftwaffe, or whatever) is to win. Let it be assumed further that the primary goal of most individuals on the front lines is to get home alive. Then there appears to be an important conflict in goals—personally rational behavior by those at the bottom will endanger goal attainment by those at the top.

But not necessarily! It depends on how the reward system is set up. The Vietnam war was indeed a study of disobedience and rebellion, with terms such as "fragging" (killing one's own commanding officer) and "search and evade" becoming part of the military vocabulary. The difference in subordinates' acceptance of authority between World War II and Vietnam is reported to be considerable, and veterans of the Second World War often

---

[1] In Simon's (10, pp. 76-77) terms, a decision is "subjectively rational" if it maximizes an individual's valued outcomes so far as his knowledge permits. A decision is "personally rational" if it is oriented toward the individual's goals.

have been quoted as being outraged at the mutinous actions of many American soldiers in Vietnam.

Consider, however, some critical differences in the reward system in use during the two conflicts. What did the GI in World War II want? To go home. And when did he get to go home? When the war was won! If he disobeyed the orders to clean out the trenches and take the hills, the war would not be won and he would not go home. Furthermore, what were his chances of attaining his goal (getting home alive) if he obeyed the orders compared to his chances if he did not? What is being suggested is that the rational soldier in World War II, *whether patriotic or not*, probably found it expedient to obey.

Consider the reward system in use in Vietnam. What did the man at the bottom want? To go home. And when did he get to go home? When his tour of duty was over! This was the case *whether or not* the war was won. Furthermore, concerning the relative chance of getting home alive by obeying orders compared to the chance if they were disobeyed, it is worth noting that a mutineer in Vietnam was far more likely to be assigned rest and rehabilitation (on the assumption that fatigue was the cause) than he was to suffer any negative consequence.

In his description of the "zone of indifference," Barnard stated that "a person can and will accept a communication as authoritative only when . . . at the time of his decision, he believes it to be compatible with his personal interests as a whole" (1, p. 165). In light of the reward system used in Vietnam, would it not have been personally irrational for some orders to have been obeyed? Was not the military implementing a system which *rewarded* disobedience, while *hoping* that soldiers (despite the reward system) would obey orders?

Medicine

Theoretically, a physician can make either of two types of error, and intuitively one seems as bad as the other. A doctor can pronounce a patient sick when he is actually well, thus causing him needless anxiety and expense, curtailment of enjoyable foods and activities, and even physical danger by subjecting him to needless medication and surgery. Alternately, a doctor can label a sick person well, and thus avoid treating what may be a serious, even fatal ailment. It might be natural to conclude that physicians seek to minimize both types of error.

Such a conclusion would be wrong.[2] It is estimated that numerous Americans are presently afflicted with iatrogenic (physican *caused*) illnesses (9). This occurs when the doctor is approached by someone complaining of a few stray symptoms. The doctor classifies and organizes these symptoms, gives them a name, and obligingly tells the patient what further symptoms may be

---

[2] In one study (4) of 14,867 films for signs of tuberculosis, 1,216 positive readings turned out to be clinically negative; only 24 negative readings proved clinically active, a ratio of 50 to 1.

expected. This information often acts as a self-fulfilling prophecy, with the result that from that day on the patient for all practical purposes is sick.

Why does this happen? Why are physicians so reluctant to sustain a type 2 error (pronouncing a sick person well) that they will tolerate many type 1 errors? Again, a look at the reward system is needed. The punishments for a type 2 error are real: guilt, embarrassment, and the threat of lawsuit and scandal. On the other hand, a type 1 error (labeling a well person sick) "is sometimes seen as sound clinical practice, indicating a healthy conservative approach to medicine" (9, p. 69). Type 1 errors also are likely to generate increased income and a stream of steady customers who, being well in a limited physiological sense, will not embarrass the doctor by dying abruptly.

Fellow physicians and the general public therefore are really *rewarding* type 1 errors and at the same time *hoping* fervently that doctors will try not to make them.

GENERAL ORGANIZATIONAL EXAMPLES

Rehabilitation Centers and Orphanages

In terms of the prime beneficiary classification (2, p. 42) organizations such as these are supposed to exist for the "public-in-contact," that is, clients. The orphanage therefore theoretically is interested in placing as many children as possible in good homes. However, often orphanages surround themselves with so many rules concerning adoption that it is nearly impossible to pry a child out of the place. Orphanages may deny adoption unless the applicants are a married couple, both of the same religion as the child, without history of emotional or vocational instability, with a specified minimum income and a private room for the child, etc.

If the primary goal is to place children in good homes, then the rules ought to constitute means toward that goal. Goal displacement results when these "means become ends-in-themselves that displace the original goals" (2, p. 229).

To some extent these rules are required by law. But the influence of the reward system on the orphanage's management should not be ignored. Consider, for example, that the:

1. Number of children enrolled often is the most important determinant of the size of the allocated budget.
2. Number of children under the director's care also will affect the size of his staff.
3. Total organizational size will determine largely the director's prestige at the annual conventions, in the community, etc.

Therefore, to the extent that staff size, total budget, and personal prestige are valued by the orphanage's executive personnel, it becomes rational for them to make it difficult for children to be adopted. After all, who wants to be the director of the smallest orphanage in the state?

If the reward system errs in the opposite direction, paying off only for placements, extensive goal displacement again is likely to result. A common example of vocational rehabilitation in many states, for example, consists of placing someone in a job for which he has little interest and few qualifications, for two months or so, and then "rehabilitating" him again in another position. Such behavior is quite consistent with the prevailing reward system, which pays off for the number of individuals placed in any position for 60 days or more. Rehabilitation counselors also confess to competing with one another to place relatively skilled clients, sometimes ignoring persons with few skills who would be harder to place. Extensively disabled clients find that counselors often prefer to work with those whose disabilities are less severe.[3]

Universities

Society *hopes* that teachers will not neglect their teaching responsibilities but *rewards* them almost entirely for research and publications. This is most true at the large and prestigious universities. Cliches such as "good research and good teaching go together" notwithstanding, professors often find that they must choose between teaching and research oriented activities when allocating their time. Rewards for good teaching usually are limited to outstanding teacher awards, which are given to only a small percentage of good teachers and which usually bestow little money and fleeting prestige. Punishments for poor teaching also are rare.

Rewards for research and publications, on the other hand, and punishments for failure to accomplish these, are commonly administered by universities at which teachers are employed. Furthermore, publication oriented resumés usually will be well received at other universities, whereas teaching credentials, harder to document and quantify, are much less transferable. Consequently it is rational for university teachers to concentrate on research, even if to the detriment of teaching and at the expense of their students.

By the same token, it is rational for students to act based upon the goal displacement which has occurred within universities concerning what they are rewarded for. If it is assumed that a primary goal of a university is to transfer knowledge from teacher to student, then grades become identifiable as a means toward that goal, serving as motivational, control, and feedback devices to expedite the knowledge transfer. Instead, however, the grades themselves have become much more important for entrance to graduate school, successful employment, tuition refunds, parental respect, etc., than the knowledge or lack of knowledge they are supposed to signify.

It therefore should come as no surprise that information has surfaced in recent years concerning fraternity files for examinations, term paper writing services, organized cheating at the service academies, and the like. Such

---

[3] Personal interviews conducted during 1972-1973.

5

activities constitute a personally rational response to a reward system which pays off for grades rather than knowledge.

BUSINESS RELATED EXAMPLES

Ecology

Assume that the president of XYZ Corporation is confronted with the following alternatives:

1. Spend $11 million for antipollution equipment to keep from poisoning fish in the river adjacent to the plant; or
2. Do nothing, in violation of the law, and assume a one in ten chance of being caught, with a resultant $1 million fine plus the necessity of buying the equipment.

Under this not unrealistic set of choices it requires no linear program to determine that XYZ Corporation can maximize its probabilities by flouting the law. Add the fact that XYZ's president is probably being rewarded (by creditors, stockholders, and other salient parts of his task environment) according to criteria totally unrelated to the number of fish poisoned, and his probable course of action becomes clear.

Evaluation of Training

It is axiomatic that those who care about a firm's well-being should insist that the organization get fair value for its expenditures. Yet it is commonly known that firms seldom bother to evaluate a new GRID, MBO, job enrichment program, or whatever, to see if the company is getting its money's worth. Why? Certainly it is not because people have not pointed out that this situation exists; numerous practitioner oriented articles are written each year to just this point.

The individuals (whether in personnel, manpower planning, or wherever) who normally would be responsible for conducting such evaluations are the same ones often charged with introducing the change effort in the first place. Having convinced top management to spend the money, they usually are quite animated afterwards in collecting arigorous vignettes and anecdotes about how successful the program was. The last thing many desire is a formal, systematic, and revealing evaluation. Although members of top management may actually *hope* for such systematic evaluation, their reward systems continue to *reward* ignorance in this area. And if the personnel department abdicates its responsibility, who is to step into the breach? The change agent himself? Hardly! He is likely to be too busy collecting anecdotal "evidence" of his own, for use with his next client.

Miscellaneous

Many additional examples could be cited of systems which in fact are rewarding behaviors other than those supposedly desired by the rewarder. A few of these are described briefly below.

Most coaches disdain to discuss individual accomplishments, preferring to speak of teamwork, proper attitude, and a one-for-all spirit. Usually, however, rewards are distributed according to individual performance. The college basketball player who feeds his teammates instead of shooting will not compile impressive scoring statistics and is less likely to be drafted by the pros. The ballplayer who hits to right field to advance the runners will win neither the batting nor home run titles, and will be offered smaller raises. It therefore is rational for players to think of themselves first, and the team second.

In business organizations where rewards are dispensed for unit performance or for individual goals achieved, without regard for overall effectiveness, similar attitudes often are observed. Under most Management by Objectives (MBO) systems, goals in areas where quantification is difficult often go unspecified. The organization therefore often is in a position where it *hopes* for employee effort in the areas of team building, interpersonal relations, creativity, etc., but it formally *rewards* none of these. In cases where promotions and raises are formally tied to MBO, the system itself contains a paradox in that it "asks employees to set challenging, risky goals, only to face smaller paychecks and possibly damaged careers if these goals are not accomplished" (5, p. 40).

It is *hoped* that administrators will pay attention to long run costs and opportunities and will institute programs which will bear fruit later on. However, many organizational reward systems pay off for short run sales and earnings only. Under such circumstances it is personally rational for officials to sacrifice long term growth and profit (by selling off equipment and property, or by stifling research and development) for short term advantages. This probably is most pertinent in the public sector, with the result that many public officials are unwilling to implement programs which will not show benefits by election time.

As a final, clear-cut example of a fouled-up reward system, consider the cost-plus contract or its next of kin, the allocation of next year's budget as a direct function of this year's expenditures. It probably is conceivable that those who award such budgets and contracts really hope for economy and prudence in spending. It is obvious, however, that adopting the proverb "to him who spends shall more be given." rewards not economy, but spending itself.

TWO COMPANIES' EXPERIENCES

A Manufacturing Organization

A midwest manufacturer of industrial goods had been troubled for some time by aspects of its organizational climate it believed dysfunctional. For research purposes, interviews were conducted with many employees and a questionnaire was administered on a companywide basis, including plants and offices in several American and Canadian locations. The company strongly encouraged employee participation in the survey, and made available time and space during the workday for completion of the instrument. All employees in attendance during the day of the survey completed the questionnaire. All instruments were collected directly by the researcher, who personally administered each session. Since no one employed by the firm handled the questionnaires, and since respondent names were not asked for, it seems likely that the pledge of anonymity given was believed.

A modified version of the Expect Approval scale (7) was included as part of the questionnaire. The instrument asked respondents to indicate the degree of approval or disapproval they could expect if they performed each of the described actions. A seven point Likert scale was used, with one indicating that the action would probably bring strong disapproval and seven signifying likely strong approval.

Although normative data for this scale from studies of other organizations are unavailable, it is possible to examine fruitfully the data obtained from this survey in several ways. First, it may be worth noting that the questionnaire data corresponded closely to information gathered through interviews. Furthermore, as can be seen from the results summarized in Table 1, sizable differences between various work units, and between employees at different job levels within the same work unit, were obtained. This suggests that response bias effects (social desirability in particular loomed as a potential concern) are not likely to be severe.

Most importantly, comparisons between scores obtained on the Expect Approval scale and a statement of problems which were the reason for the

TABLE 1

Summary of Two Divisions' Data Relevant to Conforming and Risk-Avoidance Behaviors (Extent to Which Subjects Expect Approval)

Dimension	Item	Division and Sample	Total Responses	Percentage of Workers Responding		
				1, 2, or 3 Disapproval	4	5, 6, or 7 Approval
Risk Avoidance	Making a risky decision based on the best information available at the time, but which turns out wrong.	A, levels 1-4 (lowest)	127	61	25	14
		A, levels 5-8	172	46	31	23
		A, levels 9 and above	17	41	30	30
		B, levels 1-4 (lowest)	31	58	26	16
		B, levels 5-8	19	42	42	16
		B, levels 9 and above	10	50	20	30

TABLE 1 (Continued)

Dimension	Item	Division and Sample	Total Responses	Percentage of Workers Responding		
				1, 2, or 3 Disapproval	4	5, 6, or 7 Approval
Risk Avoidance (Continued)	Setting extremely high and challenging standards and goals, and then narrowly failing to make them.	A, levels 1-4	122	47	28	25
		A, levels 5-8	168	33	26	41
		A, levels 9+	17	24	6	70
		B, levels 1-4	31	48	23	29
		B, levels 5-8	18	17	33	50
		B, levels 9+	10	30	0	70
	Setting goals which are extremely easy to make and then making them.	A, levels 1-4	124	35	30	35
		A, levels 5-8	171	47	27	26
		A, levels 9+	17	70	24	6
		B, levels 1-4	31	58	26	16
		B, levels 5-8	19	63	16	21
		B, levels 9+	10	80	0	20
Conformity	Being a "yes man" and always agreeing with the boss.	A, levels 1-4	126	46	17	37
		A, levels 5-8	180	54	14	31
		A, levels 9+	17	88	12	0
		B, levels 1-4	32	53	28	19
		B, levels 5-8	19	68	21	11
		B, levels 9+	10	80	10	10
	Always going along with the majority.	A, levels 1-4	125	40	25	35
		A, levels 5-8	173	47	21	32
		A, levels 9+	17	70	12	18
		B, levels 1-4	31	61	23	16
		B, levels 5-8	19	68	11	21
		B, levels 9+	10	80	10	10
	Being careful to stay on the good side of everyone, so that everyone agrees that you are a great guy.	A, levels 1-4	124	45	18	37
		A, levels 5-8	173	45	22	33
		A, levels 9+	17	64	6	30
		B, levels 1-4	31	54	23	23
		B, levels 5-8	19	73	11	16
		B, levels 9+	10	80	10	10

survey revealed that the same behaviors which managers in each division thought dysfunctional were those which lower level employees claimed were rewarded. As compared to job levels 1 to 8 in Division B (see Table 1), those in Division A claimed a much higher acceptance by management of "conforming" activities. Between 31 and 37 percent of Division A employees at levels 1-8 stated that going along with the majority, agreeing with the boss, and staying on everyone's good side brought approval; only once (level 5-8 responses to one of the three items) did a majority suggest that such actions would generate disapproval.

Furthermore, responses from Division A workers at levels 1-4 indicate that behaviors geared toward risk avoidance were as likely to be rewarded as to be punished. Only at job levels 9 and above was it apparent that the reward system was positively reinforcing behaviors desired by top management. Overall, the same "tendencies toward conservatism and applepolishing at the lower levels" which divisional management had complained about during the interviews were those claimed by subordinates to be the most rational course of action in light of the existing reward system. Management apparently was not getting the behaviors it was *hoping* for, but it certainly was getting the behaviors it was perceived by subordinates to be *rewarding*.

An Insurance Firm

The Group Health Claims Division of a large eastern insurance company provides another rich illustration of a reward system which reinforces behaviors not desired by top management.

Attempting to measure and reward accuracy in paying surgical claims, the firm systematically keeps track of the number of returned checks and letters of complaint received from policyholders. However, underpayments are likely to provoke cries of outrage from the insured, while overpayments often are accepted in courteous silence. Since it often is impossible to tell from the physician's statement which of two surgical procedures, with different allowable benefits, was performed, and since writing for clarifications will interfere with other standards used by the firm concerning "percentage of claims paid within two days of receipt," the new hire in more than one claims section is soon acquainted with the informal norm: "When in doubt, pay it out!"

The situation would be even worse were it not for the fact that other features of the firm's reward system tend to neutralize those described. For example, annual "merit" increases are given to all employees, in one of the following three amounts:

1. If the worker is "outstanding" (a select category, into which no more than two employees per section may be placed): 5 percent
2. If the worker is "above average" (normally all workers not "outstanding" are so rated): 4 percent

3. If the worker commits gross acts of negligence and irresponsibility
   for which he might be discharged in many other companies: 3 percent.
Now, since (a) the difference between the 5 percent theoretically attainable
through hard work and the 4 percent attainable merely by living until the
review date is small and (b) since insurance firms seldom dispense much
of a salary increase in cash (rather, the worker's insurance benefits increase,
causing him to be further overinsured), many employees are rather indifferent to the possibility of obtaining the extra one percent reward and
therefore tend to ignore the norm concerning indiscriminant payments.

However, most employees are not indifferent to the rule which states that,
should absences or latenesses total three or more in any six-month period,
the entire 4 or 5 percent due at the next "merit" review must be forfeited.
In this sense the firm may be described as *hoping* for performance, while
rewarding attendance. What it gets, of course, is attendance. (If the absence-
lateness rule appears to the reader to be stringent, it really is not. The
company counts "times" rather than "days" absent, and a ten-day absence
therefore counts the same as one lasting two days. A worker in danger of
accumulating a third absence within six months merely has to remain ill
(away from work) during his second absence until his first absence is more
than six months old. The limiting factor is that at some point his salary
ceases, and his sickness benefits take over. This usually is sufficient to get
the younger workers to return, but for those with 20 or more years' service,
the company provides sickness benefits of 90 percent of normal salary,
tax-free! Therefore . . . .)

CAUSES

Extremely diverse instances of systems which reward behavior A
although the rewarder apparently hopes for behavior B have been given.
These are useful to illustrate the breadth and magnitude of the phenomenon,
but the diversity increases the difficulty of determining commonalities and
establishing causes. However, four general factors may be pertinent to an
explanation of why fouled up reward systems seem to be so prevelant.

Fascination with an "Objective" Criterion

It has been mentioned elsewhere that:

> Most "objective" measures of productivity are objective only in that their
> subjective elements are a) determined in advance, rather than coming into play
> at the time of the formal evaluation, and b) well concealed on the rating
> instrument itself. Thus industrial firms seeking to devise objective rating
> systems first decide, in an arbitrary manner, what dimensions are to be rated,
> . . . usually including some items having little to do with organizational
> effectiveness while excluding others that do. Only then does Personnel Division
> churn out official-looking documents on which all dimensions chosen to be
> rated are assigned point values, categories, or whatever (6, p. 92).

Nonetheless, many individuals seek to establish simple, quantifiable standards against which to measure and reward performance. Such efforts may

be successful in highly predictable areas within an organization, but are likely to cause goal displacement when applied anywhere else. Overconcern with attendance and lateness in the insurance firm and with number of people placed in the vocational rehabilitation division may have been largely responsible for the problems described in those organizations.

Overemphasis on Highly Visible Behaviors

Difficulties often stem from the fact that some parts of the task are highly visible while other parts are not. For example, publications are easier to demonstrate than teaching, and scoring baskets and hitting home runs are more readily observable than feeding teammates and advancing base runners. Similarly, the adverse consequences of pronouncing a sick person well are more visible than those sustained by labeling a well person sick. Team-building and creativity are other examples of behaviors which may not be rewarded simply because they are hard to observe.

Hypocrisy

In some of the instances described the rewarder may have been getting the desired behavior, notwithstanding claims that the behavior was not desired. This may be true, for example, of management's attitude toward apple-polishing in the manufacturing firm (a behavior which subordinates felt was rewarded, despite management's avowed dislike of the practice). This also may explain politicians' unwillingness to revise the penalties for disobedience of ecology laws, and the failure of top management to devise reward systems which would cause systematic evaluation of training and development programs.

Emphasis on Morality or Equity Rather than Efficiency

Sometimes consideration of other factors prevents the establishment of a system which rewards behaviors desired by the rewarder. The felt obligation of many Americans to vote for one candidate or another, for example, may impair their ability to withhold support from politicians who refuse to discuss the issues. Similarly, the concern for spreading the risks and costs of wartime military service may outweigh the advantage to be obtained by commiting personnel to combat until the war is over.

It should be noted that only with respect to the first two causes are reward systems really paying off for other than desired behaviors. In the case of the third and fourth causes the system *is* rewarding behaviors desired by the rewarder, and the systems are fouled up only from the standpoints of those who believe the rewarder's public statements (cause 3), or those who seek to maximize efficiency rather than other outcomes (cause 4).

CONCLUSIONS

Modern organization theory requires a recognition that the members of organizations and society possess divergent goals and motives. It therefore is unlikely that managers and their subordinates will seek the same outcomes. Three possible remedies for this potential problem are suggested.

Selection

It is theoretically possible for organizations to employ only those individuals whose goals and motives are wholly consonant with those of management. In such cases the same behaviors judged by subordinates to be rational would be perceived by management as desirable. State-of-the-art reviews of selection techniques, however, provide scant grounds for hope that such an approach would be successful (for example, see 12).

Training

Another theoretical alternative is for the organization to admit those employees whose goals are not consonant with those of management and then, through training, socialization, or whatever, alter employee goals to make them consonant. However, research on the effectiveness of such training programs, though limited, provides further grounds for pessimism (for example, see 3).

Altering the Reward System

What would have been the result if:

1. Nixon had been assured by his advisors that he could not win re-election except by discussing the issues in detail?
2. Physicians' conduct was subjected to regular examination by review boards for type 1 errors (calling healthy people ill) and to penalties (fines, censure, etc.) for errors of either type?
3. The President of XYZ Corporation had to choose between (a) spending $11 million dollars for antipollution equipment, and (b) incurring a fifty-fifty chance of going to jail for five years?

Managers who complain that their workers are not motivated might do well to consider the possibility that they have installed reward systems which are paying off for behaviors other than those they are seeking. This, in part, is what happened in Vietnam, and this is what regularly frustrates societal efforts to bring about honest politicians, civic-minded managers, etc. This certainly is what happened in both the manufacturing and the insurance companies.

A first step for such managers might be to find out what behaviors currently are being rewarded. Perhaps an instrument similar to that used in the manufacturing firm could be useful for this purpose. Chances are excellent that these managers will be surprised by what they find—that their firms are not rewarding what they assume they are. In fact, such undesirable behavior by organizational members as they have observed may be explained largely by the reward systems in use.

This is not to say that all organizational behavior is determined by formal rewards and punishments. Certainly it is true that in the absence of formal reinforcement some soldiers will be patriotic, some presidents will be ecology minded, and some orphanage directors will care about children. The point, however, is that in such cases the rewarder is not *causing* the behaviors desired but is only a fortunate bystander. For an organization to *act* upon its members, the formal reward system should positively reinforce desired behaviors, not constitute an obstacle to be overcome.

It might be wise to underscore the obvious fact that there is nothing really new in what has been said. In both theory and practice these matters have been mentioned before. Thus in many states Good Samaritan laws have been installed to protect doctors who stop to assist a stricken motorist. In states without such laws it is commonplace for doctors to refuse to stop, for fear of involvement in a subsequent lawsuit. In college basketball additional penalties have been instituted against players who foul their opponents deliberately. It has long been argued by Milton Friedman and others that penalties should be altered so as to make it irrational to disobey the ecology laws, and so on.

By altering the reward system the organization escapes the necessity of selecting only desirable people or of trying to alter undesirable ones. In Skinnerian terms (as described in 11, p. 704), "As for responsibility and goodness—as commonly defined—no one . . . would want or need them. They refer to a man's behaving well despite the absence of positive reinforcement that is obviously sufficient to explain it. Where such reinforcement exists, 'no one needs goodness.' "

REFERENCES

1. Barnard, Chester I. *The Functions of the Executive* (Cambridge, Mass.: Harvard University Press, 1964).
2. Blau, Peter M., and W. Richard Scott. *Formal Organizations* (San Francisco: Chandler, 1962).
3. Fiedler, Fred E. "Predicting the Effects of Leadership Training and Experience from the Contingency Model," *Journal of Applied Psychology*, Vol. 56 (1972), 114-119.
4. Garland, L. H. "Studies of the Accuracy of Diagnostic Procedures," *American Journal Roentgenological, Radium Therapy Nuclear Medicine*, Vol. 82 (1959), 25-38.
5. Kerr, Steven. "Some Modifications in MBO as an OD Strategy," *Academy of Management Proceedings*, 1973, pp. 39-42.
6. Kerr, Steven. "What Price Objectivity?" *American Sociologist*, Vol. 8 (1973), 92-93.
7. Litwin, G. H., and R. A. Stringer, Jr. *Motivation and Organizational Climate* (Boston: Harvard University Press, 1968).
8. Perrow, Charles. "The Analysis of Goals in Complex Organizations," in A. Etzioni (Ed.), *Readings on Modern Organizations* (Englewood Cliffs, N. J.: Prentice-Hall, 1969).
9. Scheff, Thomas J. "Decision Rules, Types of Error, and Their Consequences in Medical Diagnosis," in F. Massarik and P. Ratoosh (Eds.), *Mathematical Explorations in Behavioral Science* (Homewood, Ill.: Irwin, 1965).
10. Simon, Herbert A. *Administrative Behavior* (New York: Free Press, 1957).

11. Swanson, G. E. "Review Symposium: Beyond Freedom and Dignity," *American Journal of Sociology*, Vol. 78 (1972), 702-705.
12. Webster, E. *Decision Making in the Employment Interview* (Montreal: Industrial Relations Center, McGill University, 1964).

Part B

Perceiving Ourselves and the Work Situation

12. The Self-Perception of Motivation[1]

Barry M. Staw

Within the area of interpersonal perception, it has been noted (Heider, 1958) that an individual may infer the causes of another's actions to be a function of personal and environmental force:

$$Action = f (personal\ force + environmental\ force)$$

This is quite close to saying that individuals attempt to determine whether another person is intrinsically motivated to perform an activity (action due to personal force), or extrinsically motivated (action due to environmental force), or both. The extent to which an individual will infer intrinsic motivation on the part of another is predicted to be affected by the clarity and strength of external forces within the situation (Jones & Davis, 1965; Jones & Nisbett, 1971; Kelley, 1967). When there are strong forces bearing on the individual to perform an activity, there is little reason to assume that a behavior is self-determined, whereas a high level of intrinsic motivation might be inferred if environmental force is minimal. Several studies dealing with interpersonal perception have supported this general conclusion (Jones, Davis, & Gergen, 1961; Jones & Harris, 1967; Strickland, 1958; Thibaut & Riecken, 1955).

Bem (1967a, b) extrapolated this interpersonal theory of causal attribution to the study of self-perception or how one views his *own* behavior within a social context. Bem hypothesized that the extent to which external pressures are sufficiently strong to account for one's behavior will determine the likelihood that a person will attribute his own actions to internal causes. Thus if a person acts under strong external rewards or punishments, he is likely to assume that his behavior is under external control. However, if extrinsic contingencies are not strong

157

or salient, the individual is likely to assume that his behavior is due to his own interest in the activity or that his behavior is intrinsically motivated. De Charms has made a similar point in his discussion of an individual's perception of personal causation (1968, p. 328):

> As a first approximation, we propose that whenever a person experiences himself to be the locus of causality for his own behavior (to be an Origin), he will consider himself to be intrinsically motivated. Conversely, when a person perceives the locus of causality for his behavior to be external to himself (that he is a Pawn), he will consider himself to be extrinsically motivated.

De Charms emphasized that the individual may attempt psychologically to label his actions on the basis of whether or not he has been instrumental in affecting his own behavior; that is, whether his behavior has been intrinsically or extrinsically motivated.

THE CASE FOR A NEGATIVE RELATIONSHIP BETWEEN INTRINSIC AND EXTRINSIC MOTIVATION

The self-perception approach to intrinsic and extrinsic motivation leads to the conclusion that there may be a negative interrelationship between these two motivational factors. The basis for this prediction stems from the assumption that individuals may work backward from their own actions in inferring sources of causation (Bem 1967a, b; 1972). For example, if external pressures on an individual are so high that they would ordinarily cause him to perform a given task regardless of the internal characteristics of the activity, then the individual might logically infer that he is extrinsically motivated. In contrast, if external reward contingencies are extremely low or nonsalient, the individual might then infer that his behavior is intrinsically motivated. What is important is the fact that a person, in performing an activity, may *seek out* the probable cause of his own actions. Since behavior has no doubt been caused by something, it makes pragmatic, if not scientific, sense

for the person to conclude that the cause is personal (intrinsic) rather than extrinsic if he can find no external reasons for his actions.

Two particular situations provide robust tests of the self-perception prediction. One is a situation in which there is insufficient justification for a person's actions, a situation in which the intrinsic rewards for an activity are very low (e.g., a dull task) and there are no compensating extrinsic rewards (e.g., monetary payment, verbal praise). Although rationally, one ordinarily tries to avoid these situations, there are occasions when one is faced with the difficult question of "why did I do that?". The self-perception theory predicts that in situations of insufficient justification, the individual may cognitively reevaluate the intrinsic characteristics of an activity in order to justify or explain his own behavior. For example, if the individual performed a dull task for no external reward, he may "explain" his behavior by thinking that the task was not really so bad after all.

Sometimes a person may also be fortunate enough to be in a situation in which his behavior is oversufficiently justified. For example, a person may be asked to perform an interesting task and at the same time be lavishly paid for his efforts. In such situations, the self-perception theory predicts that the individual may actually reevaluate the activity in a downward direction. Since the external reward would be sufficient to motivate behavior by itself, the individual may mistakenly infer that he was extrinsically motivated to perform the activity. He may conclude that since he was forced to perform the task by an external reward, the task probably was not terribly satisfying in and of itself.

Figure 12.1 graphically depicts the situations of insufficient and overly sufficient justification. From the figure, we can see that the conceptual framework supporting self-perception theory raises several interesting issues. First, it appears from this analysis that there are only two fully stable attributions of behavior: (1) the perception of extrinsically motivated behavior in which the internal rewards associated with performing an activity

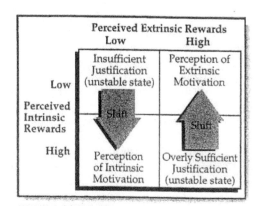

	Level of Extrinsic Rewards	
	Low	**High**
Low	Insufficient Justification (unstable perception)	Perception of Extrinsically Motivated Behavior
Level of Intrinsic Rewards **High**	Perception of Intrinsically Motivated Behavior	Overly Sufficient Justification (unstable perception)

FIGURE 12.1
A Conceptual of Self-Perception Theory

	Perceived Extrinsic Rewards	
	Low	**High**
Low	Insufficient Justification (unstable state)	Perception of Extrinsic Motivation
Perceived Intrinsic Rewards **High**	Perception of Intrinsic Motivation	Overly Sufficient Justification (unstable state)

FIGURE 12.2
A Schematic Analysis of the Self-Perception of Intrinsic and Extrinsic Motivation

are low while external rewards are high; and (2) the perception of intrinsically motivated behavior in which the task is inherently rewarding but external rewards are low. Furthermore, it appears that situations of insufficient justification (where intrinsic and extrinsic rewards are both low) and oversufficient justification (where intrinsic and extrinsic rewards are both high) involve unstable attribution states. As shown in Figure 12.2, individuals apparently resolve this attributional instability by altering their perceptions of intrinsic rewards associated with the task.

An interesting question posed by the self-perception analysis is why individuals are predicted to resolve an unstable attribution state by cognitively reevaluating a task in terms of its intrinsic rewards rather than changing their perceptions of extrinsic factors. The answer to this question may lie in the relative clarity of extrinsic as compared with intrinsic rewards, and the individual's relative ability to distort the two aspects of the situation. Within many settings (and especially within laboratory experiments) extrinsic rewards are generally quite salient and specific, whereas an individual must judge the intrinsic nature of a task for himself. Any shifts in the perception of intrinsic and extrinsic rewards may therefore be more likely to occur in the intrinsic factor. As shown in Figure 12.2 it is these predicted shifts in perceived intrinsic rewards that may theoretically underlie a negative relationship between intrinsic and extrinsic motivation.

Empirical Evidence: Insufficient Justification

Several studies have shown that when an individual is induced to commit an unpleasant act for little or no external justification, he may subsequently conclude that the act was not so unpleasant after all. Actually, the first scientific attempt to account for this phenomenon was the theory of cognitive dissonance (Festinger, 1957). It was predicted by dissonance theorists (Aronson, 1966; Festinger, 1957) that, since performing an unpleasant act for little or no reward would be an inconsistent (and seemingly irrational) thing to do, an individual might subsequently change his attitude toward the action in order to reduce the inconsistency or to appear rational. Bem's self-perception theory yields the same predictions but does not require one to posit that there is a motivating state such as dissonance reduction or self-rationalization. To Bem, since the individual examines his own behavior in light of the forces around him, he is simply more likely to come to the conclusion that his actions were intrinsically satisfying if they were performed under minimal external force.

In general, two types of experiments have been designed to assess the consequences of insufficient justification. One type of design has involved the performance of a dull task with varied levels of reward (Brehm & Cohen, 1962; Freedman, 1963; Weick, 1964; Weick & Penner, 1965). A second and more popular design has involved some form of counterattitudinal advocacy, either in terms of lying to a fellow subject about the nature of an experiment or writing an essay against one's position on an important issue (Carlsmith, Collins, & Helmreich, 1966; Festinger & Carlsmith, 1959; Linder, Cooper, & Jones, 1967). Fundamentally, the two types of designs are not vastly different. Both require subjects to perform an intrinsically dissatisfying act under varied levels of external inducement, and both predict that, in the low payment condition, the subject will change his attitude toward the activity (i.e., think more favorably of the task or begin to believe the position advocated).

The most well-known experiment designed to test the insufficient justification paradigm was conducted by Festinger and Carlsmith (1959). Subjects participated in a repetitive and dull task (putting spools on trays and turning pegs) and were asked to tell other waiting subjects that the experiment was enjoyable, interesting, and exciting. Half the experimental subjects were paid $1, and half were paid $20 for the counterattitudinal advocacy (and to be "on call" in the future), while control subjects were not paid and did not perform the counterattitudinal act. As predicted, the smaller the reward used to induce subjects to perform the counterattitudinal act, the greater the positive change in their attitudes toward the task. Although the interpretation of the results of this study have been actively debated (e.g., between dissonance and self-perception theorists) the basic findings have been replicated by a number of different researchers. It should be noted, however, that several mediating variables have also been isolated as being necessary for the attainment of this dissonance or self-perception effect: free choice (Linder, Cooper, & Jones, 1967), commitment or

irrevocability of behavior (Brehm & Cohen, 1962), and substantial adverse consequences (Calder, Ross, & Insko, 1973; Collins & Hoyt, 1972).

Recently, a strong test of the insufficient justification paradigm was also conducted outside the laboratory (Staw, 1974a). A natural field experiment was made possible by the fact that many young men had joined an organization (Army ROTC) in order to avoid being drafted, *and* these same young men subsequently received information (a draft lottery number) that changed the value of this organizational reward. Of particular relevance was the fact that those who joined ROTC did so not because of their intrinsic interest in the activities involved (e.g., drills, classes, and summer camp), but because they anticipated a substantial extrinsic reward (draft avoidance). As a result, those who received draft numbers that exempted them from military service subsequently faced a situation of low extrinsic as well as intrinsic rewards, a situation of insufficient justification. In contrast, persons who received draft numbers that made them vulnerable to military call-up found their participation in ROTC perfectly justified—they were still successfully avoiding the draft by remaining in the organization. To test the insufficient justification effect, both the attitudes and the performance of ROTC cadets were analyzed by draft number before and after the national draft lottery. The results showed that those in the insufficient justification situation enhanced their perception of ROTC and even performed somewhat better in ROTC courses after the lottery. It should be recognized, however, that this task enhancement occurred only under circumstances very similar to those previously found necessary for the dissonance or self-perception effect (i.e., high commitment, free choice, and adverse consequences).

Empirical Evidence: Overly Sufficient Justification

There have been several empirical studies designed to test the self-perception prediction within the context of overly sufficient justification. Generally, a situation in which an extrinsic reward is added to an intrinsically rewarding task has been experimentally contrived for this purpose. Following self-perception theory, it is predicted that an increase in external justification will cause indivduals to lose confidence in their intrinsic interest in the experimental task. Since dissonance theory cannot make this prediction (it is neither irrational nor inconsistent to perform an activity for too many rewards), the literature on overly sufficient justification provides the most important data on the self-perception prediction. For this reason, we will examine the experimental evidence in some detail.

In an experiment specifically designed to test the effect of overly sufficient justification on intrinsic motivation, Deci (1971) enlisted a number of college students to participate in a problem-solving study. All the students were asked to work on a series of intrinsically interesting puzzles for three experimental sessions. After the first session, however, half of the students (the experimental group) were told that they would also be given an extrinsic reward (money) for correctly solving the second set of puzzles, while the other students (the control group) were not told anything about the reward. In the third session, neither the experimental nor the control subjects were rewarded. This design is schematically outlined in Table 12.1.

Deci had hypothesized that the payment of money in the second experimental session might decrease subjects' intrinsic motivation to perform the task. That is, the introduction of an external force (money) might cause participants to alter their self-perception about why they are working on the puzzles. Instead of being intrinsically motivated to solve the interesting puzzles, they might find themselves working primarily to get the money provided by the experimenter. Thus Deci's goal in conducting the study was to compare the changes in subjects' intrinsic motivation from the first to third sessions for both the experimental and control groups. If the self-perception hypothesis was correct, the intrinsic motivation of the previously paid experimental subjects would decrease in the third session, whereas the intrinsic motivation of the unpaid controls should remain unchanged.

As a measure of intrinsic motivation, Deci used the amount of free time participants spent on the puzzle task. To obtain this measure, the experimenter left the room during each session, supposedly to feed some data into the computer. As the experimenter left the room, he told the subjects they could do anything they wanted with their free time. In addition to the puzzles, current issues of *Time*, *The New Yorker*, and *Playboy* were placed near the subjects. However, while the first experimenter was out of the laboratory, a second experimenter, unknown to the subjects, observed their behavior through a one-way mirror. It was reasoned that if the subject worked on the puzzles during this free time period, he must be intrinsically motivated to perform the task. As shown in Table 12.2, the amount of free time spent on the task decreased for those who were previously paid to perform the activity, while there was a slight increase for the unpaid controls. Although the difference between the experimental and control groups was only marginally significant, the results are suggestive of the fact that an overly sufficient extrinsic reward may decrease one's intrinsic motivation to perform a task.

TABLE 12.1
Basic Design of Deci (1971) Study

	TIME 1	TIME 2	TIME 3
Experimental group	No payment	No payment	No payment
Control group	No payment	No payment	No payment

TABLE 12.2

Mean Number of Seconds Spent Working on the Puzzles during the Free Time Periods

Group	Time 1	Time 2	Time 3	Time 3 – Time 1
Experimental (n = 12)	248.2	313.9	198.5	−49.7
Control (n = 12)	213.9	202.7	241.8	27.9

Source: E. L. Deci, "The Effects of Externally Mediated Rewards as Intrinsic Motivation," *Journal of Personality and Social Psychology* 18 (1971) 105–15. Copyright © 1971 by the American Psychological Association. Reprinted by permission.

Lepper, Greene, and Nisbett (1973) also conducted a study that tested the self-perception prediction in a situation of overly sufficient justification. Their study involved having nursery school children perform an interesting activity (playing with Magic Markers) with and without the expectation of an additional extrinsic reward. Some children were induced to draw pictures with the markers by promising them a Good Player Award consisting of a big gold star, a bright red ribbon, and a place to print their name. Other children either performed the activity without any reward or were told about the reward only after completing the activity. Children who participated in these three experimental conditions (expected reward, no reward, unexpected reward) were then covertly observed during the following week in a free-play period. As in the Deci (1971) study, the amount of time children spent on the activity when they could do other interesting things (i.e., playing with other toys) was taken to be an indicator of intrinsic motivation.

The findings of the Lepper, Greene, and Nisbett study showed that the introduction of an extrinsic reward for performing an already interesting activity caused a significant decrease in intrinsic motivation. Children who played with Magic Markers with the expectations of receiving the external reward did not spend as much subsequent free time on the activity as did the children who were not given a reward or those who were unexpectedly offered the reward. Moreover, the rated quality of drawings made by children with the markers was significantly poorer in the expected-reward group than either the no-reward or unexpected-reward groups.

The results of the Lepper et al. study help to increase our confidence in the findings of the earlier Deci experiment. Not only are the earlier findings replicated with a different task and subject population, but an important methodological problem is minimized. By reexamining Table 12.1, we can see that the second time period in the Deci experiment was the period in which payment was expected by subjects for solving the puzzles. However, we can also see that in time 2 there was a whopping increase in the free time subjects spent on the puzzles. Deci explained this increase as an attempt by subjects to practice puzzle solving to increase their chances of earning money. However, what Deci did not discuss is the possibility that the subsequent decrease in time 3 was due not to the prior administration of rewards but to the effect of satiation or fatigue. One contribution of the Lepper et al. study is that its results are not easily explained by this alternative. In the Lepper et al. experiment, there was over one week's time between the session in which an extrinsic reward was administered and the final observation period.

Although both the Deci and Lepper et al. studies support the notion that the expectation of an extrinsic reward may decrease intrinsic interest in an activity, there is still one important source of ambiguity in both these studies. You may have noticed that the decrease in intrinsic motivation follows not only the prior administration of an extrinsic reward, but also the withdrawal of this reward. For example, in the Deci study, subjects were not paid in the third experimental session in which the decrease in intrinsic motivation was reported. Likewise, subjects were not rewarded when the final observation of intrinsic motivation was taken by Lepper, Greene, and Nisbett. It is therefore difficult to determine whether the decrease in intrinsic interest is due to a change in the self-perception of motivation following the application of an extrinsic reward or merely to frustration following the removal of the reward. An experiment by Kruglanski, Freedman, and Zeevi (1971) helps to resolve this ambiguity.

Kruglanski et al. induced a number of teenagers to volunteer for some creativity and memory tasks. To manipulate extrinsic rewards, the experimenters told half the participants that because they had volunteered for the study, they would be taken on an interesting tour of the psychology laboratory; the other participants were not offered this extrinsic reward. The results showed that teenagers offered the reward were less satisfied with the experimental tasks and were less likely to volunteer for future experiments of a similar nature than were teenagers who were not offered the extrinsic reward. In addition, the extrinsically rewarded group did not perform as well on the experimental task (in terms of recall, creativity, and the Zeigarnik effect) as the nonrewarded group. These findings are similar to those of Deci (1971) and Lepper et al. (1973), but they cannot be as easily explained by a frustration effect. Since in the Kruglanski et al. study the reward was never withdrawn for the experimental group, the differences between the experimental (reward) and control (no reward) conditions are better explained by a change in self-perception than by a frustration effect.

The designs of the three overly sufficient justification studies described above have varying strengths and weaknesses (Calder & Staw, 1975a), but taken together, their results can be interpreted as supporting the notion that extrinsic rewards added to an already interesting task can decrease intrinsic motivation. This effect, if true, has important ramifications for educational, industrial, and other work settings. There are many situations in which people are offered extrinsic rewards (grades, money, special privileges) for accomplishing a task which may already be intrinsically interesting. The self-perception effect means that, by offering external rewards, we may sometimes be sacrificing an important source of task motivation and not necessarily increasing either the satisfaction or the performance of the participant. Obviously, because the practical implications of the self-perception effect are large, we should proceed with caution. Thus, in addition to scrutinizing the validity of the findings themselves (as we have done above), we should also attempt to determine the exact conditions under which they might be expected to hold.

Earlier, Deci (1971, 1972) had hypothesized that only rewards contingent on a high level of task performance are likely to have an adverse effect on intrinsic motivation. He had reasoned that a reward contingent upon specific behavioral demands is most likely to cause an individual to infer that his behavior is extrinsically rather than intrinsically motivated and that a decrease in intrinsic motivation may result from this change in self-perception. Although this assumption seems reasonable, there is not a great deal of empirical support for it. Certainly in the Kruglanski et al. and Lepper et al. studies all that was necessary to cause a decrease in intrinsic motivation was for rewards to be contingent upon the completion of an activity. In each of these studies what seemed to be important was the cognition that one was performing an activity in order to get an extrinsic reward rather than a prescribed goal for a particular level of output. Thus as long as it is salient, a reward contingency based upon the completion of an activity may decrease intrinsic motivation just like a reward contingency based on the quality or quantity of performance.

Ross (1975) recently conducted two experiments that dealt specifically with the effect of the salience of rewards on changes in intrinsic motivation. In one study, children were asked to play a musical instrument (drums) for either no reward, a nonsalient reward, or a salient reward. The results showed that intrinsic motivation, as measured by the amount of time spent on the drums versus other activities in a free-play situation, was lowest for the salient reward condition. Similar results were found in a second study in which some children were asked to think either of the reward (marshmallows) while playing a musical instrument, think of an extraneous object (snow), or not think of anything in particular. The data for this second study showed that intrinsic motivation was lowest when children consciously thought about the reward while performing the task.

In addition to the salience of an external reward, there has been empirical research on one other factor mediating the self-perception effect, the existing norms of the task situation. In examining the prior research using situations of overly sufficient justification, Staw, Calder, and Hess (1976) reasoned that there is one common element which stands out. Always, the extrinsic reward appears to be administered in a situation in which persons are not normally paid or otherwise reimbursed for their actions. For example, students are not normally paid for laboratory participation, but the Deci (1971) and Kruglanski et al. (1971) subjects were. Likewise, nursery school children are not normally enticed by special recognition or rewards to play with an interesting new toy, but both the Lepper et al. (1973) and Ross (1975) subjects were. Thus Staw, Calder, and Hess (1976) manipulated norms for payment as well as the actual payment of money for performing an interesting task. They found an interaction of norms and payment such that the introduction of an extrinsic reward decreased intrinsic interest in a task only when there existed a situational norm for no payment. From these data and the findings of the Ross study, it thus appears that an extrinsic reward must be both salient and situationally inappropriate for there to be a reduction in intrinsic interest.

Reassessing the Self-Perception Effect

At present there is growing empirical support for the notion that intrinsic and extrinsic motivation *can* be negatively interrelated. The effect of extrinsic rewards on intrinsic motivation has been replicated by several researchers using different classes of subjects (males, females, children, college students) and different activities (puzzles, toys), and the basic results appear to be internally valid. As we have seen, however, the effect of extrinsic rewards is predicated on certain necessary conditions (e.g., situational norms and reward salience), as is often the case with psychological findings subjected to close examination.

To date, the primary data supporting the self-perception prediction have come from situations of insufficient and overly sufficient justification. Empirical findings have shown that individuals may cognitively reevaluate intrinsic rewards in an upward direction when their behavior is insufficiently justified and in a downward direction when there is overly sufficient justification. In general, it can be said that the data of these two situations are consistent with the self-perception hypothesis. Still, theoretically, it is not immediately clear why previous research has been restricted to these two particular contexts. No doubt it is easier to show an increase in intrinsic motivation when intrinsic interest is initially low (as under insufficient justification) or a decrease when intrinsic interest is initially high (as under overly sufficient justification). Nevertheless, the theory should support a negative interrelationship of intrinsic and extrinsic factors at *all levels*, since it makes the rather general prediction that the greater the extrinsic rewards, the less likely is the individual to infer that he is intrinsically motivated.

One recent empirical study has tested the self-perception hypothesis by manipulating *both* intrinsic and extrinsic motivation. Calder and Staw (1975b) experimentally manipulated both the intrinsic characteristics of a task as well as extrinsic rewards in an attempt to examine the interrelationship of these two factors at more than one level. In the study male college students were asked to solve one of two sets of puzzles identical in all respects except the potential for intrinsic interest. One set of puzzles contained an assortment of pictures highly rated by students (chiefly from *Life* magazine but including several *Playboy* centerfolds); another set of puzzles was blank and rated more neutrally. To manipulate extrinsic rewards, half the subjects were promised $1 for their 20 minutes of labor (and the dollar was placed prominently in view), while for half of the subjects, money was neither mentioned nor displayed. After completing the task, subjects were asked to fill out a questionnaire on their reactions to the puzzle-solving activity. The two primary dependent variables included in the questionnaire were a measure of task satisfaction and a measure of subjects' willingness to volunteer for additional puzzle-solving exercises. The latter consisted of a sign-up sheet on which subjects could indicate the amount of time they would be willing to spend (without pay or additional course credit) in future experiments of a similar nature.

The results of the Calder and Staw experiment showed a significant interaction between task and payment on subjects' satisfaction with the activity and a marginally significant interaction on subjects' willingness to volunteer for additional work without extrinsic reward. These data provided empirical support for the self-perception effect in a situation of overly sufficient justification, but not under other conditions. Specifically, when the task was initially interesting (i.e., using the picture puzzle activity), the introduction of money caused a reduction of task satisfaction and volunteering. However, when the task was initially more neutral (i.e., using the blank puzzle activity), the introduction of money increased satisfaction and subjects' intentions to volunteer for additional work. Thus if we consider Calder and Staw's dependent measures as indicators of intrinsic interest, the first finding is in accord with the self-perception

hypothesis, while the latter result is similar to what one might predict from a reinforcement theory. The implications of these data, together with previous findings, are graphically depicted in Figure 12.3.

As shown in the figure, self-perception effects have been found *only* at the extremes of insufficient and overly sufficient justification. Thus it may be prudent to withhold judgment on the general hypothesis that there is a uniformly negative relationship between intrinsic and extrinsic motivation. Perhaps we should no longer broadly posit that the greater external rewards and pressures, the weaker the perception of intrinsic interest in an activity; and the lower external pressures, the stronger intrinsic interest. Certainly, under conditions other than insufficient and overly sufficient justification, reinforcement effects of extrinsic rewards on intrinsic task satisfaction have readily been found (Cherrington, 1973; Cherrington, Reitz, & Scott, 1971; Greene, 1974).

At present it appears that only in situations of insufficient or overly sufficient reward will there be attributional instability of such magnitude that shifts will occur in the perception of intrinsic rewards. We might therefore speculate that either no attributional instability is evoked in other situations or it is just not strong enough to overcome a countervailing force. This writer

FIGURE 12.3
The Relative Potency of Self-Perception and Reinforcement Mechanisms

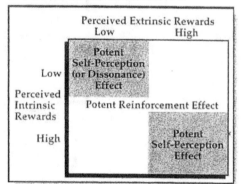

would place his confidence in the latter theoretical position. It seems likely that both self-perception *and* reinforcement mechanisms hold true, but that their relative influence over an individual's task attitudes and behavior varies according to the situational context. For example, only in situations with insufficient or overly sufficient justification will the need to resolve attributional instability probably be strong enough for external rewards to produce a decrease in intrinsic motivation. In other situations we might reasonably expect a more positive relationship between intrinsic and extrinsic factors, as predicted by reinforcement theory.

Although this new view of the interrelationship between intrinsic and extrinsic motivation remains speculative, it does seem reasonable in light of recent theoretical and empirical work. Figure 12.4 graphically elaborates this model and shows how the level of intrinsic and extrinsic

motivation may depend on the characteristics of the situation. In the figure, secondary reinforcement is depicted to be a general force for producing a positive relationship between intrinsic and extrinsic motivation. However, under situations of insufficient and overly sufficient justification, self-perception (and dissonance) effects are shown to provide a second but still potentially effective determinant of a negative interrelationship between intrinsic and extrinsic motivation. Figure 12.4 shows the joint operation of these two theoretical mechanisms and illustrates their ultimate effect on individuals' satisfaction, persistence, and performance on a task.

IMPLICATIONS OF INTRINSIC AND EXTRINSIC MOTIVATION

In this discussion we have noted that the administration of both intrinsic and extrinsic

FIGURE 12.4
The Interrelationship of Intrinsic and Extrinsic Motivation as a Function of Situational Characteristics

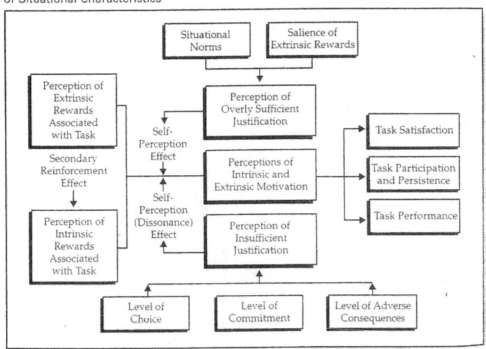

rewards can have important effects on a person's task attitudes and behavior. Individually, extrinsic rewards may direct and control a person's activity on a task and provide an important source of satisfaction. By themselves, intrinsic rewards can also motivate task-related behavior and bring gratification to the individual. As we have seen, however, the joint effect of intrinsic and extrinsic rewards may be quite complex. Not only may intrinsic and extrinsic factors not be additive in their overall effect on motivation and satisfaction, but the interaction of intrinsic and extrinsic factors may under some conditions be positive and under other conditions negative. As illustrated in Figures 12.3 and 12.4, a potent reinforcement effect will often cause intrinsic and extrinsic motivation to be positively interrelated, although on occasion a self-perception mechanism may be so powerful as to create a negative relationship between these two factors.

The reinforcement predictions of Figures 12.3 and 12.4 are consistent with our common sense. In practice, extrinsic rewards are relied upon heavily to induce desired behaviors, and most allocators of rewards (administrators, teachers, parents) operate on the theory that extrinsic rewards will positively affect an individual's intrinsic interest in a task. We should therefore concentrate on those situations in which our common sense may be in error—those situations in which there may in fact be a negative relationship between intrinsic and extrinsic motivation.

Motivation in Educational Organizations

One of the situations in which intrinsic and extrinsic motivation may be negatively interrelated is our schools. As Lepper and Greene (1975) have noted, many educational tasks are inherently interesting to students and would probably be performed without any external force. However, when grades and other extrinsic inducements are added to the activity, we may, via overly sufficient justification, be converting an interesting activity into work. That is,

by inducing students to perform educational tasks with strong extrinsic rewards or by applying external force, we may be converting learning activities into behaviors that will not be performed in the future without some additional outside pressure or extrinsic force.

Within the educational context, a negative relationship between intrinsic and extrinsic motivation poses a serious dilemma for teachers who allocate external rewards. For example, there is no doubt that grades, gold stars, and other such incentives can alter the direction and vigor of specific "in school" behaviors (e.g., getting students to complete assigned exercises by a particular date). But because of their effect on intrinsic motivation, extrinsic rewards may also weaken a student's general interest in learning tasks and decrease voluntary learning behavior that extends beyond the school setting. In essence, then, the extrinsic forces that work so well at motivating and controlling specific task behaviors may actually cause the extinction of these same behaviors within situations devoid of external reinforcers. This is an important consideration for educational organizations, since most of an individual's learning activity will no doubt occur outside the highly regulated and reinforced setting of the classroom.[2]

In order to maintain students' intrinsic motivation in learning activities it is recommended that the use of extrinsic rewards be carefully controlled. As a practical measure, it is recommended that when a learning task is inherently interesting (and would probably be performed without any external force) all external pressures on the individual be minimized. Only when a task is so uninteresting that individuals would not ordinarily perform it should extrinsic rewards be applied. In addition, it is suggested that the student role be both enlarged and enriched to increase rather directly the level of intrinsic motivation. The significance of learning tasks, responsibility for results, feedback, and variety in student activities are all areas of possible improvement.

Motivation in Work Organizations

Voluntary work organizations are very much like educational organizations; their members are often intrinsically motivated to perform certain tasks and extrinsic rewards are generally not necessary to induce the performance of many desired behaviors. Moreover, if for some reason extrinsic rewards were to be offered to voluntary workers for performing their services we would expect to find, as in the educational setting, a decrease in intrinsic motivation. As in the educational context, we would expect an external reward to decrease self-motivated (or voluntary) behavior in settings free from external reinforcement, although the specific behaviors which are reinforced might be increased. As a concrete example, let us imagine a political candidate who decides to "motivate" his volunteer campaign workers by paying them for distributing flyers to prospective voters. In this situation, we might expect that the administration of an extrinsic reward will increase the number of flyers distributed. However, the political workers' subsequent interest in performing other campaign activities *without pay* may subsequently be diminished. Similarly, the volunteer hospital worker who becomes salaried may no longer have the same intrinsic interest in his work. Although the newly professionalized worker may exert a good deal of effort on the job and be relatively satisfied with it, his satisfaction may stem from extrinsic rather than intrinsic sources of reward.

Let us now turn to the implications of intrinsic and extrinsic motivation for nonvoluntary work organizations. Deci (1972), in reviewing his research on intrinsic motivation, cautioned strongly against the use of contingent monetary rewards within industrial organizations. He maintained that paying people contingently upon the performance of specific tasks may reduce intrinsic motivation for these activities, and he recommended noncontingent reinforces in their stead. As we have seen, however, a decrease in intrinsic motivation does not always occur following the administration of extrinsic rewards; certain necessary conditions must be present before there is a negative relationship between intrinsic and extrinsic motivation. Generally, industrial work settings do not meet these necessary conditions.

First, within industrial organizations, a large number of jobs are not inherently interesting enough to foster high intrinsic motivation. Persons would not ordinarily perform many of the tasks of the industrial world (e.g., assembly line work) without extrinsic inducements, and this initial lack of intrinsic interest will probably preclude the effect of overly sufficient justification. Second, even when an industrial job is inherently interesting, there exists a powerful norm for extrinsic payment. Not only do workers specifically join and contribute their labor in exchange for particular inducements, but the instrumental relationship between task behavior and extrinsic rewards is supported by both social and legal standards. Thus the industrial work situation is quite unlike that of either a voluntary organization or an educational system. In the latter cases, participants may be initially interested in performing certain tasks without external force, and the addition of overly sufficient rewards may convey information that the task is not intrinsically interesting. Within industrial organizations, on the other hand, extrinsic reinforcement is the norm, and tasks may often be perceived to be even more interesting when they lead to greater extrinsic rewards.

The very basic distinction between nonvoluntary work situations and other task settings (e.g., schools and voluntary organizations) is that, without extrinsic rewards, nonvoluntary organizations would be largely without participants. The important question for industrial work settings is therefore not one of payment versus nonpayment, but of the recommended degree of contingency between reward and performance. On the basis of current evidence, it would seem prudent to suggest that, within industrial organizations, rewards continue to be made contingent upon behavior. This could be accomplished through performance evaluation, profit sharing, or piece-rate incentive schemes.

In addition, intrinsic motivation should be increased directly via the planned alteration of specific job characteristics (e.g., by increasing task variety, complexity, social interaction, task identity, significance, responsibility for results, and knowledge of results).

A FINAL COMMENT

Although the study of the interaction of intrinsic and extrinsic motivation is a relatively young era within psychology, it has been the intent of this paper to outline a theoretical model and provide some practical suggestions based upon the research evidence available to date. As we have seen, the effects of intrinsic and extrinsic motivation are not always simple, and several moderating variables must often be taken into account before specific predictions can be made. Thus in addition to providing "answers" to theoretical and practical problems, this paper may illustrate the complexities involved in drawing conclusions from a limited body of research data. The main caution for the reader is to regard these theoretical propositions and practical recommendations as working statements subject to the influence of future empirical evidence.

NOTES

1. The author wishes to express his gratitude to Bobby J. Calder and Greg R. Oldham for their critical reading of the manuscript, and to the Center for Advanced Study at the University of Illinois for the resources and facilities necessary to complete this work.
2. It is interesting to note that Kazdin and Bootzen (1972) have made a quite similar point in their recent review of research on token economies. They noted that while operant conditioning procedures have been quite effective in altering focal behaviors within a controlled setting, seldom have changes been found to generalize to natural, nonreinforcing environments.

REFERENCES

Aronson, E. "The Psychology of Insufficient Justification: An Analysis of Some Conflicting Data." In *Cognitive Consistency: Motivational Antecedents and Behavior Consequences*, edited by S. Feldman. Academic Press, 1966.

Bem, D. J. "Self-perception: An Alternative Interpretation of Cognitive Dissonance Phenomena." *Psychological Review* 74 (1967a): 183–200.

_____. "Self-perception: The Dependent Variable of Human Performance." *Organizational Behavior and Human Performance* 2 (1967b): 105–21.

_____. "Self-perception Theory." In *Advances in Experimental Social Psychology*, Vol. 6, edited by L. Berkowitz. New York: Academic Press, 1972.

Brehm, J. W., and Cohen, A. R. *Explorations in Cognitive Dissonance*. New York: Wiley, 1962.

Calder, B. J., Ross, M., and Insko, C. A. "Attitude Change and Attitude Attribution: Effects of Incentive, Choice, and Consequences." *Journal of Personality and Social Psychology* 25 (1973): 84–100.

_____, and Staw, B. M. "The Interaction of Intrinsic and Extrinsic Motivation: Some Methodological Notes." *Journal of Personality and Social Psychology* 31 (1975a): 76–80.

_____, and Staw, B. M. "Self-perception of Intrinsic and Extrinsic Motivation." *Journal of Personality and Social Psychology* 31 (1975b): 599–605.

Carlsmith, J. M., Collins, B. E., and Helmreich, R. L. "Studies in Forced Compliance: The Effect of Pressure of Compliance on Attitude Change Produced by Face-to-Face Role Playing and Anonymous Essay Writing." *Journal of Personality and Social Psychology* 4 (1966): 1–13.

Cherrington, D. J. "The Effects of a Central Incentive—Motivational State on Measures of Job Satisfaction." *Organizational Behavior and Human Performance* 10 (1973): 27–89.

_____, Reitz, H. J., and Scott, W. E. "Effects of Reward and Contingent Reinforcement on Satisfaction and Task Performance." *Journal of Applied Psychology* 55 (1971): 531–36.

Collins, B. E., and Hoyt, M. F. "Personal Responsibility-for-Consequences: An Integration and Extension of the Forced Compliance Literature." *Journal of Experimental Social Psychology* 8 (1972): 558–94.

de Charms, R: *Personal Causation: The Internal Affective Determinants of Behavior.* New York: Academic Press, 1968.

Deci, E. L. "The Effects of Externally Mediated Rewards on Intrinsic Motivation." *Journal of Personality and Social Psychology* 18 (1971): 105–15.

_____. "The Effects of Contingent and Noncontingent Rewards and Controls on Intrinsic Motivation." *Organizational Behavior and Human Performance* 8 (1972): 217–29.

Festinger, L. *A Theory of Cognitive Dissonance.* Palo Alto: Stanford University Press, 1957.

_____, and Carlsmith, J. M. "Cognitive Consequences of Forced Compliance." *Journal of Abnormal and Social Psychology* 58 (1959): 203–10.

Freedman, J. L. "Attitudinal Effects of Inadequate Justification." *Journal of Personality* 31 (1963): 371–85.

Greene, C. N. "Causal Connections Among Manager's Merit Pay, Job Satisfaction, and Performance." *Journal of Applied Psychology* 58 (1974): 95–100.

Heider, F. *The Psychology of Interpersonal Relations.* New York: Wiley, 1958.

Jones, E. E., and Davis, K. E. "From Acts to Dispositions: The Attribution Process in Person Perception." In *Advances in Experimental Psychology*, Vol. 2, edited by L. Berkowitz. New York: Academic Press, 1965.

_____, Davis, K. E., and Gergen, K. E. "Role Playing Variations and Their Informational Value for Person Perception." *Journal of*

Abnormal and Social Psychology 63 (1961): 302–10.

_____, and Harris, V. A. "The Attribution of Attitudes." *Journal of Experimental Social Psychology* 3 (1967): 1–24.

_____, and Nisbett, R. E. *The Actor and the Observer: Divergent Perceptions of the Causes of Behavior.* New York: General Learning Press, 1971.

Kazdin, A. E., and Bootzen, R. R. "The Token Economy: An Evaluative Review." *Journal of Applied Behavior Analysis* 5 (1972): 343–72.

Kelley, H. H. "Attribution Theory in Social Psychology." In *Nebraska Symposium on Motivation*, Vol. 15, edited by D. Levine. University of Nebraska Press, 1967.

Kruglanski, A. W., Freedman, I., and Zeevi, G. "The Effects of Extrinsic Incentives on Some Qualitative Aspects of Task Performance." *Journal of Personality* 39 (1971): 606–17.

Lepper, M. R., and Greene, D. "Turning Play into Work: Effects of Adult Surveillance and Extrinsic Rewards on Children's Intrinsic Motivation." *Journal of Personality and Social Psychology*, in press.

_____, Greene, D., and Nisbett, R. E. "Undermining Children's Intrinsic Interest with Extrinsic Rewards: A Test of the 'Overjustification' Hypothesis." *Journal of Personality and Social Psychology* 28 (1973): 129–37.

Linder, D. E., Cooper, J., and Jones, E. E. "Decision Freedom as a Determinant of the Role of Incentive Magnitude in Attitude Change." *Journal of Personality and Social Psychology* 6 (1967): 245–54.

Ross, M. "Salience of Reward and Intrinsic Motivation." *Journal of Personality and Social Psychology* 32 (1975): 245–54.

Staw, B. M. "Attitudinal and Behavioral Consequences of Changing a Major Organizational Reward: A Natural Field Experiment." *Journal of Personality and Social Psychology* 6 (1974a): 742–51.

_____. "Notes Toward a Theory of Intrinsic and Extrinsic Motivation." Paper presented at Eastern Psychological Association, 1974b.

_____, Calder, B. J., and Hess, R. "Intrinsic Motivation and Norms About Payment."

Working paper, Northwestern University, 1975.

Strickland, L. H. "Surveillance and Trust." *Journal of Personality* 26 (1958): 200–15.

Thibaut, J. W., and Riecken, H. W. "Some Determinants and Consequences of the Perception of Social Causality." *Journal of Personality* 24 (1955): 113–33.

Weick, K. E. "Reduction of Cognitive Dissonance Through Task Enhancement and Effort Expenditure." *Journal of Abnormal and Social Psychology* 68 (1964): 533–39.

———, and Penner, D. D. "Justification and Productivity." Unpublished manuscript, University of Minnesota, 1965.

Six Dangerous Myths About Pay

by Jeffrey Pfeffer

Harvard Business Review

Reprint 98309

Harvard Business Review

MAY–JUNE 1998

Reprint Number

*Many managers have bought into expensive
fictions about compensation. Have you?*

SIX DANGEROUS
MYTHS ABOUT PAY

BY JEFFREY PFEFFER

CONSIDER TWO GROUPS *of steel minimills. One group
pays an average hourly wage of $18.07. The second pays
an average of $21.52 an hour. Assuming that other direct-
employment costs, such as benefits, are the same for the two
groups, which group has the higher labor costs?*

• • • •

*An airline is seeking to compete in the low-cost, low-frills seg-
ment of the U.S. market where, for obvious reasons, labor productivity and efficiency are crucial for competitive success.
The company pays virtually no one on the basis of individual
merit or performance. Does it stand a chance of success?*

• • • •

*A company that operates in an intensely competitive segment
of the software industry does not pay its sales force on commission. Nor does it pay individual bonuses or offer stock
options or phantom stock, common incentives in an industry
heavily dependent on attracting and retaining scarce pro-
gramming talent. Would you invest in this company?*

• • • •

Every day, organizational leaders confront decisions about pay.
Should they adjust the company's compensation system to encourage some set of behaviors? Should they retain consultants
to help them implement a performance-based pay system?
How large a raise should they authorize?

In general terms, these kinds of questions come down to four decisions about compensation:

- how much to pay employees;
- how much emphasis to place on financial compensation as a part of the total reward system;
- how much emphasis to place on attempting to hold down the rate of pay; and
- whether to implement a system of individual incentives to reward differences in performance and productivity and, if so, how much emphasis to place on these incentives.

For leaders, there can be no delegation of these matters. Everyone knows decisions about pay are important. For one thing, they help establish a company's culture by rewarding the business activities, behaviors, and values that senior managers hold dear. Senior management at Quantum, the

Managers are bombarded with advice about pay. Unfortunately, much of that advice is wrong.

disk drive manufacturer in Milpitas, California, for example, demonstrates its commitment to teamwork by placing all employees, from the CEO to hourly workers, on the same bonus plan, tracking everyone by the same measure – in this case, return on total capital.

Compensation is also a concept and practice very much in flux. Compensation is becoming more variable as companies base a greater proportion of it on stock options and bonuses and a smaller proportion on base salary, not only for executives but also for people further and further down the hierarchy. As managers make organization-defining decisions about pay systems, they do so in a shifting landscape while being bombarded with advice about the best routes to stable ground.

Unfortunately, much of that advice is wrong. Indeed, much of the conventional wisdom and public discussion about pay today is misleading, incorrect, or sometimes both at the same time. The result is that businesspeople end up adopting wrongheaded notions about how to pay people and why. They believe in six dangerous myths about pay – fictions

Jeffrey Pfeffer is the Thomas D. Dee Professor of Organizational Behavior at the Stanford Graduate School of Business in Stanford, California. He is the author of The Human Equation: Building Profits by Putting People First (Harvard Business School Press, 1998).

about compensation that have somehow come to be seen as the truth.

Do you think you have managed to avoid these myths? Let's see how you answered the three questions that open this article. If you said the second set of steel minimills had higher labor costs, you fell into the common trap of confusing labor *rates* with labor *costs*. That is Myth #1: that labor rates and labor costs are the same thing. But how different they really are. The second set of minimills paid its workers at a rate of $3.45 an hour more than the first. But according to data collected by Fairfield University Professor Jeffrey Arthur, its labor costs were much lower because the productivity of the mills was higher. The second set of mills actually required 34% fewer labor hours to produce a ton of steel than the first set and also generated 63% less scrap. The second set of mills could have raised workers' pay rate by 19% and still had lower labor costs.

Connected to the first myth are three more myths that draw on the same logic. When managers believe that labor costs and labor rates are the same thing, they also tend to believe that they can cut labor costs by cutting labor rates. That's Myth #2. Again, this leaves out the important matter of productivity. I may replace my $2,000-a-week engineers with ones that earn $500 a week, but my costs may skyrocket because the new, lower-paid employees are inexperienced, slow, and less capable. In that case, I would have increased my costs by cutting my rates.

Managers who mix up labor rates and labor costs also tend to accept Myth #3: that labor costs are a significant portion of total costs. Sometimes, that's true. It is, for example, at accounting and consulting firms. But the ratio of labor costs to total costs varies widely in different industries and companies. And even where it is true, it's not as important as many managers believe. Those who swallow Myth #4 – that low labor costs are a potent competitive strategy – may neglect other, more effective ways of competing, such as through quality, service, delivery, and innovation. In reality, low labor costs are a slippery way to compete and perhaps the least sustainable competitive advantage there is.

Those of you who believed that the airline trying to compete in the low-cost, low-frills segment of the U.S. market would not succeed without using individual incentives succumbed to Myth #5: that the most effective way to motivate people to work productively is through individual incentive compensation. But Southwest Airlines has never used such a system, and it is the cost *and* productivity leader in its industry. Southwest is not alone, but still it takes smart, informed managers to buck the trend of offering individual rewards.

Would you have invested in the computer software company that didn't offer its people bonuses, stock options, or other financial incentives that could make them millionaires? You should have because it has succeeded mightily, growing over the past 21 years at a compound annual rate of more than 25%. The company is the SAS Institute of Cary, North Carolina. Today it is the largest privately held company in the software industry, with 1997 revenues of some $750 million.

Rather than emphasize pay, SAS has achieved an unbelievably low turnover rate below 4% – in an industry where the norm is closer to 20% – by offering intellectually engaging work; a family-friendly environment that features exceptional benefits; and the opportunity to work with fun, interesting people using state-of-the-art equipment.

In short, SAS has escaped Myth #6: that people work primarily for money. SAS, operating under the opposite assumption, demonstrates otherwise. In the last three years, the company has lost *none* of its 20 North American district sales managers. How many software companies do you know could make that statement, even about the last three months?

Every day, I see managers harming their organizations by believing in these myths about pay. What I want to do in these following pages is explore some factors that help account for why the myths are so pervasive, present some evidence to disprove their underlying assumptions, and suggest how leaders might think more productively and usefully about the important issue of pay practices in their organizations.

Why the Myths Exist

On October 10, 1997, the *Wall Street Journal* published an article expressing surprise that a "contrarian Motorola" had chosen to build a plant in Germany to make cellular phones despite the notoriously high "cost" of German labor. The *Journal* is not alone in framing business decisions about pay in this way. The *Economist* has also written articles about high German labor "costs," citing as

evidence labor rates (including fringe benefits) of more than $30 per hour.

The semantic confusion of labor rates with labor costs, endemic in business journalism and everyday discussion, leads managers to see the two as

Many executives spend too much time thinking about compensation when other managerial tools work just as well – or better.

equivalent. And when the two seem equivalent, the associated myths about labor costs seem to make sense, too. But, of course, labor rates and labor costs simply aren't the same thing. A labor rate is total salary divided by time worked. But labor costs take productivity into account. That's how the second set of minimills managed to have lower labor costs than the mills with the lower wages. They made more steel, and they made it faster and better.

Another reason why the confusion over costs and rates persists is that labor rates are a convenient target for managers who want to make an impact. Labor rates are highly visible, and it's easy to compare the rates you pay with those paid by your competitors or with those paid in other parts of the world.

TRUTH AND CONSEQUENCES:
THE SIX DANGEROUS MYTHS ABOUT COMPENSATION

Myth	Reality
1. Labor rates and labor costs are the same thing.	1. They are not, and confusing them leads to a host of managerial missteps. For the record, labor rates are straight wages divided by time – a Wal-Mart cashier earns $5.15 an hour, a Wall Street attorney $2,000 a day. Labor costs are a calculation of how much a company pays its people and how much they produce. Thus German factory workers may be paid at a rate of $30 an hour and Indonesians $3, but the workers' relative costs will reflect how many widgets are produced in the same period of time.
2. You can lower your labor costs by cutting labor rates.	2. When managers buy into the myth that labor rates and labor costs are the same thing, they usually fall for this myth as well. Once again, then, labor costs are a function of labor rates and productivity. To lower labor costs, you need to address *both*. Indeed, sometimes lowering labor rates increases labor costs.
3. Labor costs constitute a significant proportion of total costs.	3. This is true – but only sometimes. Labor costs as a proportion of total costs vary widely by industry and company. Yet many executives assume labor costs are the biggest expense on their income statement. In fact, labor costs are only the most immediately malleable expense.
4. Low labor costs are a potent and sustainable competitive weapon.	4. In fact, labor costs are perhaps the most slippery and least sustainable way to compete. Better to achieve competitive advantage through quality; through customer service; through product, process, or service innovation; or through technology leadership. It is much more difficult to imitate these sources of competitive advantage than to merely cut costs.
5. Individual incentive pay improves performance.	5. Individual incentive pay, in reality, undermines performance – of both the individual and the organization. Many studies strongly suggest that this form of reward undermines teamwork, encourages a short-term focus, and leads people to believe that pay is not related to performance at all but to having the "right" relationships and an ingratiating personality.
6. People work for money.	6. People do work for money – but they work even more for meaning in their lives. In fact, they work to have fun. Companies that ignore this fact are essentially bribing their employees and will pay the price in a lack of loyalty and commitment.

In addition, labor rates often appear to be a company's most malleable financial variable. It seems a lot quicker and easier to cut wages than to control costs in other ways, like reconfiguring manufacturing processes, changing corporate culture, or altering product design. Because labor costs appear to be the lever closest at hand, managers mistakenly assume it is the one that has the most leverage.

For the myths that individual incentive pay drives creativity and productivity, and that people are primarily motivated by money, we have economic theory to blame. More specifically, we can blame the economic model of human behavior widely taught in business schools and held to be true in the popular press. This model presumes that behavior is rational – driven by the best information available at the time and designed to maximize the individual's self-interest. According to this model, people take jobs and decide how much effort to expend in those jobs based on their expected financial return. If pay is not contingent on performance, the theory goes, individuals will not devote sufficient attention and energy to their jobs.

Additional problems arise from such popular economic concepts as agency theory (which contends that there are differences in preference and perspective between owners and those who work for them) and transaction-cost economics (which tries to identify which transactions are best organized by markets and which by hierarchies). Embedded in both concepts is the idea that individuals not only pursue self-interest but do so on occasion with guile and opportunism. Thus agency theory suggests that employees have different objectives than their employers and, moreover, have opportunities to misrepresent information and divert resources to their personal use. Transaction-cost theory suggests that people will make false or empty threats and promises to get better deals from one another.

All of these economic models portray work as hard and aversive – implying that the only way people can be induced to work is through some combination of rewards and sanctions. As professor James N. Baron of Stanford Business School has written, "The image of workers in these models is somewhat akin to Newton's first law of motion: employees remain in a state of rest unless compelled to change that state by a stronger force impressed upon them – namely, an optimal labor contract."

Similarly, the language of economics is filled with terms such as *shirking* and *free riding*. Language is powerful, and as Robert Frank, himself an economist, has noted, theories of human behavior become self-fulfilling. We act on the basis of these theories, and through our own actions produce in others the behavior we expect. If we believe people will work hard only if specifically rewarded for doing so, we will provide contingent rewards and thereby condition people to work only when they are rewarded. If we expect people to be untrustworthy, we will closely monitor and control them and by doing so will signal that they can't be trusted – an expectation that they will most likely confirm for us.

So self-reinforcing are these ideas that you almost have to avoid mainstream business to get away from them. Perhaps that's why several companies known to be strongly committed to managing through trust, mutual respect, and true decentralization – such as AES Corporation, Lincoln Electric, the Men's Wearhouse, the SAS Institute, ServiceMaster, Southwest Airlines, and Whole Foods Market – tend to avoid recruiting at conventional business schools.

There's one last factor that helps perpetuate all these myths: the compensation-consulting industry. Unfortunately, that industry has a number of perverse incentives to keep these myths alive.

First, although some of these consulting firms have recently broadened their practices, compensation remains their bread and butter. Suggesting that an organization's performance can be improved in

It's simpler for managers to tinker with compensation than to change the company's culture.

some way other than by tinkering with the pay system may be empirically correct but is probably too selfless a behavior to expect from these firms.

Second, if it's simpler for managers to tinker with the compensation system than to change an organization's culture, the way work is organized, and the level of trust and respect the system displays, it's even easier for consultants. Thus both the compensation consultants and their clients are tempted by the apparent speed and ease with which reward-system solutions can be implemented.

Third, to the extent that changes in pay systems bring their own new predicaments, the consultants will continue to have work solving the problems that the tinkering has caused in the first place.

From Myth to Reality:
A Look at the Evidence

The media are filled with accounts of companies attempting to reduce their labor costs by laying off people, moving production to places where labor rates are lower, freezing wages, or some combination of the above. In the early 1990s, for instance, Ford decided not to award merit raises to its white-collar workers as part of a new cost-cutting program. And in 1997, General Motors endured a series of highly publicized strikes over the issue of outsourcing. GM wanted to move more of its work to nonunion, presumably lower-wage, suppliers to reduce its labor costs and become more profitable.

Ford's and GM's decisions were driven by the myths that labor rates and labor costs are the same thing, and that labor costs constitute a significant portion of total costs. Yet hard evidence to support those contentions is slim. New United Motor Manufacturing, the joint venture between Toyota and General Motors based in Fremont, California, paid the highest wage in the automobile industry when it began operations in the mid-1980s, and it also offered a guarantee of secure employment. With productivity some 50% higher than at comparable GM plants, the venture could afford to pay 10% more and still come out ahead.

Yet General Motors apparently did not learn the lesson that what matters is not pay rate but productivity. In May 1996, as GM was preparing to confront the union over the issue of outsourcing, the "Harbour Report," the automobile industry's bible of comparative efficiency, published some interesting data suggesting that General Motors' problems had little to do with labor rates. As reported in the *Wall Street Journal* at the time, the report showed that it took General Motors some 46 hours to assemble a car, while it took Ford just 37.92 hours, Toyota 29.44, and Nissan only 27.36. As a way of attacking cost problems, officials at General Motors should have asked why they needed 21% more hours than Ford to accomplish the same thing or why GM was some 68% less efficient than Nissan.

For more evidence of how reality really looks, consider the machine tool industry. Many of its senior managers have been particularly concerned with low-cost foreign competition, believing that the cost advantage has come from the lower labor rates available offshore. But for machine tool companies that stop fixating on labor rates and focus in-

Most merit-pay systems share two attributes: they absorb vast amounts of management time and make everybody unhappy.

stead on their overall management system and manufacturing processes, there are great potential returns. Cincinnati Milacron, a company that had virtually surrendered the market for low-end machine tools to Asian competitors by the mid-1980s, overhauled its assembly process, abolished its stockroom, and reduced job categories from seven to one. Without any capital investment, those changes in the production *process* reduced labor hours by 50%, and the company's productivity is now higher than its competitors' in Taiwan.

Even U.S. apparel manufacturers lend support to the argument that labor costs are not the be-all and

end-all of profitability. Companies in this industry are generally obsessed with finding places where hourly wages are low. But the cost of direct labor needed to manufacture a pair of jeans is actually only about 15% of total costs, and even the direct labor involved in producing a man's suit is only about $12.50.[1]

Compelling evidence also exists to dispute the myth that competing on labor costs will create any sustainable advantage. Let's start close to home. One day, I arrived at a large discount store with a shopping list. Having the good fortune to actually find a sales associate, I asked him where I could locate the first item on my list. "I don't know," he replied. He gave a similar reply when queried about the second item. A glance at the long list I was holding brought the confession that because of high employee turnover, the young man had been in the store only a few hours himself. What is that employee worth to the store? Not only can't he sell the merchandise, he can't even find it! Needless to say, I wasn't able to purchase everything on my list because I got tired of looking and gave up. And I haven't returned since. Companies that compete on cost alone eventually bump into consumers like me. It's no accident that Wal-Mart combines its low-price strategy with friendly staff members greeting people at the door and works assiduously to keep turnover low.

Another example of a company that understands the limits of competing solely on labor costs is the Men's Wearhouse, the enormously successful off-price retailer of tailored men's clothing. The company operates in a fiercely competitive industry in which growth is possible primarily by taking sales from competitors, and price wars are intense. Still, less than 15% of the company's staff is part-time, wages are higher than the industry average, and the company engages in extensive training. All these policies defy conventional wisdom for the retailing industry. But the issue isn't what the Men's Wearhouse's employees cost, it's what they can do: sell very effectively because of their product knowledge and sales skills. Moreover, by keeping inventory losses and employee turnover low, the company saves money on shrinkage and hiring. Companies that miss this point—that costs, particularly labor costs, aren't everything—often overlook ways of succeeding that competitors can't readily copy.

Evidence also exists that challenges the myth about the effectiveness of individual incentives. This evidence, however, has done little to stem the tide of individual merit pay. A survey of the pay practices of the *Fortune* 1,000 reported that between 1987 and 1993, the proportion of companies using individual incentives for at least 20% of their workforce increased from 38% to 50% while the proportion of companies using profit sharing – a more collective reward – decreased from 45% to 43%. Between 1981 and 1990, the proportion of retail salespeople that were paid solely on straight salary, with no commission, declined from 21% to 7%. And this trend toward individual incentive compensation is not confined to the United States. A study of pay practices at plants in the United Kingdom reported that the proportion using some form of merit pay had increased every year since 1986 such that by 1990 it had reached 50%.[2]

Despite the evident popularity of this practice, the problems with individual merit pay are numerous and well documented. It has been shown to undermine teamwork, encourage employees to focus on the short term, and lead people to link compensation to political skills and ingratiating personalities rather than to performance. Indeed, those are among the reasons why W. Edwards Deming and other quality experts have argued strongly against using such schemes.

Consider the results of several studies. One carefully designed study of a performance-contingent pay plan at 20 Social Security Administration offices found that merit pay had no effect on office performance. Even though the merit pay plan was contingent on a number of objective indicators, such as the time taken to settle claims and the accuracy of claims processing, employees exhibited no difference in performance after the merit pay plan was introduced as part of a reform of civil service pay practices. Contrast that study with another that examined the elimination of a piecework system and its replacement by a more group-oriented compensation system at a manufacturer of exhaust system components. There, grievances decreased, product quality increased almost tenfold, and perceptions of teamwork and concern for performance all improved.[3]

Surveys conducted by various consulting companies that specialize in management and compensation also reveal the problems and dissatisfaction with individual merit pay. For instance, a study by the consulting firm William M. Mercer reported that 73% of the responding companies had made major changes to their performance-management plans in the preceding two years, as they experimented with different ways to tie pay to individual

performance. But 47% reported that their employees found the systems neither fair nor sensible, and 51% of the employees said that the performance-management system provided little value to the company. No wonder Mercer concluded that most individual merit or performance-based pay plans share two attributes: they absorb vast amounts of management time and resources, and they make everybody unhappy.

One concern about paying on a more group-oriented basis is the so-called free-rider problem, the worry that people will not work hard because they know that if rewards are based on collective performance and their colleagues make the effort,

If you could reliably measure and reward individual contributions, organizations wouldn't be needed.

they will share in those rewards regardless of the level of their individual efforts. But there are two reasons why organizations should not be reluctant to design such collective pay systems.

First, much to the surprise of people who have spent too much time reading economics, empirical evidence from numerous studies indicates that the extent of free riding is quite modest. For instance, one comprehensive review reported that "under the conditions described by the theory as leading to free riding, people often cooperate instead."[4]

Second, individuals do not make decisions about how much effort to expend in a social vacuum; they are influenced by peer pressure and the social relations they have with their workmates. This social influence is potent, and although it may be somewhat stronger in smaller groups, it can be a force mitigating against free riding even in large organizations. As one might expect, then, there is evidence that organizations paying on a more collective basis, such as through profit sharing or gain sharing, outperform those that don't.

Sometimes, individual pay schemes go so far as to affect customers. Sears was forced to eliminate a commission system at its automobile repair stores in California when officials found widespread evidence of consumer fraud. Employees, anxious to meet quotas and earn commissions on repair sales, were selling unneeded services to unsuspecting customers. Similarly, in 1992, the *Wall Street Journal* reported that Highland Superstores, an electronics and appliance retailer, eliminated commissions because they had encouraged such aggressive behavior on the part of salespeople that customers were alienated.

Enchantment with individual merit pay reflects not only the belief that people won't work effectively if they are not rewarded for their individual efforts but also the related view that the road to solving organizational problems is largely paved with adjustments to pay and measurement practices. Consider again the data from the Mercer survey: nearly three-quarters of all the companies surveyed had made *major* changes to their pay plans in just the past two years. That's tinkering on a grand scale. Or take the case of Air Products and Chemicals of Allentown, Pennsylvania. When on October 23, 1996, the company reported mediocre sales and profits, the stock price declined from the low $60s to the high $50s. Eight days later, the company announced a new set of management-compensation and stock-ownership initiatives designed to reassure Wall Street that management cared about its shareholders and was demonstrating that concern by changing compensation arrangements. The results were dramatic. On the day of the announcement, the stock price went up 1¼ points, and the next day it rose an additional 4¾ points. By November 29, Air Products' stock had gone up more than 15%. According to Value Line, this rise was an enthusiastic reaction by investors to the new compensation system. No wonder managers are so tempted to tamper with pay practices!

But as Bill Strusz, director of corporate industrial relations at Xerox in Rochester, New York, has said, if managers seeking to improve performance or

I would not necessarily say that external rewards backfire, but they do create their own problems.

solve organizational problems use compensation as the only lever, they will get two results: nothing will happen, and they will spend a lot of money. That's because people want more out of their jobs than just money. Numerous surveys – even of second-year M.B.A. students, who frequently graduate with large amounts of debt – indicate that money is far from the most important factor in choosing a job or remaining in one.

Why has the SAS Institute had such low turnover in the software industry despite its tight labor market? When asked this question, employees said

they were motivated by SAS's unique perks – plentiful opportunities to work with the latest and most up-to-date equipment and the ease with which they could move back and forth between being a manager and being an individual contributor. They also cited how much variety there was in the projects they worked on, how intelligent and nice the people they worked with were, and how much the organization cared for and appreciated them. Of course, SAS pays competitive salaries, but in an industry in which people have the opportunity to become millionaires through stock options by moving to a competitor, the key to retention is SAS's culture, not its monetary rewards.

People seek, in a phrase, an enjoyable work environment. That's what AES, the Men's Wearhouse, SAS, and Southwest have in common. One of the core values at each company is *fun.* When a colleague and I wrote a business school case on Southwest, we asked some of the employees, a number of whom had been offered much more money to work elsewhere, why they stayed. The answer we heard repeatedly was that they knew what the other environments were like, and they would rather be at a place, as one employee put it, where *work* is not a four-letter word. This doesn't mean work has to be easy. As an AES employee noted, fun means working in a place where people can use their gifts and skills and can work with others in an atmosphere of mutual respect.

There is a great body of literature on the effect of large external rewards on individuals' intrinsic motivation. The literature argues that extrinsic rewards diminish intrinsic motivation and, moreover, that large extrinsic rewards can actually decrease performance in tasks that require creativity and innovation. I would not necessarily go so far as to say that external rewards backfire, but they certainly create their own problems. First, people receiving such rewards can reduce their own motivation through a trick of self-perception, figuring, "I must not like the job if I have to be paid so much to do it" or "I make so much, I must be doing it for the money." Second, they undermine their own loyalty or performance by reacting against a sense of being controlled, thinking something like, "I will show the company that I can't be controlled just through money."

But most important, to my mind, is the logic in the idea that any organization believing it can solve its attraction, retention, and motivation problems solely by its compensation system is probably not spending as much time and effort as it should on the work environment – on defining its jobs, on creating its culture, and on making work fun and meaningful. It is a question of time and attention, of scarce managerial resources. The time and attention spent managing the reward system are not available to devote to other aspects of the work environment that in the end may be much more critical to success.

Some Advice About Pay

Since I have traipsed you through a discussion of what's wrong with the way most companies approach compensation, let me now offer some advice about how to get it right.

The first, and perhaps most obvious, suggestion is that managers would do well to keep the difference between labor rates and labor costs straight. In doing so, remember that only labor costs – and not labor rates – are the basis for competition, and that labor costs may not be a major component of total costs. In any event, managers should remember that the issue is not just what you pay people, but also what they produce.

To combat the myth about the effectiveness of individual performance pay, managers should see what happens when they include a large dose of collective rewards in their employees' compensation package. The more aggregated the unit used to measure performance, the more reliably performance can be assessed. One can tell pretty accurately how well an organization, or even a subunit, has done with respect to sales, profits, quality, productivity, and the like. Trying to parcel out who, specifically, was responsible for exactly how much of that productivity, quality, or sales is frequently much more difficult or even impossible. As Herbert Simon, the Nobel-prize-winning economist, has recognized, people in organizations are interdependent, and therefore organizational results are the consequence of collective behavior and performance. If you could reliably and easily measure and reward individual contributions, you probably would not need an organization at all as everyone would enter markets solely as individuals.

In the typical individual-based merit pay system, the boss works with a raise budget that's some percentage of the total salary budget for the unit. It's

inherently a zero-sum process: the more I get in my raise, the less is left for my colleagues. So the worse my workmates perform, the happier I am because I know I will look better by comparison. A similar dynamic can occur across organizational units in which competition for a fixed bonus pool discourages people from sharing best practices and learning from employees in other parts of the organization. In November 1995, for example, *Fortune* magazine reported that at Lantech, a manufacturer of packaging machinery in Louisville, Kentucky, individual incentives caused such intense rivalry that the chairman of the company, Pat Lancaster, said,

People seek an enjoyable work environment, one where *work* is not a four-letter word.

"I was spending 95% of my time on conflict resolution instead of on how to serve our customers."

Managers can fight the myth that people are primarily motivated by money by de-emphasizing pay and not portraying it as the main thing you get from working at a particular company. How? Consider the example of Tandem Computer which, in the years before it was acquired by Compaq, would not even tell you your salary before expecting you to accept a job. If you asked, you would be told that Tandem paid good, competitive salaries. The company had a simple philosophy – if you came for money, you would leave for money, and Tandem wanted employees who were there because they liked the work, the culture, and the people, not something – money – that every company could offer. Emphasizing pay as the primary reward encourages people to come and to stay for the wrong rea-

Pay cannot substitute for a working environment high on trust, fun, and meaningful work.

sons. AES, a global independent power producer in Arlington, Virginia, has a relatively short vesting period for retirement-plan contributions and tries not to pay the highest salaries for jobs in its local labor market. By so doing, it seeks to ensure that people are not locked into working at a place where they don't want to be simply for the money.

Managers must also recognize that pay has substantive and symbolic components. In signaling what and who in the organization is valued, pay both reflects and helps determine the organization's culture. Therefore, managers must make sure that the messages sent by pay practices are intended. Talking about teamwork and cooperation and then not having a group-based component to the pay system matters because paying solely on an individual basis signals what the organization believes is actually important – individual behavior and performance. Talking about the importance of *all* people in the organization and then paying some disproportionately more than others belies that message. One need not go to the extreme of Whole Foods Market, which pays no one more than eight times the average company salary (the result being close to $1 billion in sales at a company where the CEO makes less than $200,000 a year). But paying large executive bonuses while laying off people and asking for wage freezes, as General Motors did in the 1980s, may not send the right message, either. When Southwest Airlines asked its pilots for a five-year wage freeze, CEO Herb Kelleher voluntarily asked the compensation committee to freeze his salary for at least four years as well. The message of shared, common fate is powerful in an organization truly seeking to build a culture of teamwork.

Making pay practices public also sends a powerful symbolic message. Some organizations reveal pay distributions by position or level. A few organizations, such as Whole Foods Market, actually make data on individual pay available to all members who are interested. Other organizations try to maintain a high level of secrecy about pay. What message do those organizations send? Keeping salaries secret suggests that the organization has something to hide or that it doesn't trust its people with the information. Moreover, keeping things secret just encourages people to uncover the secrets – if something is worth hiding, it must be important and interesting enough to expend effort discovering. Pay systems that are more open and transparent send a positive message about the equity of the system and the trust that the company places in its people.

Managers should also consider using other methods besides pay to signal company values and focus behavior. The head of North American sales and operations for the SAS Institute has a useful perspective on this issue. He didn't think he was smart enough to design an incentive system that couldn't be gamed. Instead of using the pay system to signal what was important, he and other SAS managers simply told people what was important for the company and why. That resulted in much more nuanced and rapid changes in behavior because the company didn't have to change the compensation system every time business priorities altered a little. What a novel idea – actually talking to people about what is important and why, rather than trying to send some subtle signals through the compensation system!

Perhaps most important, leaders must come to see pay for what it is: just one element in a set of management practices that can either build or reduce commitment, teamwork, and performance. Thus my final piece of advice about pay is to make sure that pay practices are congruent with other management practices and reinforce rather than oppose their effects.

Breaking with Convention To Break the Myths

Many organizations devote enormous amounts of time and energy to their pay systems, but people, from senior managers to hourly workers, remain unhappy with them. Organizations are trapped in unproductive ways of approaching pay, which they find difficult to escape. The reason, I would suggest, is that people are afraid to challenge the myths about compensation. It's easier and less controversial to see what everyone else is doing and then to do the same. In fact, when I talk to executives at companies about installing pay systems that actually work, I usually hear, "But that's different from what most other companies are saying and doing."

It must certainly be the case that a company cannot earn "abnormal" returns by following the crowd. That's true about marketplace strategies, and it's true about compensation. Companies that are truly exceptional are not trapped by convention but instead see and pursue a better business model.

Companies that have successfully transcended the myths about pay know that pay cannot substitute for a working environment high on trust, fun, and meaningful work. They also know that it is more important to worry about what people do than what they cost, and that zero-sum pay plans can set off internal competition that makes learning from others, teamwork, and cross-functional cooperation a dream rather than the way the place works on an everyday basis.

There is an interesting paradox in achieving high organizational performance through innovative pay practices – if it were easy to do, it wouldn't provide as much competitive leverage as it actually does. So while I can review the logic and evidence and offer some alternative ways of thinking about

pay, it is the job of leaders to exercise both the judgment and the courage necessary to break with common practice. Those who do will develop organizations in which pay practices actually contribute rather than detract from building high-performance management systems. Those who are stuck in the past are probably doomed to endless tinkering with pay; at the end of the day, they won't have accomplished much, but they will have expended a lot of time and money doing it.

1. John T. Dunlop and David Weil, "Diffusion and Performance of Modular Production in the U.S. Apparel Industry," *Industrial Relations,* July 1996, p. 337.

2. For the survey of the pay practices of *Fortune* 1,000 companies, see Gerald E. Ledford, Jr., Edward E. Lawler III, and Susan A. Mohrman, "Reward Innovations in *Fortune* 1,000 Companies," *Compensation and Benefits Review,* April 1995, p. 76; for the salary and commission data, see Gregory A. Patterson, "Distressed Shoppers, Disaffected Workers Prompt Stores to Alter Sales Commissions," the *Wall Street Journal,* July 1, 1992, p. B1; for the study of U.K. pay practices, see Stephen Wood, "High Commitment Management and Payment Systems," *Journal of Management Studies,* January 1996, p. 53.

3. For the Social Security Administration study, see Jone L. Pearce, William B. Stevenson, and James L. Perry, "Managerial Compensation Based on Organizational Performance: A Time Series Analysis of the Effects of Merit Pay," *Academy of Management Journal,* June 1985, p. 261; for the study of group-oriented compensation, see Larry Hatcher and Timothy L. Ross, "From Individual Incentives to an Organization-Wide Gainsharing Plan: Effects on Teamwork and Product Quality," *Journal of Organizational Behavior,* May 1991, p. 169.

4. Gerald Marwell, "Altruism and the Problem of Collective Action," in V.J. Derlega and J. Grzelak, eds., *Cooperation and Helping Behavior: Theories and Research* (New York: Academic Press, 1982), p. 208.

Reprint 98309   To place an order, call 1-800-988-0886.

Harvard Business Review

CASE STUDIES AND
HARVARD BUSINESS REVIEW
ARTICLE REPRINTS

Many readers have asked for an easy way to order case studies and article reprints or to obtain permission to copy. In response, we have established a Customer Service Team to grant permission, send rush copies in paper form, deliver files in Acrobat (PDF) format electronically (*Harvard Business Review* articles only), or customize collections.

Please contact the Customer Service Team:

Phone: 617-496-1449
United States and Canada: 800-668-6780
(8 A.M.–6 P.M. weekdays, voice mail after hours)
Fax: 617-496-1029 (24 hours, 7 days a week)
E-mail: custserv@hbsp.harvard.edu
(24 hours, 7 days a week)
Web Site: http://www.hbsp.harvard.edu

Prices (minimum order, $10):

Harvard Business Review Reprints
(Discounts apply to multiple copies of the same article.)

1–9 copies	$5 each
10–99	$4
100–499	$3.50
Electronic	$3.50 each

Harvard Business School Case Studies
$5 each

For quantity estimates or quotes on customized products, call
Frank Tamoshunas at 617-495-6198.
Fax: 617-496-8866

PERMISSIONS

For information on permission to quote or translate Harvard Business School Publishing material, contact:

Customer Service Department
Harvard Business School
   Publishing Corporation
60 Harvard Way
Boston, MA 02163

Phone: 617-496-1449
United States and Canada: 800-668-6780
Fax: 617-495-6985
E-mail: custserv@hbsp.harvard.edu

HARVARD BUSINESS REVIEW
SUBSCRIPTION SERVICE

United States and Canada
Phone: 800-274-3214
Rates per year: United States, $85;
Canada, U.S.$95

International and Mexico
Phone: 44-1858-435324
Fax: 44-1858-468969
Rates per year: international, U.S.$145;
Mexico, U.S.$95
Orders, inquiries, and address changes:
Harvard Business Review
Tower House, Sovereign Park
Lathkill Street, Market Harborough
Leicestershire LE16 9EF
England

International customer service E-mail address: harvard@subscription.co.uk

Payments accepted: Visa, MasterCard, American Express; checks at current exchange rate payable to
Harvard Business Review.
Bills and other receipts may be issued.

CATALOGS

Harvard Business School Publishing Media Catalog
This 32-page, full-color catalog features more than 40 management development video and interactive CD-ROM programs.

Harvard Business School Press
This latest full-color catalog features books for the fast-paced business world where you live and work.

Harvard Business School Publishing Catalog of Best-Selling Teaching Materials
This collection of teaching materials contains those items most requested by our customers.

Harvard Business School Publishing Catalog of New Teaching Materials
Designed for individuals looking for the latest materials in case method teaching.

BRIEF CASES

2175

APRIL 11, 2008

MICHAEL BEER

ELIZABETH COLLINS

Engstrom Auto Mirror Plant: Motivating in Good Times and Bad

There had been several rough quarters at the Engstrom Auto Mirror plant in Richmond, Indiana, a privately owned business that manufactured mirrors for trucks and automobiles and employed 209 people. For more than a year, plant manager Ron Bent and his assistant, Joe Haley, had focused their Friday meetings on the troubling numbers, but the tenor of their May 14, 2007, meeting was different. Both men sensed that they now faced a crisis at the plant.

Bent was talking animatedly to Haley: "This is the third productivity problem in, what, two weeks? We can't climb out of this downturn with performance like that." He scowled as he signed the authorization to air-freight a large order to the Toyota plant where Sam Martinez managed the assembly line. The difference in cost was astronomical, and it had been necessitated by the slow pace of productivity at Engstrom, which meant in this case that a job due for completion on Monday wasn't completed until Thursday. But Bent couldn't afford to make a late delivery to Martinez; he was a prized but demanding customer who had designated Engstrom as a certified supplier one year earlier. Only one other supplier for Martinez's plant had achieved certified supplier status—a recognition of both extraordinary reliability and quality.

The worry lines on Bent's face deepened. Certified status meant that Martinez had personally authorized Engstrom products to be used on the auto lines without a quality inspection. Along with productivity problems, product-quality issues had also been creeping into the work done at Engstrom. Bent hoped that he was not paying to air-expedite defective mirrors to Martinez.

Haley said, "Ron, we both know the employees have been complaining for months, but yesterday and today the talk has been pretty hostile. I'm not saying there's a definite connection between nearly late delivery and the grumbling I heard, but you've got to wonder."

Bent knew that Haley, in just four months at the plant, had developed good relationships with several workers and could pick up useful information about the mood. Haley said, "They've had it with the Scanlon Plan. You hear the griping everywhere: 'What's the point of having a bonus plan if no bonus is paid for months?' And it's not just the people who've always been active in UAW

[United Auto Workers], although the union could start taking a more belligerent position at their next meeting."

Bent held up the expedite authorization. "It's a vicious cycle. We're paying a stiff price for slips in productivity—and that's money I would far rather be paying to workers as a reward for high performance."

After Haley left, Bent sat for a moment staring out the window in his office. Back in 1998 he had faced a similar crisis, marked by low employee morale. At the time, he had rated the average worker productivity at a dismal 40% of expectation. After studying the turnaround of two other plants in Indiana, Bent had painstakingly built the support needed from both employees and the Engstrom family to institute a Scanlon Plan at the plant. The choice proved propitious: the Scanlon Plan, which paid bonuses to workers for increased productivity, had been the primary catalyst of Engstrom's own turnaround.

Business had been good; over a seven-year period: sales had quadrupled. In 2005, however, a downturn hit the industry. In June 2006, Bent had been forced to lay off 46 of his 255 employees. Those who remained had not received a Scanlon bonus in seven months. Bent wondered: Had the plan outlived its usefulness? Was it a victim of its own success? The workers had become accustomed to the plan's substantial bonuses, perceiving the additional hundreds of dollars as part of their regular compensation. Therefore, when the bonuses stopped, the workers responded with anger and suspicion, as if something that rightfully belonged to them had been taken away. Now, Bent had to determine whether to scrap Scanlon, change it, or look elsewhere for solutions to sustaining productivity and ensuring quality until the downturn ended.

Understanding Scanlon Plans

The Scanlon Plan is the oldest organization-wide incentive plan still in use in the United States. Many employee incentive plans (for example, the typical bonus paid to sales representatives) are keyed to an individual's performance. Other plans base incentives on the performance of the functional work group to which an employee belongs. Organization-wide plans such as Scanlon reinforce teamwork and cooperation *across* work groups while they focus attention on cost savings and motivating employees to "work smarter, not harder."

The first Scanlon Plan was developed in the 1930s by Joseph Scanlon, a cost accountant by training and a steelworkers' union official at a steel mill facing bankruptcy. Scanlon worked with the mill owner to enlist the plant workers in identifying ideas for increasing productivity. Ultimately, the plant was saved. Although Scanlon was oriented to helping small, distressed companies, variants of his "gainsharing" plan have been adopted by a diversity of organizations.

The heart of these plans is the concept of participative management. Scanlon believed that individuals will work hard to help achieve their organization's goals so long as they have an opportunity to take responsibility for their actions and apply their skills. A key tactic is to communicate financial and other business data through all levels of the organization. While this is a symbolic motivator for many workers, the tactic also has a practical basis: everyone is encouraged to suggest ways to improve the plant's productivity.

The three plan components—the submission of suggestions for improvement by employees at all levels, the structure of the company committees that evaluate the suggestions, and then the sharing of the fruits of increased productivity through monthly bonuses—ideally work together to drive big changes in behavior and attitudes. When things are working properly, teamwork and knowledge-sharing typically improve in Scanlon organizations: collaboration fosters innovation and creativity, which in turn drive improvements in productivity, thereby ensuring the payment of bonuses. The culture in a Scanlon plant also typically becomes more change-friendly, as workers have the opportunity to make more money by changing the status quo for the better.

While all Scanlon plans share these characteristics, the plans can be tailored to support an organization's specific strategy. Plants like Engstrom were focused on cost savings, which means producing more per hour of labor spent. The bonus for everyone at Engstrom was therefore based on that ratio—production per labor hour. Organizations with different strategies base their Scanlon bonuses on different factors, but at Engstrom, pursuing higher productivity that drove labor savings was the linchpin. **Exhibit 1** shows the basic financial and structural components of the plan at Engstrom.

The Path to Plan Adoption at Engstrom

Engstrom Auto Mirror, which had operated since 1948 and enjoyed considerable success for much of its lifetime, had become mired in unprofitability by the late 1990s. The plant at that time was redesigning its production lines to incorporate new technology. The transition was not smooth, and increasingly long production delays irritated and eventually alienated customers. The plant manager lacked the sophistication with technology necessary to find solutions quickly and was inept at working with an increasingly militant union (he claimed that the union was "laying in wait" for him to make mistakes and "wanted to hurt management financially on grievances"). Embittered and tired of conflict, the manager resigned in 1998. Ron Bent, a successful manager in his mid-40s, was hired away from a camshaft production plant to attempt a turnaround.

Bent believed strongly in the power of worker incentive programs and wanted to establish one at Engstrom. Owing to his experience with different types of programs and further study he subsequently undertook, he held strong opinions about which type of plan might work best at Engstrom. At the camshaft plant, he had experienced an incentive plan that rewarded individuals—not groups or the employees as a whole—for performance. He didn't care for the results: "Individual incentive plans require a lot of manpower. You're often arguing with the union. In my experience, any time you set a rate on an operator, he will figure out a way to beat that rate." The cumulative effect of numerous small changes in tools and methods could result in incentive standards that had little relationship to workers' tasks. In support of his position, Bent claimed that the plan at the camshaft plant had "gotten so out of line" that the average worker earned 150% of the day rate.

Bent has similarly strong feelings about group incentive plans: "If you are going to change your operations or institute a new technology, product, or manufacturing line, the process to get that installed and operational is much longer under an individual or a group incentive plan."

A Scanlon Plan, Bent thought, was the best for Engstrom, given the challenges that the plant faced: "With Scanlon, workers are receptive to new methods and new machinery because they feel they are a part of the company-wide program. When you've established a Scanlon plan properly, you've also built a good communications network throughout your organization."

Though Bent had worked at and visited plants with multiple incentive plans in place, he felt that Engstrom was too small to accommodate the complexity of multiple plans. By early 1999, he and his management team began talking about the Scanlon concept around the plant, focusing on the potential benefits for workers. They also posted information about Scanlon on bulletin boards, and Bent spent many hours jawboning workers whom he had heard were opinion leaders.

In addition, Bent organized a trip for a group of workers to visit another plant that had implemented Scanlon. As Bent explained:

Our bargaining committee mingled casually with the other plant's bargaining committee, and some of our people attended the Scanlon meeting there. My management team kept in the background and let the workers develop their own sense of the situation. The workers came back enthused, and they set the stage for acceptance of Scanlon by their fellows at Engstrom.

Throughout these months of campaigning, Bent included a single consistent message in every communication he had with any employee at Engstrom: the Scanlon Plan would be adopted at the plant only if a substantial majority of workers wanted it.

In December 1999, a formal statement of the plan was prepared to be presented to all plant employees for discussion and, ultimately, a vote. The bar was high: management had insisted that, because strong employee buy-in was critical, a 75% "yea" vote was necessary. On December 10, 81% of the workers voted for the plan. Every employee then signed a Scanlon Bonus Plan Agreement. Following are its key provisions:

- The labor savings would be split 75% to employees and 25% to the company.

- A reserve would be established to cover months when productivity fell below the base ratio. Before the monthly payment of 75% to employees and 25% to the company, 25% of all bonus (both the employees' and the company's share) would be set aside as a reserve in case of a deficit month – that is, a month when total payroll costs exceeded allowed payroll.

- The structure of the Scanlon Production and Screening Committees—set up to stimulate and then evaluate employees' suggestions—was presented in detail, and methods for appointing or electing members were established.

- Conditions under which management could adjust the base ratio were made explicit. Changes in wages, sales volume, pricing, product mix, subcontracting, or technology were identified as potentially leading to increases or decreases in selling prices or standard costs and therefore as factors that might cause the base ratio to be changed.

The trickiest part of the plan adoption was the calculation of the plant's base Scanlon ratio. A benchmark was needed. Plant management selected a ratio of payroll cost to sales volume of production. Their strategy was to start with the total sales revenues generated during a specified period and then establish a percentage of that total as a standard or normative cost of labor, including managerial support. A ratio of 0.50 to 1, for example, would mean that the normative payroll cost was 50% of total sales revenue—and that employees would be paid a bonus for any month in which the payroll cost was less than 50% of total sales revenue (with the size of the bonus based on the percentage of savings achieved).

Bent remembered two of the reasons why establishing the ratio raised protracted arguments among the management team, a Scanlon consultant hired by Bent, and worker representatives:

The idea was to examine the historical ratio over a representative period of the plant's business cycle, including all ups and downs that are likely to occur. But we found it hard to identify a recent period we felt was representative, given the troubles at the plant. And we needed to consider that employees had been performing at unacceptable levels. We wanted to motivate them to excel, not just to perform less poorly.

The best reconstruction of actual performance showed that the ratio had varied between 30.5% and 68.2% over the previous fiscal year. The average for the 12 months was 43.7%. Though the Scanlon consultant suggested a target of 44%, the ratio was eventually set at 38.0%.

Scanlon's Track Record at Engstrom

The institution of the plan led quickly to an increase in productivity, as measured by the bonus ratio (payroll cost to sales value of production). While few of the early suggestions that employees made increased productivity in any meaningful way; the committees accepted as many as possible (276 out of 305 in the first year). Bent said, "We really wanted to support the submission of these suggestions."

Bent also immediately instituted monthly communication meetings open to all employees.

> We covered the results of the prior month in detail, praising the workers for improvements they suggested. We also shared our perception of business conditions, identified new customers we were working with, described new equipment that was coming into the plant— anything that we felt would be of interest to workers. They had never been exposed to this kind of communication before. Then we opened the floor for questions, and it was no-holds-barred. I set only two restrictions: no talking about anyone else's personality and no discussion of any individual's pay rate. If I couldn't answer a question, I'd ask one of my staff to answer it. I wanted the workers to see we weren't trying to conceal anything.

Tension and conflict in the plant eased, as most plant employees seemed to accept the serious intent of the plan. At the same time as the plant was achieving growth, higher profits, and consistent quality standards, the employees were also receiving good financial rewards. Scanlon bonuses were paid every month of every year following plan adoption, in addition to normal wage increases. (**Exhibit 1** includes an example of a worker's paycheck showing the bonus). "It's not just the money—though don't get me wrong, the money is great," said Jim Lutz, a worker on one of the plant's lines. "I'm getting rewarded for thinking, not just for performing the same tasks every day. To me, that means the plant values the knowledge I have about how my line runs."

Some of the most important cultural changes, according to Bent, were not apparent in the quantitative measures:

> If, say, a polisher's machine went down, he called the maintenance man, who came over to examine the machine and then went back to his area to get a tool – one tool. If that was the wrong tool, he'd go back for a different one. Sometimes he'd go back and forth three or four times. Why? Because it didn't affect his pay, or matter in any other aspect of his work, whether the machine was running or not. Now the maintenance man brings his whole tool cart over. And the machine operator helps out, almost like a surgical nurse, instead of standing around with his hands in his pockets.

At Scanlon meetings, workers regularly expressed satisfaction with these changes in their working conditions. Dori Andrews, a veteran of 10 years at the plant, said, "People see themselves as a more cooperative workforce—Engstrom is now a better place to work than it was before we brought in Scanlon. And this is the first place I've ever worked where management does not automatically say 'no' to workers. They listen."

Over time, however, enthusiasm waned and dissatisfaction grew with certain aspects of Scanlon. Suggestion rates dropped precipitously, down from hundreds to 50 a year. And two consistent themes were heard in worker complaints:

- **Distrust of bonus calculations:** Although all employees received a detailed explanation of the process and could easily access the bonus calculations, some employees thought that the company might be "playing with" the numbers. The complex nature of the calculation itself, which some felt was "full of bean-counter jargon," also caused distrust.

Before the plan was adopted, production achievement was measured by total units produced. However, the Scanlon bonus was influenced by many other factors, including the length of the month, sales mix, overtime, and product returns. Conceivably, a low Scanlon bonus could be paid following a month in which a record number of units were produced.

Another point of distrust shared by some employees was suspicion whenever the management team changed the ratio, which occurred four times between 2000 and 2005 (the final reduction was to 32.6%). Some workers accused management of creating a "moving carrot," despite their explanations for the reductions.

- **Question of fairness:** Some employees felt that supervisors should have received a reduced bonus because they were "not working as hard as we are."

These reactions did not surprise Bent: "A Scanlon program won't perpetuate itself. You have to give it a shot in the arm every so often—whenever the work force needs it."

Before Bent could decide how to provide that "shot in the arm," the industry downturn that began in 2005 gradually dragged down the workforce's morale along with the sales figures. The atmosphere in Bent's monthly meetings with employees grew increasingly charged, as he talked about possible layoffs and the causes for declines in productivity. It was clear that every month without a bonus further chilled labor-management relations (see **Exhibit 2** for a description of how the plan handled so-called deficit months). Bent's exhortations—about preserving the culture of the plant and the danger the Engstrom family might close that plant unless profitability trends were reversed— increasingly fell on deaf ears.

The layoffs, when they finally occurred in mid-2006, shook the confidence of even the most fervent Scanlon proponents among the workforce. The event served as an emotional lightning rod in the plant and as a temporal dividing line between good and bad times in the plant. By the time Joe Haley joined the management team in January 2007, there was increasing evidence of worker disaffection. For example, Haley's review of inventory reports led him to suspect pilfering, and his conversations with workers only deepened his suspicions.

Now, in May 2007, Bent felt he urgently needed to make changes before conditions deteriorated further. But he wondered what kind of change might work. In all the reading and listening he'd done he hadn't heard of any alternative incentive plan that motivated superior employee performance in both good times and bad – so he saw no reason to replace Scanlon with another plan. Could he revise Scanlon in some way that worked better during a downturn? Could he try to identify and change organizational factors that might be undermining Scanlon at the plant?

As Bent's uncertainty about these issues deepened, personal doubts arose about his own performance. He felt a heightened recognition of Scanlon as more a process of organizational development than a plan prescribing specific steps to follow. Had he and his top managers done everything they could to make Scanlon a sustainable success? Had they thought of it too narrowly as a bonus plan instead of a broader opportunity to build a different workplace culture? Or was there something else he was missing?

Exhibit 1 Financial and Structural Components of the Scanlon Plan at Engstrom

Suggestion plan process

1. Employees suggest ways to improve productivity at the plant. Suggestion categories include methods (e.g., eliminating unnecessary operations); machinery and equipment (e.g., reducing machine set-up time); and paperwork (e.g., simplifying or combining forms).

2. Eight production committees, each composed of a supervisor and two elected employee representatives, review the suggestions, passing along disputed suggestions or suggestions costing more than a specified amount to the screening committee.

3. The screening committee determines how to handle all suggestions passed from the production committees and also reviews the monthly bonus calculations from plant management. This committee is composed of

   - Five employees elected from the production committees.

   - Four management representatives appointed by the plant manager.

   - The plant manager.

Bonus plan

- Bonus paid monthly as part of regular paycheck

- Calculated as (total payroll costs plus vacation and holiday accruals)/sales value of production

- The base ratio represents the normal or expected total payroll cost to produce one dollar's worth of sales, expressed as a percentage of the sales value of production

Sample bonus calculation:

Sales value of production[a]	$4,000,000
Allowed payroll at 38% (or 38% of sales value)[b]	1,520,000
Actual payroll	1,280,000
Scanlon bonus pool	240,000
25% set aside for reserve[c]	60,000
Bonus balance	180,000
Company share: 25%	45,000
Employee share: 75%	135,000
Participating payroll[d]	1,260,000
Bonus % (employee share/participating payroll)	10.71%

a. Management adjusted this value for returns, increases, or decreases in inventory—number is not equivalent to shipments.

b. The normal total labor cost is 38% of the sales value of production, or 38¢ for each $1 of product produced at sales value.

c. 25% set aside before bonus distribution to form a reserve to cover deficit months.

d. Actual payroll minus payroll for employees on paid nonworking days (vacation, holidays, jury duty, etc.) or on job less than 60 days

Example of a Scanlon bonus in a floor worker's monthly paycheck

Name	Hours	Overtime Hours	Hourly Rate	Total Pay	Bonus %	Bonus	Total Earnings
J. Smith	184	36	$15	$3,570	10.71	$382	$3,952

Exhibit 2 Deficit Months under the Scanlon Plan

At the end of each Scanlon year, which is June 30, all money remaining in the reserve accounts is distributed 75% to the people and 25% to the company in what is referred to as a thirteenth monthly Scanlon bonus check. In the event a Scanlon year ends with a deficit balance in the reserve account, the entire deficit is absorbed by the company and is not charged against any future bonus. The reserve account example illustrates how this works and shows the effect of a deficit month.

Reserve Account Example

Month	Add This Montth	Reserve Total
January	$22,000	$22,000
February	34,550	56,550
March (Deficit month)	(12,000)	44,550
April	19,982	64,532
May	28,890	93,422
June	26,578	120,000
	Company Share—25%	$30,000
	Employees Share—75%	90,000
	TOTAL	$120,000

Deficit Month Example

Value of Productivity	$2,100,000
Allowed Payroll at 37%	777,000
Actual Payroll	795,000
Bonus Pool	$18,000
Reserve for Deficit Months	(-$18,000)

In this example, the actual payroll was greater than the allowed payroll, which results in a deficit bonus pool. This is charged against the bonus reserve account and reduces the amount left in the reserve at the end of the Scanlon year.

Dave Armstrong (A)

Dave Armstrong is the disguised name of the 29-year old second year MBA student who wrote this case.

I grew up in Dumas, Texas, population 9000, graduating from a small liberal arts college in central Texas. Immediately upon graduation I went to work for Thorne Enterprises in Austin, Texas, as a computer programmer. After 6 months Mr. Thorne made me president of a subsidiary company that sold conveyor belt scales. The subsidiary had 6 employees including myself. As a practical matter, I was the chief salesman. Belt scale sales had been flat through the 1973-1974 recession and did not improve much under my management. After eighteen months I quit to go into the life insurance business in Amarillo.

In five years with nothing more than a secretary and a telephone, my income was around $60,000 a year. It was a comfortable living, but the problem was I was a one-man band. When I took a vacation or even the afternoon off, the entire sales process came to a screeching halt. There was no momentum built up in the way I operated.

I applied to the Harvard Business School to see if I could get in. I hadn't considered what I would do if I got accepted. But when I was accepted, I decided that I had to go. I would still be receiving renewal income from my old policyholders, so my wife and I would not have to make too much of a sacrifice in our lifestyle.

But now, it's early March. I'm three months from graduation and I have to figure out what to do next. For the last several months I've been trying to sell a producing oil lease for an exploration company in Kentucky. It's a pretty good deal from my standpoint. They pay my expenses if I don't sell it, and an 8% commission (about $30,000) if I do sell it. If this deal sells, the 30K would make quite a difference in my plans.

At this point, I've got three job prospects. I'll call them Job A, Job B, and Job C. Job A is the one I really want, since it has the most upside potential. But I'd say it has a pretty good

Professor George Wu prepared this case as the basis for class discussion rather than to illustrate effective or ineffective handling of an administrative situation. It is based on an earlier case by Professor David E. Bell.

1

chance of not working out at all. Job B had better odds of working out but doesn't have quite the same excitement as Job A. Job C is what I would call a traditional job.

Job A

Mr. Thorne called me last fall about an idea he has for a piggyback rail terminal to be located halfway between Dallas and Houston. I got a group of second year students at the B-school to do a feasibility study of the idea. Thorne's idea is to develop a rail terminal on 9,000 acres he owns there and ship truck trailers into and out of Texas via rail. The idea of a truck trailer riding "piggyback" on a rail car is not new. But what is new is the idea of a hub serving two major cities. This terminal would draw business from both Dallas and Houston and would be built on land that is 1/100 the cost of Dallas or Houston industrial property. That's where the economies come in. Thorne also owns a railroad that already serves the proposed terminal site. Hopefully this terminal will transform the surrounding real estate into an attractive industrial site.

Mr. Thorne suggested that the terminal could be segregated from the rest of his business in order to provide a cleaner way for me to participate in the equity. At this stage, we think it will require around $1 million to get started: $300K for equipment and $700K for one year's operating expenses. I'd put in as much money as I could and Mr. Thorne would supply the rest. In addition to profit sharing, I'd be paid $50-70K, salary and bonus, to start-up and run the facility.

I have to give Mr. Thorne an answer by the end of March.

Job B

Robert Irwin owns an oil exploration company in Houston. I met him during the course of trying to sell the Kentucky oil property. Irwin and I have talked about setting up a corporation that would actively seek out producing oil leases that might be for sale. The oil and gas business has been in a severe recession for eighteen months now and a large number of producing properties have been forced on the market at fire sale prices. I would have two petroleum engineers working for me to evaluate these properties. Irwin's exploration company would receive a standard investment banking fee. I would put up a third of the equity ($100K). In addition, I would receive annual compensation equal to the greater of $60,000 or one-third of the profits.

This is really only a short-term deal. Within two years, the oil and gas glut will be gone and the attractiveness of this business will disappear also.

If the oil and gas glut dries up before we got our business launched, I would probably stay on with Irwin as an agent or broker to sell oil and gas properties. There would be no equity role for me in this but commission at 8% would add up fast if I'm good. This would also give me an opportunity to develop many contacts with prospective buyers and sellers.

2

Hopefully I would develop a strong relationship with a single buyer and then enter into an equity deal with him at some point in the future.

Job C

The third possibility is what I'd call a conventional job. Earlier this spring Mr. Irwin put me in touch with a large pension fund management company in Houston. They have plans to begin an oil and gas investment fund for key executives in the firm. I have interviewed for a position where I'd be working with two or three others to evaluate oil and gas properties for the fund.

This position doesn't open up for another 6-12 months, but they'll put me on in the interim as a securities analyst for around $45K until the fund is started. I'm going to Houston in three weeks for another series of interviews and will have to let them know if I'm serious or not.

The Decision

I've never been faced with a hard choice before. When I graduated from college, working for Thorne as a computer programmer seemed like a great opportunity. And going to Harvard Business School looked like the obvious thing to do once I was accepted. Now, for the first time in my life, things aren't so clear. Thorne needs a decision in a couple of weeks. Some days, when I think of all the financial upside, I'm tempted to reach for the phone and tell Thorne yes. But I decide to sleep on it and wake up frightened about the $200K to $300K that I might have to put into Thorne's project. All of a sudden I think about all the contacts I might develop working with Irwin and Job B looks pretty good. f course, I've asked my wife for her opinion. She's been after me to take Job C and thinks that I'm cra y for "gambling" our money on these other deals. But really all she want is that I be happy in my work that's what it comes down to.

Part B of the Dave Armstrong case should be brought to lecture class.

It is not necessary to read or review to complete your Case Memo HW. Do not include any information from Part B in your Case Memo.

Dave Armstrong (B)

One night after having browsed through my three cases for the next day, I just couldn't bring myself to do any work. I picked up the managerial decision making case for that night again. It was about some quant jock from Wharton who had used preference analysis to assist his father in making a major career change. Since I was facing a major career choice of my own, I tried again to finish the case. About half way through, I decided I should do this stuff for myself and forget about this guy's dad. So I put the unfinished case aside and drew up **Exhibit 1**.

Exhibit 1 is my rough cut analysis of what makes a job "good." I started by listing all of the attributes that the ideal job would have, such as a high salary, a bonus, equity, etc. Then I made an assessment of how each job I was considering measured up relative to each other. Since I knew that both Job A and Job B had uncertain outcomes depending on the economy and my own ability, I created a Hi and Lo scenario for each of these. Job C was a traditional job and as such had only one scenario to consider. So for each attribute, I now had five scenarios to assess.

For each attribute, I gave the best scenario a raw score of 100 and the worst a raw score of 0. For example, the salary for Job A is poor compared to the salary for Job B or Job C. But the bonus for Job A is better than the bonus for Job B, provided that we are talking about the Hi scenarios for both. However, Job C has a small bonus that is better then the bonus for either Job A-Lo or Job B-Lo.

Travel was easy to assess. Job A has limited travel, just about the right amount, and therefore gets a score of 100. Job C has no travel, which seems confining to me. Job B requires extensive travel. I would prefer extensive travel to no travel, so Job B gets a score of 50 and Job C a score of 0.

The most attractive feature of Job C is the contacts I would make in the Houston business community. Conversely, one of the biggest drawbacks to Job A is that I would be

---

Professor George Wu prepared this case as the basis for class discussion rather than to illustrate effective or ineffective handling of an administrative situation. It is based on an earlier case by Professor David E. Bell.

involved in a prosaic industry (railroading) and would make very few contacts outside of the central Texas area. This "contact" issue is one of the most difficult aspects of this whole career decision to assess and as such is one of the motivating factors for doing this analysis.

The next step was to assign weights to each attribute and then to produce "weighted assessments" by multiplying each "raw assessment" by its weight. If I understand this, these weighted assessments mean, for example, that the improvement in quality of Contacts between Job A and Job B (either Hi or Lo) is equal to the improvement in Work Flexibility between Job C and Job B-Hi scenario.

To risk adjust each scenario, I assigned probabilities to each. Job A-Hi has only a 20% chance of working out. I am almost positive that Job C will work out so I've given it a 1.0 chance.

So after all the math is complete, I end up with overall expected preference scores of 366, 356, and 206. This seems to confirm my view that I should forget Job C. I am kind of surprised that Job A and Job B end up so close. In my heart, I want to do the piggyback deal (Job A).

I showed this table to my wife. She was really interested and understood what was going on. She asks what's wrong with Job C. The other jobs both seem awfully risky to her, but again she tells me that she wants me to be happy with my work.

One other thing. She'd like to stay in Boston rather than move to some unknown place. We have a house in Belmont and our two kids are in school. It may sound strange but Boston would be a good location from which to pursue the oil and gas deal (Job B). Being from the oil patch (Texas) adds credibility up here. Since most of the action is on the phone or involves flying, it doesn't matter a whole lot where you're based. I think the main thing is she wants to resolve the uncertainty about where we'll live. She wants our next move to be our last move, at least for a while.

2

Exhibit 1

		RAW ASSESSMENTS					WEIGHTED ASSESSMENTS				
		JOB A		JOB B		JOB C	JOB A		JOB B		JOB C
Weight	Objective Description	HI	LO	HI	LO		HI	LO	HI	LO	
0.1	Salary	0	0	100	80	80	0	0	10	8	8
0.9	Bonus	100	0	80	0	20	90	0	72	0	18
1.0	Equity	100	0	80	0	0	100	0	80	0	0
0.9	Fun	100	60	50	60	0	90	54	45	54	0
0.6	Travel	100	100	50	50	0	60	60	30	30	0
0.8	Contacts	0	0	60	60	100	0	0	48	48	80
1.0	Ideas	0	0	40	40	100	0	0	40	40	100
0.6	Work Flexibility	100	30	80	30	0	60	18	48	18	0
0.3	Title	100	100	80	80	0	30	30	24	24	0
0.8	# of Employees	100	100	80	80	0	80	80	64	64	0
0.7	Location	100	100	0	0	0	70	70	0	0	0
	Subtotals (Not Risk Adjusted)						580	312	461	286	206
	times probabilities						×.2	×.8	×.4	×.6	×1.0
	Intermediate products						116	250	184	172	206
	Risk adjusted Preferences						**366**		**356**		**206**

Foundations
of Group Behavior

From Chapter 9 of *Organizational Behavior*, Seventeenth Edition. Stephen P. Robbins, Timothy A. Judge. Copyright © 2017 by Pearson Education, Inc. All rights reserved.

Foundations of Group Behavior

LEARNING OBJECTIVES

After studying this chapter, you should be able to:

1 Distinguish between the different types of groups.

2 Describe the punctuated-equilibrium model of group development.

3 Show how role requirements change in different situations.

4 Demonstrate how norms exert influence on an individual's behavior.

5 Show how status and size differences affect group performance.

6 Describe how issues of cohesiveness and diversity can be integrated for group effectiveness.

7 Contrast the strengths and weaknesses of group decision making.

MyManagementLab®
★ **Chapter Warm Up**

If your professor has chosen to assign this, go to the Assignments section of **mymanagementlab.com** to complete the chapter warm up.

CRUSHED BY THE HERD

Answer quickly: If you were an employee of this car's manufacturer and could have prevented the accident that killed two people and injured a third, would you?

No doubt you answered "yes" automatically, but if we took a few minutes to think about it, we might have to honestly answer "maybe." When we are members of groups as powerful as those in General Motors (GM), it can be very difficult to predict our behavior. Our perceptions of right and wrong can become skewed, making even straightforward ethical decisions like this one confusing.

Courtland Kelley of GM (which made the Chevrolet Cobalt in the photo) learned firsthand the pressures groups can exert on an individual. As the leader of GM's U.S. safety inspection program, he expected his workgroups to act upon the serious safety flaws he found in the vehicle. Instead, "Group after group and committee after committee within GM that reviewed the issue failed to take action or acted too slowly," a later report noted. Kelley's colleague, auditor William McAleer, agreed that management refused to acknowledge safety issues with vehicles. "Any time you had a problem, you ran into resistance," he said. "Nobody owns [the] defect. And the plant can say, 'It was working when it left here.' And the supplier can say, 'My part was good.' It relieves everybody of responsibility."

When Kelley pushed harder to have the Cobalt's faulty ignition switch addressed, management actively discouraged his efforts. The group ordered him to stay quiet about defects and rename them as mere convenience issues. At one point, his direct supervisor forbade him to share data on serious defects with McAleer and threatened to transfer him to a lesser position on the outskirts of town, while the management group tried to stifle the information. Kelley said, "I heard them have many discussions about not wanting to notify the government, not putting voice mails out to dealers, because the government could get them" and learn of the defects.

When Kelley couldn't be silenced, the group pressured him into toning down the wording in his reports and shuffled him into less responsible jobs. McAleer, who suffered similar circumstances until he was laid off in 2004, observed, "The system acts as if raising a safety issue internally were an act of corporate treason." Kelley landed off the organization chart in a "special assignment job," where he was told to "come up with charts, predict warranty for the vehicle, but not find every problem that GM might have." McAleer said of Kelley, "He still has a job—he doesn't have a career. He has no possibility of promotion." Kelley was not fired likely only because he brought lawsuits against GM.

On the positive side, Kelley's efforts have doubtlessly saved lives. After 13 deaths and 54 crashes, 2,084,000 Cobalts were recalled, as were almost 70,000 other vehicles with defects he found. From this standpoint, the battle he fought and his years in a "GM purgatory" job have been worth it. "I felt morally responsible to fix a problem that I found in a vehicle," he said of his work on the Chevy Trailblazer. However, his heroic efforts have cost him many court battles, and he has developed chest pains, panic attacks, depression, and insomnia. "I clearly saw him age drastically," his doctor, Van Alstine, said. "You just knew he was under a tremendous amount of stress. . . . It shook him to the core."

Sources: G. Gutierrez and R. Gardella, " 'Willful Ignorance' Ex-Auditor Blasts GM for Cutting Safety Program," *NBC News,* July 9, 2014, http://www.nbcnews.com/storyline/gm-recall/willful-ignorance-ex-auditor-blasts-gm-cutting-safety-program-n152311; T. Higgins and N. Summers, "If Only They Had Listened," *Bloomberg Businessweek,* June 2014, 48–53; and S. McEachern, "General Motors 'Whistleblower' Was Told to Back Off after Finding Safety Flaws," *GM Authority,* June 19, 2014, http://gmauthority.com/blog/2014/06/general-motors-whistleblower-was-told-to-back-off-after-finding-safety-flaws/.

The story of Courtland Kelley's attempts to counter the effects of group pressure provides us with a powerful example of the ways groups can (mis)behave. Even though Kelley resisted for all the right ethical reasons, sometimes countering group pressure can mean costly consequences for the individual, as he found.

Groups have their place—and their pitfalls. Some groups can exert a powerful positive influence, and others can be tragically negative. The objective of this chapter is to familiarize you with group and team concepts, provide you with a foundation for understanding how groups and teams work, and show you how to create effective working units. Let's begin by defining a *group*.

Defining and Classifying Groups

1 Distinguish between the different types of groups.

group Two or more individuals, interacting and interdependent, who have come together to achieve particular objectives.

formal group A designated workgroup defined by an organization's structure.

informal group A group that is neither formally structured nor organizationally determined; such a group appears in response to the need for social contact.

In organizational behavior, a **group** is two or more individuals, interacting and interdependent, who have come together to achieve particular objectives. Groups can be either formal or informal. A **formal group** is defined by the organization's structure, with designated work assignments and established tasks. In formal groups, the behaviors team members should engage in are stipulated by and directed toward organizational goals. The six members of an airline flight crew are a formal group, for example. In contrast, an **informal group** is neither formally structured nor organizationally determined. Informal groups in the work environment meet the need for social contact. Three employees from different departments who regularly have lunch or coffee together are an informal group. These types of interactions among individuals, though informal, deeply affect their behavior and performance.

Social Identity

social identity theory Perspective that considers when and why individuals consider themselves members of groups.

People often feel strongly about their groups partly because, as research indicates, shared experiences amplify our perception of events.[1] Also, according to research in Australia, sharing painful experiences, in particular, increases our felt bond and trust with others.[2] Why do people form groups, and why do they feel so strongly about them? Consider the celebrations that follow when a sports team wins a national championship. The winner's supporters are elated, and sales of team-related shirts, jackets, and hats skyrocket. Fans of the losing team feel dejected, even embarrassed. Why? Even though fans have little to do with the actual performance of the sports team, their self-image can be wrapped up in their identification with the group. Our tendency to personally invest in the accomplishments of a group is the territory of **social identity theory**.

Jeffrey Webster, director of human resources at a Nissan plant in Mississippi, also serves as the director of the plant's gospel choir. Choir members are a diverse group of employees who identify with each other as they all share a love of singing and performing for fellow workers, company executives, state officials, and community events.
Source: Rogelio V. Solis/AP Images

Social identity theory proposes that people have emotional reactions to the failure or success of their group because their self-esteem gets tied to whatever happens to the group.[3] When your group does well, you bask in reflected glory, and your own self-esteem rises. When your group does poorly, you might feel bad about yourself, or you might reject that part of your identity like "fair-weather fans." Furthermore, if your group is devalued and disrespected, your social identity might feel threatened, and you might endorse deviant behaviors to "get even" and restore your group's standing.[4] Social identities can even lead people to experience pleasure as a result of seeing another group suffer. We often see these feelings of *schadenfreude* in the joy fans experience when a hated team loses.[5]

People develop many identities through the course of their lives. You might define yourself in terms of the organization you work for, the city you live in, your profession, your religious background, your ethnicity, and/or your gender. Over time, some groups you belong to may become more significant to you than others. A U.S. expatriate working in Rome might be very aware of being from the United States, for instance, but doesn't give national identity a second thought when transferring from Tulsa to Tucson.[6] We may thus pick and choose which of our social identities are salient to the situation, or we may find that our social identities are in conflict, such as the identities of business leader and parent.[7]

Our social identities help us understand who we are and where we fit in with other people, and research indicates they bring us better health and lower levels of depression because we become less likely to attribute negative situations to internal or insurmountable reasons.[8] However, to experience these good outcomes, we need to feel our social identities are positive.[9]

Until now, we've discussed social identities primarily in a cultural context. However, the identity we may feel with respect to our organization is only one aspect of our work-related identities (see OB Poll). Within our organizations and workgroups, we can develop many identities through: (1) *relational* identification, when we connect with others because of our roles, and (2) *collective* identification, when we connect with the aggregate characteristics of our groups.

OB POLL

Most People Report Drinking with Coworkers Is Acceptable

At a meal during a job interview — Never
At a meal with coworkers — 22%
4% 14%
At the celebration of a company milestone — 28%
At a retirement party — 32%
At a meal with a client or customer — 40%
At a holiday party — 70%

Note: Society for Human Resources Management (SHRM) survey of 501 individuals and how drinking is viewed in their organization at a range of work-related activities.
Source: Based on S. M. Heathfield, "To Drink or Not to Drink: Does Alcohol Drinking Mix Safely with Work Events?" *About.com Guide,* 2013, http://humanresources.about.com/od/networking/qt/drink_i3.htm.

Often, our identification with our workgroups is stronger than with our organizations, but both are important to positive outcomes in attitudes and behaviors. Additionally, if we have low identification in relation to the group, there may be increased among by group members. If we have low identification with our organizations, we may experience decreased satisfaction and engage in fewer organizational citizenship behaviors (OCBs).[10]

Ingroups and Outgroups

ingroup favoritism Perspective in which we see members of our ingroup as better than other people, and people not in our group as all the same.

Ingroup favoritism occurs when we see members of our group as better than other people, and people not in our group as all the same. Recent research suggests that people with low openness and/or low agreeableness are more susceptible to ingroup favoritism.[11]

outgroup The inverse of an ingroup, which can mean everyone outside the group, but more usually an identified other group.

Whenever there is an ingroup, there is by necessity an **outgroup**, which is sometimes everyone else, but is usually an identified group known by the ingroup's members. For example, if my ingroup is the Republican party in U.S. politics, my outgroup might be anyone in the world who is not a Republican, but it's more likely to be the other U.S. political parties, or perhaps just Democrats.

When there are ingroups and outgroups, there is often animosity between them. One of the most powerful sources of ingroup–outgroup feelings is the practice of religion, even in the workplace. One global study, for instance, found that when groups became heavily steeped in religious rituals and discussions, they became especially discriminatory toward outgroups and aggressive if the outgroups had more resources.[12] Consider an example from another study of a U.K. Muslim organization that supported Al-Qaeda and identified moderate U.K. Muslims as its outgroup. The Al-Qaeda ingroup was not neutral toward the moderate outgroup; instead, the ingroup denounced the moderates, denigrating them as deviant and threatening outward aggression.[13]

Social Identity Threat

Ingroups and outgroups pave the way for *social identity threat*, which is akin to stereotype threat. With social identity threat, individuals believe they will be personally negatively evaluated due to their association with a devalued group, and they may lose confidence and performance effectiveness. One study found, for example, that when subjects from high and low socioeconomic backgrounds took a high-pressure math test, the low-status subjects who felt social identity threat could be as confident as the high-status subjects only when they were first deliberately encouraged about their abilities.[14]

Stages of Group Development

> ○ **WATCH IT!**
> If your professor has assigned this, go to the Assignments section of **mymanagementlab.com** to complete the video exercise titled *Witness.org: Managing Groups & Teams*.

2 Describe the punctuated-equilibrium model of group development.

Temporary groups with finite deadlines pass through a unique sequencing of actions (or inaction): (1) Their first meeting sets the group's direction, (2) the first phase of group activity is one of inertia and thus slower progress, (3) a transition takes place exactly when the group has used up half its allotted time, (4) this transition initiates major changes, (5) a second phase of inertia follows the transition, and (6) the group's last meeting is characterized by markedly

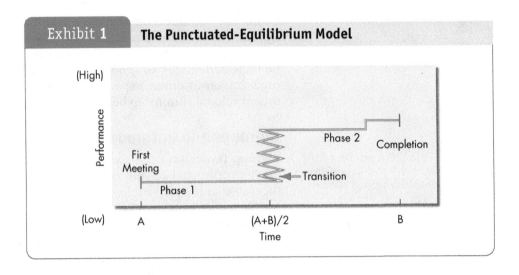

Exhibit 1   **The Punctuated-Equilibrium Model**

punctuated-equilibrium model   A set of phases that temporary groups go through that involves transitions between inertia and activity.

accelerated activity.[15] This pattern, called the **punctuated-equilibrium model**, is shown in Exhibit 1.

Let's discuss each stage of the model. At the first meeting, the group's general purpose and direction is established, and then a framework of behavioral patterns and assumptions through which the group will approach its project emerges, sometimes in the first few seconds of the group's existence. Once set, the group's direction is solidified and is unlikely to be reexamined throughout the first half of its life. This is a period of inertia—the group tends to stand still or become locked into a fixed course of action even if it gains new insights that challenge initial patterns and assumptions.

One of the most interesting discoveries in studies was that groups experienced a transition precisely halfway between the first meeting and the official deadline—whether members spent an hour on their project or 6 months. The midpoint appears to work like an alarm clock, heightening members' awareness that their time is limited and they need to get moving. This transition ends phase 1 and is characterized by a concentrated burst of changes, dropping of old patterns, and adoption of new perspectives. The transition sets a revised direction for phase 2, a new equilibrium or period of inertia in which the group executes plans created during the transition period.

The group's last meeting is characterized by a final burst of activity to finish its work. In summary, the punctuated-equilibrium model characterizes groups as exhibiting long periods of inertia interspersed with brief revolutionary changes triggered primarily by members' awareness of time and deadlines. This is not the only model of group stages by far, but it is a dominant theory with strong support. Keep in mind, however, that this model doesn't apply to all groups but is suited to the finite quality of temporary task groups working under a time deadline.[16]

Group Property 1: Roles

3   Show how role requirements change in different situations.

Workgroups shape members' behavior, and they also help explain individual behavior as well as the performance of the group itself. Some defining group properties are *roles, norms, status, size, cohesiveness, and diversity*. We'll discuss each in the sections that follow. Let's begin with the first group property, roles.

Shakespeare said, "All the world's a stage, and all the men and women merely players." Using the same metaphor, all group members are actors, each playing

role A set of expected behavior patterns attributed to someone occupying a given position in a social unit.

a **role**, a set of expected behavior patterns attributed to someone occupying a given position in a social unit. We are required to play a number of diverse roles, both on and off our jobs. As we'll see, one of the tasks in understanding behavior is grasping the role a person is currently playing.

Bill is a plant manager with EMM Industries, a large electrical equipment manufacturer in Phoenix. He fulfills a number of roles—employee, member of middle management, and electrical engineer. Off the job, Bill holds more roles: husband, father, Catholic, tennis player, member of the Thunderbird Country Club, and president of his homeowners' association. Many of these roles are compatible; some create conflicts. How does Bill's religious commitment influence his managerial decisions regarding layoffs, expense padding, and provision of accurate information to government agencies? A recent offer of promotion requires Bill to relocate, yet his family wants to stay in Phoenix. Can the role demands of his job be reconciled with the demands of his husband and father roles?

Different groups impose different role requirements on individuals. Like Bill, we all play a number of roles, and our behavior varies with each. But how do we know each role's requirements? We draw upon our role perceptions to frame our ideas of appropriate behaviors, and learn the expectations of our groups.

Role Perception

role perception An individual's view of how he or she is supposed to act in a given situation.

Our view of how we're supposed to act in a given situation is a **role perception**. We get role perceptions from stimuli all around us—for example, friends, books, films, and television, as when we form an impression of politicians from *House of Cards*. Apprenticeship programs allow beginners to watch an expert so they can learn to act as they should.

Role Expectations

role expectations How others believe a person should act in a given situation.

psychological contract An unwritten agreement that sets out what management expects from an employee and vice versa.

Role expectations are the way others believe you should act in a given context. A U.S. federal judge is viewed as having propriety and dignity, while a football coach is seen as aggressive, dynamic, and inspiring to the players.

In the workplace, we look at role expectations through the perspective of the **psychological contract**: an unwritten agreement that exists between employees and employers. This agreement sets out mutual expectations.[17] Management

Les Hatton, manager of a Recreational Equipment, Inc., store in Manhattan, pumps up employees before the store's grand opening. Part of the psychological contract between REI and its employees is the expectation that salespeople will display enthusiasm and generate excitement while welcoming and serving customers.
Source: Matt Payton/AP Images

is expected to treat employees justly, provide acceptable working conditions, clearly communicate what is a fair day's work, and give feedback on how well an employee is doing. Employees are expected to demonstrate a good attitude, follow directions, and show loyalty to the organization.

What happens if management is derelict in its part of the bargain? We can expect negative effects on employee performance and satisfaction. One study among restaurant managers found that violations of the psychological contract were related to greater intentions to quit, while another study of a variety of different industries found psychological contracts were associated with lower levels of productivity, higher levels of theft, and greater work withdrawal.[18]

There is evidence that perceptions of psychological contracts vary across cultures. In France, where people are individualistic and power is more asymmetric, contracts are perceived as self-interested yet favoring the more powerful party. In Canada, where people are individualistic but power is more symmetric, contracts are perceived as self-interested yet focused on balanced reciprocity. In China, where people are collectivistic and power is more asymmetric, contracts are perceived as going beyond the work context into employees' lives. And in Norway, where people are collectivistic but power is more symmetric, contracts are perceived as more relational and based on trust.[19]

Role Conflict

When compliance with one role requirement may make it difficult to comply with another, the result is **role conflict**.[20] At the extreme, two or more role expectations may be contradictory. For example, if as a manager you were to provide a performance evaluation of a person you mentored, your roles as evaluator and mentor may conflict. Similarly, we can experience **interrole conflict**[21] when the expectations of our different, separate groups are in opposition. An example can be found in work–family conflict, which Bill experiences when expectations placed on him as a husband and father differ from those placed on him as an executive with EMM Industries. Bill's wife and children want to remain in Phoenix, while EMM expects its employees to be responsive to the company's needs and requirements. Although it might be in Bill's financial and career interests to accept a relocation, the conflict centers on choosing between family and work role expectations. Indeed, a great deal of research demonstrates that work–family conflict is one of the most significant sources of stress for most employees.[22]

Within organizations, most employees are simultaneously in occupations, workgroups, divisions, and demographic groups, and these identities can conflict when the expectations of one clash with the expectations of another.[23] During mergers and acquisitions, employees can be torn between their identities as members of their original organization and of the new parent company.[24] Multinational organizations also have been shown to lead to dual identification—with the local division and with the international organization.[25]

Role Play and Assimilation

The degree to which we comply with our role perceptions and expectations—even when we don't agree with them initially—can be surprising. One of the most illuminating role and identity experiments was done a number of years ago by psychologist Philip Zimbardo and his associates.[26] They created a "prison" in the basement of the Stanford psychology building; hired emotionally stable, physically healthy, law-abiding students who scored "normal average" on personality tests; randomly assigned them the role of either "guard" or "prisoner"; and established some basic rules.

It took little time for the "prisoners" to accept the authority positions of the "guards" and for the mock guards to adjust to their new authority roles. Consistent with social identity theory, the guards came to see the prisoners as a negative outgroup, and they developed stereotypes about the "typical" prisoner personality type. After the guards crushed a rebellion attempt on the second day, the prisoners became increasingly passive. Whatever the guards "dished out," the prisoners took. The prisoners actually began to believe and act like they were inferior and powerless. Every guard, at some time during the simulation, engaged in abusive, authoritative behavior. One said, "I was surprised at myself. . . . I made them call each other names and clean the toilets out with their bare hands. I practically considered the prisoners cattle, and I kept thinking: 'I have to watch out for them in case they try something.'" Surprisingly, during the entire experiment—even after days of abuse—not one prisoner said, "Stop this. I'm a student like you. This is just an experiment!" The researchers had to end the study after only 6 days because of the participants' pathological reactions.

What can we conclude from this study? Like the rest of us, the participants had learned stereotyped conceptions of guard and prisoner roles from the mass media and their own personal experiences in power and powerless relationships gained at home (parent–child), in school (teacher–student), and in other situations. This background allowed them easily and rapidly to assume roles and, with a vague notion of the social identity of their roles and no prior personality pathology or training for the parts they were playing, to execute extreme forms of behavior consistent with those roles.

Myth or Science?

Gossip and Exclusion Are Toxic for Groups

This is not necessarily true. But it's certainly counterintuitive, so let's explore the conditions.

What is gossip? Most of us might say gossip is talking about others, sharing rumors, and speculating about others' behaviors; gossip affects a person's reputation. We might also say gossip is malicious, but according to researchers, it can serve positive social functions, too. Prosocial gossip can expose behavior that exploits other people, which can lead to positive changes. For example, if Julie tells Chris that Alex is bullying Summer, then Chris has learned about Alex's poor behavior through gossiping. Chris might refuse to partner with Alex on a work project, which might limit Alex's opportunities with the organization, preventing him from bullying more people. Alternatively, as the gossip spreads, Alex might feel exposed for his behavior and conform to group expectations against bullying behavior. In fact,

according to research, Alex is likely to cooperate with the group in response to the gossip, and others hearing and spreading the gossip are likely also to cooperate by not acting on their impulses toward bad behavior.

What about excluding Alex? There are two types of exclusion in the workplace: leaving someone out of a group, and ostracizing an individual. Both lead to the same end—the person isn't part of the group—but while simply leaving someone out of a group might not send a message of exclusion, ostracism certainly does. Ostracism is more of a felt punishment than gossip since it is more direct. Research indicates that ostracized individuals cooperate to a greater degree when they are around the group to show a willingness to conform, hoping to be invited back into the group.

Can gossip and ostracism work together? Yes, according to a recent study. When subjects were given an

opportunity to gossip about the work of another subject, that subject cooperated more than before; when the opportunity to gossip was paired with the ability to ostracize, that subject cooperated to a much greater degree.

Thus, gossip and exclusion may provide groups with benefits, at least when the gossip is confined to truthful work-related discussion, when the opportunity still exists to rejoin the group with full standing, and when the group norms are positive.

Sources: M. Cikara and J. J. Van Bavel, "The Neuroscience of Intergroup Relations: An Integrative Review," *Perspectives on Psychological Science* 9, no. 3 (2014): 245–74; M. Feinberg, R. Willer, and M. Schultz, "Gossip and Ostracism Promote Cooperation in Groups," *Psychological Science* 25, no. 3 (2014): 656–64; and I. H. Smith, K. Aquino, S. Koleva, and J. Graham, "The Moral Ties That Bind...Even to Out-Groups: The Interactive Effect of Moral Identity and the Binding Moral Foundations," *Psychological Science* (2014): 1554–62.

A follow-up reality television show was conducted by the BBC.[27] The BBC results were dramatically different from those of the Stanford experiment, partially because the show used a less intense simulated prison setting. The "guards" were far more careful in their behavior, limiting their aggressive treatment of "prisoners" and expressing concerns about how their actions might be perceived. In short, they did not fully take on their authority roles, possibly because they knew their behavior was being observed by millions of viewers. These results suggest that less intense situations evoke less extreme behavior, and abuse of roles can be limited when people are made conscious of their behavior.

Group Property 2: Norms

4 Demonstrate how norms exert influence on an individual's behavior.

norms Acceptable standards of behavior within a group that are shared by the group's members.

Did you ever notice that golfers don't speak while their partners are putting? Why not? The answer is norms.

All groups have established **norms**—acceptable standards of behavior shared by members that express what they ought and ought not to do under certain circumstances. It's not enough for group leaders to share their opinions—even if members adopt the leaders' views, the effect may last only 3 days![28] When agreed to by the group, norms influence behavior with a minimum of external controls. Different groups, communities, and societies have different norms, but they all have them.[29] Let's discuss the levels of influence norms can exert over us, starting with our emotions.

Norms and Emotions

Have you ever noticed how the emotions of one member of your family, especially strong emotions, can influence the emotions of the other members? A family can be a highly normative group. So can a task group whose members work together on a daily basis, because frequent communication can increase the power of norms. A recent study found that, in a task group, individuals' emotions influenced the group's emotions and vice versa. This may not be surprising, but researchers also found that norms dictated the *experience* of emotions for the individuals and for the groups—in other words, people grew to interpret their shared emotions in the same way.[30] Our emotions and moods can shape our perspective, so the normative effect of groups can powerfully influence group attitudes and outcomes.

Norms and Conformity

conformity The adjustment of one's behavior to align with the norms of the group.

As a member of a group, you desire acceptance by the group. Thus, you are susceptible to conforming to group norms. Considerable evidence suggests that groups can place strong pressures on individual members to change their attitudes and behaviors to match the group's standard.[31] The impact that group pressures for **conformity** can have on an individual member's judgment was demonstrated in studies by Solomon Asch and others.[32] Asch made up groups of seven or eight people who were asked to compare two cards. One card had one line, and the other had three lines of varying length, one of which was identical to the line on the one-line card, as Exhibit 2 shows. The difference in line length was obvious; in fact, under ordinary conditions, subjects were incorrect less than 1 percent of the time in announcing which of the three lines matched the single line.

The experiment began with sets of matching exercises. Everyone gave the right answers. On the third set, however, the first subject, who was part of the

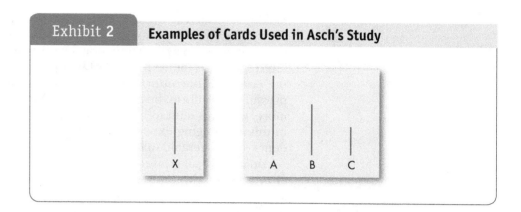

Exhibit 2   **Examples of Cards Used in Asch's Study**

research team, gave an obviously wrong answer—for example, saying "C" in Exhibit 2. The next subject, also on the research team, gave the same wrong answer, and so forth. Now the dilemma confronting the subject, who didn't know any of the subjects were on the research team, was this: publicly state a perception that differed from the announced position of the others, or give an incorrect answer that agreed with the others.

The results over many experiments showed 75 percent of subjects gave at least one answer that conformed—that they knew was wrong but was consistent with the replies of other group members—and the average conformer gave wrong answers 37 percent of the time. This suggests that we feel the pressure toward conformity with group norms. Other recent research with moral decision

An Ethical Choice

Using Peer Pressure as an Influence Tactic

We've all experienced peer pressure, and it can be hard to behave differently from your friends and coworkers. As more work in organizations is performed in groups and teams, the possibilities and pitfalls of such pressure have become an increasingly important ethical issue for managers.

Peer pressure can be a positive force in some ways. In groups where high effort and performance are the norms, peer pressure from coworkers, whether direct or indirect, can encourage high performance from those not meeting expectations. A group with a norm toward behaving ethically could also use peer pressure to minimize negative behavior. Thus, peer pressure can promote all sorts of good behaviors, from donating to charity to volunteering at the local soup kitchen.

However, peer pressure can also be destructive. It can create a feeling of exclusion in those who do not go along with group norms and can be very stressful and hurtful for those who don't see eye-to-eye with the rest of the group. Peer pressure itself can be an unethical practice that unduly influences workers' behavior and thoughts. And while groups might pressure others into good behavior, they can just as easily sway them to bad behavior.

Should you use group peer pressure? As a leader, you may need to. One survey found that only 6 percent of leaders reported being able to successfully influence their employees on their own. Peer pressure hastens a group toward consensus, and levels of peer pressure predict how much the leader can control the group. If you use peer pressure to encourage

individuals to work toward team goals and behave consistently with organizational values, it can enhance ethical performance. But your behavior should emphasize acceptance and rewarding of positive behavior, rather than rejection and exclusion, as a means of getting everyone to behave consistently in the group.

Sources: E. Estrada and E. Vargas-Estrada, "How Peer Pressure Shapes Consensus, Leadership, and Innovations in Social Groups," *Scientific Reports* 3 (2013), article number 2905; A. Verghese, "The Healing Power of Peer Pressure," *Newsweek,* March 14, 2011, www.newsweek.com; J. Meer, "Brother, Can You Spare a Dime? Peer Pressure in Charitable Solicitation," *Journal of Public Economics* 95, no. 7–8 (2011): 926–41; and L. Potter, "Lack Influence at Work? Why Most Leaders Struggle to Lead Positive Change," *Yahoo,* May 14, 2013, http://finance.yahoo.com/news/lack-influence-why-most-leaders-121500672.html.

making indicated an even stronger effect of conformity when subjects found the nonconforming ideas not just incorrect but objectionable.[33] Does that mean we are mere robots? Certainly not. The flip side of the 37 percent of conforming responses is the 63 percent of independent responses, and 95 percent gave the correct (nonconforming) response at least once. Therefore, we feel the pressure to conform, but it is not a perfect predictor of what we will do. Furthermore, we don't tend to like the pressure. Asch wrote, "Those who participated in this challenging experiment agreed nearly without exception that independence was preferable to conformity."[34]

Do individuals conform to the pressures of all groups to which they belong? Obviously not, because people belong to many groups, and their norms vary and sometimes are contradictory. People conform to their **reference groups**, in which a person is aware of other members, defines himself or herself as a member or would like to be a member, and feels group members are significant to him or her. The implication, then, is that all groups do not impose equal conformity pressures on their members.

Norms and Behavior

Norms can cover any aspect of group behavior.[35] As we've mentioned, norms in the workplace significantly influence employee behavior. This may seem intuitive, but full appreciation of the influence of norms on worker behavior did not occur until the Hawthorne Studies conducted between 1924 and 1932 at the Western Electric Company's Hawthorne Works in Chicago.[36]

In the studies, the researchers first examined the relationship between the physical environment and productivity. As they increased the light level for the experimental group of workers, output rose for that unit and the control group. But as they dropped the light level, productivity continued to increase. In fact, productivity in the experimental group decreased only when the light intensity

reference groups Important groups to which individuals belong or hope to belong and with whose norms individuals are likely to conform.

From studies of employees at the Western Electric Company's Hawthorne Works in Chicago, researchers gained valuable insights into how individual behavior is influenced by group norms. They also learned that money was less of a factor in determining worker output than were group standards, sentiments, and security.
Source: Hawthorne Museum of Morton College

had been reduced to that of moonlight, leading researchers to believe that group dynamics, rather than the environment, influenced behavior.

The researchers next isolated a small group of women assembling telephones so their behavior could be more carefully observed. Over the next several years, this small group's output increased steadily, and the number of personal and sick absences was approximately one-third of that in the regular production department. It became evident this group's performance was significantly influenced by its "special" status. The members thought they were in an elite group, and that management showed concern about their interests by engaging in experimentation. In essence, workers in both the illumination and assembly experiments were really reacting to the increased attention they received.

A wage incentive plan was then introduced in the bank wiring observation room. The most important finding was that employees did not individually maximize their output. Rather, their role performance became controlled by a group norm. Members were afraid that if they significantly increased their output, the unit incentive rate might be cut, the expected daily output might be increased, layoffs might occur, or slower workers might be reprimanded. So the group established its idea of a fair output—neither too much nor too little. Members helped each other ensure their reports were nearly level, and the norms the group established included a number of behavioral "don'ts." *Don't* be a rate-buster, turning out too much work. *Don't* be a chiseler, turning out too little work. *Don't* squeal on any of your peers. The group enforced its norms with name-calling, ridicule, and even punches to the upper arms of violators. It thus operated well below its capability, using norms that were tightly established and strongly enforced.

Positive Norms and Group Outcomes

One goal of every organization with corporate social responsibility (CSR) initiatives is for its values to hold normative sway over employees. After all, if employees aligned their thinking with positive norms, these norms would become stronger and the probability of positive impact would grow exponentially. We might expect the same outcomes from political correctness (PC) norms. But what *is* the effect of strong positive norms on group outcomes? The popular thinking is that to increase creativity in groups, for instance, norms should be loosened. However, research on gender-diverse groups indicates that strong PC norms increase group creativity. Why? Clear expectations about male-female interactions reduce uncertainty about group expectations,[37] which allows the members to more easily express their creative ideas without combatting stereotype norms.

Positive group norms may well beget positive outcomes, but only if other factors are present, too. For instance, in a recent study a high level of group extraversion predicted helping behaviors more strongly when there were positive cooperation norms.[38] As powerful as norms can be, though, not everyone is equally susceptible to positive group norms. Individual personalities factor in, too, as well as the level of a person's social identity with the group. Also, a recent study in Germany indicated that the more satisfied people were with their groups, the more closely they followed group norms.[39]

Negative Norms and Group Outcomes

LeBron is frustrated by a coworker who constantly spreads malicious and unsubstantiated rumors about him. Lindsay is tired of a member of her workgroup who, when confronted with a problem, takes out his frustration by yelling and screaming at her and other members. And Mi-Cha recently quit her job as a dental hygienist after being sexually harassed by her employer.

deviant workplace behavior Voluntary behavior that violates significant organizational norms and, in so doing, threatens the well-being of the organization or its members. Also called antisocial behavior or workplace incivility.

What do these illustrations have in common? They represent employees exposed to acts of deviant workplace behavior.[40] Counterproductive work behavior (CWB) or **deviant workplace behavior** (also called *antisocial behavior* or *workplace incivility*) is voluntary behavior that violates significant organizational norms and, in so doing, threatens the well-being of the organization or its members. Exhibit 3 provides a typology of deviant workplace behaviors, with examples of each.

Few organizations will admit to creating or condoning conditions that encourage and maintain deviant behaviors. Yet they exist. For one, as we discussed before, a workgroup can become characterized by positive or negative attributes. When those attributes are negative, such as when a workgroup is high in psychopathy and aggression, the characteristics of deceit, amorality, and intent to harm others are pronounced.[41] Second, employees have been reporting an increase in rudeness and disregard toward others by bosses and coworkers in recent years. Workplace incivility, like many other deviant behaviors, has many negative outcomes for the victims.[42] Nearly half of employees who have suffered this incivility say it has led them to think about changing jobs; 12 percent actually quit because of it.[43] Also, a study of nearly 1,500 respondents found that in addition to increasing turnover intentions, incivility at work increased reports of psychological stress and physical illness.[44] Third, research suggests that a lack of sleep, which is often caused by heightened work demands and which hinders a person's ability to regulate emotions and behaviors, can lead to deviant behavior. As organizations have tried to do more with less, pushing their employees to work extra hours, they may indirectly be facilitating deviant behavior.[45]

Like norms in general, employees' antisocial actions are shaped by the group context within which they work. Evidence demonstrates deviant workplace behavior is likely to flourish where it's supported by group norms.[46] For example, workers who socialize either at or outside work with people who are frequently absent from work are more likely to be absent themselves.[47] Thus when deviant workplace norms surface, employee cooperation, commitment, and motivation are likely to suffer.

Exhibit 3	Typology of Deviant Workplace Behavior

Category	Examples
Production	Leaving early Intentionally working slowly Wasting resources
Property	Sabotage Lying about hours worked Stealing from the organization
Political	Showing favoritism Gossiping and spreading rumors Blaming coworkers
Personal aggression	Sexual harassment Verbal abuse Stealing from coworkers

Sources: S. H. Appelbaum, G. D. Iaconi, and A. Matousek, "Positive and Negative Deviant Workplace Behaviors: Causes, Impacts, and Solutions," *Corporate Governance* 7, no. 5 (2007): 586–98; and R. W. Griffin, and A. O'Leary-Kelly, *The Dark Side of Organizational Behavior* (New York: Wiley, 2004).

What are the consequences of workplace deviance for groups? Some research suggests a chain reaction occurs in groups with high levels of dysfunctional behavior.[48] The process begins with negative behaviors like shirking, undermining coworkers, or being generally uncooperative. As a result of these behaviors, the group collectively starts to have negative moods. These negative moods then result in poor coordination of effort and lower levels of group performance.

Norms and Culture

Do people in collectivist cultures have different norms than people in individualist cultures? Of course they do. But did you know that our orientation may be changed, even after years of living in one society? In a recent experiment, an organizational role-playing exercise was given to a neutral group of subjects; the exercise stressed either collectivist or individualist norms. Subjects were then given a task of their personal choice or were assigned one by an ingroup or outgroup person. When the individualist-primed subjects were allowed personal choice of the task, or the collectivist-primed subjects were assigned the task by an ingroup person, they became more highly motivated.[49]

Group Property 3: Status, and Group Property 4: Size and Dynamics

5 Show how status and size differences affect group performance.

We've discussed how the roles we play and the norms we internalize tend to dictate our behavior in groups. However, those are not the only two factors that influence who we are in a group and how the group functions. Have you ever noticed how groups tend to stratify into higher- and lower-status members? Sometimes the status of members reflects their status outside the group setting, but not always. Also, status often varies between groups of different sizes. Let's examine how these factors affect a workgroup's efficacy.

Group Property 3: Status

status   A socially defined position or rank given to groups or group members by others.

Status—a socially defined position or rank given to groups or group members by others—permeates every society. Even the smallest group will show differences in member status over time. Status is a significant motivator and has major behavioral consequences when individuals perceive a disparity between what they believe their status is and what others perceive it to be.

status characteristics theory
A theory that states that differences in status characteristics create status hierarchies within groups.

What Determines Status?   According to **status characteristics theory**, status tends to derive from one of three sources:[50]

1. **The power a person wields over others**. Because they likely control the group's resources, people who control group outcomes tend to be perceived as high status.
2. **A person's ability to contribute to a group's goals**. People whose contributions are critical to the group's success tend to have high status.
3. **An individual's personal characteristics**. Someone whose personal characteristics are positively valued by the group (good looks, intelligence, money, or a friendly personality) typically has higher status than someone with fewer valued attributes.

Status and Norms   Status has some interesting effects on the power of norms and pressures to conform. High-status individuals may be more likely to deviate from norms when they have low identification (social identity) with the

Aaron Rodgers has high status as the quarterback of the Green Bay Packers football team. His status derives from his ability to contribute to his team's success in winning games. Rodgers's teammates and coaches value his character, leadership skills, expertise in calling plays, and ability to accurately throw touchdown passes on the move.

Source: Matt Ludtke/AP Images

group.[51] They also eschew pressure from lower-ranking members of other groups. For instance, physicians actively resist administrative decisions made by lower-ranking medical insurance company employees.[52] High-status people are also better able to resist conformity pressures than their lower-status peers. An individual who is highly valued by a group but doesn't need or care about the group's social rewards is particularly able to disregard conformity norms.[53] In general, bringing high-status members into a group may improve performance, but only up to a point, perhaps because these members may introduce counter-productive norms.[54]

Status and Group Interaction People tend to become more assertive when they seek to attain higher status in a group.[55] They speak out more often, criticize more, state more commands, and interrupt others more often. Lower-status members tend to participate less actively in group discussions; when they possess expertise and insights that could aid the group, failure to fully utilize these members reduces the group's overall performance. But that doesn't mean a group of only high-status individuals would be preferable. Adding *some* high-status individuals to a group of mid-status individuals may be advantageous because group performance suffers when too many high-status people are in the mix.[56]

Status Inequity It is important for group members to believe the status hierarchy is equitable. Perceived inequity creates disequilibrium, which inspires various types of corrective behaviors. Hierarchical groups can lead to resentment among those at the lower end of the status continuum. Large differences in status within groups are also associated with poorer individual performance, lower health, and higher intentions for the lower-status members to leave the group.[57]

Groups generally agree within themselves on status criteria; hence, there is usually high concurrence on group rankings of individuals. Business executives may use personal income or the growth rate of their companies as determinants of status. Government bureaucrats may use the size of their budgets, and blue-collar workers may use their years of seniority. Managers who occupy central positions in their social networks are typically seen as higher in status by their subordinates, and this position actually translates into greater influence over the group's functioning.[58]

Groups generally form an informal status order based on ranking and command of needed resources.[59] Individuals can find themselves in conflicts when they move between groups whose status criteria are different, or when they join groups whose members have heterogeneous backgrounds. Cultures also differ in their criteria for conferring status upon individuals. When groups are heterogeneous, status differences may initiate conflict as the group attempts to reconcile the separate hierarchies. This can be a problem when management creates teams of employees from varied functions.

Status and Stigmatization   Although it's clear that your own status affects the way people perceive you, the status of people with whom you are affiliated can also affect others' views of you. Studies have shown that people who are stigmatized can "infect" others with their stigma. This "stigma by association" effect can result in negative opinions and evaluations of the person affiliated with the stigmatized individual, even if the association is brief and purely coincidental. Of course, many of the foundations of cultural status differences have no merit in the first place. For example, men interviewing for a job were viewed as less qualified when they were sitting next to an obese woman in a waiting room. Another study looking at the effects of being associated with an overweight person found that even when onlookers were told the target person and the overweight person were unrelated, the target person was still devalued.[60]

Group Status   Early in life, we acquire an "us and them" mentality.[61] You may have correctly surmised that if you are in an outgroup, your group is of lower status in the eyes of the associated ingroup's members. Culturally, sometimes ingroups represent the dominant forces in a society and are given high status, which can create discrimination against their outgroups. Low-status groups, perhaps in response to this discrimination, are likely to leverage ingroup favoritism to compete for higher status.[62] When high-status groups then feel the discrimination from low-status groups, they may increase their bias against the outgroups.[63] With each cycle, the groups become more polarized.

Group Property 4: Size and Dynamics

Does the size of a group affect the group's overall behavior? Yes, but the effect depends on what dependent variables we examine. Groups with a dozen or more members are good for gaining diverse input. If the goal is fact-finding or idea-generating, then, larger groups should be more effective. Smaller groups of about seven members are better at doing something productive.

social loafing The tendency for individuals to expend less effort when working collectively than when working individually.

One of the most important findings about the size of a group concerns **social loafing**, the tendency for individuals to expend less effort when working collectively than when alone.[64] Social loafing directly challenges the assumption that the productivity of the group as a whole should at least equal the sum of the productivity of the individuals in it, no matter what the group size.

What causes social loafing? It may be a belief that others in the group are not carrying their fair share. If you see others as lazy or inept, you can reestablish equity by reducing your effort. But simply failing to contribute may not be enough for someone to be labeled a "free rider." Instead, the group must believe the social loafer is acting in an exploitive manner (benefitting at the expense of other team members).[65] Another explanation for social loafing is the diffusion of responsibility. Because group results cannot be attributed to any single person, the relationship between an individual's input and the group's output is clouded. Individuals may then be tempted to become free riders and coast on the group's efforts.

The implications for OB are significant. When managers use collective work situations, they must also be able to identify individual efforts. Furthermore, greater performance diversity creates greater social loafing the longer a group is together, which decreases satisfaction and performance.[66]

Social loafing appears to have a Western bias. It's consistent with individualist cultures, such as the United States and Canada, that are dominated by self-interest. It is *not* consistent with collectivist societies, in which individuals are motivated by group goals. For example, in studies comparing U.S. employees with employees from China and Israel (both collectivist societies), the Chinese and Israelis showed no propensity to engage in social loafing and actually performed better in a group than alone.

Research indicates that the stronger an individual's work ethic is, the less likely that person is to engage in social loafing.[67] Also, the greater the level of conscientiousness and agreeableness in a group, the more likely that performance will remain high whether there is social loafing or not.[68] There are ways to prevent social loafing: (1) set group goals, so the group has a common purpose to strive toward; (2) increase intergroup competition, which focuses on the shared group outcome; (3) engage in peer evaluations; (4) select members who have high motivation and prefer to work in groups; and (5) base group rewards in part on each member's unique contributions.[69] Recent research indicates that social loafing can be counteracted by publicly posting individual performance ratings for group members, too.[70] Although no magic bullet will prevent social loafing, these steps should help minimize its effect.

Young employees of Alibaba's Tmall online shopping site celebrate their group's achievement of increasing the volume of sales orders during China's "Singles Day" shopping event. Although social loafing is consistent with individualistic cultures, in collectivist societies such as China, employees are motivated by group goals and perform better in groups than they do by working individually.
Source: Han Chuanhao Xinhua News Agency/Newscom

Group Property 5: Cohesiveness, and Group Property 6: Diversity

6 Describe how issues of cohesiveness and diversity can be integrated for group effectiveness.

For a group to be highly functioning, it must act cohesively as a unit, but not because all the group members think and act alike. In some ways, the properties of cohesiveness and diversity need to be valued way back at the tacit establishment of roles and norms—will the group be inclusive of all its members, regardless of differences in backgrounds? Let's discuss the importance of group cohesiveness first.

Group Property 5: Cohesiveness

cohesiveness The degree to which group members are attracted to each other and are motivated to stay in the group.

Groups differ in their **cohesiveness**—the degree to which members are attracted to each other and motivated to stay in the group. Some workgroups are cohesive because the members have spent a great deal of time together, the group's small size or purpose facilitates high interaction, or external threats have brought members close together.

Cohesiveness affects group productivity. Studies consistently show that the relationship between cohesiveness and productivity depends on the group's performance-related norms.[71] If norms for quality, output, and cooperation with outsiders are high, a cohesive group will be more productive than a less cohesive group. But if cohesiveness is high and performance norms are low, productivity will be low. If cohesiveness is low and performance norms are high, productivity increases, but less than in the high-cohesiveness/high-norms situation. When cohesiveness and performance-related norms are both low, productivity tends to fall into the low-to-moderate range. These conclusions are summarized in Exhibit 4.

What can you do to encourage group cohesiveness? (1) Make the group smaller, (2) encourage agreement with group goals, (3) increase the time members spend together, (4) increase the group's status and the perceived difficulty of attaining membership, (5) stimulate competition with other groups, (6) give rewards to the group rather than to individual members, and (7) physically isolate the group.[72]

Group Property 6: Diversity

diversity The extent to which members of a group are similar to, or different from, one another.

The final property of groups we consider is **diversity** in the group's membership, or the degree to which members of the group are similar to, or different from, one another. Overall, studies identify both costs and benefits from group diversity.

Exhibit 4	Relationship Between Group Cohesiveness, Performance Norms, and Productivity

		Cohesiveness	
		High	Low
Performance Norms	High	High productivity	Moderate productivity
	Low	Low productivity	Moderate to low productivity

Diversity appears to increase group conflict, especially in the early stages of a group's tenure; this often lowers group morale and raises dropout rates. One study compared groups that were culturally diverse and homogeneous (composed of people from the same country). On a wilderness survival test, the groups performed equally well, but the members from the diverse groups were less satisfied with their groups, were less cohesive, and had more conflict.[73] Another study examined the effect of differences in tenure on the performance of 67 engineering research and development groups.[74] When most people had roughly the same level of tenure, performance was high, but as tenure diversity increased, performance dropped off. There was an important qualifier: Higher levels of tenure diversity were not related to lower performance for groups when there were effective team-oriented human resources (HR) practices. More specifically, groups in which members' values or opinions differ tend to experience more conflict, but leaders who can get the group to focus on the task at hand and encourage group learning are able to reduce these conflicts and enhance discussion of group issues.[75] Gender diversity can also be a challenge to a group, but if inclusiveness is stressed, group conflict and dissatisfaction are lowered.[76]

You may have correctly surmised that the type of group diversity matters. Surface-level diversity—in observable characteristics such as national origin, race, and gender—alerts people to possible deep-level diversity—in underlying attitudes, values, and opinions. One researcher argues, "The mere presence of diversity you can see, such as a person's race or gender, actually cues a team that there's likely to be differences of opinion."[77] Surface-level diversity may subconsciously cue team members to be more open-minded in their views.[78] For example, two studies of MBA student groups found surface-level diversity led to greater openness. The effects of deep-level diversity are less understood. Research in Korea indicates that putting people with a high need for *power* with those with a low need for power can reduce unproductive group competition, whereas putting individuals with a similar need for *achievement* may increase task performance.[79]

Although differences can lead to conflict, they also provide an opportunity to solve problems in unique ways. One study of jury behavior found diverse juries were more likely to deliberate longer, share more information, and make fewer factual errors when discussing evidence. Altogether, the impact of diversity on groups is mixed. It is difficult to be in a diverse group in the short term. However, if members can weather their differences, over time diversity may help them be more open-minded and creative and to do better. But even positive effects are unlikely to be especially strong. As one review stated, "The business case (in terms of demonstrable financial results) for diversity remains hard to support based on the extant research."[80] Yet, other researchers argue that we shouldn't overlook the effects of homogeneity, many of which can be detrimental.[81]

✪ PERSONAL INVENTORY ASSESSMENTS

Communicating Supportively

Are you a supportive person? Take this PIA to find out if you communicate supportively.

faultlines The perceived divisions that split groups into two or more subgroups based on individual differences such as sex, race, age, work experience, and education.

One possible side effect in diverse teams—especially those that are diverse in terms of surface-level characteristics—is **faultlines**, or perceived divisions that split groups into two or more subgroups based on individual differences such as sex, race, age, work experience, and education.

For example, let's say group A is composed of three men and three women. The three men have approximately the same amount of work experience and backgrounds in marketing. The three women have about the same amount of work experience and backgrounds in finance. Group B has three men and three women, but they all differ in terms of their experience and backgrounds. Two of the men are experienced, while the other is new. One of the women has worked at the company for several years, while the other two are new. In addition, two of the men and one woman in group B have backgrounds in marketing, while the other man and the remaining two women have backgrounds in finance. It is thus likely that a faultline will result in subgroups of males and females in group A but not in group B, based on the differentiating characteristics.

Research on faultlines has shown that splits are generally detrimental to group functioning and performance. Subgroups may compete with each other, which takes time away from core tasks and harms group performance. Groups that have subgroups learn more slowly, make more risky decisions, are less creative, and experience higher levels of conflict. Subgroups may not trust each other. Finally, satisfaction with subgroups is generally high, but the overall group's satisfaction is lower when faultlines are present.[82]

Are faultlines ever a good thing? One study suggested that faultlines based on differences in skill, knowledge, and expertise could be beneficial when the groups were in organizational cultures that strongly emphasized results. Why? A results-driven culture focuses people's attention on what's important to the company rather than on problems arising from subgroups.[83] Another study showed that problems stemming from strong faultlines based on gender and educational major were counteracted when their roles were cross-cut and the group as a whole was given a common goal to strive for. Together, these strategies force collaboration between members of subgroups and focus their efforts on accomplishing a goal that transcends the boundary imposed by the faultline.[84]

Overall, although research on faultlines suggests that diversity in groups is potentially a double-edged sword, recent work indicates they can be strategically employed to improve performance.

Group Decision Making

7 Contrast the strengths and weaknesses of group decision making.

The belief—characterized by juries—that two heads are better than one has long been accepted as a basic component of the U.S. legal system and those of many other countries. Many decisions in organizations are made by groups, teams, or committees. We'll discuss the advantages of group decision making, along with the unique challenges group dynamics bring to the decision-making process. Finally, we'll offer some techniques for maximizing the group decision-making opportunity.

Groups versus the Individual

Decision-making groups may be widely used in organizations, but are group decisions preferable to those made by an individual alone? The answer depends on a number of factors. Let's begin by looking at the strengths and weaknesses of group decision making.

Strengths of Group Decision Making Groups generate *more complete information and knowledge.* By aggregating the resources of several individuals, groups bring more input as well as heterogeneity into the decision process. They offer *increased diversity of views.* This opens up the opportunity to consider more approaches and alternatives. Finally, groups lead to increased *acceptance of a solution*. Group members who participate in making a decision are more likely to enthusiastically support and encourage others to accept it later.

Weaknesses of Group Decision Making   Group decisions are time-consuming because groups typically take more time to reach a solution. There are *conformity pressures*. The desire by group members to be accepted and considered an asset to the group can squash any overt disagreement. Group discussion can be *dominated by one or a few members*. If they're low- and medium-ability members, the group's overall effectiveness will suffer. Finally, group decisions suffer from *ambiguous responsibility*. In an individual decision, it's clear who is accountable for the final outcome. In a group decision, the responsibility of any single member is diluted.

Effectiveness and Efficiency   Whether groups are more effective than individuals depends on how you define effectiveness. Group decisions are generally more *accurate* than the decisions of the average individual in a group, but less accurate than the judgments of the most accurate person.[85] In terms of *speed*, individuals are superior. If *creativity* is important, groups tend to be more effective. And if effectiveness means the degree of *acceptance* of achievable solutions, the nod again goes to the group.[86]

But we cannot consider effectiveness without also assessing efficiency. With few exceptions, group decision making consumes more work hours than having an individual tackle the same problem. The exceptions tend to be instances in which, to achieve comparable quantities of diverse input, the single decision maker must spend a great deal of time reviewing files and talking to other people. In deciding whether to use groups, then, managers must assess whether increases in effectiveness are more than enough to offset the reductions in efficiency.

In summary, groups are an excellent vehicle for performing many steps in the decision-making process and offer both breadth and depth of input for information gathering. If group members have diverse backgrounds, the alternatives generated should be more extensive and the analysis more critical. When the final solution is agreed on, there are more people in a group decision to support and implement it. These pluses, however, may be more than offset by the time consumed by group decisions, the internal conflicts they create, and the pressures they generate toward conformity. We must be careful to define the types of conflicts, however. Research in Korea indicates that group conflicts about tasks may increase group performance, while conflicts in relationships may decrease performance.[87] In some cases, therefore, we can expect individuals to make better decisions than groups.

Groupthink and Groupshift

Two by-products of group decision making, groupthink and groupshift, can affect a group's ability to appraise alternatives objectively and achieve high-quality solutions.

Groupthink relates to norms and describes situations in which group pressures for conformity deter the group from critically appraising unusual, minority, or unpopular views. Groupthink attacks many groups and can dramatically hinder their performance. **Groupshift** describes the way group members tend to exaggerate their initial positions when discussing a given set of alternatives to arrive at a solution. In some situations, caution dominates and there is a conservative shift, while in other situations groups tend toward a risky shift. Let's look at each phenomenon in detail.

groupthink   A phenomenon in which the norm for consensus overrides the realistic appraisal of alternative courses of action.

groupshift   A change between a group's decision and an individual decision that a member within the group would make; the shift can be toward either conservatism or greater risk but it generally is toward a more extreme version of the group's original position.

Career OBjectives

Can I fudge the numbers and not take the blame?

I've got a great workgroup, except for one thing: the others make me omit negative information about our group's success that I'm in charge of as the treasurer. They gang up on me, insult me, and threaten me, so in the end I report what they want. They say omitting the negative information is not really wrong, and it doesn't violate our organization's rules, but on my own I would report everything. I need to stay in the group or I'll lose my job. If we are called out on the numbers, can I just put the blame on the whole group?

— *Jean-Claude*

Dear Jean-Claude:

The short answer is that, since you are in a leadership role in the group, you may not have the option of blaming the others. Further, you may be held individually accountable as a leader for the outcomes of this situation.

Your dilemma is not unusual. Once we think of ourselves as part of a collective, we want to stay in the group and can become vulnerable to pressures to conform. The pressure you're getting from multiple members can make you aware that you're in the minority in the group, and taunting can make you feel like an outsider or lesser member; therefore threats to harm your group standing may feel powerful.

So you have a choice: Submit to the pressure and continue misrepresenting your group's success, or adhere to the responsibility you have as the treasurer and come clean. From an ethical standpoint, we hope you don't consider the first option an acceptable choice. To make a change, you may be able to use social identification to your advantage. Rather than challenging the group as a whole, try meeting with individual group members to build trust, talking to each as fellow members of a worthy group that can succeed without any ethical quandaries. Don't try to build a coalition; instead, build trust with individuals and change the climate of the group to value ethical behavior. Then the next time you need to report the numbers, you can call upon the group's increased ethical awareness to gain support for your leadership decisions.

_____

Sources: M. Cikara and J. J. Van Bavel, "The Neuroscience of Intergroup Relations: An Integrative Review," *Perspectives on Psychological Science* 9, no. 3 (2014): 245–74; M. A. Korsgaard, H. H. Brower, and S. W. Lester, "It Isn't Always Mutual: A Critical Review of Dyadic Trust," *Journal of Management* 41, no. 1 (2015): 47–70; R. L. Priem and P. C. Nystrom, "Exploring the Dynamics of Workgroup Fracture: Common Ground, Trust-With-Trepidation, and Warranted Distrust," *Journal of Management* 40, no. 3 (2014): 674–795.

The opinions provided here are of the managers and authors only and do not necessarily reflect those of their organizations. The authors or managers are not responsible for any errors or omissions, or for the results obtained from the use of this information. In no event will the authors or managers, or their related partnerships or corporations thereof, be liable to you or anyone else for any decision made or action taken in reliance on the opinions provided here.

Groupthink Groupthink appears closely aligned with the conclusions Solomon Asch drew in his experiments with a lone dissenter. Individuals who hold a position different from that of the dominant majority are under pressure to suppress, withhold, or modify their true feelings and beliefs. As members of a group, we find it more pleasant to be in agreement—to be a positive part of the group—than to be a disruptive force, even if disruption would improve effectiveness. Groups that are more focused on performance than learning are especially likely to fall victim to groupthink and to suppress the opinions of those who do not agree with the majority.[88]

Does groupthink attack all groups? No. It seems to occur most often when there is a clear group identity, when members hold a positive image of their group they want to protect, and when the group perceives a collective threat to its positive image.[89] One study showed that those influenced by groupthink were more confident about their course of action early on;[90] however, groups that believe too strongly in the correctness of their course of action are more likely to suppress dissent and encourage conformity than groups that are more skeptical about their course of action.

What can managers do to minimize groupthink?[91] First, they can monitor group size. People grow more intimidated and hesitant as group size increases, and although there is no magic number that will eliminate groupthink, individuals are likely to feel less personal responsibility when groups get larger than about 10 members. Managers should also encourage group leaders to play an impartial role. Leaders should actively seek input from all members and avoid expressing their own opinions, especially in the early stages of deliberation. In addition, managers should appoint one group member to play the role of devil's advocate, overtly challenging the majority position and offering divergent perspectives. Yet another suggestion is to use exercises that stimulate active discussion of diverse alternatives without threatening the group or intensifying identity protection. Have group members delay discussion of possible gains so they can first talk about the dangers or risks inherent in a decision. Requiring members to initially focus on the negatives of an alternative makes the group less likely to stifle dissenting views and more likely to gain an objective evaluation.

Groupshift or Group Polarization   There are differences between group decisions and the individual decisions of group members.[92] In groups, discussion leads members toward a more extreme view of the position they already held. Conservatives become more cautious, and more aggressive types take on more risk. We can view this group polarization as a special case of groupthink. The group's decision reflects the dominant decision-making norm—toward greater caution or more risk—that develops during discussion.

The shift toward polarization has several explanations.[93] It's been argued, for instance, that discussion makes the members more comfortable with each other and thus more willing to express extreme versions of their original positions. Another argument is that the group diffuses responsibility. Group decisions free any single member from accountability for the group's final choice, so a more extreme position can be taken. It's also likely that people take extreme positions because they want to demonstrate how different they are from the outgroup.[94] People on the fringes of political or social movements take on ever-more-extreme positions just to prove they are really committed to the cause, whereas those who are more cautious tend to take moderate positions to demonstrate how reasonable they are.

So how should you use the findings on groupshift? Recognize that group decisions exaggerate the initial position of individual members, that the shift has been shown more often to be toward greater risk, and that which way a group will shift is a function of the members' pre-discussion inclinations.

We now turn to the techniques by which groups make decisions. These reduce some of the dysfunctional aspects of group decision making.

Group Decision-Making Techniques

interacting groups   Typical groups in which members interact with each other face to face.

The most common form of group decision making takes place in **interacting groups**. Members meet face to face and rely on both verbal and nonverbal interaction to communicate. But as our discussion of groupthink demonstrated, interacting groups often censor themselves and pressure individual members toward conformity of opinion. Brainstorming and the nominal group technique can reduce problems inherent in the traditional interacting group.

brainstorming   An idea-generation process that specifically encourages any and all alternatives while withholding any criticism of those alternatives.

Brainstorming   **Brainstorming** can overcome the pressures for conformity that dampen creativity[95] by encouraging any and all alternatives while withholding criticism. In a typical brainstorming session, a half-dozen to a dozen people sit around a table. The group leader states the problem in a clear manner so all participants understand. Members then freewheel as many alternatives as they can in a given length of time. To encourage members to "think the unusual," no criticism is allowed, even of the most bizarre suggestions, and all ideas are recorded for later discussion and analysis.

Exhibit 5	Evaluating Group Effectiveness

Effectiveness Criteria	Type of Group		
	Interacting	Brainstorming	Nominal
Number and quality of ideas	Low	Moderate	High
Social pressure	High	Low	Moderate
Money costs	Low	Low	Low
Speed	Moderate	Moderate	Moderate
Task orientation	Low	High	High
Potential for interpersonal conflict	High	Low	Moderate
Commitment to solution	High	Not applicable	Moderate
Development of group cohesiveness	High	High	Moderate

Brainstorming may indeed generate ideas—but not in a very efficient manner. Research consistently shows individuals working alone generate more ideas than a group in a brainstorming session. One reason for this is "production blocking." When people are generating ideas in a group, many are talking at once, which blocks individuals' thought process and eventually impedes the sharing of ideas.[96]

nominal group technique A group decision-making method in which individual members meet face to face to pool their judgments in a systematic but independent fashion.

Nominal Group Technique The **nominal group technique** may be more effective. This technique restricts discussion and interpersonal communication during the decision-making process. Group members are all physically present, as in a traditional meeting, but they operate independently. Specifically, a problem is presented and then the group takes the following steps:

1. **Before any discussion takes place,** each member independently writes down ideas about the problem.
2. **After this silent period,** each member presents one idea to the group. No discussion takes place until all ideas have been presented and recorded.
3. **The group discusses the ideas** for clarity and evaluates them.
4. **Each group member silently and independently rank-orders** the ideas. The idea with the highest aggregate ranking determines the final decision.

The chief advantage of the nominal group technique is that it permits a group to meet formally but does not restrict independent thinking. Research generally shows nominal groups outperform brainstorming groups.[97]

Each of the group-decision techniques has its own set of strengths and weaknesses. The choice depends on the criteria you want to emphasize and the cost–benefit trade-off. As Exhibit 5 indicates, an interacting group is good for achieving commitment to a solution, brainstorming develops group cohesiveness, and the nominal group technique is an inexpensive means for generating a large number of ideas.

Summary

We can draw several implications from our discussion of groups. First, norms control behavior by establishing standards of right and wrong. Second, status inequities create frustration and can adversely influence productivity and willingness to remain with an organization. Third, the impact of size on a group's performance depends on the type of task. Fourth, cohesiveness may influence a group's level of productivity, depending on the group's performance-related norms. Fifth, diversity appears to have a mixed impact on group performance, with some studies suggesting that diversity can help performance and others suggesting the opposite. Sixth, role conflict is associated with job-induced tension and job dissatisfaction.[98] Groups can be carefully managed toward positive organizational outcomes and optimal decision-making.

Implications for Managers

- Recognize that groups can dramatically affect individual behavior in organizations, to either positive or negative effect. Therefore, pay special attention to roles, norms, and cohesion—to understand how these are operating within a group is to understand how the group is likely to behave.
- To decrease the possibility of deviant workplace activities, ensure that group norms do not support antisocial behavior.
- Pay attention to the status aspect of groups. Because lower-status people tend to participate less in group discussions, groups with high status differences are likely to inhibit input from lower-status members and reduce their potential.
- Use larger groups for fact-finding activities and smaller groups for action-taking tasks. With larger groups, provide measures of individual performance.
- To increase employee satisfaction, make certain people perceive their job roles accurately.

People Are More Creative When They Work Alone

POINT   **COUNTERPOINT**

I know groups are all the rage. Businesses are knocking down walls and cubicles to create more open, "collaborative" environments. Students in universities are constantly working on group projects, and even young children are learning in small groups.

I also know *why* groups are all the rage. Work, they say, has become too complex for individuals to perform alone. Groups are better at brainstorming and coming up with creative solutions to complicated problems. Groups also produce higher levels of commitment and satisfaction—so long as group members develop feelings of cohesiveness and trust one another.

But for every group that comes up with a creative solution, I'll show you twice as many individuals who would come up with a better solution had they only been left alone. Consider creative geniuses like DaVinci, Newton, and Picasso. Or more recently, Steve Wozniak, the co-founder of Apple Computer. All were introverts who toiled by themselves. According to Wozniak, "I'm going to give you some advice that might be hard to take. That advice is: Work alone ... not on a committee. Not on a team."

But enough anecdotal evidence. Research has also shown that groups can kill creativity. One study found that computer programmers at companies that give them privacy and freedom from interruptions outperformed their counterparts at companies that forced more openness and collaboration. Or consider Adrian Furnham, an organizational psychologist whose research led him to conclude that "business people must be insane to use brainstorming groups." People slack off in groups, and they're afraid to communicate any ideas that might make them sound dumb. These problems don't exist when people work alone.

So heed Picasso's advice: "Without great solitude, no serious work is possible."

I'll grant you there are circumstances in which groups can hinder creative progress, but if the right conditions are put in place, groups are simply much better at coming up with novel solutions to problems than are individuals. Using strategies such as the nominal group technique, brainstorming, and ensuring that individuals do not evaluate others' ideas until all have been generated are just a few ways you can set up groups for creative success.

The fact of the matter is that problems *are* too complex these days for individuals to effectively perform alone. Consider the Rovers launched by NASA to roam around Mars collecting data. An accomplishment like that is made possible only by a group, not a lone individual. Steve Wozniak's collaboration with Steve Jobs is what really made Apple sail as a company. And could you assemble a car all by yourself?

In addition, the most influential research is conducted by groups of academics, rather than individuals. Indeed, if you look at recent Nobel Prize winners in areas such as economics, physics, and chemistry, the majority have been won by academics who collaborated on the research.

So if you want creativity (and who doesn't?), two heads are in fact better than one.

Sources: S. Cain, "The Rise of the New Groupthink," *The New York Times,* January 15, 2012, 1, 6; and C. Faure, "Beyond Brainstorming: Effects of Different Group Procedures on Selection of Ideas and Satisfaction with the Process," *Journal of Creative Behavior* 38 (2004): 13–34.

CHAPTER REVIEW

QUESTIONS FOR REVIEW

1 What are the different types of groups?

2 What are the key components of the punctuated-equilibrium model?

3 How do role requirements change in different situations?

4 How do group norms influence an individual's behavior?

5 How do status and size differences affect group performance?

6 How can cohesiveness and diversity support group effectiveness?

7 What are the strengths and weaknesses of group (versus individual) decision making?

EXPERIENTIAL EXERCISE Surviving the Wild: Join a Group or Go It Alone?

You are a member of a hiking party. After reaching base camp on the first day, you decide to take a quick sunset hike by yourself. After a few exhilarating miles, you decide to return to camp. On your way back, you realize you are lost. You shout for help, to no avail. It is now dark. And getting cold.

Your Task

Without communicating with anyone else in your group, read the following scenarios and choose the best answer. Keep track of your answers on a sheet of paper. You have 10 minutes to answer the 10 questions.

8. The first thing you decide to do is to build a fire. However, you have no matches, so you use the bow-and-drill method. What is the bow-and-drill method?
   a. A dry, soft stick is rubbed between the hands against a board of supple green wood.
   b. A soft green stick is rubbed between the hands against a hardwood board.
   c. A straight stick of wood is quickly rubbed back and forth against a dead tree.
   d. Two sticks (one being the bow, the other the drill) are struck to create a spark.

9. It occurs to you that you can also use the fire as a distress signal. How do you form the international distress signal with fire?
   a. 2 fires
   b. 4 fires in a square

   c. 4 fires in a cross
   d. 3 fires in a line

10. You are very thirsty. You go to a nearby stream and collect some water in the small metal cup you have in your backpack. How long should you boil the water?
    a. 15 minutes
    b. A few seconds
    c. 1 minute
    d. It depends on the altitude.

11. You are very hungry, so you decide to eat what appear to be edible berries. When performing the universal edibility test, what should you do?
    a. Do not eat for 2 hours before the test.
    b. If the plant stings your lip, confirm the sting by holding it under your tongue for 15 minutes.
    c. If nothing bad has happened 2 hours after digestion, eat half a cup of the plant and wait again.
    d. Separate the plant into its basic components and eat each component, one at a time.

12. Next, you decide to build a shelter for the evening. In selecting a site, what do you *not* have to consider?
    a. It must contain material to make the type of shelter you need.
    b. It must be free of insects, reptiles, and poisonous plants.

c. It must be large enough and level enough for you to lie down comfortably.

d. It must be on a hill so you can signal rescuers and keep an eye on your surroundings.

13. In the shelter, you notice a spider. You heard from a fellow hiker that black widow spiders populate the area. How do you identify a black widow spider?
   a. Its head and abdomen are black; its thorax is red.
   b. It is attracted to light.
   c. It runs away from light.
   d. It is dark with a red or orange marking on the female's abdomen.

14. After getting some sleep, you notice that the night sky has cleared, so you decide to try to find your way back to base camp. You believe you can use the North Star for navigation. How do you locate the North Star?
   a. Hold your right hand up as far as you can and look between your index and middle fingers.
   b. Find Sirius and look 60 degrees above it and to the right.
   c. Look for the Big Dipper and follow the line created by its cup end.
   d. Follow the line of Orion's belt.

15. You come across a fast-moving stream. What is the best way to cross it?
   a. Find a spot downstream from a sandbar, where the water will be calmer.
   b. Build a bridge.
   c. Find a rocky area, because the water will be shallow and you will have hand- and footholds.
   d. Find a level stretch where it breaks into a few channels.

16. After walking for about an hour, you feel several spiders in your clothes. You don't feel any pain, but you know some spider bites are painless. Which of these spider bites is painless?
   a. Black widow
   b. Brown recluse
   c. Wolf spider
   d. Harvestman (daddy longlegs)

17. You decide to eat some insects. Which insects should you avoid?
   a. Adults that sting or bite
   b. Caterpillars and insects that have a pungent odor
   c. Hairy or brightly colored ones
   d. All the above

Group Task

Next, break into groups of five or six people. Once the group comes to an agreement for what to do in each situation, write your decision on the same sheet of paper you used for your individual answers.

Scoring Your Answers

Your instructor will provide you with the correct answers, which are based on expert judgments in these situations. Once you have received the answers, calculate (A) your individual score; (B) your group's score; (C) the average individual score in the group; and (D) the best individual score in the group. Write these down and consult with your group to ensure they are accurate.

   A. Your individual score _____
   B. Your group's score _____
   C. Average individual score in group _____
   D. Best individual score in group _____

Discussion Questions

18. How did your group (B) perform relative to yourself (A)?

19. How did your group (B) perform relative to the average individual score in the group (C)?

20. How did your group (B) perform relative to the best individual score in the group (D)?

21. Compare your results with those of other groups. Did some groups do a better job of outperforming individuals than others?

22. What do these results tell you about the effectiveness of group decision making?

23. What can groups do to make group decision making more effective?

24. What circumstances might cause a group to perform worse than its best individual?

ETHICAL DILEMMA Is Social Loafing Unethical?

As we discussed in this chapter, social loafing is one potential downside of working in groups. Research suggests that regardless of the type of task, when working in a group, most individuals contribute less than if they were working on their own. Sometimes these people are labeled shirkers because they don't fulfill their responsibilities as group members. Other times, social loafing is overlooked, and industrious employees do the work to meet the group's performance goals. Either way, social loafing creates an ethical dilemma.

Whether in class projects or in jobs we've held, most of us have experienced social loafing in groups. We may even have been guilty ourselves. Although limiting group size, holding individuals responsible for their contributions, setting group goals, and rewarding both individual and group performance might help reduce the occurrence of social loafing, in many cases people just try to work around shirkers rather than motivate them to perform at higher levels.

Managers must determine what level of social loafing for groups and for individual employees will be tolerated in terms of nonproductive meetings, performance expectations, and counterproductive work behaviors. Employees must decide what limits to social loafing they will impose on themselves and what tolerance they have for social loafers in their workgroups.

Questions

25. Do group members have an ethical responsibility to report shirkers to leadership? If you were working on a group project for a class and a group member was loafing, would you communicate this information to the instructor? Why or why not?

26. Do you think social loafing is always shirking (failing to live up to your responsibilities)? Are there times when shirking is ethical or even justified?

27. Social loafing has been found to be higher in individualist nations than in other countries. Do you think this means we should tolerate shirking on the part of U.S. students and workers to a greater degree than if someone else does it?

CASE INCIDENT 1 The Calamities of Consensus

When it is time for groups to reach a decision, many turn to consensus. Consensus, a situation of agreement, seems like a good idea. To achieve consensus, groups must cooperate and collaborate, which ultimately will produce higher levels of camaraderie and trust. In addition, if everyone agrees, the prevailing wisdom says everyone will be more committed to the decision.

However, the need for consensus can sometimes be detrimental to group functioning. Consider the "fiscal cliff" faced by the U.S. government toward the end of 2012. The White House and Congress needed to reach a deal that would reduce the swelling budget deficit. However, many Republicans and Democrats stuck to their party lines, refusing to compromise. Many viewed the end product that achieved consensus as a less-than-optimal solution. The public gave Congress an approval rating of only 13 percent, expressing frustration with the lack of compromise, but the group may not have been able to function well partly because of the need for consensus in the face of partisanship.

If consensus is reached, does that mean the decision is the right one? Critics of consensus-based methods argue that any decisions ultimately reached are inferior to decisions using other methods such as voting or having team members provide input to their leader, who then makes the final decision. Critics also argue that because of pressures to conform, groupthink is much more likely, and decisions reached through consensus are simply those everyone dislikes the least.

Questions

28. Is consensus a good way for groups to make decisions? Why or why not?

29. Can you think of a time when a group of which you were a part relied on consensus? How do you think the decision turned out?

30. Martin Luther King Jr. once proclaimed, "A genuine leader is not a seeker of consensus but a modeler of consensus." What do you think he meant by that statement? Do you agree with it? Why or why not?

Sources: D. Leonhardt, "When the Crowd Isn't Wise," *The New York Times*, July 8, 2012, SR BW 4; and K. Jensen, "Consensus Is Poison! Who's with Me?" *Forbes*, May 20, 2013, downloaded on May 30, 2013, from www.forbes.com.

CASE INCIDENT 2   Intragroup Trust and Survival

When 10 British Army soldiers on a 10-day training exercise descended into Low's Gully, a narrow chasm that cuts through Mt. Kinabalu in Borneo, each knew "the golden rule for such expeditions—never split up." Yet, the fittest three struggled out of the jungle with a concussion, malaria, and infected wounds 19 days later; two more terribly ill soldiers found a village the next day; and the remaining five emaciated and injured men were rescued from a cave by a helicopter on day 33. What happened?

On a surface level, the near-tragic fracturing of the group began with a logical division of labor, according to the training's initiators, Lieutenant Colonel Neill and Major Foster:

> Because the group would be one of mixed abilities, and the young British and NCOs [non-commissioned officers] were likely to be fitter and more experienced than the Hong Kong soldiers, the team would work in two halves on the harder phases of the descent. The British, taking advantage of Mayfield's expertise (in rock climbing), would set up ropes on the difficult sections, while he [Neill] and Foster would concentrate on bringing the Hong Kong soldiers down. Every now and then the recce (reconnaissance) party would report back, and the expedition would go on down in one unit until another reconnaissance party became necessary.

The men reported that from then on, perilous climbing conditions, debilitating sickness, and monsoon rains permanently divided the group. A review board found differently, blaming Neill's and Foster's leadership and their decision to take some less-experienced soldiers on the exercise.

No rulings were made about the near-catastrophic decision to divide the group, but closer inquiries show that this temporary workgroup of diverse members who were not previously acquainted started out with a high level of intragroup trust that dissolved over time. The resulting faultlines, based on members' similarities and differences and the establishment of ad hoc leaders, may have been inevitable.

Initially, all group members shared the common ground of soldier training, clear roles, and volunteer commitment to the mission. When the leaders ignored the soldiers' concerns about the severity of conditions, lack of preparation, and low level of communication, however, trust issues divided the group into subgroups. The initial reconnaissance party established common ground and trust that allowed them to complete the mission and reach safety, even though they divided yet again. Meanwhile, the main group that stayed with the leaders in the cave under conditions of active distrust fractured further.

We will never know whether it would have been better to keep the group together. However, we do know that this small group of soldiers trained to stay together for survival fractured into at least four subgroups because they didn't trust their leaders or their group, endangering all their lives.

Questions

31. How was the common ground established by the reconnaissance subgroups different from the common ground established by the cave subgroups? See the leaders' description.

32. Do you think the group should have fractured as it did? Why or why not?

33. When the exercise was designed, Neill created a buddy system based on similarity of soldiers' backgrounds (rank, unit, age, fitness, skills level). The first group out of the jungle were assigned buddies and one other: two lance corporals and one corporal from the same unit (regular army); ages 24–26 with good fitness levels; all top roping and abseiling (TR&A) instructors. The second group out were assigned buddies: a sergeant and a lance corporal from the same unit (elite regular army); ages 25 and 37; good fitness levels; both with Commando Brigade skills. The group left in the cave split into: a lieutenant colonel and a major (buddies); one from the regular army and one from the part time territorial army; ages 46 and 54; fair fitness level; one TR&A and one ski instructor. The second faction was the three from the Hong Kong unit—a lance corporal and two privates, all from the Hong Kong unit; ages 24–32; fair to good fitness levels; one with jungle training and two novices. Would you have set up the buddy system Neill did? Why or why not, and if not, what would you have changed?

Sources: M. A. Korsgaard, H. H. Brower, and S. W. Lester, "It Isn't Always Mutual: A Critical Review of Dyadic Trust," *Journal of Management* 41, no. 1 (2014): 47–70; R. L. Priem and P. C. Nystrom, "Exploring the Dynamics of Workgroup Fracture: Common Ground, Trust-with-Trepidation, and Warranted Distrust," *Journal of Management* 40, no. 3 (2014): 764–95; and "The Call of Malaysia's 'Conquerable' Mount Kinabalu," *BBC*, June 5, 2015, http://www.bbc.com/news/world-asia-33020356.

MyManagementLab

Go to **mymanagementlab.com** for Auto-graded writing questions as well as the following Assisted-graded writing questions:

34. Considering Case Incident 1, what are some ways groups can improve the effectiveness of consensus methods to make decisions?

35. After reading Case Incident 2, do you feel subgroups are good or bad? Why or why not? What might be the alternative?

36. MyManagementLab Only – comprehensive writing assignment for this chapter.

ENDNOTES

[1] E. J. Boothby, M. S. Clark, and J. A. Bargh, "Shared Experiences are Amplified," *Psychological Science* 25, no. 12 (2014): 2209–16.

[2] B. Bastien, J. Jetten, and L. J. Ferris, "Pain as Social Glue: Shared Pain Increases Cooperation," *Psychological Science* 25, no. 11 (2014): 2079–85.

[3] N. Karelaia and L. Guillen, "Me, a Woman and a Leader: Positive Social Identity and Identity Conflict," *Organizational Behavior and Human Decision Processes* 125, no. 2 (2014): 204–19.

[4] P. Belmi, R. C. Barragan, M. A. Neale, and G. L. Cohen, "Threats to Social Identity Can Trigger Social Deviance," *Personality and Social Psychological Bulletin* 41, no. 4 (2015): 467–84.

[5] H. Takahashi, M. Kato, M. Matsuura, D. Mobbs, T. Suhara, and Y. Okubo, "When Your Gain Is My Pain and Your Pain Is My Gain: Neural Correlates of Envy and Schadenfreude," *Science* 323, no. 5916 (2009): 937–39; and C. W. Leach, R. Spears, N. R. Branscombe, and B. Doosje, "Malicious Pleasure: Schadenfreude at the Suffering of Another Group," *Journal of Personality and Social Psychology* 84, no. 5 (2003): 932–43.

[6] O. Yakushko, M. M. Davidson, and E. N. Williams, "Identity Salience Model: A Paradigm for Integrating Multiple Identities in Clinical Practice," *Psychotherapy* 46, no. 2 (2009): 180–92; and S. M. Toh and A. S. Denisi, "Host Country Nationals as Socializing Agents: A Social Identity Approach," *Journal of Organizational Behavior* 28, no. 3 (2007): 281–301.

[7] N. Karelaia and L. Guillen, "Me, a Woman and a Leader: Positive Social Identity and Identity Conflict."

[8] T. Cruwys, E. I. South, K. H. Greenaway, and S. A. Haslam, "Social Identity Reduces Depression by Fostering Positive Attributions," *Social Psychological and Personality Science* 6, no. 1 (2015): 65–74.

[9] T. Schmader, K. Block, and B. Lickel, "Social Identity Threat in Response to Stereotypic Film Portrayals: Effects on Self-Conscious Emotion and Implicit Ingroup Attitudes," *Journal of Social Issues* 71, no. 1 (2015): 54–72.

[10] S. Zhang, G. Chen, X.-P. Chen, D. Liu, and M. D. Johnson, "Relational versus Collective Identification within Workgroups: Conceptualization, Measurement Development, and Nomological Network Building," *Journal of Management* 40, no. 6 (2014): 1700–31.

[11] G. J. Lewis and T. C. Bates, "Common Heritable Effects Underpin Concerns over Norm Maintenance and In-Group Favoritism: Evidence from Genetic Analyses of Right-Wing Authoritarianism and Traditionalism," *Journal of Personality* 82, no. 4 (2014): 297–309.

[12] S. L. Neuberg, C. M. Warner, S. A. Mistler, A. Berlin, E. D. Hill, J. D. Johnson, J. Schober, et al., "Religion and Intergroup Conflict: Findings from the Global Group Relations Project," *Psychological Science* 25, no. 1 (2014): 198–206.

[13] W. M. L. Finlay, "Denunciation and the Construction of Norms in Group Conflict: Examples from and Al-Qaeda-Supporting Group," *British Journal of Social Psychology* 53, no. 4 (2014): 691–710.

[14] T. C. Dennehy, A. Ben-Zeev, and N. Tanigawa, "'Be Prepared:' An Implemental Mindset for Alleviating Social-Identity Threat," *British Journal of Social Psychology* 53 (2014): 585–94.

[15] M. J. Garfield and A. R. Denis, "Toward an Integrated Model of Group Development: Disruption of Routines by Technology-Induced Change," *Journal of Management Information Systems* 29, no. 3 (2012): 43–86; M. J. Waller, J. M. Conte, C. B. Gibson, and M. A. Carpenter, "The Effect of Individual Perceptions of Deadlines on Team Performance," *Academy of Management Review* (October 2001): 586–600; and A. Chang, P. Bordia, and J. Duck, "Punctuated Equilibrium and Linear Progression: Toward a New Understanding of Group Development," *Academy of Management Journal* (February 2003): 106–17.

[16] M. M. Kazmer, "Disengaging from a Distributed Research Project: Refining a Model of Group Departures," *Journal of the American Society for Information Science and Technology* (April 2010): 758–71.

[17] K. Giese and A. Thiel, "The Psychological Contract in Chinese-African Informal Labor Relations," *International Journal of Human Resource Management* 26, no. 14 (2015): 1807–26; L. Sels, M. Janssens, and I. Van den Brande, "Assessing the Nature of Psychological Contracts: A Validation of Six Dimensions," *Journal of Organizational Behavior* (June 2004): 461–88; and C. Hui, C. Lee, and D. M. Rousseau, "Psychological Contract and Organizational Citizenship Behavior in China: Investigating Generalizability and Instrumentality," *Journal of Applied Psychology* (April 2004): 311–21.

[18] M. D. Collins, "The Effect of Psychological Contract Fulfillment on Manager Turnover Intentions and Its Role as a Mediator in a Casual, Limited-Service Restaurant Environment," *International Journal of Hospitality Management* 29, no. 4 (2010): 736–42; J. M. Jensen, R. A. Opland, and A. M. Ryan, "Psychological Contracts and Counterproductive Work Behaviors: Employee Responses to Transactional and Relational Breach," *Journal of Business and Psychology* 25, no. 4 (2010): 555–68.

[19] D. C. Thomas, S. R. Fitzimmons, E. C. Ravlin, K. Y. Au, B. Z. Ekelund, and C. Barzantny, "Psychological Contracts across Cultures," *Organization Studies* 31 (2010): 1437–58.

[20] K. S. Wilson and H. M. Baumann, "Capturing a More Complete View of Employees' Lives outside of Work: The Introduction and Development of New Interrole Conflict Constructs," *Personnel Psychology* 68, no. 2 (2015): 235–82.

[21] Ibid.

[22] See, for example, F. T. Amstad, L L. Meier, U. Fasel, A. Elfering, and N. K. Semmer, "A Meta-Analysis of Work-Family Conflict and Various Outcomes with a Special Emphasis on Cross-Domain Versus Matching-Domain Relations," *Journal of Occupational Health Psychology* 16, no. 2 (2011): 151–69.

[23] K. S. Wilson and H. M. Baumann, "Capturing a More Complete View of Employees' Lives outside of Work: The Introduction and Development of New Interrole Conflict Constructs."

[24] D. Vora and T. Kostova. "A Model of Dual Organizational Identification in the Context of the Multinational Enterprise," *Journal of Organizational Behavior* 28 (2007): 327–50.

[25] C. Reade, "Dual Identification in Multinational Corporations: Local Managers and Their Psychological Attachment

to the Subsidiary versus the Global Organization," *International Journal of Human Resource Management,* 12, no. 3 (2001): 405–24.

[26]S. Drury, S. A. Hutchens, D. E. Shuttlesworth, and C. L. White, "Philip G. Zimbardo on His Career and the Stanford Prison Experiment's 40th Anniversary," *History of Psychology* 15, no. 2 (2012): 161–70; and S. A. Haslam and S. D. Reicher, "Contesting the 'Nature' of Conformity: What Milgram and Zimbardo's Studies Really Show," *Plos Biology* 10, no. 11 (2012): e1001426.

[27]S. A. Haslam and S. Reicher, "Stressing the Group: Social Identity and the Unfolding Dynamics of Responses to Stress," *Journal of Applied Psychology* 91, no. 5 (2006): 1037–52; S. Reicher and S. A. Haslam, "Rethinking the Psychology of Tyranny: The BBC Prison Study," *British Journal of Social Psychology* 45, no. 1 (2006): 1–40; and P. G. Zimbardo, "On Rethinking the Psychology of Tyranny: The BBC Prison Study," *British Journal of Social Psychology* 45, no. 1 (2006): 47–53.

[28]Y. Huang, K. M. Kendrick, and R. Yu, "Conformity to the Opinions of Other People Lasts for No More Than 3 Days," *Psychological Science* 25, no. 7 (2014): 1388–93.

[29]M. S. Hagger, P. Rentzelas, and N. K. D. Chatzisrantis, "Effects of Individualist and Collectivist Group Norms and Choice on Intrinsic Motivation," *Motivation and Emotion* 38, no. 2 (2014): 215–23; and M. G. Ehrhart and S. E. Naumann, "Organizational Citizenship Behavior in Work Groups: A Group Norms Approach," *Journal of Applied Psychology* (December 2004): 960–74.

[30]E. Delvaux, N. Vanbeselaere, and B. Mesquita, "Dynamic Interplay between Norms and Experiences of Anger and Gratitude in Groups," *Small Group Research* 46, no. 3 (2015): 300–23.

[31]R. B. Cialdini and N. J. Goldstein, "Social Influence: Compliance and Conformity," *Annual Review of Psychology* 55 (2004): 591–621.

[32]P. Kundu and D. D. Cummins, "Morality and Conformity: The Asch Paradigm Applied to Moral Decisions," *Social Influence* 8, no. 4 (2013): 268–79.

[33]Ibid.

[34]R. A. Griggs, "The Disappearance of Independence in Textbook Coverage of Asch's Social Pressure Experiments," *Teaching of Psychology* 42, no. 2 (2015): 137–42.

[35]S. Sansfacon and C. E. Amiot, "The Impact of Group Norms and Behavioral Congruence on the Internalization of an Illegal Downloading Behavior," *Group Dynamics-Theory Research and Practice* 18, no. 2 (2014): 174–88; and L. Rosh, L. R. Offermann, and R. Van Diest, "Too Close for Comfort? Distinguishing between Team Intimacy and Team Cohesion," *Human Resource Management Review* (June 2012): 116–27.

[36]J. S. Hassard, "Rethinking the Hawthorne Studies: The Western Electric Research in Its Social, Political, and Historical Context," *Human Relations* 65, no. 11 (2012): 1431–61.

[37]J. A. Goncalo, J. A. Chatman, M. M. Duguid, and J. A. Kennedy, "Creativity from Constraint? How the Political Correctness Norm Influences Creativity in Mixed-Sex Work Groups," *Administrative Science Quarterly* 60, no. 1 (2015): 1–30.

[38]E. Gonzalez-Mule, D. S. DeGeest, B. W. McCormick, et al., "Can We Get Some Cooperation Around Here? The Mediating Role of Group Norms on the Relationship between Team Personality and Individual Helping Behaviors," *Journal of Applied Psychology* 99, no. 5 (2014): 988–99.

[39]T. Masson and I. Fritsche, "Adherence to Climate Change-Related Ingroup Norms: Do Dimensions of Group Identification Matter?" *European Journal of Social Psychology* 44, no. 5 (2014): 455–65.

[40]See R. J. Bennett and S. L. Robinson, "The Past, Present, and Future of Workplace Deviance," in J. Greenberg (ed.), *Organizational Behavior: The State of the Science,* 2nd ed. (Mahwah, NJ: Erlbaum, 2003), 237–71; and C. M. Berry, D. S. Ones, and P. R. Sackett, "Interpersonal Deviance, Organizational Deviance, and Their Common Correlates: A Review and Meta-Analysis," *Journal of Applied Psychology* 92, no. 2 (2007): 410–24.

[41]M. A. Baysinger, K. T. Scherer, and J. M. LeBreton, "Exploring the Disruptive Effects of Psychopathy and Aggression on Group Processes and Group Effectiveness," *Journal of Applied Psychology* 99, no. 1 (2014): 48–65.

[42]T. C. Reich and M. S. Hershcovis, "Observing Workplace Incivility," Journal of Applied Psychology 100, no. 1 (2015): 203–15; and Z. E. Zhou, Y. Yan, X. X. Che, and L. L. Meier, "Effect of Workplace Incivility on End-of-Work Negative Affect: Examining Individual and Organizational Moderators in a Daily Diary Study," *Journal of Occupational Health Psychology* 20, no. 1 (2015): 117–30.

[43]See C. Pearson, L. M. Andersson, and C. L. Porath, "Workplace Incivility," in S. Fox and P. E. Spector (eds.), *Counterproductive Work Behavior: Investigations of Actors and Targets* (Washington, DC: American Psychological Association, 2005), 177–200.

[44]S. Lim, L. M. Cortina, and V. J. Magley, "Personal and Workgroup Incivility: Impact on Work and Health Outcomes," *Journal of Applied Psychology* 93, no. 1 (2008): 95–107.

[45]M. S. Christian and A. P. J. Ellis, "Examining the Effects of Sleep Deprivation on Workplace Deviance: A Self-Regulatory Perspective," *Academy of Management Journal* 54, no. 5 (2011): 913–34.

[46]Robinson and O'Leary-Kelly, "Monkey See, Monkey Do"; and T. M. Glomb and H. Liao, "Interpersonal Aggression in Workgroups: Social Influence, Reciprocal, and Individual

Effects," *Academy of Management Journal* 46 (2003): 486–96.

[47]P. Bamberger and M. Biron, "Group Norms and Excessive Absenteeism: The Role of Peer Referent Others," *Organizational Behavior and Human Decision Processes* 103, no. 2 (2007): 179–96; and A. Väänänen, N. Tordera, M. Kivimäki, A. Kouvonen, J. Pentti, A. Linna, and J. Vahtera, "The Role of Work Group in Individual Sickness Absence Behavior," *Journal of Health & Human Behavior* 49, no. 4 (2008): 452–67.

[48]M. S. Cole, F. Walter, and H. Bruch, "Affective Mechanisms Linking Dysfunctional Behavior to Performance in Work Teams: A Moderated Mediation Study," *Journal of Applied Psychology* 93, no. 5 (2008): 945–58.

[49]M. S. Hagger, P. Rentzelas, and N. K. D. Chatzisrantis, "Effects of Individualist and Collectivist Group Norms and Choice on Intrinsic Motivation."

[50]J. Dippong and W. Kalkhoff, "Predicting Performance Expectations from Affective Impressions: Linking Affect Control Theory and Status Characteristics Theory," *Social Science Research* 50 (2015): 1–14; and A. E. Randel, L. Chay-Hoon, and P. C. Earley, "It's Not Just about Differences: An Integration of Role Identity Theory and Status Characteristics Theory," in M. C. T. Hunt (ed.), *Research on Managing Groups and Teams* (2005), 23–42.

[51]A. E. Randel, L. Chay-Hoon, and P. C. Earley, "It's Not Just about Differences: An Integration of Role Identity Theory and Status Characteristics Theory."

[52]R. R. Callister and J. A. Wall Jr., "Conflict across Organizational Boundaries: Managed Care Organizations versus Health Care Providers," *Journal of Applied Psychology* 86, no. 4 (2001): 754–63; and P. Chattopadhyay, W. H. Glick, and G. P. Huber, "Organizational Actions in Response to Threats and Opportunities," *Academy of Management Journal* 44, no. 5 (2001): 937–55.

[53]P. F. Hewlin, "Wearing the Cloak: Antecedents and Consequences of Creating Facades of Conformity," *Journal of Applied Psychology* 94, no. 3 (2009): 727–41.

[54]B. Groysberg, J. T. Polzer, and H. A. Elfenbein, "Too Many Cooks Spoil the Broth: How High-Status Individuals Decrease Group Effectiveness," *Organization Science* (May–June 2011): 722–37.

[55]C. Bendersky and N. P. Shah, "The Cost of Status Enhancement: Performance Effects of Individuals' Status Mobility in Task Groups," *Organization Science* 23, no. 2 (2012): 308–22.

[56]B. Groysberg, J. T. Polzer, and H. A. Elfenbein, "Too Many Cooks Spoil the Broth: How High-Status Individuals Decrease Group Effectiveness," Organization Science 22, no. 3 (2011): 722–37.

[57]A. M. Christie and J. Barling, "Beyond Status: Relating Status Inequality to Performance and Health in Teams," *Journal of Applied Psychology* 95, no. 5 (2010): 920–34; and

L. H. Nishii and D. M. Mayer, "Do Inclusive Leaders Help to Reduce Turnover in Diverse Groups? The Moderating Role of Leader-Member Exchange in the Diversity to Turnover Relationship," *Journal of Applied Psychology* 94, no. 6 (2009): 1412–26.

[58]V. Venkataramani, S. G. Green, and D. J. Schleicher, "Well-Connected Leaders: The Impact of Leaders' Social Network Ties on LMX and Members' Work Attitudes," *Journal of Applied Psychology* 95, no. 6 (2010): 1071–84.

[59]H. van Dijk and M. L. van Engen, "A Status Perspective on the Consequences of Work Group Diversity," *Journal of Occupational and Organizational Psychology* (June 2013): 223–41.

[60]Based on J. B. Pryor, G. D. Reeder, and A. E. Monroe, "The Infection of Bad Company: Stigma by Association," *Journal of Personality and Social Psychology*. 102, no. 2 (2012): 224–41; E. Goffman, *Stigma: Notes on the Management of Spoiled Identity* (Touchstone Digital, 2009); and M. R. Hebl, and L. M. Mannix, "The Weight of Obesity in Evaluating Others: A Mere Proximity Effect," *Personality and Social Psychology Bulletin* 29 (2003): 28–38.

[61]M. Cikara and J. J. Van Bavel, "The Neuroscience of Intergroup Relations: An Integrative Review," *Perspectives on Psychological Science* 9, no. 3 (2014): 245–74.

[62]M. Rubin, C. Badea, and J. Jetten, "Low Status Groups Show In-Group Favoritism to Compensate for Their Low Status and Compete for Higher Status," *Group Processes & Intergroup Relations* 17, no. 5 (2014): 563–76.

[63]C. L. Wilkins, J. D. Wellman, L. G. Babbitt, N. R. Toosi, and K. D. Schad, "You Can Win but I Can't Lose: Bias against High-Status Groups Increases Their Zero-Sum Beliefs about Discrimination," *Journal of Experimental Social Psychology* 57 (2014): 1–14.

[64]R. B. Lount, Jr. and S. L. Wilk, "Working Harder or Hardly Working? Posting Performance Eliminates Social Loafing and Promotes Social Laboring in Workgroups," *Management Science* 60, no. 5 (2014): 1098–106; S. M. Murphy, S. J. Wayne, R. C. Liden, and B. Erdogan, "Understanding Social Loafing: The Role of Justice Perceptions and Exchange Relationships," *Human Relations* (January 2003): 61–84; and R. C. Liden, S. J. Wayne, R. A. Jaworski, and N. Bennett, "Social Loafing: A Field Investigation," *Journal of Management* (April 2004): 285–304.

[65]A. W. Delton, L. Cosmides, M. Guemo, T. E. Robertson, and J. Tooby, "The Psy-

chosemantics of Free Riding: Dissecting the Architecture of a Moral Concept," *Journal of Personality and Social Psychology* 102, no. 6 (2012): 1252–70.

[66]C. Rubino, D. R. Avery, S. D. Volpone, et al., "Does Teaming Obscure Low Performance? Exploring the Temporal Effects of Team Performance Diversity," *Human Performance* 27, no. 5 (2014): 416–34.

[67]D. L. Smrt and S. J. Karau, "Protestant Work Ethic Moderates Social Loafing," *Group Dynamics-Theory Research and Practice* (September 2011): 267–74.

[68]M. C. Schippers, "Social Loafing Tendencies and Team Performance: The Compensating Effect of Agreeableness and Conscientiousness," *Academy of Management Learning & Education* 13, no. 1 (2014): 62–81.

[69]A. Gunnthorsdottir and A. Rapoport, "Embedding Social Dilemmas in Intergroup Competition Reduces Free-Riding," *Organizational Behavior and Human Decision Processes* 101 (2006): 184–99; and E. M. Stark, J. D. Shaw, and M. K. Duffy, "Preference for Group Work, Winning Orientation, and Social Loafing Behavior in Groups," *Group and Organization Management* 32, no. 6 (2007): 699–723.

[70]R. B. Lount, Jr. and S. L. Wilk, "Working Harder or Hardly Working? Posting Performance Eliminates Social Loafing and Promotes Social Laboring in Workgroups."

[71]A. Gunnthorsdottir and A. Rapoport, "Embedding Social Dilemmas in Intergroup Competition Reduces Free-Riding;" and E. M. Stark, J. D. Shaw, and M. K. Duffy, "Preference for Group Work, Winning Orientation, and Social Loafing Behavior in Groups."

[72]L. L. Greer, "Group Cohesion: Then and Now," *Small Group Research* (December 2012): 655–61.

[73]D. S. Staples and L. Zhao, "The Effects of Cultural Diversity in Virtual Teams Versus Face-to-Face Teams," *Group Decision and Negotiation* (July 2006): 389–406.

[74]N. Chi, Y. Huang, and S. Lin, "A Double-Edged Sword? Exploring the Curvilinear Relationship between Organizational Tenure Diversity and Team Innovation: The Moderating Role of Team-Oriented HR Practices," *Group and Organization Management* 34, no. 6 (2009): 698–726.

[75]K. J. Klein, A. P. Knight, J. C. Ziegert, B. C. Lim, and J. L. Saltz, "When Team Members' Values Differ: The Moderating Role of Team Leadership," *Organizational Behavior and*

Human Decision Processes 114, no. 1 (2011): 25–36; and G. Park and R. P. DeShon, "A Multilevel Model of Minority Opinion Expression and Team Decision-Making Effectiveness," *Journal of Applied Psychology* 95, no. 5 (2010): 824–33.

[76]J. S. Chun and J. N. Choi, "Members' Needs, Intragroup Conflict, and Group Performance," *Journal of Applied Psychology* 99, no. 3 (2014): 437–50.

[77]M. Rigoglioso, "Diverse Backgrounds and Personalities Can Strengthen Groups," *Stanford Knowledgebase*, August 15, 2006, www.stanford.edu/group/knowledgebase/.

[78]K. W. Phillips and D. L. Loyd, "When Surface and Deep-Level Diversity Collide: The Effects on Dissenting Group Members," *Organizational Behavior and Human Decision Processes* 99 (2006): 143–60; and S. R. Sommers, "On Racial Diversity and Group Decision Making: Identifying Multiple Effects of Racial Composition on Jury Deliberations," *Journal of Personality and Social Psychology* (April 2006): 597–612.

[79]J. S. Chun and J. N. Choi, "Members' Needs, Intragroup Conflict, and Group Performance."

[80]E. Mannix and M. A. Neale, "What Differences Make a Difference? The Promise and Reality of Diverse Teams in Organizations," *Psychological Science in the Public Interest* (October 2005): 31–55.

[81]E. P. Apfelbaum, K. W. Phillips, and J. A. Richeson, "Rethinking the Baseline in Diversity Research: Should We Be Explaining the Effects of Homogeneity?" *Perspectives on Psychological Science* 9, no. 3 (2014): 235–44.

[82]See M. B. Thatcher and P. C. Patel, "Group Faultlines: A Review, Integration, and Guide to Future Research," *Journal of Management* 38, no. 4 (2012): 969–1009.

[83]K. Bezrukova, S. M. B. Thatcher, K. A. Jehn, and C. S. Spell, "The Effects of Alignments: Examining Group Faultlines, Organizational Cultures, and Performance," *Journal of Applied Psychology* 97, no. 1 (2012): 77–92.

[84]R. Rico, M. Sanchez-Manzanares, M. Antino, and D. Lau, "Bridging Team Faultlines by Combining Task Role Assignment and Goal Structure Strategies," *Journal of Applied Psychology* 97, no. 2 (2012): 407–20.

[85]B. L. Bonner, S. D. Sillito, and M. R. Baumann, "Collective Estimation: Accuracy, Expertise, and Extroversion as Sources of Intra-Group Influence," *Organizational*

Behavior and Human Decision Processes 103 (2007): 121–33.

[86]J. E. Kammer, W. Gaissmaier, T. Reimer, and C. C. Schermuly, "The Adaptive Use of Recognition in Group Decision Making," *Cognitive Science* 38, no. 5 (2014): 911–42.

[87]J. S. Chun and J. N. Choi, "Members' Needs, Intragroup Conflict, and Group Performance."

[88]G. Park and R. P. DeShon, "A Multilevel Model of Minority Opinion Expression and Team Decision-Making Effectiveness," *Journal of Applied Psychology* 95, no. 5 (2010): 824–33.

[89]R. Benabou, "Groupthink: Collective Delusions in Organizations and Markets," *Review of Economic Studies* (April 2013): 429–62.

[90]J. A. Goncalo, E. Polman, and C. Maslach, "Can Confidence Come Too Soon? Collective Efficacy, Conflict, and Group Performance over Time," *Organizational Behavior and Human Decision Processes* 113, no. 1 (2010): 13–24.

[91]See N. Richardson Ahlfinger and J. K. Esser, "Testing the Groupthink Model: Effects of Promotional Leadership and Conformity Predisposition," *Social Behavior & Personality* 29, no. 1 (2001): 31–41; and S. Schultz-Hardt, F. C. Brodbeck, A. Mojzisch, R. Kerschreiter, and D. Frey, "Group Decision Making in Hidden Profile Situations: Dissent as a Facilitator for Decision Quality," *Journal of Personality and Social Psychology* 91, no. 6 (2006): 1080–93.

[92]See I. Yaniv, "Group Diversity and Decision Quality: Amplification and Attenuation of the Framing Effect," *International Journal of Forecasting* (January–March 2011): 41–49.

[93]M. P. Brady and S. Y. Wu, "The Aggregation of Preferences in Groups: Identity, Responsibility, and Polarization," *Journal of Economic Psychology* 31, no. 6 (2010): 950–63.

[94]Z. Krizan and R. S. Baron, "Group Polarization and Choice-Dilemmas: How Important Is Self-Categorization?" *European Journal of Social Psychology* 37, no. 1 (2007): 191–201.

[95]See R. P. McGlynn, D. McGurk, V. S. Effland, N. L. Johll, and D. J. Harding, "Brainstorming and Task Performance in Groups Constrained by Evidence," *Organizational Behavior and Human Decision Processes* (January 2004): 75–87; and R. C. Litchfield, "Brainstorming Reconsidered: A Goal-Based View," *Academy of Management Review* 33, no. 3 (2008): 649–68.

[96]N. L. Kerr and R. S. Tindale, "Group Performance and Decision-Making," *Annual Review of Psychology* 55 (2004): 623–55.

[97]C. Faure, "Beyond Brainstorming: Effects of Different Group Procedures on Selection of Ideas and Satisfaction with the Process," *Journal of Creative Behavior* 38 (2004): 13–34.

[98]P. L. Perrewe, K. L. Zellars, G. R. Ferris, A. M. Rossi, C. J. Kacmar, and D. A. Ralston, "Neutralizing Job Stressors: Political Skill as an Antidote to the Dysfunctional Consequences of Role Conflict," *Academy of Management Journal* (February 2004): 141–52.

GLOSSARY

brainstorming   An idea-generation process that specifically encourages any and all alternatives while withholding any criticism of those alternatives.

cohesiveness   The degree to which group members are attracted to each other and are motivated to stay in the group.

conformity   The adjustment of one's behavior to align with the norms of the group.

deviant workplace behavior   Voluntary behavior that violates significant organizational norms and, in so doing, threatens the well-being of the organization or its members. Also called antisocial behavior or workplace incivility. Referred to often in relation to counterproductive work behavior (CWB).

diversity   The extent to which members of a group are similar to, or different from, one another.

faultlines   The perceived divisions that split groups into two or more subgroups based on individual differences such as sex, race, age, work experience, and education.

formal group   A designated work group defined by an organization's structure.

group   Two or more individuals, interacting and interdependent, who have come together to achieve particular objectives.

groupshift   A change between a group's decision and an individual decision that a member within the group would make; the shift can be toward either conservatism or greater risk but it generally is toward a more extreme version of the group's original position.

groupthink   A phenomenon in which the norm for consensus overrides the realistic appraisal of alternative courses of action.

informal group   A group that is neither formally structured nor organizationally determined; such a group appears in response to the need for social contact.

ingroup favoritism   Perspective in which we see members of our ingroup as better than other people, and people not in our group as all the same.

interacting groups   Typical groups in which members interact with each other face to face.

interrole conflict   A situation in which the expectations of an individual's different, separate groups are in opposition.

nominal group technique   A group decision-making method in which individual members meet face to face to pool their judgments in a systematic but independent fashion.

norms   Acceptable standards of behavior within a group that are shared by the group's members.

psychological contract   An unwritten agreement that sets out what management expects from an employee and vice versa.

punctuated-equilibrium model   A set of phases that temporary groups go through that involves transitions between inertia and activity.

reference groups   Important groups to which individuals belong or hope to belong and with whose norms individuals are likely to conform.

role   A set of expected behavior patterns attributed to someone occupying a given position in a social unit.

role conflict   A situation in which an individual is confronted by divergent role expectations.

role expectations   How others believe a person should act in a given situation.

role perception   An individual's view of how he or she is supposed to act in a given situation.

social identity theory   The tendency to personally invest in the accomplishments of a group.

social loafing   The tendency for individuals to expend less effort when working collectively than when working individually.

status   A socially defined position or rank given to groups or group members by others.

status characteristics theory   A theory that states that differences in status characteristics create status hierarchies within groups.

Understanding Work Teams

From Chapter 10 of *Organizational Behavior*, Seventeenth Edition. Stephen P. Robbins, Timothy A. Judge. Copyright © 2017 by Pearson Education, Inc. All rights reserved.

Understanding Work Teams

LEARNING OBJECTIVES

After studying this chapter, you should be able to:

1 Analyze the continued popularity of teams in organizations.

2 Contrast groups and teams.

3 Contrast the five types of team arrangements.

4 Identify the characteristics of effective teams.

5 Explain how organizations can create team players.

6 Decide when to use individuals instead of teams.

 **Chapter Warm Up**

If your professor has chosen to assign this, go to the Assignments section of **mymanagementlab.com** to complete the chapter warm up.

TEAMS THAT PLAY TOGETHER STAY TOGETHER

At SmugMug, an online photo sharing company, every day is a photo opportunity. If you're hired there, you might be expected to enjoy photography, have extensive Web knowledge, and be willing to work in teams. You might even be expected to become a subject in photos the organization posts. But would you anticipate having to crawl through muddy trenches under barbed wire with your team as these employees have? They've just finished the hard-core 10–12-mile obstacle course experience provided by Tough Mudder, an organization that creates physical challenges for organizational teams like those at SmugMug.

The mission of Tough Mudder is simple: solidify teams through a shared experience. Co-founder Chris MacAskill said, "You get muddy and tired and beat up. It is like the Marines and boot camp. The more athletic help the less athletic because you want to finish together as a team. At the end, you are arm in arm, and there are big smiles and high-fives." Tough Mudder events like the one pictured here teach values like mental grit by providing fun, success, and thrills. It seems to work, according to Lynn Gruber of *Fortune*, who remarked, "The teamwork and camaraderie out there was amazing." To date, the organization boasts a track record of over 100 events, 1.5 million participants, 4,000 Tough Mudder tattoos, and a 95 percent participation rate.

Is Tough Mudding not your cup of tea? Then perhaps you should consider employment at Grid Connect Inc., a software firm in Illinois. The game there is ping pong, and "Everybody plays, nobody can opt out. You can take your frustrations out playing ping pong. When you aren't playing, you can root for the underdogs," said founder and CEO Mike Justice. He is the trophy holder and his father is the official scorekeeper, but still, he says, the organization's tournaments enhance team building for his employees. "It's a real confidence booster. It was one of the best things we ever did for morale."

Perhaps old-fashioned athletic leagues are more your thing? Most companies have leagues for organized sports, which may or may not enhance their work teams. At Offerpop, a social-marketing firm, "The sports teams help to make everyone more comfortable with each other," said CEO Wendell Landsford, although he says the real team building happens during postgame drinks. Jerry Schranz of public-relations agency Beckerman personally learned an important job skill while captain of the softball team. He observed, "It is very difficult to give up the ball as a starting pitcher, where you think that no one can pitch as well as you. It was something I had to learn to do: delegate to others and let it unfold."

For all the good that intentional team-building recreation can do, note that programs such as Tough Mudder's may be more successful than off-hours sports leagues. John Pinkham of PAN Communications Inc. was in charge of the Boston PR firm's casual soccer team. He said, "Turns out the fun league we signed up for was super competitive, with ex-college players and Europeans who kicked the ball faster than I thought was possible." In response, losers either tried to out-strategize the perpetual winners or quit. Those that stayed tried to have fun no matter the score. Pinkham said, "I think everyone was glad they played, and it brought us more together as colleagues and friends—just maybe not as teammates."

Sources: B. Haislip, "Play Ball!" *The Wall Street Journal,* June 12, 2014, R4; M. L. Shuffler, D. DiazGranados, and E. Salas, "There's a Science for That: Team Development Interventions in Organizations," *Current Directions in Psychological Science* 20, no. 6 (2011): 365–72; and *Tough Mudder* website, www.toughmudder.com, accessed June 23, 2015.

Do teams that play together stay together, as the opening discussion suggests? There is definitely an upside to shared experiences, as we will find in this chapter. There may also be something about unique, unexpected challenges that bring teams together, as Tough Mudder claims. We are, however, cautioned to consider the effects of these "play" exercises, including possible discrimination against employees who are disabled or physically unfit. We will consider more types of team-building strategies, and teams in general, in this chapter.

Why Have Teams Become So Popular?

1 Analyze the continued popularity of teams in organizations.

Why are teams popular? In short, because we believe they are effective. "A team of people happily committed to the project and to one another will outperform a brilliant individual every time," writes *Forbes* publisher Rich Karlgaard.[1] In some ways, he's right. Teams can sometimes achieve feats an individual could never accomplish.[2] Teams are more flexible and responsive to changing events than traditional departments or other forms of permanent groupings. They can quickly assemble, deploy, refocus, and disband. They are an effective means to democratize organizations and increase employee involvement. And finally, research indicates that our involvement in teams positively shapes the way we think as individuals, introducing a collaborative mindset about even our personal decision making.[3]

The fact that organizations have embraced teamwork doesn't necessarily mean teams are always effective. Team members, as humans, can be swayed by fads and herd mentality that can lead them astray from the best decisions. What conditions affect their potential? How do members work together? Do we even like teams? Maybe not, according to the OB Poll. To answer these questions, let's first distinguish between groups and teams.

Differences Between Groups and Teams

2 Contrast groups and teams.

workgroup A group that interacts primarily to share information and to make decisions to help each group member perform within his or her area of responsibility.

Groups and teams are not the same thing. We define a *group* as two or more individuals, interacting and interdependent, who work together to achieve particular objectives. A **workgroup** is a group that interacts primarily to share information and make decisions to help each member perform within his or her area of responsibility.

Workgroups have no need or opportunity to engage in collective work with joint effort, so the group's performance is merely the summation of each member's individual contribution. There is no positive synergy that would create an overall level of performance greater than the sum of the inputs. A workgroup

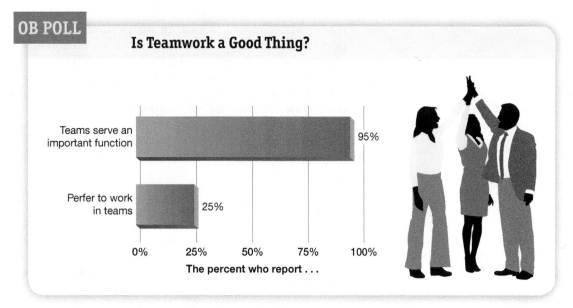

OB POLL

Is Teamwork a Good Thing?

The percent who report . . .

Teams serve an important function — 95%

Perfer to work in teams — 25%

Source: "University of Phoenix Survey Reveals Nearly Seven-in-Ten Workers Have Been Part of Dysfunctional Teams," downloaded on June 9, 2013, from www.prnewswire.com

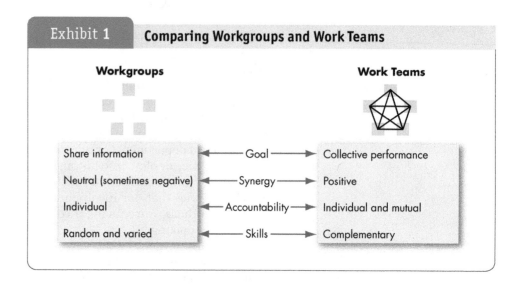

Exhibit 1 **Comparing Workgroups and Work Teams**

Workgroups		Work Teams
Share information	← Goal →	Collective performance
Neutral (sometimes negative)	← Synergy →	Positive
Individual	← Accountability →	Individual and mutual
Random and varied	← Skills →	Complementary

work team A group whose individual efforts result in performance that is greater than the sum of the individual inputs.

is a collection of individuals doing their work, albeit with interaction and/or dependency.

A **work team**, on the other hand, generates positive synergy through coordination. The individual efforts result in a level of performance greater than the sum of the individual inputs.

In both workgroups and work teams, there are often behavioral expectations of members, collective normalization efforts, active group dynamics, and some level of decision making (even if just informally about the scope of membership). Both may generate ideas, pool resources, or coordinate logistics such as work schedules; for the workgroup, however, this effort will be limited to information-gathering for decision makers outside the group.

Whereas we can think of a work team as a subset of a workgroup, the team is constructed to be purposeful (symbiotic) in its member interaction. The distinction between a workgroup and a work team should be kept even when the terms are mentioned interchangeably in differing contexts. Exhibit 1 highlights the differences between them.

The definitions help clarify why organizations structure work processes by teams. Management is looking for positive synergy that will create increased performance. The extensive use of teams creates the *potential* for an organization to generate greater outputs with no increase in employee headcount. Notice, however, that we said *potential*. There is nothing magical that ensures the achievement of positive synergy in the creation of teams. Merely calling a *group* a *team* doesn't automatically improve its performance. As we show later, effective teams have certain common characteristics. If management hopes to gain increases in organizational performance through the use of teams, their teams must possess these characteristics.

Types of Teams

3 Contrast the five types of team arrangements.

Teams can make products, provide services, negotiate deals, coordinate projects, offer advice, and make decisions.[4] In this section, first we describe four common types of teams in organizations: *problem-solving teams, self-managed work teams, cross-functional teams,* and *virtual teams* (see Exhibit 2). Then we will discuss *multiteam systems,* which utilize a "team of teams" and are becoming increasingly widespread as work increases in complexity.

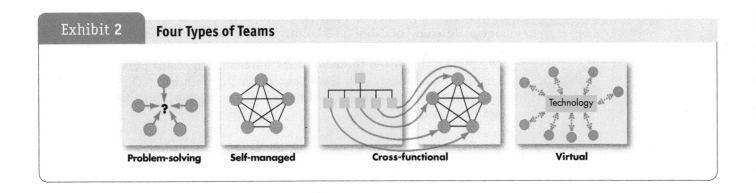

Exhibit 2   **Four Types of Teams**

Problem-solving   Self-managed   Cross-functional   Virtual

Problem-Solving Teams

Quality-control teams have been in use for many years. Originally seen most often in manufacturing plants, these were permanent teams that generally met at a regular time, sometimes weekly or daily, to address quality standards and any problems with the products made. Also, the medical field in particular has recently implemented quality teams to improve their services in patient care. **Problem-solving teams** like these rarely have the authority to unilaterally implement their suggestions, but if their recommendations are paired with implementation processes, some significant improvements can be realized.

Self-Managed Work Teams

As we discussed, problem-solving teams only make recommendations. Some organizations have gone further and created teams that also implement solutions and take responsibility for outcomes.

Self-managed work teams are groups of employees (typically 10 to 15 in number) who perform highly related or interdependent jobs; these teams take on some supervisory responsibilities.[5] Typically, the responsibilities include planning and scheduling work, assigning tasks to members, making operating decisions, taking action on problems, and working with suppliers and customers. Fully self-managed work teams even select their own members who evaluate each other's performance. When these teams are established, former supervisory positions take on decreased importance and are sometimes eliminated.

Research results on the effectiveness of self-managed work teams have not been uniformly positive. Some research indicates that self-managed teams may be more or less effective based on the degree to which team-promoting behaviors are rewarded. For example, one study of 45 self-managing teams found that when team members perceived that economic rewards such as pay were dependent on input from their teammates, performance improved for both individuals and the team as a whole.[6]

A second area of research focus has been the impact of conflict on self-managed work team effectiveness. Some research indicates that self-managed teams are not effective when there is conflict. When disputes arise, members often stop cooperating and power struggles ensue, which lead to lower group performance.[7] However, other research indicates that when members feel confident they can speak up without being embarrassed, rejected, or punished by other team members—in other words, when they feel psychologically safe—conflict can be beneficial and boost team performance.[8]

Thirdly, research has explored the effect of self-managed work teams on member behavior. Here again the findings are mixed. Although individuals on teams report higher levels of job satisfaction than other individuals, stud-

problem-solving teams   Groups of 5 to 12 employees from the same department who meet for a few hours each week to discuss ways of improving quality, efficiency, and the work environment.

self-managed work teams   Groups of 10 to 15 people who take on responsibilities of their former supervisors.

ies indicate they sometimes have higher absenteeism and turnover rates. One large-scale study of labor productivity in British establishments found that although using teams improved individual (and overall) labor productivity, no evidence supported the claim that self-managed teams performed better than traditional teams with less decision-making authority.[9] On the whole, it appears that for self-managing teams to be advantageous, a number of facilitating factors must be in place.

Cross-Functional Teams

cross-functional teams Employees from about the same hierarchical level, but from different work areas, who come together to accomplish a task.

Starbucks created a team of individuals from production, global PR, global communications, and U.S. marketing to develop the Via brand of instant coffee. The team's suggestions resulted in a product that would be cost-effective to produce and distribute, and that was marketed with a tightly integrated, multifaceted strategy.[10] This example illustrates the use of **cross-functional teams**, made up of employees from about the same hierarchical level but different work areas who come together to accomplish a task.

Cross-functional teams are an effective means of allowing people from diverse areas within or even between organizations to exchange information, develop new ideas, solve problems, and coordinate complex projects. However, due to the high need for coordination, cross-functional teams are not simple to manage. First, it makes sense for power shifts to occur as different expertise is needed because the members are at roughly the same level in the organization, which creates leadership ambiguity. A climate of trust thus needs to be developed before shifts can happen without undue conflict.[11] Second, the early stages of development are often long, since members need to learn to work with higher levels of diversity and complexity. Third, it takes time to build trust and teamwork, especially among people with different experiences and perspectives.

Harley-Davidson Motor Company uses cross-functional teams at all levels of its organization in creating new products, such as its first electric motorcycle, shown here. From product conception to launch, cross-functional teams include Harley employees from product planning, engineering, design, marketing, manufacturing, and purchasing.
Source: Justin Lane/EPA/Newscom

Organizations have used horizontal, boundary-spanning teams for decades, and we would be hard-pressed to find a large organization or product launch that did not use them. Major automobile manufacturers—Toyota, Honda, Nissan, BMW, GM, Ford, and Chrysler—currently use this form of team to coordinate complex projects, as do other industries. For example, Cisco relies on specific cross-functional teams to identify and capitalize on new trends in several areas of the software market. Its teams are the equivalent of social-networking groups that collaborate in real time to identify new business opportunities in the field and then implement them from the bottom up.[12]

In sum, the strength of traditional cross-functional teams is the collaborative effort of individuals with diverse skills from a variety of disciplines. When the unique perspectives of these members are considered, these teams can be very effective.

Virtual Teams

virtual teams Teams that use computer technology to tie together physically dispersed members in order to achieve a common goal.

The teams described in the preceding section do their work face-to-face, whereas **virtual teams** use computer technology to unite physically dispersed members and achieve a common goal.[13] They collaborate online—using communication links such as wide-area networks, corporate social media, videoconferencing, and e-mail—whether members are nearby or continents apart. Nearly all teams do at least some of their work remotely.

Virtual teams should be managed differently than face-to-face teams in an office, partially because virtual team members may not interact along traditional hierarchical patterns. Because of the complexity of interactions, research indicates that shared leadership of virtual teams may significantly enhance team performance, although the concept is still in development.[14] For virtual teams to be effective, management should ensure that (1) trust is established among members (one inflammatory remark in an e-mail can severely undermine team trust), (2) progress is monitored closely (so the team doesn't lose sight of its goals and no team member "disappears"), and (3) the efforts and products of the team are publicized throughout the organization (so the team does not become invisible).[15]

It would be a mistake to think virtual teams are an easy substitute for face-to-face teams. While the geographical reach and immediacy of online communication make virtual teams a natural development, managers must make certain this type of team is the optimal choice for the desired outcome and then maintain an oversight role throughout the collaboration.

Multiteam Systems

multiteam system A collection of two or more interdependent teams that share a superordinate goal; a team of teams.

The types of teams we've described so far are typically smaller, standalone teams, though their activities relate to the broader objectives of the organization. As tasks become more complex, teams often grow in size. Increases in team size are accompanied by higher coordination demands, creating a tipping point at which the addition of another member does more harm than good. To solve this problem, organizations use **multiteam systems**, collections of two or more interdependent teams that share a superordinate goal. In other words, multiteam systems are a "team of teams."[16]

To picture a multiteam system, imagine the coordination of response needed after a major car accident. There is the emergency medical services team, which responds first and transports the injured to the hospital. An emergency room team then takes over, providing medical care, followed by a recovery team. Although the emergency services team, emergency room team, and recovery

The Size of Your Meeting's Carbon Footprint

Despite being in different countries, or even on different continents, many teams in geographically dispersed locations communicate without regularly meeting face-to-face, and may never meet each other in person. Although the merits of face-to-face versus electronic communication have been debated, there may be a strong *ethical* argument for virtual teams.

Keeping team members where they are, as opposed to having them travel every time they need to meet, may be in line with corporate social responsibility (CSR) initiatives. A very large proportion of airline, rail, and car transport is for business purposes and contributes greatly to global carbon dioxide emissions. When teams are able to meet virtually rather than face-to-face, they dramatically reduce their carbon footprint.

In a globally connected world, how might you minimize your organization's environmental impact from business travel? Several tips might get you started thinking about ways that virtual teams can be harnessed for greater sustainability:

1. **Encourage all team members to think about whether a face-to-face meeting is really necessary.** Try to utilize alternative communication methods whenever possible.
2. **Communicate as much as possible through virtual means.** This includes e-mail, telephone calls, and video-conferencing.
3. **When traveling to team meetings, choose the most environmentally responsible travel methods possible.** Also, check the environmental profile of hotels before booking rooms.
4. **If the environmental savings are not enough motivation to reduce travel, consider the financial savings.** According to one survey, businesses spend about 8 to 12 percent of their entire budget on travel. Communicating electronically can therefore result in two benefits: (1) it's cheaper and (2) it's good for the environment.

Sources: P. Tilstone, "Cut Carbon...and Bills," *Director,* May 2009, 54; L. C. Latimer, "6 Strategies for Sustainable Business Travel," *Greenbiz,* February 11, 2011, www.greenbiz.com; and F. Gebhart, "Travel Takes a Big Bite out of Corporate Expenses," *Travel Market Report,* May 30, 2013, downloaded June 9, 2013, from www.travelmarketreport.com.

team are technically independent, their activities are interdependent, and the success of one depends on the success of the others. Why? Because they all share the higher goal of saving lives.

Some factors that make smaller, more traditional teams effective do not necessarily apply to multiteam systems and can even hinder their performance. One study showed that multiteam systems performed better when they had "boundary spanners" whose jobs were to coordinate with members of the other subteams. This reduced the need for some team member communication, which was helpful because it reduced coordination demands.[17] Leadership of multiteam systems is also much different than for standalone teams. While leadership of all teams affects team performance, a multiteam leader must both facilitate coordination between teams and lead each team. Research indicated teams that received more attention and engagement from the organization's leaders felt more empowered, which made them more effective as they sought to solve their own problems.[18]

In general, a multiteam system is the best choice either when a team has become too large to be effective, or when teams with distinct functions need to be highly coordinated.

○ **WATCH IT!**

If your professor has assigned this, go to the Assignments section of mymanagementlab.com to complete the video exercise titled *Teams (TWZ Role Play).*

Creating Effective Teams

Teams are often created deliberately but sometimes evolve organically. Take the rise of team "hives" over the past 5 years, for an organic example. Freelancing is typically the solo work of people who are highly specialized in their fields and can provide expertise to organizations on a short-term basis. The difficulty is for the freelancers to effectively market themselves to organizations, and for organizations to find freelancers who fit their needs. To bridge this gap, freelancers form teams with other freelancers from complementary specialties to present a cohesive working unit—a hive—to clients. This team-based approach has proven very successful.[19]

Many people have tried to identify factors related to team effectiveness. To help, some studies have organized what was once a large list of characteristics into a relatively focused model.[20] Exhibit 3 summarizes what we currently know about what makes teams effective.

In considering the team effectiveness model, keep in mind two points. First, teams differ in form and structure. The model attempts to generalize across all varieties of teams but avoids rigidly applying its predictions to all teams.[21] Use it as a guide. Second, the model assumes teamwork is preferable to individual work. Creating "effective" teams when individuals can do the job better is like perfectly solving the wrong problem. Third, let's consider what *team effectiveness* means in this model. Typically, team effectiveness includes objective measures

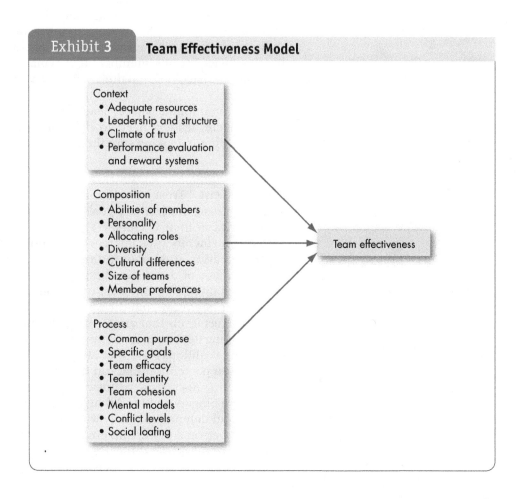

Exhibit 3   Team Effectiveness Model

Context
- Adequate resources
- Leadership and structure
- Climate of trust
- Performance evaluation and reward systems

Composition
- Abilities of members
- Personality
- Allocating roles
- Diversity
- Cultural differences
- Size of teams
- Member preferences

Process
- Common purpose
- Specific goals
- Team efficacy
- Team identity
- Team cohesion
- Mental models
- Conflict levels
- Social loafing

Team effectiveness

of the team's productivity, managers' ratings of the team's performance, and aggregate measures of member satisfaction.

We can organize the key components of effective teams into three general categories. First are the resources and other *contextual* influences that make teams effective. The second relates to the team's *composition*. Finally, *process* variables are events within the team that influence effectiveness. We will explore each of these components next.

Team Context: What Factors Determine Whether Teams Are Successful?

The four contextual factors most significantly related to team performance are adequate resources, effective leadership, a climate of trust, and a performance evaluation and reward system that reflects team contributions.

Adequate Resources   Teams are part of a larger organization system; every work team relies on resources outside the group to sustain it. A scarcity of resources directly reduces the ability of a team to perform its job effectively and achieve its goals. As one study concluded after looking at 13 factors related to group performance, "perhaps one of the most important characteristics of an effective work group is the support the group receives from the organization."[22] This support includes timely information, proper equipment, adequate staffing, encouragement, and administrative assistance.

Leadership and Structure   Teams can't function if they can't agree on who is to do what and ensure all members share the workload. Agreeing on the specifics of work and how they fit together to integrate individual skills requires leadership and structure, either from management or from team members themselves. In self-managed teams, members absorb many of the duties typically assumed by managers. A manager's job then becomes managing *outside* (rather than inside) the team.

As we mentioned before, leadership is especially important in multiteam systems. Here, leaders need to delegate responsibility to teams and play the role of facilitator, making sure the teams work together rather than against one another.[23]

Climate of Trust   Trust is the foundation of leadership; it allows a team to accept and commit to the leader's goals and decisions. Members of effective teams exhibit trust in their leaders.[24] They also trust each other. Interpersonal trust among team members facilitates cooperation, reduces the need to monitor each other's behavior, and bonds individuals through the belief that members won't take advantage of them. Members are more likely to take risks and expose vulnerabilities when they can trust others on their team. The overall level of trust in a team is important, but the way trust is dispersed among team members also matters. Trust levels that are asymmetric and imbalanced between team members can mitigate the performance advantages of a high overall level of trust—in such cases, coalitions form that often undermine the team as a whole.[25]

Trust is a perception that can be vulnerable to shifting conditions in a team environment. Also, trust is not unequivocally desirable. For instance, recent research in Singapore found that, in high-trust teams, individuals are less likely to claim and defend personal ownership of their ideas, but individuals who do still claim personal ownership are rated as lower contributors *by team members*.[26] This "punishment" by the team may reflect resentments that create negative relationships, increased conflicts, and reduced performance.

Performance Evaluation and Reward System   Individual performance evaluations and incentives may interfere with the development of high-performance teams. So, in addition to evaluating and rewarding employees for their individual contributions, management should utilize hybrid performance systems that incorporate an individual member component to recognize individual contributions and a group reward to recognize positive team outcomes.[27] Group-based appraisals, profit-sharing, small-group incentives, and other system modifications can reinforce team effort and commitment.

Team Composition

Maria Contreras-Sweet, head of the U.S. Small Business Administration, said, "When I'm building a team, I'm looking for people who are resourceful. I need people who are flexible, and I really need people who are discreet.... Discreetness also speaks to integrity."[28] These are good qualities, but not all that we should consider when staffing teams. The team composition category includes variables that relate to how teams should be staffed: the abilities and personalities of team members, allocation of roles, diversity, cultural differences, size of the team, and members' preferences for teamwork. As you can expect, opinions vary widely about the type of members leaders want on their teams.

Abilities of Members   It's true we occasionally read about an athletic team of mediocre players who, because of excellent coaching, determination, and precision teamwork, beat a far more talented group. But such cases make the news precisely because they are unusual. A team's performance depends in part on the knowledge, skills, and abilities of individual members.[29] Abilities set limits on what members can do and how effectively they will perform on a team.

Research reveals insights into team composition and performance. First, when solving a complex problem such as reengineering an assembly line, high-ability teams—composed of mostly intelligent members—do better than lower-ability teams. High-ability teams are also more adaptable to changing situations; they can more effectively apply existing knowledge to new problems.

Members of a research team at the innovation lab of Swiss bank UBS are testing digital, virtual reality, and other new technologies to attract a young generation of investors and to help current clients visualize complex investment portfolios. Team members have the technical expertise and skills needed to function as a high-ability team.
Source: Arnd Wiegmann/Reuters

Team Members Who Are "Hot" Should Make the Play

Before we tell you whether this statement is true or false, we need to take a step back and ask: "Can individuals go on 'hot' streaks?" In teams, and especially in sports, we often hear about players who are on a streak and have the "hot hand." Basketball player LeBron James scores five baskets in a row, golfer Rory McIlroy makes three birdies in a row for the European Ryder Cup team, and tennis player Serena Williams hits four aces in a row during a doubles match with her sister Venus. Most people (around 90 percent) believe LeBron, Rory, and Serena score well because they are on

a hot streak, performing above their average.

Although people *believe* in the hot hand, the scores tell the story. About half the relevant studies have shown that the hot hand is possible, while the remaining half show it is not. But perception can influence reality, so perhaps the more important question is whether belief in the hot hand affects teams' strategies. One study of volleyball players showed that coaches and players allocate more balls to players who are believed to have the hot hand. Is this a good strategy? If the hot player's performance is actually lower than her teammates', then giving her more balls to hit will hurt the team

because the better players aren't getting enough chances to hit, while she gets more chances to perform.

Considering the research to date, then, the opening statement appears to be false.

Sources: M. Raab, B. Gula, and G. Gigerenzer, "The Hot Hand Exists in Volleyball and Is Used for Allocation Decisions," *Journal of Experimental Psychology: Applied* 18, no. 1 (2012): 81–94; T Gilovich, R. Vallone, and A. Tversky, "The Hot Hand in Basketball: On the Misperception of Random Sequences," *Cognitive Psychology* 17 (1985): 295–314; and M. Bar-Eli, S. Avugos, and M. Raab, "Twenty Years of 'Hot Hand' Research: The Hot Hand Phenomenon: Review and Critique," *Psychology, Sport, and Exercise* 7 (2006): 525–53.

Finally, the ability of the team's leader matters. Smart team leaders help less intelligent team members when they struggle with a task. A less intelligent leader can, conversely, neutralize the effect of a high-ability team.[30]

Personality of Members   Personality significantly influences individual behavior. Some dimensions identified in the Big Five personality model are particularly relevant to team effectiveness.[31] Conscientiousness is especially important to teams. Conscientious people are good at backing up other team members and sensing when their support is truly needed. Conscientious teams also have other advantages—one study found that behavioral tendencies such as organization, achievement orientation, and endurance were all related to higher levels of team performance.[32]

Team composition can be based on individual personalities to good effect. Suppose an organization needs to create 20 teams of 4 people each and has 40 highly conscientious people and 40 who score low on conscientiousness. Would the organization be better off (1) forming 10 teams of highly conscientious people and 10 teams of members low on conscientiousness, or (2) "seeding" each team with 2 people who scored high and 2 who scored low on conscientiousness? Perhaps surprisingly, evidence suggests option 1 is the best choice; performance across the teams will be higher if the organization forms 10 highly conscientious teams and 10 teams low in conscientiousness. The reason is that a team with varying conscientiousness levels will not work to the peak performance of its highly conscientious members. Instead, a group normalization dynamic (or simple resentment) will complicate interactions and force the highly conscientious members to lower their expectations, thus reducing the group's performance.[33]

What about the other traits? Teams with a high level of openness to experience tend to perform better, and research indicates that constructive task conflict *enhances* the effect. Open team members communicate better with one another and throw out more ideas, which makes teams composed of open people more creative and innovative.[34] Task conflict also enhances performance for teams with high levels of emotional stability.[35] It's not so much that the conflict itself improves performance for these teams, but that teams characterized by openness and emotional stability are able to handle conflict and leverage it to improve performance. The minimum level of team member agreeableness matters, too: teams do worse when they have one or more highly disagreeable members, and a wide span in individual levels of agreeableness can lower productivity. Research is not clear on the outcomes of extraversion, but a recent study indicated that a high mean level of extraversion in a team can increase the level of helping behaviors, particularly in a climate of cooperation.[36] Thus the personality traits of individuals are as important to teams as the overall personality characteristics of the team.

Allocation of Roles Teams have different needs, and members should be selected to ensure all the various roles are filled. A study of 778 major league baseball teams over a 21-year period highlights the importance of assigning roles appropriately.[37] As you might expect, teams with more experienced and skilled members performed better. However, the experience and skill of those in core roles who handled more of the workflow of the team, and were central to all work processes (in this case, pitchers and catchers), were especially vital. In other words, put your most able, experienced, and conscientious workers in the most central roles in a team.

We can identify nine potential team roles (see Exhibit 4). Successful work teams have selected people to play all these roles based on their skills and preferences.[38] (On many teams, individuals will play multiple roles.) To increase the

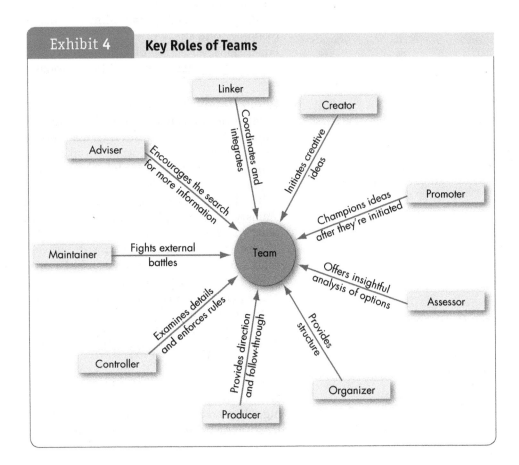

Exhibit 4   Key Roles of Teams

likelihood team members will work well together, managers need to understand the individual strengths each person can bring to a team, select members with their strengths in mind, and allocate work assignments that fit with members' preferred styles.

Diversity of Members   The effect of diversity on groups. How does *team* diversity affect *team* performance? The degree to which members of a work unit (group, team, or department) share a common demographic attribute, such as age, sex, race, educational level, or length of service in the organization, is the subject of **organizational demography**. Organizational demography suggests that attributes such as age or the date of joining should help predict turnover. The logic goes like this: Turnover will be greater among those with dissimilar experiences because communication is more difficult and conflict is more likely. Increased conflict makes membership less attractive, so employees are more likely to quit. Similarly, the losers of a conflict are more apt to leave voluntarily or be forced out.[39] The conclusion is that diversity negatively affects team performance.

Many of us hold the optimistic view that diversity should be a good thing—diverse teams should benefit from differing perspectives. Two meta-analytic reviews show, however, that demographic diversity is essentially unrelated to team performance, while a third review suggests that race and gender diversity are actually negatively related to team performance.[40] Other research findings are mixed. One qualifier is that gender and ethnic diversity have more negative effects in occupations dominated by white or male employees, but in more demographically balanced occupations, diversity is less of a problem. Diversity in function, education, and expertise are positively related to team performance, but these effects are small and depend on the situation.

Proper leadership can improve the performance of diverse teams.[41] For example, one study of 68 teams in China found that teams diverse in knowledge, skills, and ways of approaching problems were more creative, but only when their leaders were transformational and inspiring.[42]

Cultural Differences   We have discussed research on team diversity regarding a number of differences. But what about cultural differences? Evidence indicates cultural diversity interferes with team processes, at least in the short term,[43] but let's dig a little deeper: what about differences in cultural status? Though it's debatable, people with higher cultural status are usually in the majority or ruling race group of their nations. Researchers in the United Kingdom found that cultural status differences affected team performance, whereby individuals in teams with more high cultural-status members than low cultural-status members realized improved performance...for *every* member.[44] This suggests not that diverse teams should be filled with individuals who have high cultural status in their countries, but that we should be aware of how people identify with their cultural status even in diverse group settings.

In general, cultural diversity seems to be an asset for tasks that call for a variety of viewpoints. But culturally heterogeneous teams have more difficulty learning to work with each other and solving problems. The good news is that these difficulties seem to dissipate with time.

Size of Teams   Most experts agree that keeping teams small is key to improving group effectiveness.[45] Amazon CEO Jeff Bezos uses the "two-pizza" rule, saying, "If it takes more than two pizzas to feed the team, the team is too big."[46] Psychologist George Miller claimed "the magical number [is] seven, plus or

organizational demography   The degree to which members of a work unit share a common demographic attribute, such as age, sex, race, educational level, or length of service in an organization, and the impact of this attribute on turnover.

Is it wrong that I'd rather have guys on my team?

Please don't call me sexist; women are great colleagues and equally effective managers, but I'd rather have men on my team. It's more relaxing for me, and for the other guys I think, because we naturally understand each other and can talk freely. The teams with all men that I've been in have all been very productive.

—*Jorge*

Dear Jorge,

With all the talk currently focused on gender diversity in organizations, your viewpoint is refreshingly honest. And your preferences are not uncommon. Researchers who studied 8 years of employee surveys from a large U.S. organization found that individuals were happier on teams mainly of their own gender, whereas those on diverse teams reported less happiness, trust, and cooperation. Researcher Sara Fisher Ellison noted, "People are more comfortable around other people who are like them."

In some ways, the preference for our own gender in teams is an ugly truth. After all, if there hadn't been gender diversity initiatives and protections, a majority of professional positions may still be closed to women in masculine cultures like Japan, Austria, and Venezuela. The value system in many countries has fortunately changed, with increased recognition of team diversity's potential for

higher morale, trust, and satisfaction. Notice that these are *values*, as opposed to the reported *reality* from the paragraph above. Ellison concluded that there is a "mismatch between the kind of workplace people think they would like and the actual workplace that would make them happier."

Don't think this is your ticket to male-only teams, though. Happiness aside, this study found that diverse teams realized significantly greater revenues, productivity, and performance. Other research in Spain indicated that gender-diverse teams realize novel solutions and radical innovation at a greater rate. Still other research suggested that gender-diverse teams perform better than male-dominated ones in sales and profits. The contextual climate is key, though. One meta-analysis found that gender equality and collectivism were important conditions for task performance in diverse teams; a Danish study indicated that diverse top management teams realized higher financial performance only when the structure supported cross-functional team work; and a study in South Korea indicated that cooperative group norms can lower the negative effects of gender diversity.

What all this means for you is that, while you may naturally prefer to work with men, it's not good for business. You would be better off putting your

efforts into creating an egalitarian atmosphere and choosing your teammates based on what they can contribute to your team.

Sources: C. Diaz-Garcia, A. Gonzalez-Moreno, and F. Jose Saez-Martinez, "Gender Diversity within R&D Teams: Its Impact on Radicalness of Innovation," *Innovation-Management Policy & Practice* 15, no. 2 (2013): 149–60; S. Hoogedoorn, H. Oosterbeek, and M. van Praag, "The Impact of Gender Diversity on the Performance of Business Teams: Evidence from a Field Experiment," *Management Science* 59, no. 7 (2013): 1514–28; N. Opstrup and A. R. Villadsen, "The Right Mix? Gender Diversity in Top Management Teams and Financial Performance," *Public Administration Review*, 2015, 291–301; M. Schneid, R. Isidor, C. Li, et al., "The Influence of Cultural Context on the Relationship between Gender Diversity and Team Performance: A Meta-Analysis," *International Journal of Human Resource Management* 26, no. 6 (2015): 733–56; J. Y. Seong and D.-S. Hong, "Gender Diversity: How Can We Facilitate Its Positive Effects on Teams?" *Social Behavior and Personality* 41, no. 3 (2013): 497–508; and R. E. Silverman, "Do Men and Women Like Working Together?" *The Wall Street Journal*, December 16, 2014, D2.

minus two," as the ideal team size.[47] Author and *Forbes* publisher Rich Karlgaard writes, "Bigger teams almost never correlate with a greater chance of success" because the potential connections between people grow exponentially as team size increases, complicating communications.[48]

Generally speaking, the most effective teams have five to nine members. Experts suggest using the smallest number of people who can do the task. Unfortunately, managers often err by making teams too large. It may require only four or five members to develop an array of views and skills, while coordination problems can increase as team members are added. When teams have excess members, cohesiveness and mutual accountability decline, social loafing

A Japanese nurse (left) served on a seven-member medical team formed by the International Committee of the Red Cross and deployed to the Philippines after a typhoon hit Mindanoa Island. The small team of health care workers had the capacity to respond quickly and effectively in providing patients with emergency medical care.

Source: Kyodo/AP Images

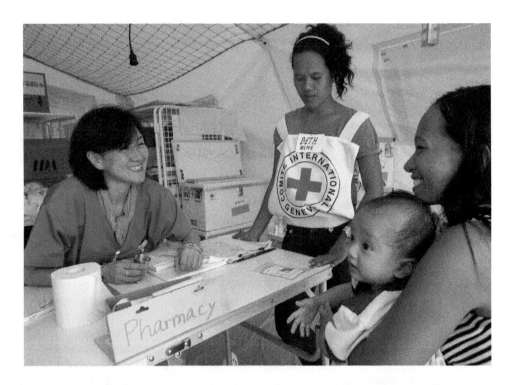

increases, and people communicate less. Members of large teams have trouble coordinating with one another, especially under time pressure. When a natural working unit is larger and you want a team effort, consider breaking the group into subteams.[49]

Member Preferences Not every employee is a team player. Given the option, many employees will select themselves *out* of team participation. When people who prefer to work alone are required to team up, there is a direct threat to the team's morale and to individual member satisfaction.[50] This suggests that, when selecting team members, managers should consider individual preferences along with abilities, personalities, and skills. High-performing teams are likely to be composed of people who prefer working as part of a group.

Team Processes

The final category related to team effectiveness includes process variables such as member commitment to a common purpose, establishment of specific team goals, team efficacy, team identity, team cohesion, mental models, a managed level of conflict, and minimized social loafing. These will be especially important in larger teams and in teams that are highly interdependent.[51]

Why are processes important to team effectiveness? Teams should create outputs greater than the sum of their inputs. Exhibit 5 illustrates how group processes can have an impact on a group's actual effectiveness.[52] Teams are often used in research laboratories because they can draw on the diverse skills of various individuals to produce more meaningful research than researchers working independently—that is, they produce positive synergy, and their process gains exceed their process losses.

Common Plan and Purpose Effective teams begin by analyzing the team's mission, developing goals to achieve that mission, and creating strategies for achieving the goals. Teams that consistently perform better have a clear sense of

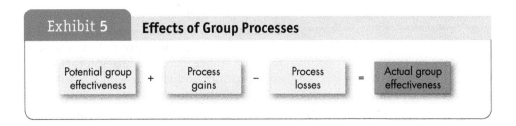

Exhibit 5   **Effects of Group Processes**

Potential group effectiveness $+$ Process gains $-$ Process losses $=$ Actual group effectiveness

what needs to be done and how.[53] This sounds obvious, but many teams ignore this fundamental process.

Members of successful teams put a tremendous amount of time and effort into discussing, shaping, and agreeing on a purpose that belongs to them collectively and individually. This common purpose, when accepted by the team, becomes what GPS is to a ship captain: It provides direction and guidance under any conditions. Like a ship following the wrong course, teams that don't have good planning skills are doomed, executing the wrong plan.[54] Teams should agree on whether their purpose is to learn about and master a task or simply to perform the task; evidence suggests that differing perspectives on learning versus performance lead to lower levels of team performance overall.[55]

reflexivity   A team characteristic of reflecting on and adjusting the master plan when necessary.

Effective teams show **reflexivity**, meaning they reflect on and adjust their purpose when necessary. A team must have a good plan, but it needs to be willing and able to adapt when conditions call for it.[56] Interestingly, some evidence suggests that teams high in reflexivity are better able to adapt to conflicting plans and goals among team members.[57]

Specific Goals   Successful teams translate their common purpose into specific, measurable, and realistic performance goals. Specific goals facilitate clear communication. They help teams maintain their focus on getting results.

Consistent with the research on individual goals, team goals should be challenging. Difficult but achievable goals raise team performance on those criteria for which they're set. So, for instance, goals for quantity tend to increase quantity, goals for accuracy increase accuracy, and so on.[58]

team efficacy   A team's collective belief that they can succeed at their tasks.

Team Efficacy   Effective teams have confidence in themselves; they believe they can succeed. We call this **team efficacy**.[59] Teams that have been successful raise their beliefs about future success, which, in turn, motivates them to work harder. In addition, teams that have a shared knowledge of individual capabilities can strengthen the link between team members' self-efficacy and their individual creativity because members can more effectively solicit informed opinions from their teammates.[60] What can management do to increase team efficacy? Two options are helping the team achieve small successes that build confidence, and providing training to improve members' technical and interpersonal skills. The greater the abilities of team members, the more likely the team will develop confidence and the ability to deliver on that confidence.

Team Identity   The important role of social identity in people's lives. When people connect emotionally with the groups they're in, they are more likely to invest in their relationship with those groups. It's the same with teams. For example, research with soldiers in the Netherlands indicated that individuals who felt included and respected by team members became more willing to work hard for their teams, even though as soldiers they were already called upon to be dedicated to their units. Therefore, by recognizing individuals' specific skills and abilities, as well as creating a climate of

team identity A team member's affinity for and sense of belongingness to his or her team.

team cohesion A situation when team members are emotionally attached to one another and motivated toward the team because of their attachment.

mental models Team members' knowledge and beliefs about how the work gets done by the team.

respect and inclusion, leaders and members can foster positive **team identity** and improved team outcomes.[61]

Organizational identity is important, too. Rarely do teams operate in a vacuum—more often teams interact with other teams, requiring interteam coordination. Individuals with a positive team identity but without a positive organizational identity can become fixed to their teams and unwilling to coordinate with other teams within the organization.[62]

Team Cohesion Have you ever been a member of a team that really "gelled," one in which team members felt connected? The term **team cohesion** means members are emotionally attached to one another and motivated toward the team because of their attachment. Team cohesion is a useful tool to predict team outcomes. For example, a large study in China recently indicated that if team cohesion is high and tasks are complex, costly investments in promotions, rewards, training, and so forth yield greater profitable team creativity. Teams with low cohesion and simple tasks, on the other hand, are not likely to respond to incentives with greater creativity.[63]

Team cohesion is a strong predictor of team performance such that when cohesion is harmed, performance may be, too. Negative relationships are one driver of reduced cohesion. To mitigate this effect, teams can foster high levels of interdependence and high-quality interpersonal interactions.

Mental Models Effective teams share accurate **mental models**—organized mental representations of the key elements within a team's environment that team members share.[64] (If team mission and goals pertain to *what* a team needs to be effective, mental models pertain to *how* a team does its work.) If team members have the wrong mental models, which is particularly likely in teams under acute stress, their performance suffers.[65] One review of 65 independent studies found that teams with shared mental models engaged in more frequent interactions with one another, were more motivated, had more positive attitudes toward their work, and had higher levels of objectively-rated performance.[66] If team

Product Hunt founder Ryan Hoover (on computer) and his entrepreneurial team are highly cohesive. The company describes itself as a "tight-knit team" whose members share a love of new tech products, care about people, and are passionate about building communities that celebrate tech creations.
Source: LiPo Ching/Bay Area News Group/TNS/Landov

members have different ideas about how to do things, however, the team will fight over methods rather than focus on what needs to be done.[67]

Individuals who normally function in *action teams*—teams with specialists engaged in intense, interdependent, and unpredictable tasks—are likely to share mental models. Even though they are often under acute stress, their performance levels can be high because the stress has been normalized through the expected context. These action teams have learned that the best way to share mental models is to voice them. An anesthetic team in a hospital is one example of an action team with shared mental models. For example, research in Switzerland found that anesthetic teams communicated two distinct types of messages while in an operation: vocally monitoring each others' performance (not to criticize but to keep a vocal record of events), and "talking to the room" (announcements to everyone such as "Patient's blood pressure is dropping"). The study found that high- and low-performing teams communicated in these ways equally often; what mattered to performance was the sequencing of the communication to maintain a shared mental model. High-performing teams followed up monitoring dialogue with assistance and instructions, and talking-to-the-room dialogue with further team dialogue.[68] The message seems simple: to maintain shared mental models, share conversation about what is happening while the team is in operation!

Conflict Levels   Conflict has a complex relationship with team performance, and it's not necessarily bad. *Relationship conflicts*—those based on interpersonal incompatibility, tension, and animosity toward others—are almost always dysfunctional. However, when teams are performing nonroutine activities, disagreements about task content—called *task conflicts*—stimulate discussion, promote critical assessment of problems and options, and can lead to better team decisions. According to one study conducted in China, moderate levels of task conflict during the initial phases of team performance were positively related to team creativity, but both very low and very high levels of task conflict were negatively related to team performance.[69] In other words, both too much and too little disagreement about how a team should initially perform a creative task can inhibit performance.

The way conflicts are resolved can make the difference between effective and ineffective teams. A study of ongoing comments made by 37 autonomous work groups showed that effective teams resolved conflicts by explicitly discussing the issues, whereas ineffective teams had unresolved conflicts that were focused more on personalities and the way things were said.[70]

Which teams are more likely to have conflicts than others? It's not a simple answer. While we may presume that diversity increases conflicts, the answer is likely to be much more subtle than that. For example, recent research in Spain found that when individual team members varied greatly in their perceptions of organizational support, task conflict increased, communication decreased, and ultimately team performance suffered.[71] If the researchers had instead compared only the average level of organizational support given to the team, rather than how members perceived the support, they would have missed the correct causal links. Thus we need to be careful not to overgeneralize.

Social Loafing   As we noted earlier, individuals can engage in social loafing and coast on the group's effort when their particular contributions (or lack thereof) can't be identified. Effective teams undermine this tendency by making members individually and jointly accountable for the team's purpose, goals, and approach.[72] Therefore, members should be clear on what they are individually and jointly responsible for on the team.

Turning Individuals into Team Players

5 Explain how organizations can create team players.

We've made a case for the value and growing popularity of teams. But many people are not inherently team players, and many organizations have historically nurtured individual accomplishments. Teams often fit well in countries that score high on collectivism, but what if an organization wants to introduce teams into a work population of individuals born and raised in an individualistic society?

Here are options for managers trying to turn individuals into team players.

Selecting: Hiring Team Players

Some people already possess the interpersonal skills to be effective team players. When hiring team members, be sure candidates can fulfill their team roles as well as technical requirements.[73]

Creating teams often means resisting the urge to hire the best talent no matter what. For example, the New York Knicks professional basketball team pays Carmelo Anthony well because he scores a lot of points for his team; but statistics show he takes more shots than other highly paid players in the league, which means fewer shots for his teammates.[74]

As a final consideration, personal traits appear to make some people better candidates for working in diverse teams. Teams made of members who like to work through difficult mental puzzles also seem more effective and able to capitalize on the multiple points of view that arise from diversity in age and education.[75]

Training: Creating Team Players

Training specialists conduct exercises that allow employees to experience the satisfaction teamwork can provide. Workshops help employees improve their problem-solving, communication, negotiation, conflict-management, and coaching skills. L'Oréal, for example, found that successful sales teams required much more than a staff of high-ability salespeople. "What we didn't account for was that many members of our top team in sales had been promoted because they had excellent technical and executional skills," said L'Oréal's senior VP David Waldock. As a result of introducing purposeful team training, Waldock says, "We are no longer a team just on paper, working independently. We have a real group dynamic now, and it's a good one."[76] An effective team doesn't develop overnight—it takes time.

Rewarding: Providing Incentives to Be a Good Team Player

A traditional organization's reward system must be reworked to encourage cooperative efforts rather than competitive ones.[77] Hallmark Cards Inc. added to its basic individual-incentive system an annual bonus based on the achievement of team goals. Whole Foods directs most of its performance-based rewards toward team performance. As a result, teams select new members carefully so they will

New engineering employees of India's Tata Consultancy Services work in teams to construct paper boats during a team-building exercise at the firm's training center. Creating team players is essential to the success of TCS as employees must collaborate and work cohesively in providing IT consulting services and business solutions for global clients.

Source: Namas Bhojani/Bloomberg via Getty Images

contribute to team effectiveness (and, thus, team bonuses).[78] It is usually best to set a cooperative tone as soon as possible in the life of a team. As we already noted, teams that switch from competitive to cooperative do not immediately share information, and they still tend to make rushed, poor-quality decisions.[79] Apparently, the low trust typical of the competitive group will not be readily replaced by high trust with a quick change in reward systems.

Promotions, pay raises, and other forms of recognition should be given to individuals who work effectively as team members by training new colleagues, sharing information, helping resolve team conflicts, and mastering needed new skills. This doesn't mean individual contributions should be ignored; rather, they should be balanced with selfless contributions to the team.

Finally, don't forget the intrinsic rewards, such as camaraderie, that employees can receive from teamwork. It's exciting to be part of a successful team. The opportunity for personal development of self and teammates can be a very satisfying and rewarding experience.

⚙ **TRY IT!**

If your professor has assigned this, go to the Assignments section of **mymanagementlab.com** to complete the **Simulation:** *Teams*.

Beware! Teams Aren't Always the Answer

6 Decide when to use individuals instead of teams.

Teamwork takes more time and often more resources than individual work. Teams have increased communication demands, conflicts to manage, and meetings to run. So, the benefits of using teams have to exceed the costs, and that's not always possible.[80]

How do you know whether the work of your group would be better done in teams?[81] You can apply three tests. First, can the work be done better by more than one person? Good indicators are the complexity of the work and the need for different perspectives. Simple tasks that don't require diverse input are probably better left to individuals. Second, does the work create a common purpose or set of goals for the people in the group that is more than the aggregate of individual goals? Many service departments of new-vehicle dealers have introduced teams that link customer-service people, mechanics, parts specialists, and sales representatives. Such teams can better manage collective responsibility for ensuring customer needs are properly met.

The final test is to determine whether the members of the group are interdependent. Using teams makes sense when there is interdependence among tasks—the success of the whole depends on the success of each one, *and* the success of each one depends on the success of the others. Soccer, for instance, is an obvious *team* sport. Success requires a great deal of coordination among interdependent players. Conversely, except possibly for relays, swim teams are not really teams. They're groups of individuals performing individually, whose total performance is merely the aggregate summation of their individual performances.

Summary

Few trends have influenced jobs as much as the massive movement of teams into the workplace. Working on teams requires employees to cooperate with others, share information, confront differences, and sublimate personal interests for the greater good of the team. Understanding the distinctions between problem-solving, self-managed, cross-functional, and virtual teams as well as multiteam systems helps determine the appropriate applications for team-based work. Concepts such as reflexivity, team efficacy, team identity, team cohesion, and mental models bring to light important issues relating to team context, composition, and processes. For teams to function optimally, careful attention must be given to hiring, creating, and rewarding team players. Still, effective organizations recognize that teams are not always the best method for getting the work done efficiently. Careful discernment and an understanding of organizational behavior are needed.

Implications for Managers

- Effective teams have adequate resources, effective leadership, a climate of trust, and a performance evaluation and reward system that reflects team contributions. These teams have individuals with technical expertise, and the right traits and skills.
- Effective teams tend to be small. They have members who fill role demands and who prefer to be part of a group.
- Effective teams have members who believe in the team's capabilities, are committed to a common plan and purpose, and have an accurate shared mental model of what is to be accomplished.
- Select individuals who have the interpersonal skills to be effective team players, provide training to develop teamwork skills, and reward individuals for cooperative efforts.
- Do not assume that teams are always needed. When tasks will not benefit from interdependency, individuals may be the better choice.

To Get the Most Out of Teams, Empower Them

POINT

If you want high-performing teams with members who like each other and their jobs, here's a simple solution: Remove the leash tied to them by management and let them make their own decisions. In other words, empower them. This trend started a long time ago, when organizations realized that creating layers of bureaucracy thwarts innovation, slows progress to a trickle, and merely provides hoops for people to jump through in order to get anything done.

You can empower teams in two ways. One way is structurally, by transferring decision making from managers to team members and giving teams the official power to develop their own strategies. The other way is psychologically, by enhancing team members' beliefs that they have more authority, even though legitimate authority still rests with the organization's leaders. Structural empowerment leads to heightened feelings of psychological empowerment, giving teams (and organizations) the best of both worlds.

Research suggests empowered teams benefit in a number of ways. Members are more motivated. They exhibit higher levels of commitment to the team and the organization. And they perform much better. Empowerment sends a signal to the team that it is trusted and doesn't have to be constantly micromanaged by upper leadership. And when teams get the freedom to make their own choices, they accept more responsibility for and take ownership of both the good and the bad.

Granted, that responsibility also means empowered teams must take the initiative to foster their ongoing learning and development, but teams entrusted with the authority to guide their own destiny do just that. So, do yourself (and your company) a favor and make sure that teams, rather than needless layers of middle managers, are the ones making the decisions that count.

COUNTERPOINT

Empowerment can do some good in certain circumstances, but it's certainly not a cure-all.

Yes, organizations have become flatter over the past several decades, paving the way for decision-making authority to seep into lower levels of the organization. But consider that many teams are "empowered" simply because the management ranks have been so thinned that there is no one left to make the key calls. Empowerment is then just an excuse to ask teams to take on more responsibility without an accompanying increase in tangible benefits like pay.

In addition, the organization's leadership already has a good idea of what it would like its teams (and individual employees) to accomplish. If managers leave teams to their own devices, how likely is it that those teams will always choose what the manager wanted? Even if the manager offers suggestions about how the team might proceed, empowered teams can easily ignore that advice. Instead, they need direction on what goals to pursue and how to pursue them. That's what effective leadership is all about.

When decision-making authority is distributed among team members, each member's role is less clear, and members lack a leader to whom they can go for advice. And finally, when teams are self-managed, they become like silos, disconnected from the rest of the organization and its mission. Simply handing people authority is no guarantee they will use it effectively. So, leave the power to make decisions in the hands of those who were assigned leadership roles. After all, they got to be leaders for a reason, and they can best guide the team to stay focused and perform at top levels to maximize organizational outcomes.

Sources: S. I. Tannenbaum, J. Mathieu, E. Salas, and D. Cohen, "Teams Are Changing: Are Research and Practice Evolving Fast Enough?" *Industrial and Organizational Psychology* 5 (2012): 2–24; and R. Ashkenas, "How to Empower Your Team for Non-Negotiable Results," *Forbes*, April 24, 2013, downloaded June 10, 2013, from www.forbes.com.

CHAPTER REVIEW

QUESTIONS FOR REVIEW

1 How do you explain the growing popularity of teams in organizations?

2 What is the difference between a group and a team?

3 What are the five types of team arrangements?

4 What conditions or context factors determine whether teams are effective?

5 How can organizations create team players?

6 When is work performed by individuals preferred over work performed by teams?

EXPERIENTIAL EXERCISE Composing the "Perfect" Team

Break into teams of four to five. Assume you work for a company that redesigns existing products to improve them, from computer keyboards to bicycle helmets to toothbrushes. As a result, creativity is a key factor in whether your company succeeds in developing a product that is marketable.

You need to staff a new team of 5 individuals, and you have a pool of 20 to choose from. For each person, you have information about the following characteristics: intelligence, work experience, conscientiousness, agreeableness, neuroticism, openness to experience, and extraversion.

Answer the following questions as a team:

7. If you could form your perfect team for this context, what would it look like? In other words, what

characteristics would you choose for each of the five members—a lot of work experience or a little; high, moderate, or low conscientiousness; and so on? Why?

8. How, if at all, would your choices change if the task required teams to make quick decisions that were not necessarily the most creative? Why?

9. Each member of your group should describe his or her ideal team member—one hypothetical person you'd most like to work with in this context (use the same criteria as in question 7). As a group, compare your responses. Does every person's ideal member share the same characteristics, or are there differences? If you could, would you compose a team entirely of your ideal individuals? Why or why not?

ETHICAL DILEMMA The Sum of the Team Is Less Than Its Members

Of the billions of tons of carbon let loose into the world's atmosphere each year, China is responsible for 21 percent, mostly due to its growth in manufacturing. And due to the billions of tons of wastewater and sewage released

into rivers and lakes by Chinese chemical firms every year, 300 million of its citizens do not have clean drinking water. Clearly, these ethical breaches represent the failure not of one individual but of scores of teams: to be exact, top management teams in organizations throughout the country. Does that mean the leaders of China's companies are all unethical? Surely not.

To increase corporate social responsibility (CSR), we need to understand the team dynamics that lead to unethical decision making. First, we examine the context. As a major emerging country, China witnessed unprecedented growth in industry that has brought opportunities for corporate profits, better salaries, and better access to services for its citizens. Millions have been able to pull themselves and their families out of poverty. Few would argue that providing jobs and services isn't a highly ethical pursuit. However, top management teams now face pressure to sustain growth at any cost. The top management team of Rongping Chemical Company made the tragic decision to cut costs and increase profits by dumping untreated chlorine into rivers, raising the level of chromium-6—a tasteless, odorless compound that causes ulcers and cancers—to over 20 times national standards. Other organizations, like Luliang Chemical Company, have done the same, endangering the health of the same citizens it helps with jobs and opportunities.

Some observers have been shocked that top management teams in a country with collectivist values, which stress a group-oriented outlook, would make decisions that don't consider everyone affected by them. One recent study indicated that the problem is competing ethical principles: duty to others v. duty to society. As management teams faced financial dissatisfaction about their firm's performance, environmental ethics and CSR actions decreased, suggesting the teams were feeling pressure from their organization's stakeholders and becoming less concerned about the environment. They may also have rationalized that providing jobs was for the greater societal good and believed that violating stakeholder expectations would cost them their own place on the management team. However, the study found that on an individual level, when a person's sense of collectivist values increased, environmental ethics also increased, suggesting that the top managers did favor CSR initiatives, but other concerns predominated in the team settings. We may conclude that these teams are likely hindering the progress of environmental awareness. When teams feel pressured to meet certain (sometimes narrow) metrics, there may be more unethical team decisions than individual members would make on their own.

Questions

10. Do you think you could be convinced to let your organization dump chemicals such as chromium-6 into the water supply? Why or why not?

11. Why might top management teams be more likely to make unethical decisions than their individual members would make?

12. The cases of Rongping and Luliang are far from isolated incidents. You may remember the case of Pacific Gas & Electric (PG&E), which dumped chromium-6 into the water supply in Hinckley, California, as recounted in the movie *Erin Brockovich.* That case resulted in a $333 million award, the largest settlement ever in a direct-action lawsuit, to help the town's 2,000 residents. In contrast, when 1,721 villagers brought suit against Rongping (more plaintiffs than ever in China, to date), the court ordered the company to pay only a total compensation of $105,000 for damage to the land. And the Chinese environmental group Friends of Nature filed the country's first-ever public-interest lawsuit, which shut down Rongping's plant in a village, but did not offer monetary restitution for the villagers. How might these outcomes affect the ethical decisions of top management teams in the future?

Sources: "Eight Cases That Mattered," *ChinaDialogue,* https://www.chinadialogue.net/article/show/single/en/4429-Eight-cases-that-mattered, accessed June 22, 2015; "Facts about Chromium," Environmental Protection Agency, http://www.epa.gov/region7/pdf/national_beef_leathers-prime_tanning_chromiumVI_Fact_Sheet.pdf, accessed June 22, 2015; EJOLT Team at School of Geography and China Centre, University of Oxford, "Heavy Metal Pollution in Quijing, Yunnan, China," *Environmental Justice Atlas,* February 25, 2015; S. Thau, R. Derfler-Rozin, M. Pitesa, M. S. Mitchell, and M. M. Pillutla, "Unethical for the Sake of the Group: Risk of Social Exclusion and Pro-Group Unethical Behavior," *Journal of Applied Psychology* 100, no. 1 (2015): 98–113; J. Steinberg, "Hinckley: No Hollywood Ending for Erin Brockovich's Tainted Town," *San Jose Mercury News,* July 7, 2013, http://www.mercurynews.com/ci_23649050/hinckley-no-hollywood-ending-erin-brockovichs-tainted-town; and X. Wang and M. N. Young, "Does Collectivism Affect Environmental Ethics? A Multi-Level Study of Top Management Teams from Chemical Firms in China," *Journal of Business Ethics* 122, no. 3 (2014): 387–94.

CASE INCIDENT 1 Tongue-Tied in Teams

Thirty-one-year-old Robert Murphy has the best intentions to participate in team meetings, but when it's "game time," he chokes. An online marketing representative, Robert cannot be criticized for lack of preparation. After being invited to a business meeting with six of his coworkers and his supervisor, Robert began doing his research on the meeting's subject matter. He compiled notes and arranged them neatly. As soon as the meeting began, however, "I just sat there like a lump, fixated on the fact that I was quiet." The entire meeting passed without Robert contributing a word.

Robert is certainly not the first person to fail to speak up during meetings, and he won't be the last. While some silent employees may not have any new ideas to contribute, the highly intelligent also freeze. One study found that if we believe our peers are smarter, we experience anxiety that temporarily blocks our ability to think effectively. In other words, worrying about what the group thinks of you makes you dumber. The study also found the effect was worse for women, perhaps because they can be more socially attuned to what others may think.

In other cases, failing to speak up may be attributed to personality. While the extraverted tend to be assertive and assured in group settings, the more introverted prefer to collect their thoughts before speaking—if they

speak at all. But again, even those who are extraverted can remain quiet, especially when they feel they cannot contribute.

You may be wondering whether it is important for everyone to speak up. Collaboration (the word comes from "laboring together" in Latin) is at the heart of organizational transformation, so yes, the more participation, the more likely the collaboration will result in higher trust, increased productivity, and enhanced creativity. Furthermore, collaboration works best when individuals know their ideas are taken seriously.

The message from research is clear: give free speech a try!

Questions

13. Recall a time when you failed to speak up during a group meeting. What were the reasons for your silence? Are they similar to or different from the reasons discussed here?
14. Can you think of strategies that can help the tongue-tied?
15. Imagine you are leading a team meeting and you notice that a couple of team members are not contributing. What specific steps might you take to try to increase their contributions?

Sources: E. Bernstein, "Speaking Up Is Hard to Do: Researchers Explain Why," *The Wall Street Journal,* February 7, 2012, D1; M. Kashtan, "Want Teamwork? Promote Free Speech," *The New York Times,* April 13, 2014, 8; and H. Leroy et al., "Behavioral Integrity for Safety, Priority of Safety, Psychological Safety, and Patient Safety: A Team-Level Study," *Journal of Applied Psychology* (November 2012): 1273–81.

CASE INCIDENT 2 Smart Teams and Dumb Teams

In this chapter, we've identified how some of the characteristics we use to describe individuals also can describe teams. For example, individuals can be high in the trait of openness, as can a team. Along the same lines, have you noticed that some teams seem to be smart, while others seem, um, dumb? This characteristic has nothing to do with the average IQ of the team members but instead reflects the functionality of the whole team. Teams that are

synergistic excel in logical analysis, brainstorming, coordination, planning, and moral reasoning. And teams that are dumb? Think of long unproductive meetings, social loafing, and interpersonal conflicts.

You might be remembering a few teams you've witnessed that are in the dumb category, but we hope you can think of a few that excelled. Smart teams tend to be smart in everything—for any task, they will find a workable solution. But what makes them smart? Researchers in an MIT study grouped 697 subjects into teams of 2–5 members to solve tasks, looking for the characteristics of smart teams (they weren't all smart). The findings were:

1. **Smart teams did not allow individual members to dominate**. Instead, there were more equal contributions from members than in other teams.
2. **Smart teams had more members who were able to read minds**. Just kidding. But the members were able to read complicated emotions by looking into the eyes of others. There is a test for this ability called Reading the Mind in the Eyes.
3. **Smart teams had more women**. It's not that smart teams had more gender equality; these teams simply had more women. This result might be partly due to the fact that more women scored higher in the Reading the Mind in the Eyes test.

The researchers recently replicated the study using 68 teams and again found that some teams were smarter than others. This study added a new angle to the research: How would teams working in person differ from teams working online? Surprisingly, there was little difference: All smart teams had more equal member communication (and plenty of it) and were good at emotion reading. When the online collaborators could not see each other, they practiced Theory of Mind, remembering and reacting to the emotional cues they were able to detect through any mode of communication. Theory of Mind is related to emotional intelligence (EI).

When we have the opportunity to hand-pick team members, we can look for those who listen as much as they speak, express empathy, and remember what others tell them about themselves. For teams to which we are assigned, we can seek these attributes in others and help guide the team toward its best self. As for IQ? Here's the good news: Recent research indicates that our membership in a team actually makes us smarter decision-makers as individuals!

Questions

16. From your experiences in teams, do you agree with the researchers' findings on the characteristics of smart teams? Why or why not?
17. On the highly functioning teams in which you've been a member, what other characteristics might have contributed to success?
18. The authors who suggested that membership in a team makes us smarter found that teams were more rational and quicker at finding solutions to difficult probability problems and reasoning tasks than were individuals. However, after participation in the study, team members were much better at decision making on their own, even up to 5 weeks later. Do you think this spillover effect would happen equally for people in smart teams and dumb teams? Why or why not?

Source: E. E. F. Bradford, I. Jentzsch, and J.-C. Gomez, "From Self to Cognition: Theory of Mind Mechanisms and Their Relation to Executive Functioning," *Cognition* 138 (2015): 21–34; B. Maciejovsky, M. Sutter, D. V. Budescu, et al., "Teams Make You Smarter: How Exposure to Teams Improves Individual Decisions in Probability and Reasoning Tasks," *Management Science* 59, no. 6 (2013): 1255–70; and A. Woolley, T. W. Malone, and C. Chabris, "Why Some Teams Are Smarter Than Others," *The New York Times,* January 18, 2015, 5.

MyManagementLab

Go to **mymanagementlab.com** for Auto-graded writing questions as well as the following Assisted-graded writing questions:

19. Regarding Case Incident 1, do you think it's necessary for everyone to speak up in a team? Why or why not?
20. In reference to Case Incident 2, do you think you can read emotions from people's eyes enough to react well to them in teams? Why or why not? There are Reading the Mind from the Eyes tests online if you want to test your skill.
21. **MyManagementLab Only** – comprehensive writing assignment for this chapter.

ENDNOTES

[1]R. Karlgaard, "Think (Really!) Small," *Forbes,* April 13, 2015, 32.

[2]J. C. Gorman, "Team Coordination and Dynamics: Two Central Issues," *Current Directions in Psychological Science* 23, no. 5 (2014): 355–60.

[3]Ibid.

[4]J. Mathieu, M. T. Maynard, T. Rapp, and L. Gilson, "Team Effectiveness 1997–2007: A Review of Recent Advancements and a Glimpse into the Future," *Journal of Management* 34, no. 3 (2008): 410–76.

[5]See, for example, A. Erez, J. A. LePine, and H. Elms, "Effects of Rotated Leadership and Peer Evaluation on the Functioning and Effectiveness of Self-Managed Teams: A Quasi-experiment," *Personnel Psychology* (Winter 2002): 929–48.

[6]G. L. Stewart, S. H. Courtright, and M. R. Barrick, "Peer-Based Control in Self-Managing Teams: Linking Rational and Normative Influence with Individual and Group Performance," *Journal of Applied Psychology* 97, no. 2 (2012): 435–47.

[7]C. W. Langfred, "The Downside of Self-Management: A Longitudinal Study of the Effects of Conflict on Trust, Autonomy, and Task Interdependence in Self-Managing Teams," *Academy of Management Journal* 50, no. 4 (2007): 885–900.

[8]B. H. Bradley, B. E. Postlethwaite, A. C. Klotz, M. R. Hamdani, and K. G. Brown, "Reaping the Benefits of Task Conflict in Teams: The Critical Role of Team Psychological Safety Climate," *Journal of Applied Psychology,* 97, no. 1 (2012): 151–58.

[9]J. Devaro, "The Effects of Self-Managed and Closely Managed Teams on Labor Productivity and Product Quality: An Empirical Analysis of a Cross-Section of Establishments," *Industrial Relations* 47, no. 4 (2008): 659–98.

[10]A. Shah, "Starbucks Strives for Instant Gratification with Via Launch," *PRWeek* (December 2009): 15.

[11]F. Aime, S. Humphrey, D. S. DeRue, and J. B. Paul, "The Riddle of Heterarchy: Power Transitions in Cross-Functional Teams," *Academy of Management Journal* 57, no. 2 (2014): 327–52.

[12]B. Freyer and T. A. Stewart, "Cisco Sees the Future," *Harvard Business Review* (November 2008): 73–79.

[13]See, for example, L. L. Martins, L. L. Gilson, and M. T. Maynard, "Virtual Teams: What Do We Know and Where Do We Go from Here?" *Journal of Management* (November 2004):

805–35; and B. Leonard, "Managing Virtual Teams," *HRMagazine,* June 2011, 39–42.

[14]J. E. Hoch and S. W. J. Kozlowski, "Leading Virtual Teams: Hierarchical Leadership, Structural Supports, and Shared Team Leadership," *Journal of Applied Psychology* 99, no. 3 (2014): 390–403.

[15]A. Malhotra, A. Majchrzak, and B. Rosen, "Leading Virtual Teams," *Academy of Management Perspectives* (February 2007): 60–70; and J. M. Wilson, S. S. Straus, and B. McEvily, "All in Due Time: The Development of Trust in Computer-Mediated and Face-to-Face Teams," *Organizational Behavior and Human Decision Processes* 19 (2006): 16–33.

[16]P. Balkundi and D. A. Harrison, "Ties, Leaders, and Time in Teams: Strong Inference about Network Structure's Effects on Team Viability and Performance," *Academy of Management Journal* 49, no. 1 (2006): 49–68; G. Chen, B. L. Kirkman, R. Kanfer, D. Allen, and B. Rosen, "A Multilevel Study of Leadership, Empowerment, and Performance in Teams," *Journal of Applied Psychology* 92, no. 2 (2007): 331–46; L. A. DeChurch and M. A. Marks, "Leadership in Multiteam Systems," *Journal of Applied Psychology* 91, no. 2 (2006): 311–29; A. Srivastava, K. M. Bartol, and E. A. Locke, "Empowering Leadership in Management Teams: Effects on Knowledge Sharing, Efficacy, and Performance," *Academy of Management Journal* 49, no. 6 (2006): 1239–51; and J. E. Mathieu, K. K. Gilson, and T. M. Ruddy, "Empowerment and Team Effectiveness: An Empirical Test of an Integrated Model," *Journal of Applied Psychology* 91, no. 1 (2006): 97–108.

[17]R. B. Davison, J. R. Hollenbeck, C. M. Barnes, D. J. Sleesman, and D. R. Ilgen, "Coordinated Action in Multiteam Systems," *Journal of Applied Psychology* 97, no. 4 (2012): 808–24.

[18]M. M. Luciano, J. E. Mathieu, and T. M. Ruddy, "Leading Multiple Teams: Average and Relative External Leadership Influences on Team Empowerment and Effectiveness," *Journal of Applied Psychology* 99, no. 2 (2014): 322–31.

[19]R. Greenwald, "Freelancing Alone—But Together," *The Wall Street Journal,* February 3, 2014, R5.

[20]V. Gonzalez-Roma and A. Hernandez, "Climate Uniformity: Its Influence on Team Communication Quality, Task Conflict, and Team Performance," *Journal of Applied Psychology* 99, no. 6 (2014): 1042–58; C. F. Peralta, P. N. Lopes, L. L. Gilson, P. R. Lourenco,

and L. Pais, "Innovation Processes and Team Effectiveness: The Role of Goal Clarity and Commitment, and Team Affective Tone," *Journal of Occupational and Organizational Psychology* 88, no. 1 (2015): 80–107; L. Thompson, *Making the Team* (Upper Saddle River, NJ: Prentice Hall, 2000), 18–33; and J. R. Hackman, *Leading Teams: Setting the Stage for Great Performance* (Boston: Harvard Business School Press, 2002).

[21]See G. L. Stewart and M. R. Barrick, "Team Structure and Performance: Assessing the Mediating Role of Intrateam Process and the Moderating Role of Task Type," *Academy of Management Journal* (April 2000): 135–48.

[22]Hyatt and Ruddy, "An Examination of the Relationship between Work Group Characteristics and Performance," 577.

[23]P. Balkundi and D. A. Harrison, "Ties, Leaders, and Time in Teams: Strong Inference about Network Structure's Effects on Team Viability and Performance," *Academy of Management Journal* 49, no. 1 (2006): 49–68; G. Chen, B. L. Kirkman, R. Kanfer, D. Allen, and B. Rosen, "A Multilevel Study of Leadership, Empowerment, and Performance in Teams," *Journal of Applied Psychology* 92, no. 2 (2007): 331–46; L. A. DeChurch and M. A. Marks, "Leadership in Multiteam Systems," *Journal of Applied Psychology* 91, no. 2 (2006): 311–29; A. Srivastava, K. M. Bartol, and E. A. Locke, "Empowering Leadership in Management Teams: Effects on Knowledge Sharing, Efficacy, and Performance," *Academy of Management Journal* 49, no. 6 (2006): 1239–51; and J. E. Mathieu, K. K. Gilson, and T. M. Ruddy, "Empowerment and Team Effectiveness: An Empirical Test of an Integrated Model," *Journal of Applied Psychology* 91, no. 1 (2006): 97–108.

[24]K. T. Dirks, "Trust in Leadership and Team Performance: Evidence from NCAA Basketball," *Journal of Applied Psychology* (December 2000): 1004–12; M. Williams, "In Whom We Trust: Group Membership as an Affective Context for Trust Development," *Academy of Management Review* (July 2001): 377–96; and J. Schaubroeck, S. S. K. Lam, and A. C. Peng, "Cognition-Based and Affect-Based Trust as Mediators of Leader Behavior Influences on Team Performance," *Journal of Applied Psychology,* Online First Publication (February 7, 2011), doi: 10.1037/a0022625.

[25]B. A. De Jong and K. T. Dirks, "Beyond Shared Perceptions of Trust and Monitoring in Teams: Implications of Asymmetry and

Dissensus," *Journal of Applied Psychology* 97, no. 2 (2012): 391–406.

[26]G. Brown, C. Crossley, and S. L. Robinson, "Psychological Ownership, Territorial Behavior, and Being Perceived as a Team Contributor: The Critical Role of Trust in the Work Environment," *Personnel Psychology* 67 (2014): 463–85.

[27]See F. Aime, C. J. Meyer, and S. E. Humphrey, "Legitimacy of Team Rewards: Analyzing Legitimacy as a Condition for the Effectiveness of Team Incentive Designs," *Journal of Business Research* 63, no. 1 (2010): 60–66; and P. A. Bamberger and R. Levi, "Team-Based Reward Allocation Structures and the Helping Behaviors of Outcome-Interdependent Team Members," *Journal of Managerial Psychology* 24, no. 4 (2009): 300–27; and M. J. Pearsall, M. S. Christian, and A. P. J. Ellis, "Motivating Interdependent Teams: Individual Rewards, Shared Rewards, or Something in Between?" *Journal of Applied Psychology* 95, no. 1 (2010): 183–91.

[28]A. Bryant, "Taking Your Skills with You," *The New York Times,* May 31, 2015, 2.

[29]R. R. Hirschfeld, M. H. Jordan, H. S. Feild, W. F. Giles, and A. A. Armenakis, "Becoming Team Players: Team Members' Mastery of Teamwork Knowledge as a Predictor of Team Task Proficiency and Observed Teamwork Effectiveness," *Journal of Applied Psychology* 91, no. 2 (2006): 467–74; and K. R. Randall, C. J. Resick, and L. A. DeChurch, "Building Team Adaptive Capacity: The Roles of Sensegiving and Team Composition," *Journal of Applied Psychology* 96, no. 3 (2011): 525–40.

[30]H. Moon, J. R. Hollenbeck, and S. E. Humphrey, "Asymmetric Adaptability: Dynamic Team Structures as One-Way Streets," *Academy of Management Journal* 47, no. 5 (October 2004): 681–95; A. P. J. Ellis, J. R. Hollenbeck, and D. R. Ilgen, "Team Learning: Collectively Connecting the Dots," *Journal of Applied Psychology* 88, no. 5 (October 2003): 821–35; C. L. Jackson and J. A. LePine, "Peer Responses to a Team's Weakest Link: A Test and Extension of LePine and Van Dyne's Model," *Journal of Applied Psychology* 88, no. 3 (June 2003): 459–75; and J. A. LePine, "Team Adaptation and Postchange Performance: Effects of Team Composition in Terms of Members' Cognitive Ability and Personality," *Journal of Applied Psychology* 88, no. 1 (February 2003): 27–39.

[31]C. C. Cogliser, W. L. Gardner, M. B. Gavin, and J. C. Broberg, "Big Five Personality Factors and Leader Emergence in Virtual Teams: Relationships with Team Trustworthiness,

Member Performance Contributions, and Team Performance," *Group & Organization Management* 37, no. 6 (2012): 752–84; and "Deep-Level Composition Variables as Predictors of Team Performance: A Meta-Analysis," *Journal of Applied Psychology* 92, no. 3 (2007): 595–615.

[32]T. A. O'Neill and N. J. Allen, "Personality and the Prediction of Team Performance," *European Journal of Personality* 25, no. 1 (2011): 31–42.

[33]S. E. Humphrey, J. R. Hollenbeck, C. J. Meyer, and D. R. Ilgen, "Personality Configurations in Self-Managed Teams: A Natural Experiment on the Effects of Maximizing and Minimizing Variance in Traits," *Journal of Applied Psychology* 41, no. 7 (2011): 1701–32.

[34]Ellis, Hollenbeck, and Ilgen, "Team Learning"; C. O. L. H. Porter, J. R. Hollenbeck, and D. R. Ilgen, "Backing Up Behaviors in Teams: The Role of Personality and Legitimacy of Need," *Journal of Applied Psychology* 88, no. 3 (June 2003): 391–403; and J. A. Colquitt, J. R. Hollenbeck, and D. R. Ilgen, "Computer-Assisted Communication and Team Decision-Making Performance: The Moderating Effect of Openness to Experience," *Journal of Applied Psychology* 87, no. 2 (April 2002): 402–10.

[35]B. H. Bradley, B. E. Postlewaite, and K. G. Brown, "Ready to Rumble: How Team Personality Composition and Task Conflict Interact to Improve Performance," *Journal of Applied Psychology* 98, no. 2 (2013): 385–92.

[36]E. Gonzalez-Mule, D. S. DeGeest, B. W. McCormick, J. Y. Seong, and K. G. Brown, "Can We Get Some Cooperation around Here? The Mediating Role of Group Norms on the Relationship between Team Personality and Individual Helping Behaviors," *Journal of Applied Psychology* 99, no. 5 (2014): 988–99.

[37]S. E. Humphrey, F. P. Morgeson, and M. J. Mannor, "Developing a Theory of the Strategic Core of Teams: A Role Composition Model of Team Performance," *Journal of Applied Psychology* 94, no. 1 (2009): 48–61.

[38]C. Margerison and D. McCann, *Team Management: Practical New Approaches* (London: Mercury Books, 2000).

[39]A. Joshi, "The Influence of Organizational Demography on the External Networking Behavior of Teams," *Academy of Management Review* (July 2006): 583–95.

[40]A. Joshi and H. Roh, "The Role of Context in Work Team Diversity Research: A Meta-Analytic Review," *Academy of Management Journal* 52, no. 3 (2009): 599–627; S. K. Horwitz and I. B. Horwitz, "The Effects of Team Diversity

on Team Outcomes: A Meta-Analytic Review of Team Demography," *Journal of Management* 33, no. 6 (2007): 987–1015; and S. T. Bell, A. J. Villado, M. A. Lukasik, L. Belau, and A. L. Briggs, "Getting Specific about Demographic Diversity Variable and Team Performance Relationships: A Meta-Analysis," *Journal of Management* 37, no. 3 (2011): 709–43.

[41]S. J. Shin and J. Zhou, "When Is Educational Specialization Heterogeneity Related to Creativity in Research and Development Teams? Transformational Leadership as a Moderator," *Journal of Applied Psychology* 92, no. 6 (2007): 1709–21; and K. J. Klein, A. P. Knight, J. C. Ziegert, B. C. Lim, and J. L. Saltz, "When Team Members' Values Differ: The Moderating Role of Team Leadership," *Organizational Behavior and Human Decision Processes* 114, no. 1 (2011): 25–36.

[42]S. J. Shin, T. Kim, J. Lee, and L. Bian, "Cognitive Team Diversity and Individual Team Member Creativity: A Cross-Level Interaction," *Academy of Management Journal* 55, no. 1 (2012): 197–212.

[43]S. Mohammed and L. C. Angell, "Surface- and Deep-Level Diversity in Workgroups: Examining the Moderating Effects of Team Orientation and Team Process on Relationship Conflict," *Journal of Organizational Behavior* (December 2004): 1015–39.

[44]Y. F. Guillaume, D. van Knippenberg, and F. C. Brodebeck, "Nothing Succeeds Like Moderation: A Social Self-Regulation Perspective on Cultural Dissimilarity and Performance," *Academy of Management Journal* 57, no. 5 (2014): 1284–308.

[45]D. Coutu, "Why Teams Don't Work" *Harvard Business Review* (May 2009): 99–105. The evidence in this section is described in Thompson, *Making the Team*, pp. 65–67. See also L. A. Curral, R. H. Forrester, and J. F. Dawson, "It's What You Do and the Way That You Do It: Team Task, Team Size, and Innovation-Related Group Processes," *European Journal of Work & Organizational Psychology* 10, no. 2 (June 2001): 187–204; R. C. Liden, S. J. Wayne, and R. A. Jaworski, "Social Loafing: A Field Investigation," *Journal of Management* 30, no. 2 (2004): 285–304.

[46]R. Karlgaard, "Think (Really!) Small."

[47]Ibid.

[48]Ibid.

[49]"Is Your Team Too Big? Too Small? What's the Right Number? *Knowledge@Wharton,* June 14, 2006, 1–5; see also A. M. Carton and J. N. Cummings, "A Theory of Subgroups in Work Teams," *Academy of Management Review* 37, no. 3 (2012): 441–70.

[50]Hyatt and Ruddy, "An Examination of the Relationship between Work Group Characteristics and Performance"; J. D. Shaw, M. K. Duffy, and E. M. Stark, "Interdependence and Preference for Group Work: Main and Congruence Effects on the Satisfaction and Performance of Group Members," *Journal of Management* 26, no. 2 (2000): 259–79; and S. A. Kiffin-Peterson and J. L. Cordery, "Trust, Individualism, and Job Characteristics of Employee Preference for Teamwork," *International Journal of Human Resource Management* (February 2003): 93–116.

[51]J. A. LePine, R. F. Piccolo, C. L. Jackson, J. E. Mathieu, and J. R. Saul, "A Meta-Analysis of Teamwork Processes: Tests of a Multidimensional Model and Relationships with Team Effectiveness Criteria," *Personnel Psychology* 61 (2008): 273–307.

[52]J. F. Dovidio, "Bridging Intragroup Processes and Intergroup Relations: Needing the Twain to Meet," *British Journal of Social Psychology* 52, no. 1 (2013): 1–24; and J. Zhou, J. Dovidio, and E. Wang, "How Affectively-Based and Cognitively-Based Attitudes Drive Intergroup Behaviours: The Moderating Role of Affective-Cognitive Consistency," *Plos One* 8, no. 11 (2013): article e82150.

[53]J. A. LePine, R. F. Piccolo, C. L. Jackson, J. E. Mathieu, and J. R. Saul, "A Meta-Analysis of Teamwork Processes: Tests of a Multidimensional Model and Relationships with Team Effectiveness Criteria"; and J. E. Mathieu and T. L. Rapp, "Laying the Foundation for Successful Team Performance Trajectories: The Roles of Team Charters and Performance Strategies," *Journal of Applied Psychology* 94, no. 1 (2009): 90–103.

[54]J. E. Mathieu and W. Schulze, "The Influence of Team Knowledge and Formal Plans on Episodic Team Process–Performance Relationships," *Academy of Management Journal* 49, no. 3 (2006): 605–19.

[55]A. N. Pieterse, D. van Knippenberg, and W. P. van Ginkel, "Diversity in Goal Orientation, Team Reflexivity, and Team Performance," *Organizational Behavior and Human Decision Processes* 114, no. 2 (2011): 153–64.

[56]A. Gurtner, F. Tschan, N. K. Semmer, and C. Nagele, "Getting Groups to Develop Good Strategies: Effects of Reflexivity Interventions on Team Process, Team Performance, and Shared Mental Models," *Organizational Behavior and Human Decision Processes* 102 (2007): 127–42; M. C. Schippers, D. N. Den Hartog, and P. L. Koopman, "Reflexivity in Teams: A Measure and Correlates," *Applied Psychology: An International Review* 56, no. 2 (2007): 189–211; and C. S. Burke, K. C. Stagl, E. Salas, L. Pierce, and D. Kendall, "Understanding Team Adaptation: A Conceptual Analysis and Model," *Journal of Applied Psychology* 91, no. 6 (2006): 1189–207.

[57]A. N. Pieterse, D. van Knippenberg, and W. P. van Ginkel, "Diversity in Goal Orientation, Team Reflexivity, and Team Performance," *Organizational Behavior and Human Decision Processes* 114, no. 2 (2011): 153–64.

[58]See R. P. DeShon, S. W. J. Kozlowski, A. M. Schmidt, K. R. Milner, and D. Wiechmann, "A Multiple-Goal, Multilevel Model of Feedback Effects on the Regulation of Individual and Team Performance," *Journal of Applied Psychology* (December 2004): 1035–56.

[59]K. Tasa, S. Taggar, and G. H. Seijts, "The Development of Collective Efficacy in Teams: A Multilevel and Longitudinal Perspective," *Journal of Applied Psychology* 92, no. 1 (2007): 17–27; D. I. Jung and J. J. Sosik, "Group Potency and Collective Efficacy: Examining Their Predictive Validity, Level of Analysis, and Effects of Performance Feedback on Future Group Performance," *Group & Organization Management* (September 2003): 366–91; and R. R. Hirschfeld and J. B. Bernerth, "Mental Efficacy and Physical Efficacy at the Team Level: Inputs and Outcomes among Newly Formed Action Teams," *Journal of Applied Psychology* 93, no. 6 (2008): 1429–37.

[60]A. W. Richter, G. Hirst, D. van Knippenberg, and M. Baer, "Creative Self-Efficacy and Individual Creativity in Team Contexts: Cross-Level Interactions with Team Informational Resources," *Journal of Applied Psychology* 97, no. 6 (2012): 1282–90.

[61]N. Ellemers, E. Sleebos, D. Stam, and D. de Gilder, "Feeling Included and Valued: How Perceived Respect Affects Positive Team Identity and Willingness to Invest in the Team," *British Journal of Management* 24 (2013): 21–37.

[62]T. A. De Vries, F. Walter, G. S. Van Der Vegt, and P. J. M. D. Essens, "Antecedents of Individuals' Interteam Coordination: Broad Functional Experiences as a Mixed Blessing," *Academy of Management Journal* 57, no. 5 (2014): 1334–59.

[63]S. Chang, L. Jia, R. Takeuchi, and Y. Cai, "Do High-Commitment Work Systems Affect Creativity? A Multilevel Combinational Approach to Employee Creativity," *Journal of Applied Psychology* 99, no. 4 (2014): 665–80.

[64]S. Mohammed, L. Ferzandi, and K. Hamilton, "Metaphor No More: A 15-Year Review of the Team Mental Model Construct," *Journal of Management* 36, no. 4 (2010): 876–910.

[65]A. P. J. Ellis, "System Breakdown: The Role of Mental Models and Transactive Memory on the Relationships between Acute Stress and Team Performance," *Academy of Management Journal* 49, no. 3 (2006): 576–89.

[66]L. A. DeChurch and J. R. Mesmer-Magnus, "The Cognitive Underpinnings of Effective Teamwork: A Meta-Analysis," *Journal of Applied Psychology* 95, no. 1 (2010): 32–53.

[67]S. W. J. Kozlowski and D. R. Ilgen, "Enhancing the Effectiveness of Work Groups and Teams," *Psychological Science in the Public Interest* (December 2006): 77–124; and B. D. Edwards, E. A. Day, W. Arthur Jr., and S. T. Bell, "Relationships among Team Ability Composition, Team Mental Models, and Team Performance," *Journal of Applied Psychology* 91, no. 3 (2006): 727–36.

[68]M. Kolbe, G. Grote, M. J. Waller, J. Wacker, B. Grande, and D. R. Spahn, "Monitoring and Talking to the Room: Autochthonous Coordination Patterns in Team Interaction and Performance," *Journal of Applied Psychology* 99, no. 6 (2014): 1254–67.

[69]J. Farh, C. Lee, and C. I. C. Farh, "Task Conflict and Team Creativity: A Question of How Much and When," *Journal of Applied Psychology* 95, no. 6 (2010): 1173–80.

[70]K. J. Behfar, R. S. Peterson, E. A. Mannix, and W. M. K. Trochim, "The Critical Role of Conflict Resolution in Teams: A Close Look at the Links between Conflict Type, Conflict Management Strategies, and Team Outcomes," *Journal of Applied Psychology* 93, no. 1 (2008): 170–88.

[71]V. Gonzalez-Roma and A. Hernandez, "Climate Uniformity: Its Influence on Team Communication Quality, Task Conflict, and Team Performance," *Journal of Applied Psychology* 99, no. 6 (2014): 1042–58.

[72]K. H. Price, D. A. Harrison, and J. H. Gavin, "Withholding Inputs in Team Contexts: Member Composition, Interaction Processes, Evaluation Structure, and Social Loafing," *Journal of Applied Psychology* 91, no. 6 (2006): 1375–84.

[73]G. Hertel, U. Konradt, and K. Voss, "Competencies for Virtual Teamwork: Development and Validation of a Web-Based Selection Tool for Members of Distributed Teams," *European Journal of Work and Organizational Psychology* 15, no. 4 (2006): 477–504.

[74]T. V. Riper, "The NBA's Most Overpaid Players," *Forbes*, April 5, 2013, http://www.forbes.com/sites/tomvanriper/2013/04/05/the-nbas-most-overpaid-players/.

[75]E. Kearney, D. Gebert, and S. C. Voelpel, "When and How Diversity Benefits Teams: The Importance of Team Members' Need for Cognition," *Academy of Management Journal* 52, no. 3 (2009): 581–98.

[76]H. M. Guttman, "The New High-Performance Player," *The Hollywood Reporter*, October 27, 2008, www.hollywoodreporter.com.

[77]C.-H. Chuang, S. Chen, and C.-W. Chuang, "Human Resource Management Practices and Organizational Social Capital: The Role of Industrial Characteristics," *Journal of Business Research* (May 2013): 678–87; and L. Prusak and D. Cohen, "How to Invest in Social Capital," *Harvard Business Review* (June 2001): 86–93.

[78]T. Erickson and L. Gratton, "What It Means to Work Here," *BusinessWeek*, January 10, 2008, www.businessweek.com.

[79]M. D. Johnson, J. R. Hollenbeck, S. E. Humphrey, D. R. Ilgen, D. Jundt, and C. J. Meyer, "Cutthroat Cooperation: Asymmetrical Adaptation to Changes in Team Reward Structures," *Academy of Management Journal* 49, no. 1 (2006): 103–19.

[80]C. E. Naquin and R. O. Tynan, "The Team Halo Effect: Why Teams Are Not Blamed for Their Failures," *Journal of Applied Psychology* (April 2003): 332–40.

[81]E. R. Crawford and J. A. Lepine, "A Configural Theory of Team Processes: Accounting for the Structure of Taskwork and Teamwork," *Academy of Management Review* (January 2013): 32–48.

GLOSSARY

cross-functional teams Employees from about the same hierarchical level, but from different work areas, who come together to accomplish a task.

mental models Team members' knowledge and beliefs about how the work gets done by the team.

multiteam system A collection of two or more interdependent teams that share a superordinate goal; a team of teams.

organizational demography The degree to which members of a work unit share a common demographic attribute, such as age, sex, race, educational level, or length of service in an organization.

problem-solving teams Groups of employees from the same department who meet for a few hours each week to discuss ways of improving quality, efficiency, and the work environment.

reflexivity A team characteristic of reflecting on and adjusting the master plan when necessary.

team cohesion A situation when members are emotionally attached to one another and motivated toward the team because of their attachment.

team efficacy A team's collective belief that they can succeed at their tasks.

team identity A team member's affinity for and sense of belongingness to his or her team.

virtual teams Teams that use computer technology to tie together physically dispersed members in order to achieve a common goal.

workgroup A group that interacts primarily to share information and to make decisions to help each group member perform within his or her area of responsibility.

work team A group whose individual efforts result in performance that is greater than the sum of the individual inputs.

TEAMWORK TURMOIL

Tony Marshall, a second-year learning team mentor, stared at his notes again. His interaction with the team last night confirmed what he suspected. Only three weeks into the first year of an MBA program at a big-name school in the eastern United States, the learning team was in trouble. From his own experience the year before, Marshall knew that a first-rate learning team made a huge difference in a student's first-year experience (see **Exhibit 1** for details on learning teams at this particular business school). The corollary was also true: a bad or difficult learning team experience could taint the entire first-year school experience. Although Marshall wanted to help, he was not at all sure how to do so. Perhaps describing the situation to his fellow peer mentors in his second-year elective class on managing teams would draw out some good ideas. In his mind, Marshall could hear himself explain the story:

Let me first describe the team members. Essentially, they were all around 26 years of age, athletic, and had professional backgrounds in finance or economics. I'll start with Tom Giffen, who was a self-professed introvert and who was passionate about the Chicago Cubs baseball team. Professionally, prior to business school, Griffin worked as a financial analyst on Wall Street for a few different firms. He spent time at the London School of Economics, but had not traveled outside the country much over the past few years. With plans to target investment banking firms for his summer internship and post-Darden career path, Griffin had been spending a lot of nights networking with banking alumni and recruiters.

Sandeep Prasad was from Bangalore, India. He received a degree in technology and worked for Intel in Bangalore for six years before coming to graduate school. Prasad spoke fluent English and was a huge cricket fan. He followed his favorite team, Bengal, passionately and was also very involved in the informal Indian club at the school and planned to make his chicken curry for the International Food Festival. After graduation, Prasad wanted to pursue a career in consulting and hoped to get sponsored for a visa to live and work in the United States permanently.

Jennifer Martin was the only woman on the learning team and came from a mixed-race family—African American and Caucasian. In 2002, Martin was awarded the crown for Miss Colorado and had been Miss Colorado Teen in 1999. Coupling brains with beauty, Martin received a dual undergraduate degree in finance and information systems. Prior to business school, she worked as an analyst for a private foundation. Martin planned to focus her career on private wealth. Despite the great amount of networking that her chosen career path required, Martin was very involved in the school community. She spent a lot of time working on projects for the Black Business Student Forum and the National Association of Women MBAs.

Daren Onyealisi was originally from Nigeria and had been living in the United States for more than 10 years. He graduated from the University of Maryland with a degree in government. Following his undergraduate degree, Onyealisi worked as a policy research analyst for the District of Columbia, then changed career paths and worked as a real estate analyst for three years before attending business school. Onyealisi was a first-generation college graduate and awarded the Robert Toigo Foundation Fellowship upon entering the MBA program.[1] While Onyealisi was not very involved in the graduate school community, through the Big Brothers Big Sisters of America organization he was a Big Brother for local youths. Onyealisi planned to target the consulting industry for his summer internship.

Rob Delery was the only scientist in the group and earned a BS in chemical engineering from Penn State. During his undergraduate years, Delery was a member of the Penn State soccer club and the team won the national championship when he was a sophomore. Before business school, Delery worked for Air and Product Chemicals in Allentown, Pennsylvania. He was hired into the competitive Engineering Career Development Program consisting of three one-year rotational assignments in varying locations and functional roles. Being single, Delery embraced the social life of the school community and could often be found at the Thursday Night Drinking Club. Like Griffin, Delery planned on going into investment banking after graduation.

This brings us to the sixth learning team member—Jason Cooper. He was also a former college athlete. While working on a degree in accounting at Washington & Lee University, Cooper was also the captain of the varsity football team. Before business school, he spent five years in real estate investment. Cooper was the only married member of the learning team, and his wife worked in the school's admissions office. He was very involved in the Christian fellowship program at the school and planned to continue his career in real estate.

Now here's what I saw that night that brought me to share this story with you. Marshall was already in the room when team members began to arrive, and Onyealisi was the last to enter. "I didn't realize you were going to be here tonight," Delery said looking up from his computer screen. "We haven't seen you all week. Where have you been?"

---

[1] The Toigo Fellowship means a lifetime commitment to excellence and a responsibility to carry the Toigo banner of ethical leadership and a spirit of inclusion. Toigo supports the interests of fellows with aspirations for careers on Wall Street in addition to sectors less easily connected to finance roles, such as real estate and pension fund management.

"I've been very busy," Onyealisi responded while smiling at Delery, "I had to head up to D.C. for an interview on Tuesday. But thanks for sending me all the answers and class notes, so I could stay caught up."

"You've already had an interview!?" This was an eye-opener for Delery who continued, "Company briefings haven't even started yet! And don't thank me. Jennifer Martin was the one who put everything together."

With that, Delery looked at Martin, nodded his head, and sat down. When it looked like everyone was ready to go, Martin cleared her throat. "Ok guys; let's do takeaways from the cases from today." Delery groaned lightly in response. With an arched eyebrow, Martin asked, "Is there something wrong?"

Delery hesitated for a moment and looked around at the other group members. "Well, we never really agreed that we should do takeaways every day. They take up at least a half hour every meeting and we might be able to make better use of that time or at least get out of here early—I'm sure that Cooper's wife would appreciate that!"

Cooper just shrugged his shoulders. "I think that takeaways are great and they should really help us when exam time rolls around." Prasad agreed with Cooper as did Griffin. Martin asked Onyealisi what his opinion was. He shrugged his shoulders and said that it didn't really matter to him either way. "Well, I guess I'm outvoted then," Delery said smiling slightly. "Let's keep going."

Martin looked at Delery, "If it helps, I can take ownership of the document and put something together at the end of the term for all of us."

"Anything that helps with exams is great," Delery responded.

Okay so none of this seems that bad right? Well please just keep listening. Martin started with her own notes of takeaways and then asked for additional ones from the rest of the group. As they worked, they passed around the table some chocolate cookies that Cooper's wife had made. Cooper gave his takeaways and stood up to draw a chart on the board, replicating something that his professor had done in class. As Prasad began covering his takeaways, his cell phone went off and he left the room to answer it. The group paused and several members started to check their e-mail.

Prasad walked back in, apologized for the interruption, and presented his takeaways. Then Martin, who had been taking notes for the group copy, asked Onyealisi if he had anything to say. Onyealisi passed because he had no input, but he looked flustered. "Who's leading the marketing case tonight?" he asked.

"Well since none of us are marketing experts," Cooper replied, "we're just going to have to struggle through this together."

"I spent some time this afternoon on the fist two questions," Griffin told the group. "Let me go through my responses and we can talk about it as a group, OK?" Martin and Cooper nodded their heads, but none of the other team members responded. Griffin started the case and made sure to mention that everyone was welcome to add anything as he worked his way through the questions. Once Griffin started to repeat himself, Prasad interrupted. "Let me share some of the stories I've heard about people having problems with OnStar technology," he looked at Griffin for approval before continuing. "I think that customer perception is a good indicator of brand awareness." Cooper spoke up with his interpretation of the case study questions. Delery, who had been sitting silent the entire time then spoke up to mention that OnStar was purchased by affluent people. "No joke," Onyealisi said, laughing sarcastically. Delery quickly turned his eyes back to his laptop.

Let me provide you some background about why this was unusual. Delery was normally the most outgoing of the team members and often shared funny anecdotes from his class sessions. That night he was very quiet. Cooper appeared to notice this because he kept looking over at Delery with a small frown on his face, but he didn't say anything.

Griffin brought them back to the case questions and provided his thoughts on the next question. Cooper waited for Griffin to finish before he spoke up:

> I really don't understand why you feel that way. I think that you are looking at this too much from a finance standpoint. I think that the important point here is that OnStar has the first mover advantage but it won't last much longer especially if they can't fix the defects in the technology.

"Isn't that pretty much what I said?" Griffin asked the group. Before Cooper could reply Prasad interrupted, "You guys do this every time! One of you thinks he has a different point and you argue about it for 15 minutes before you realize you are saying the same thing." Cooper and Delery looked at each other and neither responded to Prasad's comment. Martin looked around the table. "I think we're working really well on this case tonight so let's not let things deteriorate, OK?"

"OK, I agree," Prasad said, "Let's continue on and talk about the 4 Ps in this situation." Griffin groaned, "I am so sick of talking about the 4 Ps and we are only three weeks into class!" Delery and Martin laughed as Griffin threw his hands up in the air in disgust. "Well, I heard from a second year," Prasad smiled and said, "that understanding the components of a marketing plan will be crucial for the final."

"Well OK. Let's just do it, then," Griffin said. "So OnStar is being positioned as a luxury item for a few select brands of car. Do we think that is the right move for them to make?"

"Absolutely not," Onyealisi snorted. "After all, Toyota only has a few luxury cars and aren't they mostly lower-end 'affordable' cars?" Martin exchanged confused looks with Cooper and Delery and said, "Umm, don't you mean GM?"

"No, Toyota," Onyealisi replied, don't they own OnStar?" Shaking his head slowly Delery asked Onyealisi, "Did you even read the case for tonight?"

"What's the big deal?" Onyealisi shrugged. "I had to do other things today and besides everyone knows about OnStar." Martin was visibly upset. "I thought we all talked about how we needed to be prepared for every case," she sneered. "Otherwise you are basically just using this team to get answers to use in class tomorrow. Why should you benefit from all our work?"

"OK everyone, let's just slow down for a minute," Delery said as he waved his hands in the air. "It's been a really long week and I think that tempers are getting the best of us. Let's just finish answering these questions so we can get home and try to relax before class tomorrow." Prasad, Griffin, and Cooper mumbled their assent. Martin didn't say anything but glared at Onyealisi who said "Fine … let's talk about positioning some more." Martin proceeded to share a personal story about her grandparents love for OnStar and Onyealisi laughed calling them silly and suggested they were wasting money. Martin got defensive about her grandparents, and Cooper and Griffin told similar stories so Onyealisi stopped laughing.

Martin continued and brought up XM as a similar model to follow and again Onyealisi laughed, claiming it was a silly connection since OnStar was not an aftermarket product. The rest of the group again defended Martin's view arguing that OnStar could be an aftermarket product so that it was not specific to GM cars. Increasing sales and allowing OnStar to get better distribution through Best Buy and Circuit City made sense. Onyealisi stopped laughing and apologized to Martin for not understanding her point. Then he asked some questions about OnStar that were not in the case and that no one had the answers to. The questions concerned the current state of OnStar so he started to Google OnStar. As he did, Prasad cleared his throat and said, "I think that looking up information on the Internet would be a violation of the honor code."

"Come on, that totally doesn't make sense," Onyealisi snorted. "Why shouldn't we have information about what's going on today? We already know about the product. It hasn't been around for that long." Cooper and Delery agreed with Prasad and told Onyealisi that he definitely couldn't look any information about OnStar up on-line.

"Do you think it would be possible to sell OnStar through third parties?" Martin asked the group. "For example, having Radio Shack, Circuit City, and Best Buy carry the product. They do it with XM and Sirius radios and I think that OnStar would fit into that market."

"That is the dumbest idea I have ever heard," Onyealisi quickly sneered. Martin immediately turned to look him directly in the eye. "Really? And why do you think that, Onyealisi?" Onyealisi smirked and looked down at his computer. He didn't say anything. Breaking the tension, Delery leaned back in his chair, stretched, and said, "One more question to go. Let's jam out a positioning statement and call it a night."

"Can we spend some time talking about what a positioning statement is, and why it's important?" Cooper looked at Delery and asked. "My professor doesn't really spend much time talking about positioning statements so I'm a little confused." Delery groaned and replied. "Can we do that later? Why don't you meet with your professor on your own to talk about that stuff?"

"But I thought that the point of learning team was to help each other grasp concepts—not just work through the case questions," Cooper pressed on. "And I could use the help."

"What if we split cases?" Onyealisi suggested. "That might make us more productive in team meetings and then we can spend more time on concepts."

"I feel like I would go back and redo your work," Prasad said shaking his head. "After all, you didn't even read the case for tonight and we only have two classes tomorrow! You also haven't led any DA, operations, or accounting cases so can I trust that what you share is right?" Cooper frowned at Prasad and asked "What does any of that have to do with my concern about reviewing concepts as a team?"

"We're going to have to talk about splitting cases eventually so why not address it now?" Prasad argued. With this the team meeting quickly deteriorated into multiple side conversations as Prasad and Onyealisi continued to argue about splitting the case work. Delery and Cooper started raising their voices as they volleyed back and forth about spending time on conceptual issues. Martin sighed and looked at Griffin. She turned to me and asked, "Isn't there anything you can do to help?"

They definitely want me to step in and help but I'm not sure that I'm ready for that—I just don't know what to say or do! I could really use your help. Any ideas?

Exhibit 1

TEAMWORK TURMOIL

The Importance of Learning Teams[1]

With each incoming first-year MBA class, the director of student affairs generated team assignments and kept the members under wraps until the last day of orientation. Learning teams were selected carefully to include diversity (international students, minorities, and females) and mix different class sections with each other. The idea was to offer students an opportunity to work with individuals outside their classroom. Most teams had six or seven individuals who spent two to three hours a night working on case preparation for the following day.

While most students had group or team experiences, the learning teams were different from traditional groups. There was a fundamental difference between teams that had a formally designated leader (e.g., consulting teams, group of analysts, task forces, or project teams) and those teams that were self-managed groups of peers. In the latter, rather than power and accountability being formally situated with one person (i.e., the group manager, the project leader, the chairperson of the taskforce, the informal team leader), there was, at least theoretically, a shared power and accountability. No one was the leader; everyone lead in a learning team. Because these learning teams were self-managed, they called for a distinct set of skills in order to be effective. Rather than one particular individual holding responsibility for things like agenda setting, providing direction or vision, keeping the group focused, mediating conflicts, delegating responsibilities, and debriefing the group's activities, these and all other tasks were distributed throughout the team. Each learning team member was both a leader and a member. This basic distinction was key to understanding how learning teams were different from other teams of which most have been a member.

---

[1] More information on the purpose and design of Darden's First Year Learning Teams can be found in the note UVA-OB-0745, "Learning Teams at the Darden Business School," by Joseph Harder and Lynn Isabella.

Harnessing the Science
of Persuasion

by Robert B. Cialdini

Harvard Business Review

Reprint R0109D

Harvard Business Review

October 2001

Harnessing the Science of Persuasion

by Robert B. Cialdini

A LUCKY FEW HAVE IT; most of us do not. A handful of gifted "naturals" simply know how to capture an audience, sway the undecided, and convert the opposition. Watching these masters of persuasion work their magic is at once impressive and frustrating. What's impressive is not just the easy way they use charisma and eloquence to convince others to do as they ask. It's also how eager those others are to do what's requested of them, as if the persuasion itself were a favor they couldn't wait to repay.

The frustrating part of the experience is that these born persuaders are often unable to account for their remarkable skill or pass it on to others. Their way with people is an art, and artists as a rule are far better at doing than at explaining. Most of them can't offer much help to those of us who possess no more than the ordinary quotient of charisma and eloquence but who still have to wrestle with leadership's fundamental challenge: getting things done through others. That challenge is painfully familiar to corporate executives, who every day have to figure out how to motivate and direct a highly individualistic work force. Playing the "Because I'm the boss" card is out. Even if it weren't demeaning and demoralizing for all concerned, it would be out of place in a world where cross-functional teams, joint ventures, and intercompany partnerships have blurred the lines of authority. In such an environment, persuasion skills exert far greater influence over others' behavior than formal power structures do.

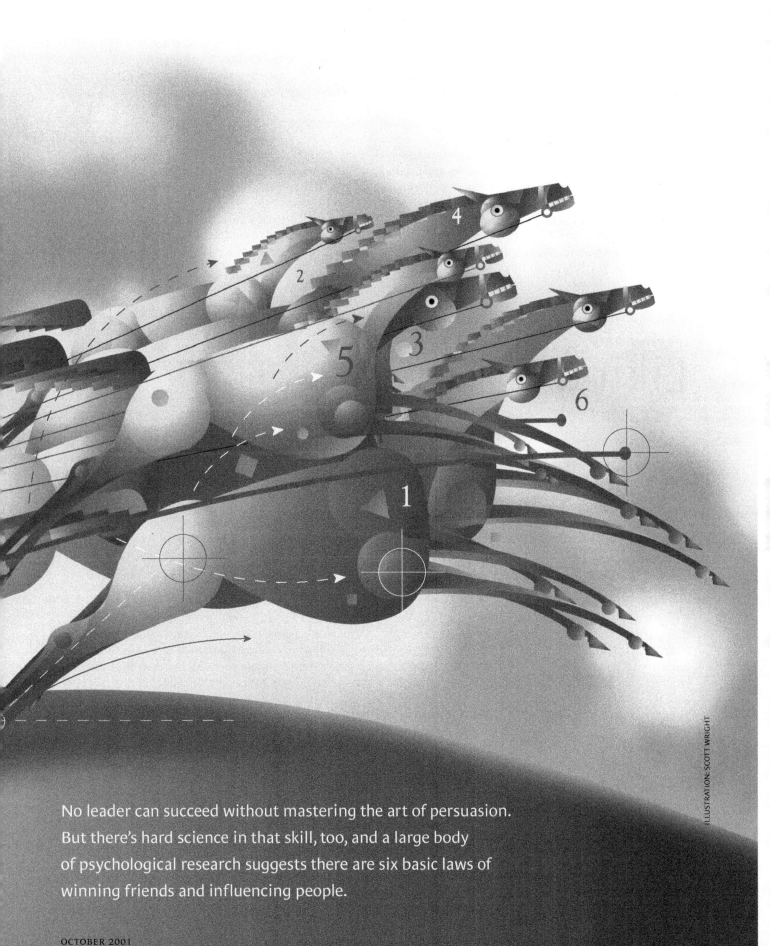

No leader can succeed without mastering the art of persuasion.
But there's hard science in that skill, too, and a large body
of psychological research suggests there are six basic laws of
winning friends and influencing people.

Which brings us back to where we started. Persuasion skills may be more necessary than ever, but how can executives acquire them if the most talented practitioners can't pass them along? By looking to science. For the past five decades, behavioral scientists have conducted experiments that shed considerable light on the way certain interactions lead people to concede, comply, or change. This research shows that persuasion works by appealing to a limited set of deeply rooted human drives and needs, and it does so in predictable ways. Persuasion, in other words, is governed by basic principles that can be taught, learned, and applied. By mastering these principles, executives can bring scientific rigor to the business of securing consensus, cutting deals, and winning concessions. In the pages that follow, I describe six fundamental principles of persuasion and suggest a few ways that executives can apply them in their own organizations.

THE PRINCIPLE OF
Liking:
People like those who like them.

THE APPLICATION:

Uncover real similarities and offer genuine praise.

The retailing phenomenon known as the Tupperware party is a vivid illustration of this principle in action. The demonstration party for Tupperware products is hosted by an individual, almost always a woman, who invites to her home an array of friends, neighbors, and relatives. The guests' affection for their hostess predisposes them to buy from her, a dynamic that was confirmed by a 1990 study of purchase decisions made at demonstration parties. The researchers, Jonathan Frenzen and Harry Davis, writing in the *Journal of Consumer Research,* found that the guests' fondness for their hostess weighed twice as heavily in their purchase decisions as their regard for the products they bought. So when guests at a Tupperware party buy something, they aren't just buying to please themselves. They're buying to please their hostess as well.

What's true at Tupperware parties is true for business in general: If you want to influence people, win friends. How? Controlled research has identified several factors that reliably increase liking, but two stand out as espe-

---

Robert B. Cialdini *is the Regents' Professor of Psychology at Arizona State University and the author of* Influence: Science and Practice *(Allyn & Bacon, 2001), now in its fourth edition. Further regularly updated information about the influence process can be found at www.influenceatwork.com.*

cially compelling – similarity and praise. Similarity literally draws people together. In one experiment, reported in a 1968 article in the *Journal of Personality,* participants stood physically closer to one another after learning that they shared political beliefs and social values. And in a 1963 article in *American Behavioral Scientists,* researcher F. B. Evans used demographic data from insurance company records to demonstrate that prospects were more willing to purchase a policy from a salesperson who was akin to them in age, religion, politics, or even cigarette-smoking habits.

Managers can use similarities to create bonds with a recent hire, the head of another department, or even a new boss. Informal conversations during the workday create an ideal opportunity to discover at least one common area of enjoyment, be it a hobby, a college basketball team, or reruns of *Seinfeld.* The important thing is to establish the bond early because it creates a presumption of goodwill and trustworthiness in every subsequent encounter. It's much easier to build support for a new project when the people you're trying to persuade are already inclined in your favor.

Praise, the other reliable generator of affection, both charms and disarms. Sometimes the praise doesn't even have to be merited. Researchers at the University of North Carolina writing in the *Journal of Experimental Social Psychology* found that men felt the greatest regard for an individual who flattered them unstintingly even if the comments were untrue. And in their book *Interpersonal Attraction* (Addison-Wesley, 1978), Ellen Berscheid and Elaine Hatfield Walster presented experimental data showing that positive remarks about another person's traits, attitude, or performance reliably generates liking in return, as well as willing compliance with the wishes of the person offering the praise.

Along with cultivating a fruitful relationship, adroit managers can also use praise to repair one that's damaged or unproductive. Imagine you're the manager of a good-sized unit within your organization. Your work frequently brings you into contact with another manager – call him Dan – whom you have come to dislike. No matter how much you do for him, it's not enough. Worse, he never seems to believe that you're doing the best you can for him. Resenting his attitude and his obvious lack of trust in your abilities and in your good faith, you don't spend as much time with him as you know you should; in consequence, the performance of both his unit and yours is deteriorating.

The research on praise points toward a strategy for fixing the relationship. It may be hard to find, but there has to be something about Dan you can sincerely admire, whether it's his concern for the people in his department, his devotion to his family, or simply his work ethic. In your next encounter with him, make an appreciative comment about that trait. Make it clear that in this case at least, you value what he values. I predict that Dan will relax his relentless negativity and give you an opening to convince him of your competence and good intentions.

THE PRINCIPLE OF
Reciprocity:

People repay in kind.

THE APPLICATION:

Give what you want to receive.

Praise is likely to have a warming and softening effect on Dan because, ornery as he is, he is still human and subject to the universal human tendency to treat people the way they treat him. If you have ever caught yourself smiling at a coworker just because he or she smiled first, you know how this principle works.

Charities rely on reciprocity to help them raise funds. For years, for instance, the Disabled American Veterans organization, using only a well-crafted fund-raising letter, garnered a very respectable 18% rate of response to its appeals. But when the group started enclosing a small gift in the envelope, the response rate nearly doubled to 35%. The gift – personalized address labels – was extremely modest, but it wasn't what prospective donors received that made the difference. It was that they had gotten anything at all.

What works in that letter works at the office, too. It's more than an effusion of seasonal spirit, of course, that impels suppliers to shower gifts on purchasing departments at holiday time. In 1996, purchasing managers admitted to an interviewer from *Inc.* magazine that after having accepted a gift from a supplier, they were willing to purchase products and services they would have otherwise declined. Gifts also have a startling effect on retention. I have encouraged readers of my book to send me examples of the principles of influence at work in their own lives. One reader, an employee of the State of Oregon, sent a letter in which she offered these reasons for her commitment to her supervisor:

> He gives me and my son gifts for Christmas and gives me presents on my birthday. There is no promotion for the type of job I have, and my only choice for one is to move to another department. But I find myself resisting trying to move. My boss is reaching retirement age, and I am thinking I will be able to move out after he retires....[F]or now, I feel obligated to stay since he has been so nice to me.

Ultimately, though, gift giving is one of the cruder applications of the rule of reciprocity. In its more sophisticated uses, it confers a genuine first-mover advantage on any manager who is trying to foster positive attitudes and productive personal relationships in the office: Managers can elicit the desired behavior from coworkers and employees by displaying it first. Whether it's a sense of trust, a spirit of cooperation, or a pleasant demeanor, leaders should model the behavior they want to see from others.

The same holds true for managers faced with issues of information delivery and resource allocation. If you lend a member of your staff to a colleague who is shorthanded and staring at a fast-approaching deadline, you will significantly increase your chances of getting help when you need it. Your odds will improve even more if you say, when your colleague thanks you for the assistance, something like, "Sure, glad to help. I know how important it is for me to count on your help when I need it."

THE PRINCIPLE OF
Social Proof:

People follow the lead of similar others.

THE APPLICATION:

Use peer power whenever it's available.

Social creatures that they are, human beings rely heavily on the people around them for cues on how to think, feel, and act. We know this intuitively, but intuition has also been confirmed by experiments, such as the one first described in 1982 in the *Journal of Applied Psychology*. A group of researchers went door-to-door in Columbia, South Carolina, soliciting donations for a charity campaign and displaying a list of neighborhood residents who had already donated to the cause. The researchers found that the longer the donor list was, the more likely those solicited would be to donate as well.

To the people being solicited, the friends' and neighbors' names on the list were a form of social evidence about how they should respond. But the evidence would not have been nearly as compelling had the names been those of random strangers. In an experiment from the 1960s, first described in the *Journal of Personality and Social Psychology*, residents of New York City were asked to return a lost wallet to its owner. They were highly likely to attempt to return the wallet when they learned that another New Yorker had previously attempted to do so. But learning that someone from a foreign country had tried to return the wallet didn't sway their decision one way or the other.

The lesson for executives from these two experiments is that persuasion can be extremely effective when it comes from peers. The science supports what most sales professionals already know: Testimonials from satisfied customers work best when the satisfied customer and the prospective customer share similar circumstances. That lesson can help a manager faced with the task of selling a new corporate initiative. Imagine that you're trying to streamline your department's work processes. A group of veteran employees is resisting. Rather than try to convince the employees of the move's merits yourself, ask an old-timer who supports the initiative to speak up for it at a team meeting. The compatriot's testimony stands a much better chance of convincing the group than yet another speech from the boss. Stated simply, influence is often best exerted horizontally rather than vertically.

THE PRINCIPLE OF

Consistency:

People align with their clear commitments.

THE APPLICATION:

Make their commitments active, public, and voluntary.

Liking is a powerful force, but the work of persuasion involves more than simply making people feel warmly toward you, your idea, or your product. People need not only to like you but to feel committed to what you want them to do. Good turns are one reliable way to make people feel obligated to you. Another is to win a public commitment from them.

My own research has demonstrated that most people, once they take a stand or go on record in favor of a position, prefer to stick to it. Other studies reinforce that finding and go on to show how even a small, seemingly trivial commitment can have a powerful effect on future actions. Israeli researchers writing in 1983 in the *Personality and Social Psychology Bulletin* recounted how they asked half the residents of a large apartment complex to sign a petition favoring the establishment of a recreation center for the handicapped. The cause was good and the request was small, so almost everyone who was asked agreed to sign. Two weeks later, on National Collection Day for the Handicapped, all residents of the complex were approached at home and asked to give to the cause. A little more than half of those who were not asked to sign the petition made a contribution. But an astounding 92% of those who did sign donated money. The residents of the apartment complex felt obligated to live up to their commitments because those commitments were active, public, and voluntary. These three features are worth considering separately.

There's strong empirical evidence to show that a choice made actively – one that's spoken out loud or written down or otherwise made explicit – is considerably more likely to direct someone's future conduct than the same choice left unspoken. Writing in 1996 in the *Personality and Social Psychology Bulletin*, Delia Cioffi and Randy Garner described an experiment in which college students in one group were asked to fill out a printed form saying they wished to volunteer for an AIDS education project in the public schools. Students in another group volunteered for the same project by leaving blank a form stating that they didn't want to participate. A few days later, when the volunteers reported for duty, 74% of those who showed up were students from the group that signaled their commitment by filling out the form.

The implications are clear for a manager who wants to persuade a subordinate to follow some particular course of action: Get it in writing. Let's suppose you want your employee to submit reports in a more timely fashion. Once you believe you've won agreement, ask him to summarize the decision in a memo and send it to you. By doing so, you'll have greatly increased the odds that he'll fulfill the commitment because, as a rule, people live up to what they have written down.

Research into the social dimensions of commitment suggests that written statements become even more powerful when they're made public. In a classic experiment, described in 1955 in the *Journal of Abnormal and Social Psychology*, college students were asked to estimate the length of lines projected on a screen. Some students were asked to write down their choices on a piece of paper, sign it, and hand the paper to the experimenter. Others wrote their choices on an erasable slate, then erased the slate immediately. Still others were instructed to keep their decisions to themselves.

The experimenters then presented all three groups with evidence that their initial choices may have been wrong. Those who had merely kept their decisions in their heads were the most likely to reconsider their original estimates. More loyal to their first guesses were the students in the group that had written them down and immediately erased them. But by a wide margin, the ones most reluctant to shift from their original choices were those who had signed and handed them to the researcher.

This experiment highlights how much most people wish to appear consistent to others. Consider again the matter of the employee who has been submitting late reports. Recognizing the power of this desire, you should, once you've successfully convinced him of the need to be more timely, reinforce the commitment by making sure it gets a public airing. One way to do that would be to send the employee an e-mail that reads, "I think your plan is just what we need. I showed it to Diane in manufacturing and Phil in shipping, and they thought it was right on target, too." Whatever way such commitments are formalized, they should never be like the New Year's resolutions people privately make and then abandon with no one the wiser. They should be publicly made and visibly posted.

More than 300 years ago, Samuel Butler wrote a couplet that explains succinctly why commitments must be voluntary to be lasting and effective: "He that complies against his will/Is of his own opinion still." If an undertaking is forced, coerced, or imposed from the outside, it's not a commitment; it's an unwelcome burden. Think how you would react if your boss pressured you to donate to the campaign of a political candidate. Would that make you more apt to opt for that candidate in the privacy of a voting booth? Not likely. In fact, in their 1981 book *Psychological Reactance* (Academic Press), Sharon S. Brehm and Jack W. Brehm present data that suggest you'd vote the opposite way just to express your resentment of the boss's coercion.

This kind of backlash can occur in the office, too. Let's return again to that tardy employee. If you want to produce an enduring change in his behavior, you should avoid using threats or pressure tactics to gain his compliance. He'd likely view any change in his behavior as the result of intimidation rather than a personal commitment to change. A better approach would be to identify something that the employee genuinely values in the workplace – high-quality workmanship, perhaps, or team spirit – and then describe how timely reports are consistent with those values. That gives the employee reasons for improvement that he can own. And because he owns them, they'll continue to guide his behavior even when you're not watching.

THE PRINCIPLE OF
Authority:

People defer to experts.

THE APPLICATION:

Expose your expertise; don't assume it's self-evident.

Two thousand years ago, the Roman poet Virgil offered this simple counsel to those seeking to choose correctly: "Believe an expert." That may or may not be good advice, but as a description of what people actually do, it can't be beaten. For instance, when the news media present an acknowledged expert's views on a topic, the effect on public opinion is dramatic. A single expert-opinion news story in the *New York Times* is associated with a 2% shift in public opinion nationwide, according to a 1993 study described in the *Public Opinion Quarterly*. And researchers writing in the *American Political Science Review* in 1987 found that when the expert's view was aired on national television, public opinion shifted as much as 4%. A cynic might argue that these findings only illustrate the docile submissiveness of the public. But a fairer explanation is

that, amid the teeming complexity of contemporary life, a well-selected expert offers a valuable and efficient shortcut to good decisions. Indeed, some questions, be they legal, financial, medical, or technological, require so much specialized knowledge to answer, we have no choice but to rely on experts.

Since there's good reason to defer to experts, executives should take pains to ensure that they establish their

> Surprisingly often, people mistakenly assume that others recognize and appreciate their experience.

own expertise before they attempt to exert influence. Surprisingly often, people mistakenly assume that others recognize and appreciate their experience. That's what happened at a hospital where some colleagues and I were consulting. The physical therapy staffers were frustrated because so many of their stroke patients abandoned their exercise routines as soon as they left the hospital. No matter how often the staff emphasized the importance of regular home exercise – it is, in fact, crucial to the process of regaining independent function – the message just didn't sink in.

Interviews with some of the patients helped us pinpoint the problem. They were familiar with the background and training of their physicians, but the patients knew little about the credentials of the physical therapists who were urging them to exercise. It was a simple matter to remedy that lack of information: We merely asked the therapy director to display all the awards, diplomas, and certifications of her staff on the walls of the therapy rooms. The result was startling: Exercise compliance jumped 34% and has never dropped since.

What we found immensely gratifying was not just how much we increased compliance, but how. We didn't fool or browbeat any of the patients. We *informed* them into compliance. Nothing had to be invented; no time or resources had to be spent in the process. The staff's expertise was real – all we had to do was make it more visible.

The task for managers who want to establish their claims to expertise is somewhat more difficult. They can't simply nail their diplomas to the wall and wait for everyone to notice. A little subtlety is called for. Outside the United States, it is customary for people to spend time interacting socially before getting down to business for the first time. Frequently they gather for dinner the night before their meeting or negotiation. These get-togethers can

Persuasion Experts, Safe at Last

Thanks to several decades of rigorous empirical research by behavioral scientists, our understanding of the how and why of persuasion has never been broader, deeper, or more detailed. But these scientists aren't the first students of the subject. The history of persuasion studies is an ancient and honorable one, and it has generated a long roster of heroes and martyrs.

A renowned student of social influence, William McGuire, contends in a chapter of the *Handbook of Social Psychology,* 3rd ed. (Oxford University Press, 1985) that scattered among the more than four millennia of recorded Western history are four centuries in which the study of persuasion flourished as a craft. The first was the Periclean Age of ancient Athens, the second occurred during the years of the Roman Republic, the next appeared in the time of the European Renaissance, and the last extended over the hundred years that have just ended, which witnessed the advent of large-scale advertising, information, and mass media campaigns. Each of the three previous centuries of systematic persuasion study was marked by a flowering of human achievement that was suddenly cut short when political authorities had the masters of persuasion killed. The philosopher Socrates is probably the best known of the persuasion experts to run afoul of the powers that be.

Information about the persuasion process is a threat because it creates a base of power entirely separate from the one controlled by political authorities. Faced with a rival source of influence, rulers in previous centuries had few qualms about eliminating those rare individuals who truly understood how to marshal forces that heads of state have never been able to monopolize, such as cleverly crafted language, strategically placed information, and, most important, psychological insight.

It would perhaps be expressing too much faith in human nature to claim that persuasion experts no longer face a threat from those who wield political power. But because the truth about persuasion is no longer the sole possession of a few brilliant, inspired individuals, experts in the field can presumably breathe a little easier. Indeed, since most people in power are interested in remaining in power, they're likely to be more interested in acquiring persuasion skills than abolishing them.

make discussions easier and help blunt disagreements – remember the findings about liking and similarity – and they can also provide an opportunity to establish expertise. Perhaps it's a matter of telling an anecdote about successfully solving a problem similar to the one that's on the agenda at the next day's meeting. Or perhaps dinner is the time to describe years spent mastering a complex discipline – not in a boastful way but as part of the ordinary give-and-take of conversation.

Granted, there's not always time for lengthy introductory sessions. But even in the course of the preliminary conversation that precedes most meetings, there is almost always an opportunity to touch lightly on your relevant background and experience as a natural part of a sociable exchange. This initial disclosure of personal information gives you a chance to establish expertise early in the game, so that when the discussion turns to the business at hand, what you have to say will be accorded the respect it deserves.

THE PRINCIPLE OF

Scarcity:

People want more of what they can have less of.

THE APPLICATION:

Highlight unique benefits and exclusive information.

Study after study shows that items and opportunities are seen to be more valuable as they become less available. That's a tremendously useful piece of information for managers. They can harness the scarcity principle with the organizational equivalents of limited-time, limited-supply, and one-of-a-kind offers. Honestly informing a coworker of a closing window of opportunity – the chance to get the boss's ear before she leaves for an extended vacation, perhaps – can mobilize action dramatically.

Managers can learn from retailers how to frame their offers not in terms of what people stand to gain but in terms of what they stand to lose if they don't act on the information. The power of "loss language" was demonstrated in a 1988 study of California home owners written up in the *Journal of Applied Psychology.* Half were told that if they fully insulated their homes, they would save a certain amount of money each day. The other half were told that if they failed to insulate, they would lose that amount each day. Significantly more people insulated their homes when exposed to the loss language. The same phenomenon occurs in business. According to a 1994 study in the journal *Organizational Behavior and Human Decision Processes,* potential losses figure far more heavily in managers' decision making than potential gains.

In framing their offers, executives should also remember that exclusive information is more persuasive than widely available data. A doctoral student of mine, Amram Knishinsky, wrote his 1982 dissertation on the purchase decisions of wholesale beef buyers. He observed that they more than doubled their orders when they were told that, because of certain weather conditions overseas, there was likely to be a scarcity of foreign beef in the near future. But their orders increased 600% when they were informed that no one else had that information yet.

The persuasive power of exclusivity can be harnessed by any manager who comes into possession of information that's not broadly available and that supports an idea or initiative he or she would like the organization to adopt. The next time that kind of information crosses your desk, round up your organization's key players. The information itself may seem dull, but exclusivity will give it a special sheen. Push it across your desk and say, "I just got this report today. It won't be distributed until next week, but I want to give you an early look at what it shows." Then watch your listeners lean forward.

Allow me to stress here a point that should be obvious. No offer of exclusive information, no exhortation to act now or miss this opportunity forever should be made unless it is genuine. Deceiving colleagues into compliance is not only ethically objectionable, it's foolhardy. If the deception is detected – and it certainly will be – it will snuff out any enthusiasm the offer originally kindled. It will also invite dishonesty toward the deceiver. Remember the rule of reciprocity.

Putting It All Together

There's nothing abstruse or obscure about these six principles of persuasion. Indeed, they neatly codify our intuitive understanding of the ways people evaluate information and form decisions. As a result, the principles are easy for most people to grasp, even those with no formal education in psychology. But in the seminars and workshops I conduct, I have learned that two points bear repeated emphasis.

First, although the six principles and their applications can be discussed separately for the sake of clarity, they should be applied in combination to compound their impact. For instance, in discussing the importance of expertise, I suggested that managers use informal, social conversations to establish their credentials. But that conversation affords an opportunity to gain information as well as convey it. While you're showing your dinner companion that you have the skills and experience your business problem demands, you can also learn about your companion's background, likes, and dislikes – information that will help you locate genuine similarities and give sincere compliments. By letting your expertise surface and also establishing rapport, you double your persuasive power. And if you succeed in bringing your dinner partner on board, you may encourage other people to sign on as well, thanks to the persuasive power of social evidence.

The other point I wish to emphasize is that the rules of ethics apply to the science of social influence just as they do to any other technology. Not only is it ethically wrong to trick or trap others into assent, it's ill-advised in practical terms. Dishonest or high-pressure tactics work only in the short run, if at all. Their long-term effects are malignant, especially within an organization, which can't function properly without a bedrock level of trust and cooperation.

That point is made vividly in the following account, which a department head for a large textile manufacturer related at a training workshop I conducted. She described a vice president in her company who wrung public commitments from department heads in a highly manipulative manner. Instead of giving his subordinates time to talk or think through his proposals carefully, he would approach them individually at the busiest moment of their workday and describe the benefits of his plan in exhaustive, patience-straining detail. Then he would move in for the kill. "It's very important for me to see you as being on my team on this," he would say. "Can I count on your support?" Intimidated, frazzled, eager to chase the man from their offices so they could get back to work, the department heads would invariably go along with his request. But because the commitments never felt voluntary, the department heads never followed through, and as a result the vice president's initiatives all blew up or petered out.

This story had a deep impact on the other participants in the workshop. Some gulped in shock as they recognized their own manipulative behavior. But what stopped everyone cold was the expression on the department head's face as she recounted the damaging collapse of her superior's proposals. She was smiling.

Nothing I could say would more effectively make the point that the deceptive or coercive use of the principles of social influence is ethically wrong and pragmatically wrongheaded. Yet the same principles, if applied appropriately, can steer decisions correctly. Legitimate expertise, genuine obligations, authentic similarities, real social proof, exclusive news, and freely made commitments can produce choices that are likely to benefit both parties. And any approach that works to everyone's mutual benefit is good business, don't you think? Of course, I don't want to press you into it, but, if you agree, I would love it if you could just jot me a memo to that effect. ⎇

Reprint R0109D

To place an order, call 1-800-988-0886.

The Necessity of Power:
You Can't Manage Without It

Excerpted from

Power, Influence, and Persuasion:
Sell Your Ideas and Make Things Happen

Harvard Business School Press
Boston, Massachusetts

ISBN-10: 1-4221-0544-X
ISBN-13: 978-1-4221-0544-3
5443BC

The Necessity of Power

You Can't Manage Without It

Key Topics Covered in This Chapter

- *Why power and power seekers are suspect*

- *The necessary role of power in organizations*

- *How dependencies restrain the concentration and autocratic use of power*

- *Three managerial approaches to power*

POWER IS A necessary feature of every social system. In military organizations, every unit has one person vested with the power to command action. Even in collegial and democratic workplaces, someone has the authority to say, "Thank you all for your input. Now, here is what must be done." Despite its necessity, however, few people have a positive view of power and are often distrustful of the people who seek it.

This chapter discusses how people feel about power, why it is an essential part of organizational life, and how it is restrained by interpersonal dependencies. It also evaluates three managerial approaches to using power.

Our Antipathy Toward Power

In many cultures, power is viewed with suspicion and fear because of its potential for coercion and corruption. People easily recall examples of power used for malignant purposes rather than for good: Villains such as Hitler, Stalin, Pol Pot, and Saddam Hussein immediately come to mind. The use of power for malicious or self-serving ends is surely what moved Britain's Lord Acton to declare in 1887, "Power tends to corrupt, and absolute power corrupts absolutely." This sentiment is so well entrenched in the public consciousness that those who seek power are viewed with suspicion and distrust. Indeed, many feel that power should be withheld from those who most actively seek it. Because of this general antipathy toward power and power seekers, writes Rosabeth Moss Kanter, "People who have it deny it; people who want it do not want to appear to hunger for it; and people who engage in its machinations do so secretly."[1]

Given our antipathy toward power and those who hold it, it is no surprise that democratic political systems contain checks on power and specify measures to distribute power in ways that prevent it from becoming absolute or concentrated in too few hands. England's Magna Carta (Great Charter), signed in 1215 by King John, provides a concrete example. It stipulated in detail the rights of the church, the barons, and freemen that could not be infringed by the power of the Crown. More than five centuries later, the founders of the American republic grappled with the same issue. Their constitutional solution was to prevent the concentration of power in one branch of government and establish mechanisms that protect the interests of minorities against the power of the majority. The U.S. Constitution's Bill of Rights checks power by specifying individual rights that government cannot abridge.

Power as Necessity

Paradoxically, neither society nor its organizations can function without the application of power. Government cannot fulfill its basic functions without the power to tax and spend, to make laws, and to enforce them. Roadways would be chaotic if police lacked the power to enforce traffic regulations. And our business organizations would quickly go to pieces if boards and managers lacked the power to make and implement strategy, to hire and fire, and to compensate employees. Recognizing the necessity of power, democratic societies allow certain individuals and institutions to have power as long as they use it within the bounds of policy, custom, or law, and in the service of ends that the majority accepts as legitimate.

Power was defined in the Introduction as the potential to allocate resources and to make and enforce decisions. In an organizational context this means that power gives someone the potential, among other things, to do the following:

- Determine compensation for subordinates

- Obtain funding, materials, or staff for key projects

- Have access to important information

- Resolve disputes

- Clear away barriers to progress

- Determine key goals and marshal resources around them

These activities are critical to the business of management; little would be accomplished in the absence of someone's power to decide or act. The power to influence others is equally important. That power can be used to rally support for important goals and to motivate individual employees. It is difficult to think of managers being successful without either type of power.

Paradoxically, societal distrust of individual power does not transfer completely to the workplace, where we expect that some people will have more power than others. In fact, many employees would rather work for managers who have organizational power ("clout") than for people who do not. The former can get them what they want: visibility, upward mobility, and resources. Working for a powerful boss also confers an aura of status on subordinates. In contrast, working for a powerless boss is like being in the outer darkness; subordinates of bosses who have no organizational clout feel powerless and are usually dissatisfied with their situations.

There is even some evidence that powerless bosses are more likely to behave tyrannically toward their underlings. According to Rosabeth Kanter, "Powerlessness . . . tends to breed bossiness rather than true leadership. In large organizations, at least, it is powerlessness that often creates ineffective, desultory management and petty, dictatorial, rules-minded managerial styles."[2] Managers who lack real power cannot obtain the resources needed to fulfill their responsibilities. This leads to frustration, poor morale, and ineffectiveness among subordinates.

Thus, power that is used wisely in workplace settings is more likely to produce effectiveness and motivation than oppression and poor morale. Consider this hypothetical case of a middle manager who, lacking organizational power, has become ineffective:

William enjoyed upward mobility during the first six years of his employment with Ultra Electronix. Hired as a market analyst, he made important contributions to the company's market research unit, and before long he was named director of market research. Thanks to his technical know-how, useful market assessments, and ability to work productively with other units, William gained progressively more organizational power and influence—and a budget to match. Morale was high among his five direct reports.

William's visibility and growing influence was abetted by his boss, Harold, the vice president of sales and marketing. Harold believed strongly in the value of market research and made sure that research played a key role in high-level product decisions.

William's standing in the company changed quickly, however, when Harold retired. Toni, Harold's successor, had built her career through the field sales organization and put little stock in formal market research. As far as she was concerned, personal relationships with customers was the be-all and end-all of marketing and market intelligence. So no one was surprised when the budget for market research was cut 20 percent, forcing William to lay off one of his analysts.

Under Toni's regime, William felt his organizational power slipping away, and with it his ability to influence other managers and motivate his subordinates. He no longer had exciting projects to offer his people nor rewards to share. Work became routine and less meaningful. His direct reports no longer looked to him for mentoring or career development.

Supervisors and managers such as William need power to do their jobs. Lacking it, they exhibit the symptoms described in table 1-1. They develop into managers for whom no one with talent or ambition wants to work. Failing to possess and use power when the situation calls for it results in indecision, delays, and sometimes mischief. As Jeffrey Pfeffer aptly put it in his book *Managing With Power*, "[O]ne can be quite content, quite happy, quite fulfilled as an organizational

TABLE 1-1

Symptoms and Sources of Powerlessness for Key Positions

Position	Symptoms	Sources
First-line supervisors	• Close, rules-minded supervision • Tendency to do things oneself, blocking of subordinates' development and information • Resistant, underproducing subordinates	• Routine, rules-minded jobs with little control over events • Limited lines of information • Few advancement prospects for oneself/ subordinates
Staff professionals	• Turf protection, information control • Retreat into professionalism • Resistance to change	• Routine tasks seen as peripheral to "real" tasks • Blocked careers • Easy replacement by outside experts
Top executives	• Focus on internal cost-cutting, producing short-term results, punishing failure • Dictatorial, top-down communication	• Uncontrollable lines of supply because of environmental changes • Limited or blocked lines of information from below

Source: Adapted from Rosabeth Moss Kanter, "Power Failure in Management Circuits," *Harvard Business Review,* July–August 1979.

hermit, but one's influence is limited and the potential to accomplish great things, which requires independent action, is almost extinguished."[3] People who will not touch the hot handle of power will not—cannot—influence what happens around them.

Of Power and Dependency

If power is essential for effective management, it doesn't necessarily come with the job. Newly minted supervisors and managers usually think that the formal authority attached to their positions will give them all the power they need to fulfill their responsibilities and carve out reputations for themselves in the organization. They believe that, like *Star Trek*'s Captain Picard, they need only describe what they want done and tell subordinates to "make it so." Then reality delivers a swift kick to the posterior. They find that they are not masters of the universe, but highly dependent on others: on their bosses, their subordinates, peers, suppliers, and others.

Dependency is a fact of life in complex organizations, and at every level, because of limited resources and the division of labor and information across many units. Dependency is not eliminated through the acquisition of formal power. Consider these examples:

- Hugh, the manager of a busy coffee and pastry bistro, depends on each crewmember doing his or her job quickly and effectively. Hugh is so busy greeting customers and running the cash register that confusion would reign if there were any laggards.

- William, the director of market research described earlier, depends heavily on the technical know-how of his professional staff to complete his unit's work. Those individuals must design research tools that accurately measure customer demand and preferences. He also depends on people who do not work for him, primarily the company's forty field sales representatives. He needs their intimate knowledge of customers to obtain customer feedback and to identify candidates for focus groups conducted by market research personnel.

- Edgar, the vice president of manufacturing, seldom sees eye-to-eye with the CEO on important issues. In fact, "contained hostility" would be a good description of their relationship. Other executives don't understand why the CEO doesn't fire Edgar and replace him with someone more compliant. The CEO knows the answer: He depends on Edgar's skill in managing the company's production assets. Edgar is hard to work with, but he delivers, and that makes the CEO look good to the board and to shareholders.

- Judith is eager to advance her career. In this she has come to depend on two individuals: her boss, who gives her assignments that broaden her skills, and Linda, a senior executive with whom she has established a mentoring relationship. Linda opens doors for Judith throughout the company and sees that she is assigned to important cross-functional teams.

Each of these examples demonstrates how individuals, even people with formal authority, depend on others for success.

Although dependency blunts the power that many feel they need in order to manage, or the power to which they aspire, it serves a crucial purpose in the modern organization. That purpose is to restrain the concentration and autocratic use of power. Lacking dependencies, leaders and managers would quickly become corrupt and tyrannical, just as Acton warned. You'll learn more about dependencies in the next chapter.

Using Power: Three Types of Managers

Assuming that people acquire the power they need to do their jobs, how do they use it, and how does power motivate their behavior? David McClelland and David Burnham studied these questions and published their findings in 2003. They found that a manager's approach to power is tightly connected to personal motivation and the way he or she defines success. In effect, they described three types of managers: affiliative managers, personal power managers, and institutional managers.[4]

Affliliative Managers

The *affiliative manager,* in the view of McClelland and Burnham, is more interested in being liked than in having and using power to get the job done. When dealing with subordinates, this manager's decisions are heavily influenced by what will make subordinates happy and put them on his side. Consequently, decisions are more ad hoc than consistent with the requirements of the work at hand. Policies and procedures are secondary to decisions that make people happy with the boss. Of the three types of managers, this one is the weakest and least effective.

In their eagerness to be liked, affiliative managers fail to use power for its intended purposes. The result is predictable: Key goals are not met. The case of General George B. McClellan (no relation to David McClelland) underscores this important point.

In the early part of the U.S. Civil War (1861–1865), General McClellan was entrusted with the Union's main army, to which he applied his exceptional talents for organizing and training. He built the Army of the Potomac into a powerful fighting machine and developed plans for seizing Richmond, the capital of the secessionist Confederacy. McClellan was popular with his soldiers and with many politicians, who affectionately called him "the Young Napoleon." McClellan basked in that popularity, even to the point of visualizing a political career.

It seems that he was popular with almost everyone except his commander in chief, President Abraham Lincoln. Lincoln repeatedly urged McClellan to use his force to engage the enemy, but the general vacillated. He complained endlessly that he needed more men, more munitions, and more time to prepare. The few campaigns he did launch were either timid, too late, or terminated too quickly. Frustrated by his general's reluctance to use his considerable force, Lincoln sacked him and turned the reins over to others. "My dear McClellan," Lincoln wrote in March 1862, "if you don't want to use the Army I should like to borrow it for a while."

McClellan enjoyed his status and his popularity with the troops and the public, but he didn't use the power he was given to pursue his primary responsibility. So he had to go. Do you know of managers like this—people who are reluctant to make tough decisions and apply their power? The reason for that reluctance, in many cases, is a fear of offending or losing popularity. These managers run the risk of getting a memo similar to the one written by Lincoln: "My dear Jones, if you are fearful of losing the friendship of your subordinates, you will be replaced by someone who has no such fear."

Working for an Affiliative Manager

As much as the affiliative manager will try to be your friend, he will likely jeopardize your career, and for two reasons. First, this manager will not be consistent in making decisions and following policy, and this means that you cannot anticipate his behavior. Second, this manager is likely to lose status in the organization relative to people who know how to acquire power and use it effectively. Consequently you'll be working for a weakened boss and may not get the resources and visibility you need to build your own career. Our advice: Look for a move.

Personal Power Managers

The *personal power manager,* per scholars David McClelland and David Burnham, is a much different creature. This manager's personal need for power exceeds his need to be liked. He seeks power for himself and for people on his team in order to get the job done. Unlike the authoritarian or coercive boss, who gains strength by making everyone around him weak, this boss generally manages in a democratic way. Subordinates like this kind of boss and often become very loyal because their boss is strong and makes them feel strong. On the negative side, these managers are power aggrandizers and turf builders, and not good institution builders. Consider this example:

> Steve, the vice president of corporate sales, is smart, aggressive, and a tough taskmaster. During his first year in his current post, he pushed out the three or four people who couldn't or wouldn't do their jobs, replacing them with individuals having solid track records. "You people are on the best team in the business," he often tells his staff and sales representatives.
>
> Steve is generous with his subordinates and stands behind them when they come into conflict with people in other departments. "We are sales," he likes to remind them during periodic pep talks. "Nothing happens in this company until one of us makes a sale. Nothing! That's something that other departments need to understand."

Although Steve has met the company's sales goals and has built high energy and morale in his unit, he has created friction with other departments—to the point that collaboration has become difficult. To Steve, every interaction with other departments is an opportunity either to defend the prerogatives of his unit from encroachment or to expand its power at another department's expense.

Do you know any managers like Steve? If you do, you know that they are not team players in the companywide sense. They are fiercely competitive and often combative in their interactions with fellow managers. And when they eventually exit the company for more powerful positions elsewhere, the subordinates they leave behind feel as though the air has been sucked out of them because their loyalties were to their boss, and not to the larger organization.

Working for the Personal Power Manager

If you work for a personal power manager, expect a high sense of team spirit within your unit. However, the boss may have so estranged other departments that collaboration with people outside your unit will be difficult. You may also find yourself forced to choose between the interests of your unit (i.e., your boss) and the interests of the company as a whole. In the long term this may endanger your career with the company, especially if and when the personal power boss departs. The best advice in these situations is as follows:

- Be loyal to your boss—this boss demands and rewards loyalty—but only as long as you are not required to do anything that is clearly against the interests of the company and its shareholders.

- Build and maintain your own broad network of contacts within the company; doing so will increase your effectiveness.

- Develop a personal reputation for high integrity and standards; that reputation will help you if and when your boss leaves the company.

Institutional Managers

The most effective managers, say McClelland and Burnham, have something in common with personal power types such as Steve (see figure 1-1). They need power more than they need to be liked. But that's where the similarity ends. These *institutional managers* deploy power in the service of the organization, and not in service of personal goals. Generally, these people

- are highly organization-minded

- have a strong work ethic

- are willing to sacrifice some self-interest for the welfare of the organization

- believe in rewarding individuals who work hard toward organizational goals.[5]

For subordinates who like to work hard and do a good job, these are the best managers to work for: They are mature—not egotistical and not defensive—and eager to reward performance.

Altering Your Management Style

Can you change your management style? Yes, according to McClelland and Burnham—but only after you become aware of your current style. You can gain this self-awareness through executive coaching or by seeking objective feedback from peers and subordinates.

Awareness must be followed by behavior change. For example, if you find that you are an affiliative manager and you want to become an institutional manager, you must adopt the behaviors of that type of person and make habits of those behaviors. Perhaps the most fruitful way to accomplish this is to identify and emulate a successful role model—someone who has the traits of an institutional manager. If you can, get yourself assigned to that person as a subordinate. If

FIGURE 1-1

Assessing the Effectiveness of Manager Types

WHICH MANAGER IS MOST EFFECTIVE?

Subordinates of managers with different motive profiles report different levels of responsibility, organizational clarity, and team spirit.

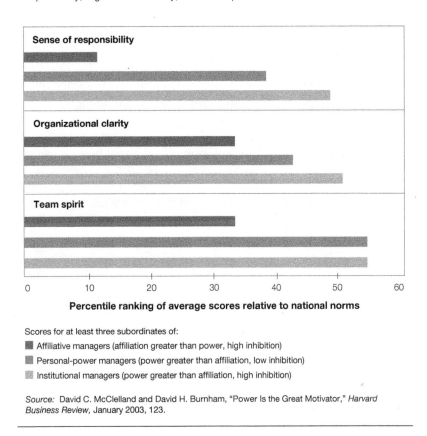

Percentile ranking of average scores relative to national norms

Scores for at least three subordinates of:

- Affiliative managers (affiliation greater than power, high inhibition)
- Personal-power managers (power greater than affiliation, low inhibition)
- Institutional managers (power greater than affiliation, high inhibition)

Source: David C. McClelland and David H. Burnham, "Power Is the Great Motivator," *Harvard Business Review,* January 2003, 123.

that is not possible, ask that manager to become your mentor. If all else fails, observe the institutional manager from a distance. Take note of how she makes decisions and works with peers, superiors, and subordinates. Then imitate what you observe.

Yes, power is necessary, and individuals embody and use it in various ways. You cannot manage without it. But if it is necessary, what are its sources? That's the subject of the next chapter.

Summing Up

- People generally distrust and fear power and those who seek it.

- Despite negative views of power, organizations cannot function without it. Most people prefer working for bosses who have and use power.

- New managers quickly discover that their power to act is limited by dependencies on others.

- According to two researchers, affiliative managers are ineffective users of power; they are more interested in being liked than in having and using power to accomplish goals.

- Personal power managers seek power and know how to use it. However, their use of power is often self-serving.

- Institutional managers, as described in this chapter, represent the ideal. They use power to advance the interests of the organization, giving those interests priority over their own.

Notes

Chapter 1

1. Rosabeth Moss Kanter, "Power Failure in Management Circuits," *Harvard Business Review*, July–August 1979, 65.

2. Ibid.

3. Jeffrey Pfeffer, *Managing With Power* (Boston: Harvard Business School Press, 1992), 9.

4. David C. McClelland and David H. Burnham, "Power Is the Great Motivator," *Harvard Business Review*, January 2003, 117–126.

5. Ibid.

15

Harvard Business Essentials

The New Manager's Guide and Mentor

The Harvard Business Essentials series is designed to provide comprehensive advice, personal coaching, background information, and guidance on the most relevant topics in business. Drawing on rich content from Harvard Business School Publishing and other sources, these concise guides are carefully crafted to provide a highly practical resource for readers with all levels of experience, and will prove especially valuable for the new manager. To assure quality and accuracy, each volume is closely reviewed by a specialized content adviser from a world-class business school. Whether you are a new manager seeking to expand your skills or a seasoned professional looking to broaden your knowledge base, these solution-oriented books put reliable answers at your fingertips.

Books in the Series:

Business Communication
Coaching and Mentoring
Creating Teams with an Edge
Crisis Management
Decision Making
Entrepreneur's Toolkit
Finance for Managers
Hiring and Keeping the Best People
Manager's Toolkit
Managing Change and Transition
Managing Creativity and Innovation
Managing Employee Performance
Managing Projects Large and Small
Marketer's Toolkit
Negotiation
Power, Influence, and Persuasion
Strategy
Time Management

BRIEF CASES

2095

MAY 1, 2008

W. EARL SASSER

HEATHER BECKHAM

Thomas Green:
Power, Office Politics, and a Career in Crisis

Another long day at the office had drawn to a close. Thomas Green felt the pulsing in his temples that usually preceded a migraine. As he stepped outside Dynamic Displays' corporate headquarters in Boston, the brisk air made him catch his breath. It was now February 5, 2008. Green could not believe that in five short months his dream promotion had turned into a disaster. When Green had been promoted to his new position in September, he was a rising star. Now, he would be lucky to celebrate his one-year anniversary with the company. His boss, Frank Davis, had sent the division vice president, Shannon McDonald, two scathing emails criticizing Green's performance. Green and Davis had yet to see eye to eye on work styles or market trends. Tension had also risen when Green did not enthusiastically endorse the sales forecasts made by Davis. Green felt the forecasts were either overly optimistic or outright fabrications.

Before he left for the day, Green had reread the series of emails regarding his performance and was certain that Davis was setting him up to be dismissed. Davis's most recent email had made it clear to Green that his position as a senior market specialist was in jeopardy. He did not have much time to rectify the situation. McDonald had emailed a formal request to him that afternoon, asking for his perspective on his performance and how he was going to improve the situation. With this in mind, Green started his commute home and began to analyze what went wrong and what he could do to save his job.

Company and Industry Background

Dynamic Displays was founded in 1990 as a provider of self-service options to banks via Automated Teller Machines (ATMs). In 1994, Dynamic Displays launched a new division aimed at the travel and hospitality industry, and deployed their first self-service check-in kiosk for Discover Airlines. In 2007, Dynamic Displays' Travel and Hospitality Division had 60% market share with over 1,500 self-service kiosks in use at more than 75 airports. Customers included regional, national, and international airline carriers, as well as various hotels and car-rental agencies. Eighty percent of the Travel and Hospitality Division's 2007 revenue came from airline carrier clients, 15% from hotels, and 5% from car-rental agencies. The company was a full service provider, offering hardware, software, engineering, and maintenance support.

Kiosks were an attractive option for airlines to quickly and easily check in passengers while reducing processing costs. Dynamic Displays' kiosks not only reduced costs but also improved customer service, shortened passenger wait times, and provided valuable information to these travelers. In 2006, Forrester Research estimated the average cost for an airline passenger to check in through an agent was $3.02, versus a range of $0.14 to $0.32 for kiosk check-in.[1] This impressive savings was realized by allowing the repetitive tasks of selecting or changing seat assignments and printing and distributing boarding passes to be handled by the passengers themselves. Airlines reduced headcount or assigned the agents to more value-added tasks, such as solving complex customer service issues and ensuring compliance with safety and security standards. The cost savings were particularly important for the airline industry during a period when margins were razor thin and fuel costs were continuing to climb.

Airlines were also aggressively promoting another self-service option for travelers. Web check-in allowed passengers to complete the entire check-in process via the internet from a remote location, utilizing their personal or office computer. Cost savings using online check-in was of even greater benefit because the airline did not have to purchase and install a kiosk, and passengers printed their own boarding passes using their own paper. According to a 2006 Forrester report, airport kiosks were a mature application with 75% of U.S. leisure passengers using kiosk in 2006. Web check-in on the other hand, was still experiencing dramatic growth, increasing from less than 45% of U.S. leisure passengers in 2005 to 64% in 2006.[2]

Thomas Green: Path to Senior Market Specialist

Thomas Green was born in 1979 in Brunswick, Georgia, the son of a postman and a school secretary. At the University of Georgia, he worked in a warehouse and washed cars while earning a bachelor's degree in Economics. His first full-time job was in sales for National Business Solutions in Atlanta. Green enjoyed impressive success in the Banking Division, focusing on ATM sales to regional banks in the Southeast. In March 2007, Dynamic Displays recruited Green for an account executive position in the Southeast territory for the Travel and Hospitality Division. To Green, Dynamic Displays seemed to present a great chance for a fast climb up the managerial ladder.

Green hit the ground running at Dynamic Displays. In his first four months as an account executive, he completed a contract for one of the largest airline carriers, Journey Airlines, to accelerate rollout of kiosks in 20 airports and purchase upgraded software for kiosks in the majority of their locations.

Green had told a close friend, "I wanted to come in and dazzle them at Dynamic Displays. This was no easy feat. But I wanted more than an account executive position. I had heard there was a lot of opportunity for fresh talent at corporate headquarters and I made it my mission to get noticed immediately."

Senior executives at Dynamic Displays quickly took notice of Green's performance and were eager to strengthen his relationship with the company. In July 2007, Green attended a week-long training session at corporate headquarters. Shannon McDonald, the division vice president, and Mary Jacobs, the national sales director, made a concerted effort to get to know him better. Green and McDonald

---

[1] Harteveldt and Epps, "Self-Service Check-In Clicks with Travelers," *Forrester Report*, February 23, 2007

[2] Ibid.

BRIEFCASES | HARVARD BUSINESS SCHOOL

were both University of Georgia alumni and Georgia natives. They had an instant connection, and McDonald seemed to take Green under her wing. McDonald had several informal meetings with Green, and by the end of the week Green became aware of an open position for a senior market specialist. Green aggressively campaigned to be considered for this position. Over the next month, Green made several trips to corporate headquarters to meet with McDonald. Green discussed his various client relationships, and McDonald agreed that in a short time he had developed unique insights into their markets. Following a dinner meeting at which Green offered lengthy explanations of the client opportunities he perceived and his strategies for winning them, McDonald promoted him to the position of senior market specialist.

McDonald told Green, "Tom, you are obviously a bright and ambitious account executive. You have a great rapport with your clients. You have made a strong case for your promotion and I'm willing to take a chance on you. I think this group needs a fresh perspective. However, I do have a couple of reservations about your lack of managerial experience. You have only held sales roles, and the senior market specialist position is very different. This new job will require you to think strategically as well as tactically, and you will have to coordinate between several different functions and layers of corporate management. I am hoping you compensate for your lack of experience by seeking out guidance from some of our more seasoned managers."

Green was assigned to work out of corporate headquarters in Boston. The division's organizational structure is shown in **Exhibit 1**. The promotion had been a giant step upward for Green; an account executive interested in joining the marketing team usually moved first to a market specialist position and then put in a number of years in the field before reaching "senior" status. The other senior market specialists in the division were in their forties. Green was 28. His salary was now $125,000, a 50% increase over his previous salary.

Senior market specialists were responsible for identifying industry trends, evaluating new business opportunities, and establishing sales goals. In addition, specialists developed general market and specific client strategies to help the account executives obtain a sale. Green directly supervised the two market specialists in his region. Green reported to Frank Davis, the marketing director. Davis had recently been promoted from the position that Green assumed (see **Exhibit 2** for relevant bios).

After Green's Promotion

Green's promotion became effective on September 10, 2007. McDonald stopped by Green's office that first day and told Green, "Tom, you are walking into a tricky situation with Frank Davis. Frank had expected to choose the new senior market specialist and it would not have been you. You'll have to deal with any fallout that might result from that. You are getting an unusual opportunity with this promotion. Don't let me down."

Green used most of his first week to review 2006 and 2007 year-to-date sales. He spent the next week with his boss, Frank Davis, making a rapid tour of major airline industry clients. At the end of the week, Davis told Green, "We had some good meetings this week and the clients responded well to your ideas. However, I think we would have been more effective if we had been able to provide the clients with some market data. When you are on your own I expect you to spend a significant amount of time preparing for client meetings and developing supporting detail for your proposals. I know you will need a little time to get up to speed on your new position, but I expect you to start developing some new market strategies for your region soon."

Green next visited clients, market specialists, and account executives in New York, Atlanta, and Orlando. In addition to the travel, Green's personal life was very busy. He was searching for a house in Boston, arranging to move belongings there, and still trying to maintain a relationship with his girlfriend in Atlanta.

On October 8, Green attended the 2008 Budget Plan meeting in which Davis presented sales projections for the upcoming year. This was the first time Green had been exposed to the planning and forecasting process. Since Davis had held Green's position when the estimates were due, the numbers for the Eastern region had been developed without input from Green. At the meeting, Davis assigned 2008 performance commitments for all senior marketing specialists and their teams. Performance reviews would be based upon their ability to meet or exceed the objectives. Green was surprised by the numbers that Davis was proposing. Davis estimated 10% growth in the Eastern region.

According to Green, "Frank Davis was way off base with his pro forma numbers. I had been talking with our account execs and there was no way we could achieve double-digit growth in 2008. The sales goals Frank set for my region were totally unrealistic. In the meeting I expressed my concern that my goals would be impossible to meet. I couldn't believe I was the only one with the guts to speak up. After the meeting, Frank stopped me in the hall and told me about all these big opportunities for the market. I listened politely, but the time I'd spent out on the road with clients gave me every reason to doubt Frank's expectations."

Davis was visibly upset that Green openly challenged him at the meeting. Davis commented to McDonald, "Thomas's negative attitude is not what we need on this team. Corporate expects this division to be a growth engine for the company. We've realized a 10% CAGR over the past 5 years. The market indicators are positive, and with the right sales strategy my projections are attainable. The hotel and car-rental markets are virtually untapped right now. Thomas's problem is that he's too conservative in his outlook. He is thinking like an account exec who is only concerned with the sales target. In the senior market specialist position, he has to think outside the box and develop strategies to capture that aggressive growth target."

Meeting with Frank Davis

It was customary for employees at Dynamic Displays to have an informal evaluation in the first or second month after a promotion. When Green saw a meeting with Davis regarding his performance pop up on his Outlook calendar, he was not the least bit worried. On October 15, 2007, Green met with Davis to discuss his performance to date. Quite to Green's surprise, Davis had prepared a list of problems he had encountered with Green's work in the first month after his promotion.

Davis sternly looked Green in the eye and began. "Thomas, you have not done a good job of keeping me informed of your schedule. For example, this past Thursday, I was trying to locate you and your Outlook calendar said you were in Orlando. I needed you to send me some information on one of our accounts. You didn't answer your cell phone. I ended up calling the account exec in Orlando and was told you had left the previous day. To make matters worse, I had asked you to deliver on that same day a brief report on that new kiosk opportunity in Tampa—and I didn't receive it."

Flabbergasted, Green responded, "I decided to go to Atlanta a day early because I had run out of good opportunities in Orlando. I was able to get a meeting with the VP of purchasing at a client in Atlanta and thought that would be more productive than sitting around Orlando talking to nobodies."

Davis continued, "On September 20, I asked you to check why VIP Hotel Group had not purchased any of our kiosks. After three reminders, I still have not received a good answer from you. In the same vein, two weeks ago, I requested the status of the regional jet division of Journey Airlines. I have not received any update from you yet. I also asked for organizational charts on two clients in Charlotte and Raleigh. Do you remember your reply? You said, 'What's the value of charts like that? I have that information in my head.' Thomas, we can make good use of those charts—they can help us lay out a strategy for getting to the decision makers in a company. I expect the charts on my desk by end of the week."

Davis and Green spent the next two hours going over various incidents and discussing a plan to improve the situation.

Later, Green told a manager outside his group, "I can't shake this nagging suspicion that Frank's criticisms of my performance are a direct result of my questioning the validity of his forecasts in the Budget Plan meeting. I was blindsided by his negative assessment of my work. Frank spent two hours picking apart my work style. You would think he would be concerned with bigger issues than how often I update my Outlook calendar."

A few days after the meeting, Davis wrote an email to McDonald, who had promoted Green, outlining the points covered in the meeting and copied Green on the communication (**Exhibit 3**).

Three Months Later: Trouble Continues

After the October 15 meeting, Green met with the national sales director and director of software development. Green was focused on developing a new up-selling and cross-selling software program that would allow airline passengers to upgrade seating; have meals, magazines, or books delivered to the flight; and book hotel rooms or cars at their destination. According to Green, "The only way for us to capture growth is if we can convince the airlines that our products have revenue-generating opportunity and other advantages over web check-in. However, these programs may take months to develop and will not impact our sales in 2008."

Green spent most of November, December, and January working independently on his special software project and traveling to meet with his market specialists and various clients. According to one of the market specialists who accompanied Green to several meetings, "Thomas is great when it comes to selling the clients on his ideas. He is very charismatic and can think quickly on his feet. I can tell he has put a lot of thought into his strategies and I really like working for him. However, the clients are starting to ask me for hard data to back up his claims of cost savings. They are also requiring memos and presentations to bring to their superiors that justify the expenditure. Thomas doesn't really work that way. He would rather talk through the issues face to face."

During this time, Green avoided interactions with Davis whenever he could. Green continued to tell people outside the group he did not agree with his boss's projections for 2008. Green stated, "With the continued financial distress in the airline industry and preference for web check-in, I don't foresee a lot of growth in spending next year. Davis is holding firm with his upbeat projections. I deliberately steer clear of him. I know my mood is terrible. The excitement's gone from work. I must say, though, I've had a couple of good chats with managers from another part of Dynamic Displays, and they're supportive. They told me to stand my ground. "

On January 28, Davis held another performance review meeting with Green, focusing on the continuing deficiencies in Green's work and attitude. After the meeting, Davis sent an email to McDonald outlining his issues with Green (**Exhibit 4**). Green was not copied on this email, but someone sent him a copy by interoffice mail. McDonald met with Davis the following day to flesh out

---

the issue. Davis told McDonald, "I am truly disappointed with Thomas's work. He is an intelligent and capable young man, but I do not believe he is making a strong effort."

In response to Davis's complaints, McDonald sent a short email to Green (**Exhibit 5**) asking for his point of view on the situation.

Green told a close friend, "It's clear that Frank intends to get rid of me. He's just putting his argument together."

Green's Next Move

As Green entered I-93 on the way to his new home in North Andover, he replayed in his head the series of events and subsequent emails. Green recognized that he had not paid much attention to office politics when he'd taken on his job. He had met one-on-one with McDonald only twice since he moved to the corporate headquarters. He had been preoccupied with the job itself, and with living up to McDonald's expectations. Now it seemed as though he had no allies in the company. McDonald's email today struck a nerve. Because McDonald sponsored his promotion, Green had taken for granted that she would watch out for him. If Davis was indeed trying to fire him, Green wondered who McDonald would side with.

Several questions persisted in Green's mind. What steps should he take next? Set up a meeting with McDonald? Write McDonald a detailed memo? Do what Davis tells him and keep his mouth shut, even though he was convinced that the forecasts were inflated? Was it his responsibility to expose Davis's overstated projections? Maybe contact a head hunter and start looking for another job? He had to sort through before he responded to McDonald's email. Next week, his first mortgage payment was due and the new furniture he'd picked out was scheduled to be delivered. This was certainly not a good time to be out of work, for 2008 was shaping up to be a very stressful year for Thomas Green.

Exhibit 1   Abbreviated Organization Chart, Travel and Hospitality Division of Dynamic Displays, 2007

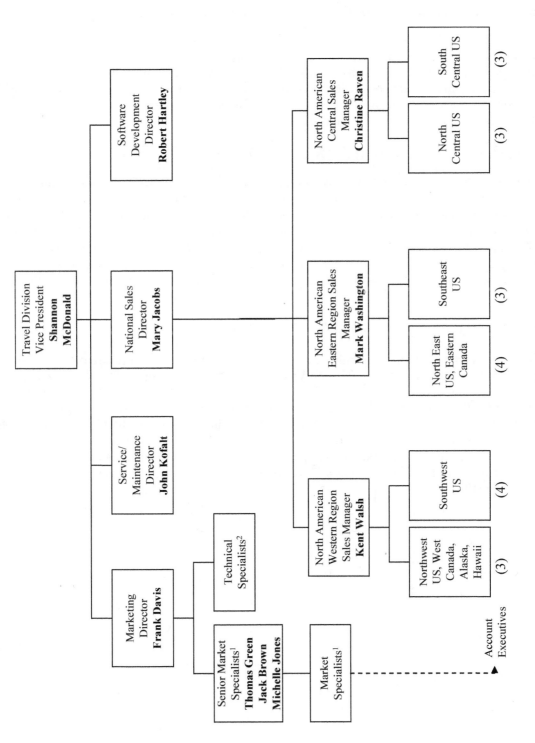

[1] There were three senior market specialists (one for each region) and six market specialists (one for each territory). Thomas Green was the market specialist for Eastern Region

[2] There were six technical specialists (one for each territory)

Exhibit 2   Relevant Bios

Thomas Green (Age 28) – Senior Market Specialist

Thomas Green began his career as an account executive for National Business Solutions in Atlanta, Georgia. He spent six years as an account executive in the Banking Division, selling ATMs to regional banks throughout the Southeast. In March 2007 he joined Dynamic Displays as an account executive in their Travel and Hospitality Division. He is currently the division's senior market specialist for the Eastern region of North America. Green graduated summa cum laude from University of Georgia with a bachelor's degree in Economics in 2001.

Frank Davis (Age 45) – Marketing Director

Frank Davis is a 17-year veteran of Dynamic Displays. He joined the company in 1990 as an account executive with the Financial Services Solutions Division. He has also held positions as an account executive, market specialist, and senior market specialist with the Travel and Hospitality Division. Frank Davis is currently the marketing director for the Travel and Hospitality Division. Prior to joining Dynamic Displays, Davis worked as a sales representative for Advanced Telecommunications Services selling PBX phone systems to large corporations. He holds a bachelors degree in history from New York University (1986) and an Executive MBA from Suffolk University, Sawyer Business School (2002).

Shannon McDonald (Age 42) – Division Vice President

Reporting to the Dynamic Displays Chairman, Chief Executive Officer and President, Sam Costello, Shannon McDonald was promoted to Division Vice President in November of 2006 and is responsible for all aspects of the Travel and Hospitality Business. Previously, McDonald was the director of national sales for the Travel and Hospitality Division (2000-2006). She was responsible for driving Dynamic Displays' self-service business with the largest airline carriers in the United States. Ms. McDonald has also held positions as a strategic consultant with Chicago Consulting Group's Travel and Tourism practice and as a marketing analyst with Quest Airlines. She holds a bachelors degree in marketing from the University of Georgia (1987) and an MBA from Northwestern's Kellogg School of Management (1992).

Exhibit 3   10/19/07 Email Regarding Green's Performance

FROM: "FRANK DAVIS" <FDAVIS@dynamicdisplays.com >

TO: "SHANNON MCDONALD" <smcdonald@dynamicdisplays.com >

CC: "THOMAS GREEN" <TGREEN@dynamicdisplays.com >

SENT: FRIDAY, OCTOBER 19, 2007 3:48:32 pM

SUBJECT: THOMAS GREEN

Since Thomas assumed the position of senior market specialist on September 10, 2007, numerous incidents of poor judgment and questionable behavior have concerned me. Thomas and I talked about most of these incidents as they occurred. However, I concluded that we needed to have an overarching discussion about his performance and to develop a strategy for improving his work style. At that meeting, held October 15, 2007, we reviewed a range of problems. Among them:

1. Thomas fails to inform me of his plans and keep me updated on his schedule.

2. He does not follow up when information is requested of him.

3. Thomas's lack of enthusiasm is troubling. He has a right and an obligation to question aspects of our plans if he finds them illogical or unfeasible, but the kind of negativity he displayed in the Budget Plan meeting on October 8 is dangerous to the organization and unacceptable to me.

Thomas seemed to accept my criticisms in a thoughtful manner and assured me he will do what is necessary to succeed in his position. He and I plan to discuss his overall performance again in mid-November. Meanwhile, he'll be expected to take the following corrective measures:

1. Plan to make focused calls when dealing with market specialists, account executives, and clients. Have a specific communication strategy going into a call, and have all sales collateral and other necessary materials available. Stop making calls purely for the purpose of meeting people.

2. Update Outlook calendar regularly and always return calls from our office promptly.

3. Provide feedback to my requests in a timely manner. Thomas says he now recognizes that my requests are not merely "reminders"; they are a call for information that I genuinely need.

4. Demonstrate a more positive attitude both inside and outside the company.

Frank R. Davis
Travel and Hospitality Marketing Director
Dynamic Displays
212-314-1420

Exhibit 4   1/30/08 Email Regarding Green's Performance

FROM: "FRANK DAVIS" <FDAVIS@dynamicdisplays.com >

TO: "SHANNON MCDONALD" <smcdonald@dynamicdisplays.com >

SENT: WEDNESDAY, January 30, 2008 4:28:12 pM

SUBJECT: THOMAS GREEN

On October 19, 2007, I sent you an email communicating my concerns with Thomas's attitude and job performance. On January 28, 2008, Thomas and I had another meeting on this subject. I would like to summarize that conversation.

Thomas wastes a great deal of time complaining about the problems of selling to our current and prospective clients and far too little time developing strategic marketing approaches and effective sales tactics. I informed him that his job is to sell the accounts, not to agree with our clients' assertions about alleged disadvantages of our products or the current excess capacity in the industry.

I told Thomas his lack of effort and enthusiasm are not consistent with the standards of Dynamic Displays and could lead to an outcome he likely would not find pleasant. Thomas then said he felt I was micromanaging his activities. It was here that I think we uncovered the root of the problem. I inquired as to what new or even slightly imaginative marketing approaches he documented in the past five months. His answer was, "None that are documented." When I see no new targets and no thoughtful, creative marketing, I feel I must micromanage, and I communicated this to Thomas.

I then pulled up several Power Point presentations, spreadsheet models, and associated emails that Michelle Jones, the Western Region senior market specialist, had used to shape her region's strategy and to support their selling efforts. As we paged through her work, Thomas stated that all those email updates and fancy presentations and models were "political" and didn't match up well with his personal approach to selling. I told him this was not only good politics, but also proved to his boss that he was working effectively.

Thomas ultimately conceded the mistakes and personal shortcomings that I explained to him.. He pledged to develop creative marketing approaches and keep me updated on his progress. I hope these promises materialize in the next 30 days. If not, I recommend we part ways with Thomas Green and quickly seek out a competent replacement for this extremely important position.

Frank R. Davis
Travel and Hospitality Marketing Director
Dynamic Displays
212-314-1420

Exhibit 5   2/5/08 Email from McDonald to Green

FROM:	"SHANNON MCDONALD" <smcdonald@dynamicdisplays.com >
TO:	"THOMAS GREEN" <TGREEN@dynamicdisplays.com >
CC:	"FRANK DAVIS" <FDAVIS@dynamicdisplays.com >
SENT:	TUESDAY, FEBRUARY 5, 2008 8:38:53 AM
SUBJECT:	PERFORMANCE

Frank Davis has explained to me his point of view on your performance. I think all of us want to improve the current situation, which is regrettable. At this point I would like to get your perspective on your recent performance and to understand your ideas about specific areas that need improvement.

I look forward to resolving this issue ASAP. I would be glad to discuss this matter with you in detail, but first I would like to receive your statement in writing.

Shannon A. McDonald
Travel and Hospitality Group Vice-President
Dynamic Displays
212-314-1415

AN INTRODUCTORY NOTE ON MANAGING PEOPLE IN ORGANIZATIONS

Ann Frost and Lyn Purdy wrote this note solely to provide material for class discussion. The authors do not intend to provide legal, tax, accounting or other professional advice. Such advice should be obtained from a qualified professional.

Version: 2015-04-21

The work of organizations is done through people. Elaborate structures, systems, rules, and reporting relationships do little more than provide guidance for such behaviour — they do not produce it. Eliciting the needed behaviour is the job of managers. Increasingly, firms are also dependent on more than mere compliance to the dictates of management. Rather, a firm's competitive success rests on its ability to respond quickly and flexibly, to innovate, and to continually improve. To achieve success, the organization requires the commitment of its members. Today's managers face the daunting task of converting their subordinates' compliance into the commitment required to meet the organization's strategic objectives.

Clearly then, the work of a manager goes beyond organizing, assigning, and deploying resources. Perhaps the most critical management skill is managing people — not only subordinates, but also superiors and peers. Your performance as a manager will be evaluated on the basis of how well you are able to do these things; yet, to do them well is a difficult task.

We often think good management skills can be reduced to effective interpersonal skills. Good interpersonal skills, however, are not enough. Being nice to people may result in higher levels of job satisfaction or at least satisfaction with the manager in question, but satisfaction is, at best, only tenuously related to performance. More critical than good interpersonal skills is the ability to understand people's interests (based on their personal characteristics as well as their place in the organization), motivations, and abilities, so that a manager can lead people to accomplish the organization's goals. Without an understanding of people and the mechanisms by which they operate, a manager is left virtually powerless to be effective in his or her role.

This chapter introduces the topic of managing people in organizations. As a survey chapter, it is by no means exhaustive or highly detailed. Rather, we have attempted to introduce you to the critical areas that apply most directly to the job of a manager and to some of the research that has produced what we know in this area. Where appropriate, we have provided citations to original sources that you may want to refer to on your own for more detail.

---

[1] *This material appears as Chapter 4 of E. Grasby, M. Crossan, A. Frost, J. Haywood-Farmer, M. Pearce and L. Purdy, Making Business Decisions, 1st ed., London, Ont.: Richard Ivey School of Business, 2008.*

ORGANIZATIONAL STRUCTURE AND DESIGN

A rapidly globalizing economy, ongoing technological change, and deregulation have all contributed to intensifying competition over the past several decades. Old sources of competitive advantage are drying up as technology is now easily copied, monopoly positions give way in the wake of deregulation, and barriers to entry fall. Organizational capabilities are one of the few remaining sources of sustainable competitive advantage. These capabilities come from the way an organization structures its work and motivates its people to achieve its strategic objectives.

This section looks at the fundamental components of organizational structure, outlines some basic organizational forms, discusses the costs and benefits associated with each of them, and highlights the conditions for which particular forms are best suited.

The Purpose of Organizational Structure

Organizational structure has two specific purposes: to divide work into various distinct tasks to be performed and to coordinate these tasks to accomplish the overall objectives of the organization. Breaking activities into smaller parts, referred to here as differentiation, makes the work easier or more efficient to do but, ultimately, results in the need to put these smaller parts back together to complete the activity. We refer to this putting back together as integration.

Differentiation

Differentiation occurs at two levels within the organization. Decision makers must first decide on the extent of horizontal and vertical specialization of an individual job — the breadth of the job in terms of how many separate tasks will be assigned to the job, as well as the depth of the job in terms of how much planning, conception, execution, and administrative activities are included. Decision makers must also determine the groupings of jobs that make the most sense for the organization based on the goods and services it produces; the geographic or client markets it serves; and the skills, knowledge, and expertise the organization needs to produce its product. Extreme differentiation or specialization creates greater expertise, builds economies of scale, and focuses attention. However, it tends to produce monotonous work, narrow interests, and the need for higher levels of integration to bring the specialized parts back together again to form a whole.

Integration

Differentiation provides the organization with efficiency through the division of labour and aligns group goals within specific areas. However, to make the organization effective, various tasks, departments, and subunits must be integrated. The greater the degree of differentiation and the greater the interdependence, the greater is the need for integration. Various mechanisms can be used to accomplish this objective. The right one will depend on the amount of integration needed.

As the need for interaction, information flow, and coordination increases, the integration process will be more resource intensive. At very low levels, rules and procedures will suffice to coordinate activities. Similarly, planning and hierarchy serve well at fairly low levels. As the need for integration rises, liaison roles, task forces, and teams become necessary to deal with more nonstandard integration needs. Finally, at the most extreme level, whole integrating departments may become necessary to oversee the coordination of activities between groups.

Organizational Structure — Basic Forms

There are three basic organizational forms: the functional, the divisional, and the matrix.[2] Each is designed to deal with different challenges (e.g., size of organization, complexity of environment, multiplicity of markets served). An organization rarely appears in the pure form of any of the following three types; however, most organizations basically conform to one of them. Knowing the basic characteristics of these forms can provide a manager with considerable insight.

The Functional Form

When organizations are grouped by function, positions are grouped based on particular skills or processes (see **Figure 1**). For example, all accountants would be grouped together, all engineers would be grouped together, and all marketing personnel would be grouped together. With this approach, the work of the organization is divided so that a single group handles each part (or function). Each function or department becomes differentiated and adopts similar values, goals, and orientation, encouraging collaboration, innovation, and quality within the department. This differentiation may, however, make coordination with other departments more difficult.

FIGURE 1: The Functional Form

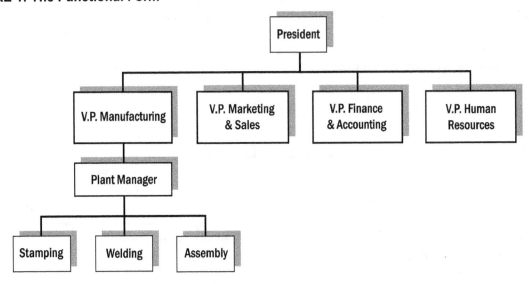

The activities of all these groups must be put together in order to accomplish the overall goal of the organization. This integration necessitates a good deal of information processing among the different functional groups. Procedures need to be developed to coordinate work in order to produce the organization's final product. In a stable environment, coordination may be relatively easy, but in a rapidly changing environment, it becomes increasingly difficult.

---

[2] Nitin Nohria, "Note on Organization Structure," Harvard Business School Publishing, Boston, 1991.

The advantages of grouping by function are:

1. Resources are used efficiently (there is no duplication of equipment or efforts).
2. Professional development is promoted (group members can learn from one another and career paths are obvious).
3. There is a comfortable setting for socialization and evaluation (there is an ease of interaction between people of similar interests and backgrounds, and evaluations are conducted by someone knowledgeable in the area).

In grouping by function several disadvantages also emerge. There is typically poor intergroup coordination; the goals of the organization often become secondary to the goals of the functional group; there is diffuse accountability for the final product or service of the organization; and the organization tends to be more formalized and less flexible, as work is strictly divided between functions. Overall, this form is best suited for small to medium-size organizations that produce a single or closely related set of products and services.

The Divisional Form

The divisional structure is organized by the outputs the organization produces. Each division is responsible for different products, geographic markets, or clients. Regardless of the basis on which it is organized, the division is a self-contained unit that contains all the functional areas necessary to serve its specified market (see **Figure 2**). For example, General Motors, a divisional organization based on product market groups, has separate divisions for cars and trucks in which each group has all the necessary marketing, sales, production, accounting, engineering, and distribution personnel it requires to produce and sell its set of products.

FIGURE 2: Divisional Form by Product

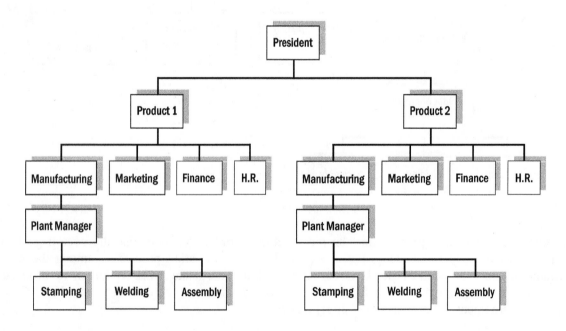

The divisional structure is excellent when the predominant goal of the organization is to respond effectively to satisfy clients in a particular market segment. Because each division has the necessary complement of skills, it can respond quickly to the changing needs of its market. Moreover, corporate control can be more effectively exerted because each division can be held accountable for its own performance.

The advantages of the divisional form are:

1. There is good coordination of activities — everyone who is responsible for a single product is grouped together and the groups are relatively small.
2. Attention is more directed at the organizational goal and less directed at the individual functional group goals.

There is increased flexibility (organizations can respond to changes in their markets by adding or deleting divisions as required with little negative impact on other parts of the organization).

The divisional form also has drawbacks. There is often duplication of resources across the organization; professional development is not as clear in terms of career paths and in terms of developing specialized talents; and the setting for socialization and evaluation is less comfortable (evaluations may become particularly problematic because individuals may be evaluated by someone with little expertise in their area). The divisional form works best in medium- or large-size organizations that operate in heterogeneous environments and produce multiple products, serve different customers, and/or sell products in different geographic regions.

The Matrix Form

Matrix structures combine both functional and divisional forms (see **Figure 3**). In some instances organizations want the benefits of both forms: the deep technological expertise within functions, as well as coordination across functions. In a matrix structure, all organizational members maintain a home base in a functional group while working on projects for specific products, regions, or clients. Individuals can be involved with several projects and with tasks for the functional group. As they complete projects, individuals return, either physically or time-wise, to their functional base for reassignment. The intention of the matrix structure is to reap the advantages of the divisional form and the functional form and to avoid the pitfalls of either one. The advantages of the matrix structure are:

3. It adapts easily to a changing workload (projects are added and deleted as required).
4. Resources are used efficiently (there is no need to duplicate specialists across projects).
5. It provides a home base for specialists (expertise can be pooled).
6. There is flexibility for workers and variety in their task assignments.
7. It promotes innovation (people with diverse backgrounds are drawn together on projects).

The matrix structure does, however, have its own set of drawbacks, including the following:

8. There is a high degree of dependency on teamwork, which may not be the preferred work mode for all individuals.
9. There is conflict for the individual (should one listen to the project manager or the functional manager if priorities conflict?), and there is often uncertainty with regard to evaluation (will the functional manager or the project managers do the evaluation?).

FIGURE 3: Matrix Form

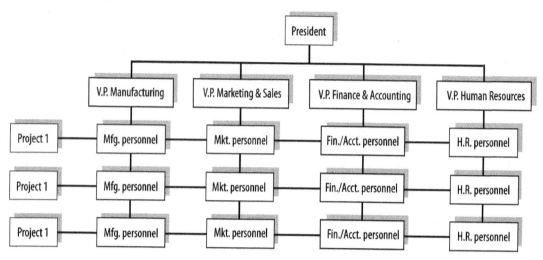

10. Power struggles often arise between project groups and between project and functional groups in determining personnel assignments to tasks.
11. There is a lack of stability in the work environment for individuals (owing to the constant change of projects and considerable variation in time demands).
12. There is a relatively high cost to administering these structures (tracking of individuals, constant renegotiation for project assignments, etc.).

The matrix structure is the ideal structure under the following conditions. First, a matrix structure is appropriate when the organization faces environmental pressures from two sources, such as function and product or function and region. In cases such as this, the dual authority structure is needed to balance these pressures. Second, it is well suited when the firm is in an uncertain and complex task environment. In such instances, the matrix provides the organization with the requisite responsiveness. Finally, the matrix form is well suited to situations in which the firm requires economies of scale in the use of internal resources.

Holacracy

The newest development in organizational structure is the advent of Holacracy[TM]. Emerging from roots in the agile movement in the software development industry, holacracy is a radical departure from the organizational designs of the past century, with their reliance on hierarchy and the need for management. Instead, holacracy seeks to distribute authority and decision making to those doing purpose driven work using a system of interlocking teams (or "circles") that form and disband as dictated by the work needing to be done. By doing so, holacracy seeks to make companies more agile and to respond better to, and to be able to benefit more from, the ongoing flux in the competitive environment.

Holacracy is the creation of Brian J. Robertson, a serial software entrepreneur turned consultant. Software engineering was one of the first settings where the hierarchical, planning-driven approach was noted to fail. In such ever-changing, dynamic environments, the traditional organizational designs proved too cumbersome and slow. In 2001, a group of 17 software developers came together to draft a set of principles outlining a "Manifesto of Agile Software Development."[3]   From that document, Robertson developed his principles of organizational design that he then implemented in his own new software company, Ternary Software.   In 2007, he published an article outlining the principles of the new organizational form.[4]

Holacracy is organized around a set of inter-related circles or teams devoted to the completion of a common task or project. Circles are linked, distributing authority throughout the organization, and keep the organization lean and adaptable as circles are formed and disbanded based on what work needs to be done. The circles are run democratically and openly with detailed procedures on how decisions are to be made and meetings are to be run. In holacracy there are no job titles, only roles. There are no managers. Decisions are made by consent, not by consensus – which means that not everyone has to agree before action is taken, only that no one can bring evidence to persuade the others that such action is a bad idea. The latter is an important distinction, enabling decisions to be made quickly and then altered if need be once disconfirming evidence comes to light. The benefits to holacracy include organizational agility and flexibility, responsiveness to an ever changing environment, and an ability to adapt as necessary to external demands.

Implications of Organizational Structure for Managers

Organizational structure is a key component in creating the unique and difficult to imitate capabilities that organizations now require for sustainable competitive advantage.[5] Organizational structure is important, too, at a more micro level. For individual managers, the redesign or restructuring of their own areas of responsibility has the potential to fundamentally change patterns of performance. Organizational design decisions define where an organization channels its resources, where and how information flows, how it defines jobs, shapes work processes, motivates performance, and moulds informal interactions between people over time. A manager will be judged on the basis of how well his or her area performs. An understanding of organizational design helps a manager in doing his or her job effectively.

ORGANIZATIONAL CULTURE

Organizational culture is a central and important feature of organizations. Its effects are pervasive and operate unconsciously, moulding the way employees see and respond to their environment. Although its abstract nature makes it difficult to understand and to study, it greatly affects the way in which an organization's members behave. This section considers culture, its manifestations, and its impact on organizational performance.

Defining Organizational Culture

Definitions of culture are difficult to agree on because of the phenomenon's inherently fuzzy nature. Culture can be broadly defined as a basic pattern of assumptions developed by a group as it learns to cope with the problems of surviving in its environment and functioning as a unit.[6] The assumptions that have

---

[3] P. Van de Kamp, "Holacracy - A Radical Approach to Organizational Design." www.researchgate.net/publication/264977984_Holacracy__A_Radical_Approach_to_Organizational_Design,   accessed March 31, 2015.

[4] B. J. Robertson "Organization at the leading edge: Introducing Holacracy TM Integral Leadership Review, 7 (3), 2007.

[5] David A. Nadler and Michael L. Tushman, Competing by Design, Oxford University Press, New York, 1997.

[6] Edgar H. Schein, "Organizational Culture," American Psychologist, 45(2) (1990): 109-19.

been found to work well enough in accomplishing these ends and are thus considered valid are then taught to new members as the correct way to perceive, think, and feel in relation to those problems. In short, culture can be thought of as the set of shared assumptions, values, beliefs, and norms that guide organizational members' behaviour.

Any definable group with a shared history can have a culture, creating the possibility for the existence of multiple subcultures within a given organization. The tendency is for these cultures to be consistent, but it is also possible for them to be independent or even inconsistent. For example, the culture within the R&D function of a large company would likely value innovativeness and the importance of new discovery. In contrast, the manufacturing function within the same organization may value cost effectiveness and high levels of efficiency.

Culture originates from the unique history of the firm. The roles and actions of leaders (especially founders) are particularly important. There are four primary mechanisms by which an organizational culture becomes embedded:

13. What leaders pay attention to, measure, and control;
14. How leaders react to organizational crises or critical incidents;
15. The deliberate coaching and modelling of behaviour; and
16. The criteria used for recruitment, selection, promotion, retirement, and termination.

Manifestations of Organizational Culture

Culture manifests itself in many different ways: from the layout of company facilities, to jargon used by members, to stories told, to the rules of the game for getting along or ahead in the organization. One gets a sense of two very different corporate cultures simply by looking at the environment the organization has designed for itself. The large, green playing fields surrounding Microsoft's Redmond, Washington, "campus" contrast markedly with the enormous skyscraper in the heart of New York City that houses GE's corporate head office. Similarly, an unabashed culture of caring is manifested throughout WestJet Airlines. The recent WestJet Christmas Miracles[7] demonstrate the extent to which WestJet is willing to go to reinforce its culture of caring. In 2013, passengers boarding a Calgary-bound flight from Hamilton were asked by Santa what they wanted for Christmas. Upon arrival at the luggage carousel, wrapped parcels came down the conveyor belt containing the gifts, big and small, that everyone had asked for. The following year, WestJet went to a town in the Dominican Republic and again asked people what they wanted for Christmas. The next day, all of the gift requests to Santa were fulfilled – from a horse, to a new motorcycle engine, to a washing machine, to a doll and skateboards. These actions as well as other acts of kindness towards customers and employees serve to illustrate the depth of the caring culture at WestJet.

Socialization Processes

Organizations must provide mechanisms by which new members can become familiar with the culture of the organization. Socialization processes are designed to do that.[8] Almost all organizations with strong cultures enact socialization processes by (1) using rigorous, multistep selection and orientation processes

---

[7] *WestJet Christmas Miracle: Real Time Giving* www.youtube.com/watch?v=zIElvi2MuEk and *WestJet Christmas Miracle: Spirit of Giving* www.youtube.com/watch?v=p-BKX3G0BpQ, accessed March 31, 2015.
[8] *Charles A. O'Reilly and Jennifer A. Chatman, "Culture as Social Control: Corporations, Cults, and Commitment," in Advances in Organizational Behavior, Vol. 18 (Greenwich, CT: JAI Press, 1996), pp.157-200.*

that develop the individual's commitment to the organization through participation in the selection process, (2) signaling that certain goals, attitudes, and behaviours are important, and (3) developing reward systems that reinforce appropriate attitudes and behaviours and provide continuous recognition. Socialization can occur in groups (as in boot camp) or individually (as in professional offices). New recruits may be taken through a formal orientation program consisting of video, written material, and lectures, or socialization may be handled more informally through on-the-job training or apprenticeship programs.[9] Regardless of the means, the individual may decide to adopt the assumptions and conform to the norms of the organization; adopt a number of core assumptions and norms, but be innovative in how he or she actually behaves in the organization; or rebel, rejecting all the assumptions of the organization. Clearly, the last option is the least desired by the organization. The organization most desires members who adopt the values, attitudes, behaviours, and norms of the organization. People are then more likely to fulfill the goals of the organization without the use of formal controls and to form a sense of commitment to the organization's goals. Employees will also benefit from "fitting in." It is more likely that people who "fit" will be recognized, rewarded, and ultimately promoted within the organization.

Maintenance of Organizational Culture

Organizational culture is maintained over time by a number of reinforcing mechanisms. Organizational design and structures, as well as organizational systems and procedures, guide behaviour and reinforce organizational values. For example, a formal and distant culture is maintained by steep hierarchies and bureaucratic systems for gaining project approval. The design of physical space and buildings also reinforces particular cultural features.

What is rewarded also sends out powerful signals of what is valued in a particular organization. The recognition of the Four Seasons Hotel bellhop who used his own money to fly out to return a guest's forgotten suitcase sent a powerful message about the value placed on excellent and unsurpassed levels of customer service.[10]

Processes of recruitment and selection also emphasize the core values of the organization. Southwest Airlines, known for its lighthearted, fun-loving, and caring culture puts up with no egos or with people who have no sense of humour. As an example, in interviewing eight potential pilot recruits, the men were teased about their formal business attire and were invited to exchange their suit pants for the standard Southwest Bermuda shorts for the duration of the day of interviews. The six who accepted the offer and continued their day in suit jackets, ties, dark socks, dress shoes, and Bermuda shorts were hired.[11] In addition, stories are told of Herb Kelleher, the highly visible, slightly over-the-top CEO of Southwest Airlines, regularly showing up armed with a box of doughnuts at maintenance facilities in the early morning, and proceeding to put on a pair of coveralls to go out to clean planes.[12] Such stories only reinforce norms of egalitarianism, cooperation, and pitching in to help one another out. Such values and norms have succeeded in making Southwest Airlines the only major U.S. airline to earn a profit throughout its entire history,[13] including the most recent financial crisis when U.S. airline carriers suffered losses in the billions of dollars.

---

[9] John Van Maanen, "People Processing: Strategies of Organizational Socialization," *Organizational Dynamics*, Vol. 7 (1978), pp. 18-36.

[10] Eileen D. Watson, "Four Seasons (A)," No. 9A88C007, Richard Ivey School of Business, London, ON, 1988.

[11] O'Reilly and Pfeffer, *Southwest Airlines (A)*.

[12] Charles O'Reilly and Jeffrey Pfeffer, "Southwest Airlines (A)," Stanford University Graduate School of Business, Stanford, CA, 1992.

[13] Roger Hallowell, "Southwest Airlines: A Case Study Linking Employee Needs Satisfaction and Organizational Capabilities to Competitive Advantage," *Human Resource Management*, 35(4) (1996): 513-34.

Organizational rites and ceremonies are important, as well, for reinforcing an organizational culture. Weekly beer bashes and barbecues were a fundamental part of maintaining the close-knit culture of Hewlett-Packard. Company Christmas parties, gifts of Christmas turkeys, family picnics, and other social gatherings also reinforce cohesive cultures.[14]

The Impact of Culture on Organizational Performance

So what does culture mean for the bottom line? Quite a lot it seems. Harvard Business School's John Kotter and James Heskett found that firms with cultures that emphasized all key stakeholders (customers, employees, and shareholders) and leadership from managers at all levels (not just the top) overwhelmingly outperformed firms that did not. Over an 11-year period, the former companies increased revenues by 682 per cent, expanded their work forces by 282 per cent, increased their share price by 901 per cent, and improved their net incomes by 756 per cent.[15] In contrast, the other firms increased revenues by 166 per cent, expanded their work forces by 36 per cent, increased their share price by 74 per cent, and improved their net incomes by only 1 per cent.

It is important to note, however, that it is not a strong culture but rather a strategically appropriate one that is critical to performance. In particular, the ability of the culture to adapt as the competitive environment shifts seems especially important. However, studies have shown repeatedly that culture is extremely difficult to change. Often, it is changed only through indirect means and over an often considerable period of time. Managers need to be conscious of what kind of culture they are seeking to establish or maintain through their actions and policies because of the profound effects it can have on organizational members' behaviour.

LEADERSHIP

Effective leadership is critical to all organizations. Because organizational tasks are divided into separate activities assigned to various individuals, an effective leader must be able to influence those individuals to work toward achieving the organization's goals. The question, What makes someone an effective leader?, has been asked for many years. In trying to answer this question, researchers have attempted to identify universal traits of leaders, to explain effective leadership by the behaviours that the leader displays, and to describe which leadership approaches are effective in various situations.

Leader Traits

Researchers have tried to identify universal traits of leaders under the premise that if a set of traits could be identified, then the organization could select the "right" person to be the leader. The basic belief was that great leaders possessed traits (e.g., ability, personality, or physical characteristics) that distinguished them from the people who followed them and that would be effective in any situation. After more than 60 years of research that has tried to identify the traits of effective leaders, many researchers have concluded that "possession of particular traits increases the likelihood that a leader will be effective, but they do not guarantee effectiveness, and the relative importance of different traits is dependent on the nature of the leadership situation."[16] In other words, although some traits are consistently associated with effective

---

[14] Harrison Trice and Janice Beyer, *The Cultures of Work Organizations*, Prentice-Hall, Englewood Cliffs, NJ, 1993.

[15] John P. Kotter and James L. Heskett, *Corporate Culture and Performance*, The Free Press, New York, 1992.

[16] Gary Yukl, *Leadership in Organizations*, 3rd ed., Prentice-Hall, Englewood Cliffs, NJ, 1994, p. 256.

leadership (e.g., decisiveness, initiative, self-confidence, adaptability to situation),[17] the specific situation — the followers, the task, and the organization — will determine which particular traits are essential for effective leadership. Thus, traits alone are insufficient to define effective leaders.

Leader Behaviours

A second stream of research has sought to determine whether effective leaders behave in distinctive ways. It was assumed that if critical behaviour patterns of effective leadership could be identified, then potential leaders could be trained in those behaviours. Over the last half century, a number of studies have been conducted to examine leaders' behaviours and their impact on the satisfaction and performance of their followers. Typically, leader behaviours have been grouped into two broad categories: task-oriented behaviours and relationship-oriented behaviours.[18] Task-oriented leaders emphasize the technical aspects of the job and the completion of group goals by, for example, establishing goals and work standards, assigning people to tasks, giving instructions, and checking performance. Relationship-oriented leaders emphasize interpersonal relationships by, for example, taking interest in followers' personal needs, accepting individual differences, and being friendly and approachable. For the most part, leaders who display both behaviours simultaneously are most effective.

Nonetheless, the specific situational context must be considered in terms of the requirements and constraints it places on the leader's behaviour. For example, in cases where the task is already highly structured, a leader who focuses mainly on task-oriented aspects of the job is often disliked. The requirements of the task are quite clear-cut, and further structuring of the task is annoying; in these cases, leaders who focus mainly on the relationship-oriented aspects of the job are more appreciated. However, leaders who demonstrate little relationship orientation do not always have dissatisfied subordinates. For example, if the task is highly unstructured, leaders high in task orientation are often appreciated despite their lack of relationship-oriented behaviours.

Table 1 presents a taxonomy of leadership behaviours.[19] The taxonomy was developed to categorize and describe more specific behaviours that are part of all leadership roles in varying degrees. These practices include behaviours that are concerned with both tasks and relationships. Some of the behaviours are clearly more task-oriented, such as monitoring and planning. Appropriate use of specific task-oriented or relationship-oriented behaviours is critical to leadership effectiveness; leaders must consider which form of the behaviour is appropriate to the particular situation and subordinate.

Table 1: Taxonomy of Leadership Behaviours

> ### 1. Making Decisions
> - *Planning and Organizing*: Determining long-term objectives and strategies, allocating resources according to priorities, determining how to use personnel and resources to accomplish a task efficiently, and determining how to improve coordination, productivity, and the effectiveness of the organizational unit.

---

[17] Ralph M. Stogdill, *Handbook of Leadership: A Survey of the Literature*, The Free Press, New York, 1974.
[18] Robert L. Kahn and Daniel Katz, "Leadership Practices in Relation to Productivity and Morale," in D. Cartwright and A. Zander (eds.), *Group Dynamics: Research and Theory*, Peterson & Co., New York: Row, 1960; Steven Kerr, Chester A. Schriesheim, Charles, J. Murphy, and Ralph M. Stogdill, "Toward a Contingency Theory of Leadership Based upon the Consideration and Initiating Structure Literature," *Organizational Behavior and Human Performance*, 12(1974): 62-82; Ralph M. Stogdill and Alvin E. Coons, *Leader Behavior: It's Description and Measurement*, Research Monograph #88, Columbus: Ohio State University, 1957.
[19] Gary Yukl, *Leadership in Organizations*, pp. 72, 69.

- *Problem Solving*: Identifying work-related problems, analyzing problems in a timely but systematic manner to identify causes and find solutions, and acting decisively to implement solutions to resolve important problems or crises.

- Consulting: Checking with people before making changes that affect them, encouraging suggestions for improvement, inviting participation in decision making, incorporating the ideas and suggestions of others in decisions.

- Delegating: Allowing subordinates to have substantial responsibility and discretion in carrying out work activities, handling problems, and making important decisions.

2. Influencing People
- Motivating and Inspiring: Using influence techniques that appeal to emotion or logic to generate enthusiasm for the work, commitment to task objectives, and compliance with requests for cooperation, assistance, support, or resources; setting an example of appropriate behavior.

- Recognizing: Providing praise and recognition for effective performance, significant achievements, and special contributions; expressing appreciation for someone's contributions and special efforts.

3. Building Relationships
- Supporting: Acting friendly and considerate, being patient and helpful, showing sympathy and support when someone is upset or anxious, listening to complaints and problems, looking out for someone's interests.

- Developing and Mentoring: Providing coaching and helpful career advice, and doing things to facilitate a person's skill acquisition, professional development, and career advancement.

- Managing Conflict and Team Building: Facilitating the constructive resolution of conflict, and encouraging cooperation, teamwork, and identification with the work unit.

4. Giving –Seeking Information
- Clarifying Roles and Objectives: Assigning tasks, providing direction in how to do the work, and communicating a clear understanding of job responsibilities, task objectives, deadlines, and performance expectations.

- Informing: Disseminating relevant information about decisions, plans, and activities to people that need to do their work, providing written materials and documents, and answering requests for technical information.

- Monitoring: Gathering information about work activities and external conditions affecting the work, checking on the progress and quality of the work, evaluating the performance of individuals and the organizational unit, analyzing trends, and forecasting external events.

Source: Gary Yukl, Leadership in Organizations, 4th ed. © 1981. Reprinted with permission of Prentice-Hall, Inc., Upper Saddle River, NJ.

Situational Leadership

A number of factors are important to understanding which leadership behaviours are effective in particular situations (e.g., the nature of the task, the ability to exert power, attitudes of followers). Numerous studies of leadership have been conducted using the situational approach. We highlight one situational theory here, the Path-Goal Theory of Leadership.

Path-Goal Theory of Leadership

In the Path-Goal Theory of Leadership the role of the leader is (1) to assist followers in attaining the followers' goals and (2) to provide the necessary direction and support to ensure that followers' goals are compatible with the organization's goals.[20] Effective leaders are those who clarify and clear the path for the followers to achieve those goals.

Leaders are effective when they provide a positive impact on followers' motivation, performance, and satisfaction. If the leader clarifies the links or paths between effort and performance and between performance and reward, and if the leader rewards the followers with things that they value (assists the followers in attaining the followers' work goals), then the followers will be motivated.

Four styles of leader behaviour are identified:

1. *Directive*: A directive leader explicitly lets followers know what is expected of them by scheduling work, maintaining performance standards, giving specific guidance about what and how work is done, etc.
2. *Supportive*: A supportive leader shows concern for followers, is friendly and approachable, and treats members as equals.
3. *Participative*: A participative leader consults followers and uses their suggestions in making decisions.
4. *Achievement oriented*: An achievement-oriented leader sets challenging goals and expects high-level performance with continual improvement.

In order to determine which of these leadership styles is appropriate, two situational variables must be considered: the personal characteristics of the followers and environmental factors. The personal characteristics of the followers that are deemed important in determining the appropriate leadership style are:

1. The followers' perceptions of their ability: whether the followers perceive that they have the relevant experience and ability to do a given task;
2. The followers' locus of control: whether the followers believe that their actions can have influence; and
3. The followers' level of authoritarianism: whether the followers are willing to accept the influence of others.

Environmental factors are beyond the control of followers, but they are important to the followers' satisfaction and ability to perform effectively. The factors considered are:

---

[20] *Robert J. House and Terence R. Mitchell, "Path-Goal Theory of Leadership," Journal of Contemporary Business, Autumn 1974, 81-97.*

4. The formal authority system in the organization — The extent to which the system is well defined through rules and a clear chain of command.
5. The nature of the work groups — The extent to which group norms and dynamics allow followers to receive necessary cues to do the job and desired rewards from someone other than the leader.
6. The nature of the tasks — The extent to which the task is clearly defined, and routine.

An effective leadership style is one that complements the personal characteristics of the followers and the environmental factors. For example, if the followers do not perceive that they have the necessary ability to do the task, they have an external locus of control (they believe that events around them are shaped by forces beyond their control), and/or they are willing to accept the influence of others, then a directive style would be appropriate. If, however, the task is clearly defined and routine, then it is unlikely that a directive style of leadership would be desired by the followers — followers are already very aware of what it is they are to do, thereby making this style redundant. Similarly, if there is no clear chain of command or if there are group norms of autonomy, then followers would not welcome a directive style. This theory assumes that the leader can portray different styles more or less simultaneously, as required by different environmental factors and follower characteristics.

Models of situational leadership contribute to our understanding of leadership behavior by considering the influence of external / situational factors on the choice of leadership style. The path-goal model evaluates leadership according to the leader's ability to influence motivation, job satisfaction, and performance. Other situational theories of leadership (i.e., The Vroom-Jago Leader-Participation Model),[21] suggest that that leaders use participatory methods when the quality of the decision is important, the acceptance by subordinates is important, and the subordinates are trusted to pay attention to organization or group goals over their own preferences. If group acceptance of a decision is not required to be successfully implemented, then leaders can make the decision on their own.

Transformational Leadership

In contrast to the above "transactional" approaches to leadership, in which leaders establish what is required of their followers, the conditions that must be abided by, and the rewards that will be received when the requirements are fulfilled, Bernard Bass presents another view of the transformational leader.[22] Bass's transformational leaders achieve superior results from their employees by employing some or all of the following four components of transformational leadership:

7. *Charismatic leadership*: Leaders are perceived as having extraordinary capabilities, persistence, and determination; are willing to take risks; are consistent; are highly ethical and moral; and are admired, respected, and trusted.
8. *Inspirational motivation*: Leaders provide meaning and challenge to their followers' work; arouse team spirit and enthusiasm; clearly articulate a vision for the future; and demonstrate clear commitment to goals.
9. *Intellectual stimulation*: Leaders stimulate followers to be innovative and creative by questioning assumptions, reframing problems, and using and encouraging novel approaches to situations.
10. *Individualized consideration*: Leaders pay special attention to followers' needs for achievement and growth by acting as coach and mentor and personalizing their interactions. Followers are continually

---

[21] *Victor Vroom and Arthur Jago, The New Leadership: Managing Participation in Organizations, Prentice-Hall, Englewood Cliffs, NJ, 1988.*
[22] *Bernard Bass, Leadership and Performance Beyond Expectations, The Free Press, New York, 1985; Bernard Bass, Transformational Leadership: Industry, Military, and Educational Impact, Lawrence Erlbaum-Assoc., Mahwah, NJ, 1990.*

encouraged to reach higher levels of achievement, and new learning opportunities are created within a supportive climate.

Thus, transformational leadership goes beyond merely fulfilling the transactional aspects of leadership. It occurs when "leaders broaden and elevate the interests of their employees, when they generate awareness and acceptance of the purposes and missions of the group, and when they stir their employees to look beyond their own self-interest for the good of the group."[23]

Leader Character

In addition to traits and behaviours, recent research has identified the importance of leader character in shaping leader effectiveness. Work of Crossan, Gandz, and Seijts,[24] done in the wake of the 2008-2009 financial crisis, identified several virtues that along with personality traits and personal values, shaped leader character and ultimately outcomes for the organizations they led. By interviewing over 300 executive level leaders on three continents about actions that either led to failure or to relative success in the wake of the crisis, the group identified character as a central construct in differentiating those who succeeded from those who failed during this period.

FIGURE 3: Leader Character Model

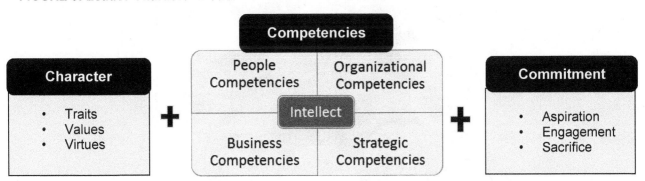

The leader character model identifies leader Character, Competencies, and Commitment as being central to the decisions leaders take (see **Figure 3**). The specific competencies effective leaders display are those scholars have long identified: competencies in business, managing people, understanding organizational complexities, and in thinking strategically. Commitment is seen as simply the desire on the leader's part to do the hard work necessary to put the competencies he or she possesses to work.

Character is the most difficult of the three to define and for many of us to talk about. Character, the authors argue, emerges from our personality traits, our personal values, and the presence or absence of a number of virtues. Many of us are familiar with personality traits and their effect on our own behavior. Personality attributes are formed early in our lives and remain stable predictors of our preferred states of being and often are important determinants of our actions. We are similarly familiar with the importance of personal values in shaping our behaviors. Those who value the feelings of others will tend to treat others with dignity and respect, for example. The virtues that helped shape character were more difficult to define and to talk about. In many instances, we tend to discuss character in its absence. However, understanding the importance of character development was central to the model Crossan, Gandz, and

---

[23] *Bernard Bass, Leadership and Performance Beyond Expectations, p. 70.*
[24] *M. Crossan, J. Gandz, and G. Seijts, "Developing Leadership Character," Ivey Business Journal, 2012.*

Seijts developed (see **Figure 4**). They argue that all individuals possess these character dimensions, but vary in the degree to which they are utilized. Interestingly, both too much of a particular character dimension as well as too little, can derail a leader. For example, a lack of Drive can just as easily ruin a leader as a surfeit – too much Drive can mean a leader lacks patience, fails to listen appropriately, or runs roughshod over those who plead for Temperance.

Subsequent work by the group identified the importance of leader candour in allowing character to be fully operational in an organizational setting. Without candour, people are unable or unwilling to have the difficult or uncomfortable conversations that are necessary to allowing the effects of leader character to be realized.[25]

FIGURE 4: Dimensions of Character

Work in this area continues with researchers interested not only in measuring character in individuals within organizations, but also understanding the organizational and interpersonal factors that create the conditions conducive to candour within workgroups and organizations. Unlike personality traits and personal values, character and candour are seen to be malleable features that can be developed over time, by gaining an understanding of what they are, where one has strengths as well as deficiencies, and how character dimensions and candour can best be used to lead successfully.

The Importance of Effective Leadership

Studies of leadership have a common thread — to determine what makes a leader effective. As the preceding discussion has revealed, there is no clear-cut answer — it depends on the situation. Yet for any organization there are many unforeseen situational factors that must be dealt with, including unexpected

---

[25] *M. Crossan and A. Byrne. "Linking Candour to Leadership Character With General Rick Hillier" Ivey Business Journal, 2013.*

changes in the environment and differences in organizational members' goals. Thus, it is important to the organization that its leaders have the ability to influence organizational members appropriately.

POWER AND INFLUENCE

Power is a fundamental concept in the study of organizational behaviour. Many authorities argue that the effective use of power is the most critical element of management.[26] Harvard professor John Kotter, who teaches a course on power, has the following to say:

> It makes me sick to hear economists tell students that their job is to maximize shareholder profits. Their job is going to be managing a whole host of constituencies: bosses, underlings, customers, suppliers, unions, you name it. Trying to get cooperation from different constituencies is an infinitely more difficult task than milking your business for money.[27]

Simply defined, power is the ability to mobilize resources to accomplish the work of the organization. Although we often associate power with domination or exacting behaviour under duress, power is not negative in and of itself. How it is used is critical in understanding its effects. Power is an essential issue for managers, since their success is fundamentally shaped by how effectively they use power. Managers who either do not have power or who cannot use it effectively ultimately are judged as poor managers.

In this section we consider different sources of power, the conditions for using power, and various influence strategies for using power.

Sources of Power

John French and Bertram Raven have identified five sources of power: reward power, coercive power, legitimate power, referent power, and expert power.[28]

11. *Reward power*. If a person controls rewards that someone else wants (e.g., pay or promotion), then that person is able to exert reward power. Reward power can be exerted only if the potential recipient values the rewards and believes that the power holder has the ability to give or withhold the reward.
12. *Coercive power*. If a person can punish someone (e.g., place a written warning in a personnel file or revoke privileges), then that power holder is able to exert coercive power. Coercive power can be exerted only if the other person dislikes the punishment and believes that the power holder has the ability to administer or terminate the punishment. Continued punishment or threat of punishment is necessary to maintain influence; if punishment or its threat is not present, then the effects will only be temporary.
13. *Legitimate power*. If a person is perceived as having the right to influence another, then that power holder is able to exert legitimate power. Typically, legitimate power is based on the position within the formal organizational hierarchy, whereby superiors have the right to influence subordinates' actions. Legitimate power can be exerted only if subordinates respect the formal hierarchy.

---

[26] David Whetten and Kim Cameron, *Developing Management Skills*, 4th ed., Addison Wesley, Reading, MA, 1998.
[27] Eric Gelman, Vicki Quade, J. M. Harrison, and Peter McAlevey, "Playing Office Politics," *Newsweek*, September 16, 1985, p. 56.
[28] John R. P. French and Bertram Raven, "The Bases of Social Power," in D. Cartwright and A. Zander (eds.), *Group Dynamics: Research and Theory*, 2nd ed., Row, Peterson, Evanston, IL, 1960, pp. 607-23.

14. *Referent power*. If a person is well liked by others and has personal qualities or characteristics that are admired, then that person is able to exert referent power. For example, individuals can exert referent power when other people seek their approval.

15. *Expert power*. If a person has information or knowledge relevant to a particular problem that another person does not have, then the power holder is able to exert expert power. In order for expert power to be used, others must acknowledge that the person actually possesses the critical information and skills. Furthermore, expert power is limited in influence, since it is situation specific.

Reward, coercive, and legitimate power are often referred to as position power — because of individuals' organizational positions, they have the ability to influence others through these avenues. Referent and expert power are often referred to as personal power — owing to individuals' attributes, they have the ability to influence others through these avenues.

Conditions for Using Power

Pfeffer identifies three necessary conditions for the use of power: interdependence, scarcity, and heterogeneous goals.[29]

16. *Interdependence*. Interdependence is a necessary precondition to the use of power. If individuals can do their work relatively independently, there is little opportunity for power to play a role. For example, if individuals have easy access to all the resources required to do their task or if they have a great deal of latitude in decision making, then they have considerably reduced (1) their reliance on other people, (2) the likelihood of conflict, and (3) the opportunity for others to exert influence over them. Conversely, as an individual's dependency on others increases, there is more opportunity for conflict and for others to use power in the relationship.

17. *Scarcity*. Scarcity is closely connected to the issue of interdependence. If there are no alternative sources of supply for a required resource and the supply is limited, the resource is deemed scarce. In situations of scarcity, dependence increases on the supplier of that resource. The situation of dependency, as noted above, results in the opportunity to exert power.

18. *Heterogeneous goals*. If everyone agrees on goals and if there is no ambiguity about these goals, the opportunity for the use of power is decreased. Under these circumstances there is likely to be little conflict or need to influence individuals' actions. However, this situation is highly unlikely in any organization. The more typical organizational situation is one where individuals or groups have different goals they wish to achieve and the goals are ambiguous. This sort of situation will likely lead to disagreements and conflict, thus allowing for the use of power.

Influence Strategies

Power is a necessary precondition for influence. Without power one cannot hope to secure the consent of others to accomplish organizational objectives. However, power must be converted to influence so that the consent of others is gained in ways that minimize their resistance and resentment. Influence strategies used by managers fall into three broad categories: retribution, reciprocity, and reason.[30] Each influence strategy relies on different mechanisms to secure compliance.

---

[29] Jeffrey Pfeffer, <u>Power Organizations</u>, Pitman Publishers, Marshfield, MA, 1981.
[30] David Whetten and Kim Cameron, Developing Management Skills.

Retribution

This strategy relies on coercive and reward power — on an explicit or implied threat to either impose a punishment or withhold a reward if the manager's request is not obeyed. This strategy is effective in producing the desired behaviour immediately and to the manager's exact specifications. It is best used when there is a significant imbalance in power between the manager and the subordinate, when commitment and quality are not important, or when resistance is likely anyway. However, this strategy also has significant drawbacks. It inevitably creates resentment on the part of the target, it often creates resistance to future requests, it requires the escalation of threats over time to maintain the same level of pressure, and it significantly reduces the target's levels of commitment and creativity. Effective managers use this technique sparingly — only in crises or as a last resort when other strategies have failed.

Reciprocity

This strategy works to satisfy the interests of both parties and is based on reward power. It has both direct and indirect forms. The direct form appears in the context of negotiation in which the parties bargain over the transaction they are making so that both are able to extract what they want from the deal. The indirect form appears as ingratiation, whereby the manager or subordinate grants favours to incur social debt or obligations that can be called on when help or support is needed. Examples in organizations include an employee's agreeing to work overtime in exchange for time off later or a subordinate doing small favours for a boss in exchange for the ability to take longer lunch hours on occasion.[31] The benefit of the reciprocity strategy is that it generates compliance without resentment or resistance. The main drawback of this strategy is that it tends to create an instrumental view of the workplace. It encourages people to believe that every request made of them is open for negotiation. The result is often that the individual will eventually do what the manager asks only when something is offered in return. It is a strategy that is best used when the parties are mutually dependent, when each has resources desired by the other, and when the parties have time to negotiate.

Reason

In exerting influence based on reason, the manager argues that compliance is warranted because of the inherent merits of the request. This strategy is most likely to be effective if subordinates see the manager as knowledgeable or as possessing attractive personal characteristics; in other words, the manager relies on expert and referent power. The major benefits of the reason strategy are the higher levels of compliance and internalized commitment it engenders, which, in turn, reduce the need for supervision and control and often increase subordinates' levels of initiative and creativity. The major drawback to this strategy, however, is the considerable time that is required to develop the necessary relationship and trust on which a reason strategy is based. It is best used when the parties have an ongoing relationship, common goals and values, and mutual respect.

Research has evaluated the effectiveness of these different strategies. Managers who rely largely on reason and logic to influence others are rated as highly effective by their superiors. In addition, they report low

---

[31] A.R. Cohen and D. L. Bradford, "Influence Without Authority: The Use of Alliances, Reciprocity, and Exchange to Accomplish Our Work," in Barry M. Staw (ed.), *Psychological Dimensions of Organizational Behavior*, MacMillan, New York, 1991, pp. 378-87.

levels of job-related stress and high levels of job satisfaction.[32] In contrast, managers who use other strategies to accomplish their objectives tend to receive lower performance ratings from their bosses and experience higher levels of both personal stress and job dissatisfaction.

ORGANIZATIONAL COMMITMENT, MOTIVATION, AND ENGAGEMENT

Organizational Commitment

Employee commitment is essential for long-term effectiveness of any organization. If employees are not committed to the goals that they are expected to pursue or to the organization as a whole, then effectiveness is decreased. Organizational commitment has been widely researched and has been found to have three components: affective, continuance, and normative.[33] Affective commitment is based on emotional connections to the organization and results in a desire to remain a member of the organization. The emotional connections can be to the people that work there, to the culture, or to the job that is being done. All of these connections lead to staying in the organization because the individual wants to stay. Continuance commitment is based on a need to stay with the organization and an awareness of the costs of leaving. Some ways in which this need can be developed are due to recognizing that other job prospects are not very good, that pay or promotion potential may be less, or that other family members will not want to be re-located. The final component of commitment is normative commitment – staying with the organization because of feeling that one ought to stay. Some ways in which normative commitment develop are from loyalty and appreciation for what others have done, and from a sense of obligation to clients or to see activities and projects through to their completion.

People will have varying degrees of commitment on each of these components but, regardless of the exact extent of each component, understanding where commitment arises from can help managers focus their actions more appropriately. When people are not committed to the organization, it is very difficult for managers to motivate them.

Motivation

The motivation of employees is critical for all managers. Managers want employees who are highly motivated — who are willing to persist in their efforts to achieve particular goals. To motivate employees, it helps to have a basic understanding of the nature of human motivation, a topic that has been the subject of considerable research over the years. Attention has been paid to what energizes people in terms of their needs and desires and how the process of motivation works.

McClelland's Need Theory

The most supported theory of what energizes people in terms of their needs and desires is McClelland's need theory.[34] Needs are important drivers of behaviour. People are motivated to fulfill those needs that are most important to them by pursuing behaviours that enable them to satisfy these needs. McClelland identifies three fundamental needs that are important to understanding motivation in organizational

[32] D. Kipnis and S. M. Schmidt, "Upward-Influence Styles: Relationship with Performance Evaluations, Salary, and Stress," *Administrative Science Quarterly*, 33(1988): 528-42.
[33] J.P. Meyer and N.J. Allen, "A Three-Component Model Conceptualization of Organizational Commitment," *Human Resource Management Review*, 1 (1991): 61-89.
[34] David C. McClelland, *Human Motivation*, Cambridge University Press, Cambridge, 1987, p. 9.

settings: the need for achievement, the need for affiliation, and the need for power. People high in any of these needs are likely to be motivated by situations in which they perceive they can satisfy these needs.

The *need for achievement* is characterized by a drive to excel. Individuals with a high need for achievement like personal responsibility for performance results, rapid feedback on performance, and moderately challenging goals. In particular, these people seek to do things better than others and to rise to challenges. If goals or tasks are too easy, such individuals are not challenged and will want to move on to something new. If goals or tasks are too difficult, such individuals will not want to engage in these tasks since they feel they will be unsuccessful. When working in a group situation, they like feedback about their task performance and they like knowing whether they are doing better than others. They care little about how well they get along with group members and are too focused on their own performance to notice the achievement orientation of others in their group.

People with a high need for achievement tend to be interested in and do well at business. Business requires dealing with moderate levels of risk, assuming personal responsibility, being innovative, and paying attention to performance feedback in terms of profits and costs. These people are particularly good at sales and entrepreneurial activity, since they are focused on managing their own performance. Nonetheless, people high in need for achievement are typically less effective as managers. They find it hard to focus on others and to delegate since they like to take personal responsibility for their tasks.

The *need for affiliation* is characterized by a desire to interact with other people. Maintaining or establishing close, friendly interpersonal relationships is what drives such individuals. People who are high in need for affiliation work harder and get better outcomes when their manager is warm and friendly. When working in groups, they prefer feedback on how well the group is getting along as opposed to feedback on how well the group is performing the task. They also learn social relationships more quickly, typically engage in more dialogue, and act to avoid conflict when possible.

Individuals with a high need for affiliation tend to be less successful as managers. Managers often must act competitively, try to influence others, and make decisions that hurt other people's feelings. These activities are difficult for people with a high need for affiliation who prefer to avoid conflict. However, if the manager's job is to be an integrator — to help people to resolve their differences and to get along — those high in need for affiliation are more successful.

The *need for power* is characterized by a desire to influence others. Being in charge, being influential, and having an impact, drive individuals high in this need. Individuals who are high in the need for power prefer situations where they can influence others, and they tend to collect symbols of power (prestige possessions). When working in a group, people with a high need for power behave in ways that make them more visible to other group members and prefer to take on dominant, controlling roles. They also prefer to surround themselves with less known or less assertive individuals who can be led. Not surprisingly, those with a high need for power are not best liked, nor are they considered to have contributed most to getting the job done. They are, however, judged to be influential and to have talked a lot. Individuals who are seen as effective managers tend to have a relatively high need for power and a lower need for affiliation.

A caveat must be added to the above discussion of needs. It must be made clear that needs and abilities are two distinct things. People with a low need for achievement are not necessarily low achievers. Rather, they could in fact be high achievers. What differentiates them from people with a high need for achievement is those with a high need for achievement require that they find outlets to satisfy their need for achievement if they are to be satisfied at work. People with a low need for achievement require no such outlets to be satisfied at work.

Equity Theory

Equity theory[35] is what is known as a process theory of motivation — a theory concerned with how individuals become motivated. Equity theory predicts that we will engage in certain activities to the extent that we perceive the situation to be fair and equitable. In general, we compare what we receive in return for our efforts with what others in similar situations receive relative to their efforts. If this comparison of input to output ratios is equal, then we perceive equity and will continue with the activity. In assessing inputs we consider factors such as effort, performance level, education, and time. In assessing outputs we consider factors such as pay, recognition, and other rewards.

Situations can be perceived as inequitable for two reasons: we are being over-rewarded or we are being under-rewarded. Often people are more comfortable with being over-rewarded than with being under-rewarded. Nonetheless, in situations of over-reward, people may feel guilty and be motivated to try to decrease the imbalance. The common means of decreasing the imbalance is to increase the level of input by increasing either the amount or the quality of the work done.

When we perceive that we are under-rewarded, we are motivated to alter the level of input to bring the situation into balance either by working less or lowering the quality of our work. In more extreme instances, we simply quit. People also may be motivated to try to alter the outcome side of the equation by seeking raises or other forms of recognition.

Although the theory seems relatively simple, the difficulty for the manager reveals itself when we recognize that equity is based on people's perceptions. People can perceptually distort either their performance or the comparison person's performance to produce equity.

Regardless of the accuracy of my perceptions of my inputs and outcomes or the other person's inputs or outcomes, I will make an assessment of the equity of the situation. I may not, in fact, know all of your inputs, nor may I weigh all the inputs in a similar fashion to you or to the manager as I am doing my mental calculations of equity. Unfortunately for the manager, though, the perceptions of equity or inequity influence how people are motivated and, hence, how they behave.

Expectancy Theory

Expectancy theory,[36] another process theory of motivation, is a probabilistic model of motivation. It can be summarized by the following equation:

Motivation = Expectancy ¥ Instrumentality ¥ Valence

Expectancy is the probability that a certain level of effort will lead to a certain level of performance as assessed by the individual; *instrumentality* is the probability that a certain level of performance will lead to a certain level of the reward as assessed by the individual; and *valence* is the attractiveness of the reward to the individual.

---

[35] *Stacey J. Adams, "Inequity in Social Exchange," in L. Berkowitz (ed.), Advances in Experimental Psychology, Academic Press, New York, 1965, pp. 267-99.*
[36] *Victor H. Vroom, Work and Motivation (New York: John Wiley & Sons, 1964); Frank J, Landy and Don A. Trumbo, "Instrumentality Theory," in R. M. Steers and L. W. Porters (eds.), Motivation and Work Behavior, McGraw-Hill, New York, 1983, pp. 72-81.*

The model suggests that for each activity a person will assess the likelihood that his or her efforts will lead to performance, that his or her performance will lead to the reward, and that he or she values the reward. If any of these relationships are assessed to be zero, there will be no motivation to engage in that activity. The activity that the person will be motivated to engage in is the one in which the product of these relationships is the greatest.

It may be somewhat difficult for managers to use this theory to motivate subordinates, since they may not know all of the activities an employee is considering engaging in or exactly what each employee values. Nonetheless, managers can ensure that the link between effort and performance is clear or attainable (increasing expectancy). They can also clarify the link between performance and reward (increasing instrumentality). Finally, they can try to determine what rewards their employees will value (increasing valence).

For example, managers at Beth Israel Hospital in Boston, Massachusetts, learned through the implementation of a gainsharing plan[37] that not all employees are equally motivated by the same program. Specifically, the valence attributed to rewards varied considerably between employee groups. Housekeepers and dietary workers, for example, were highly motivated to seek out ways to save the hospital money and to share in the payouts that such savings produced. Receiving an additional $25 or $30 per month was motivating for these relatively low paid employees. Physicians, on the other hand, who often earned hundreds of thousands of dollars per year, placed little valence on rewards of this magnitude and therefore had little motivation to seek out and implement changes that could produce savings for the hospital.

Motivating employees is a complex activity. Managers must think not only about how the process of motivation works but also about what motivates their employees, neither of which is easy to ascertain. However, if managers can try to understand what their individual employees need or value and try to deliver rewards that are equitable, they can go a long ways toward improving their employees' motivation.

Employee Engagement

Engaged employees, those who are inspired by their work and are fully committed, are important for the success of an organization and have been shown to drive bottom line results. As a manager there are several actions that one can take to help increase engagement. The 10C's of employee engagement,[38] listed in **Table 2**, are important to consider. If employees are unengaged, then the manager needs to try to consider why they are not engaged and to take actions to remedy this situation.

Table 2: 10 C's of Employee Engagement

Connect	Managers need to connect with employees and have a positive relationship with them.	**Contribute**	Managers need to let employees know how their tasks contribute to the organization in a meaningful way

---

[37] Raymond A. Friedman and Caitlin Dienard, *Prepare /21 at "Beth Israel Hospital (A),"* case 9-491-045, *Harvard Business School*, 1991, 28 pp.
[38] G.H. Seijts and D. Crim, What Engages Employees the Most or, The Ten C's of Employee Engagement, <u>Ivey Business Journal</u>, March/April 2006.

Career	Managers need to provide meaningful and challenging work for employees and provide them with career advancement opportunities	Control	Managers need to allow employees the ability to control their work and to be involved in decisions that will impact them
Clarity	Managers need to provide a clear direction for their employees	Collaborate	Managers need to foster a team environment where employees are willing to trust and collaborate with one another
Convey	Managers need to communicate their expectations and provide feedback for employees	Credibility	Managers must maintain a high standard for themselves and their employees
Congratulate	Managers need to acknowledge good performance when it happens	Confidence	Managers must create confidence in themselves and the organization for their employees

COGNITIVE DIFFERENCES

Cognitive differences importantly shape behaviour in organizations. They affect how we see the world and respond to various stimuli. As a manager, it is important to understand such individual differences in order to foresee how others might respond, to structure tasks so that they will be readily accepted, and to understand your own preconceptions in dealing with others. In this section, we highlight three important cognitive differences: personality, learning style, and perception.

Personality

Research on personality has been extensive. However, researchers in this field continue to debate a number of questions, including, How is one's personality determined? and, What are the critical dimensions of personality? What can be agreed upon, however, is that personality is defined by the stable, personal characteristics that lead to consistent behaviour. Furthermore, researchers have largely come to agree that these characteristics are inherited as well as learned and that personality is defined early in life.

Hundreds, if not thousands, of personality traits have been identified and investigated over time. We focus here on one that has been extensively studied and that has obvious organizational implications: locus of control. Locus of control refers to the degree to which individuals believe that they can control events affecting them. Individuals with a high internal locus of control believe that they largely (but not totally) determine events in their lives. In contrast, people with an external locus of control believe that events around them are largely shaped by forces beyond their control — by other people, chance, or fate.

An individual's locus of control has been shown to be significant in predicting some aspects of job behaviour.[39] For example, people with a high internal locus of control have been shown to perform better in work that requires complex information processing and learning, that requires initiative and independent

---

[39] J.B. Miner, _Industrial and Organizational Psychology_, McGraw-Hill, New York, 1992.

action, that requires high motivation, and that provides valued rewards in return for greater effort. In contrast, when the work requires compliance and conformity, individuals with a high external locus of control perform better.

Learning Style

It is also important for a manager to be aware of an individual's learning or cognitive style. Often confused with a measure of personality, the Myers-Briggs Type Indicator (MBTI) test classifies individuals into one of 16 categories based on a set of four bipolar dimensions:

Extroversion (externally directed)	–	**I**ntroversion (introspective)
Sensing (relies on facts)	–	**IN**tuitive (explores possibilities)
Thinking (logical and analytical)	–	**F**eeling (emotional and sympathetic)
Judgment (structured and organized)	–	**P**erception (adaptable)

(The boldfaced letters are used as abbreviations for the dimensions and are combined to indicate a person's category for each of the four dimensions.)

Research on the MBTI suggests that certain types (such as INTJ or ESFP) are better suited for particular occupations.[40] For example, on the sensing–intuitive dimension, over 80 per cent of steelworkers, police detectives, and factory supervisors prefer S over N. In contrast, over 80 per cent of research assistants, social scientists, writers, artists, and entertainers prefer N over S.

The extroversion–introversion dimension also has organizational implications. Extroverts need stimulation in the form of social activity, frequent change in their environment, and intense colours or noise. Introverts, in contrast, require little stimulation from the external environment. They may perform better than their extroverted counterparts on repetitive tasks or in environments that provide little sensory stimulation.

To be effective, managers need to recognize and be able to adapt to the learning styles of their subordinates. For example, learning style may affect how and the extent to which managers organize their subordinates' tasks — high Js prefer structured tasks, whereas high Ps prefer a more unstructured work environment. Similarly, a manager of a high S may need to provide the subordinate with sufficient information to accomplish the task, while a manager of a high N may not need to provide such information, but rather may allow the subordinate more latitude in exploring a range of possibilities.

The MBTI is commonly used for employee and work group development, leadership training, and career planning. By identifying individuals' preferences, the MBTI can help people in organizations to better understand their own behavior and that of others. Some of the insights that it can help to provide are: preferences in method of communication; preferences in work situations; and areas for personal development.[41]

It is unadvisable to use the MBTI for selection purposes. Due to the manner in which the MBTI questionnaire is designed, respondents are forced to choose between alternatives. For example, are you usually (a) a "good mixer," or (b) rather quiet and reserved? Thus, the scores represent the preference of

---

[40] *Isabel Briggs Myers and Mary H. MCCaulley, A Guide to the Development and Use of the Myers-Briggs Type Indicator, Consulting Psychologists Press, Palo Alto, CA, 1985.*
[41] *Sandra Krebs Hirsch and Jean Kummerow, Introduction to Type in Organizations, 2nd ed., Consulting Psychologists Press, Palo Alto, Calif.*

the individual between the alternatives and are only meaningful when making comparisons regarding a single respondent's answers.[42] It does not speak to abilities or skills. MBTI scores cannot be meaningfully correlated with job performance measures - a requirement if one were to use these scores for selection purposes.

Perception

All of us continuously engage in the process of perception. We are constantly bombarded with sensory stimuli, but we pay attention to only a small portion of them. It is through the process of perception that we organize, interpret, and give meaning to our environment. The perceptual process affects what we notice and how we interpret or make sense of our observations. Our perceptions are influenced by who we are, what we are perceiving, and the situation. Thus, different people perceive different things, and different people perceive the same thing differently.

Our motives, our experiences and expectations, and our attitudes and beliefs all influence the way we perceive targets (objects, people, or events). For example, if you are hungry and everything you see reminds you of food, your perceptions are being influenced by your motives (in this case, hunger). Similarly, if every time you complete a task your boss finds fault with it and you start to think your boss is just someone who likes to find faults no matter what the situation, your perceptions are being influenced by your past experiences and expectations. In fact, if your boss praises you, you will likely be surprised.

In addition, characteristics of the target influence our perception. If the target stands out in some way, owing to appearance or some other attribute, we are more likely to notice or perceive it. For example, advertisers often use moving or blinking signs to promote their products because they realize that we are more likely to pay attention to those signs than to ones that are not changing or moving.

Finally, the situation will influence whether and how an object or person is perceived. For example, if a person has a very loud voice, it is possible that he or she will go unnoticed at a large party but it is very likely that he or she will be noticed in the library. Thus, the background or the situation affects how the figure or the target is perceived. Similarly, the type of organizational context in which people work will influence how they perceive events and the actions of other people. If a new employee in an organization that is very cooperative displays a self-serving behaviour, not only will that behaviour be noticed, but it may also be frowned on.

Sources of Perceptual Errors

Because we are faced with so much information from our environment, we tend to use shortcuts to help process information faster. Unfortunately, many of these shortcuts result in misreading the situation, since we are making judgments using only a portion of the information available to us. Some of the sources of perceptual errors are selectivity, assumed similarity, stereotyping, the halo effect, and the recency and primacy effects.

Selectivity occurs when we attend to only a portion of the information available based on our interests, experiences, and expectations. As a result, we may miss important information that could help us to more accurately interpret events in our environment. In organizations, it is not uncommon for departments to

---

[42] *Robert Gatewood and Hubert Field, Human Resource Selection, 5th ed. Harcourt College Publishers, New York, 2001, p. 611.*

narrowly focus on resolving issues from the perspective of their own department, as opposed to using a broader approach. In doing so, the solution may fit well within the context of the one department, but it may lead to a different set of problems for another department that it must deal with.

Assumed similarity occurs when we project our beliefs, attitudes, or motives onto others. For example, if managers decide that they should give their subordinates more challenging jobs because the managers like to be challenged, they are operating under the assumption of assumed similarity. If, in fact, the subordinates do not want more challenging jobs, they may be unhappy with the changes to their work.

Stereotyping occurs when we judge others based on the group they belong to. This grouping can be on the basis of age, gender, race/ethnicity, occupation, or any other characteristic that is seen to distinguish one group of people from another. The danger with stereotyping is that there are many ways in which people may differ, despite having one area of obvious similarity. For example, one researcher found that a number of the managers in her study thought that women should be happy to receive emotional rewards in place of monetary rewards because women were motivated by noneconomic, emotional factors.[43] Clearly, making decisions based on stereotyping can lead to erroneous conclusions!

The *halo effect* occurs when we generate a general impression about someone based on a single positive characteristic. The reality may be that the person is good at that particular activity, but he or she may not be good at all other activities. For example, if a manager notices that an employee is very good at organizing his or her thoughts on paper, it would be erroneous for the manager to assume that the employee would necessarily be good at delivering a speech to a large audience. The skills required for these two activities, although overlapping, are somewhat different.

The *recency effect* occurs when we weigh the most recent information about a person more heavily than the other information that we have. The *primacy effect* occurs when we use the limited information from our first meeting with a person to form stable impressions about that person. In both cases, we are using limited information to draw general conclusions about a person which we cannot be certain will hold true over time or in different situations.

Attribution

When we try to explain the behaviours of ourselves and other people, we are making attributions. Attribution theory attempts to explain how we judge people based on the meaning we give to a behaviour.[44] There are two basic explanations of why people behave as they do:

19. *Dispositional attributions*: People behave the way they do because of factors under their control, such as their personality, ability, effort, or level of knowledge.
20. *Situational attributions*: People behave the way they do because of factors in the situation beyond their control, such as luck, chance, or something specific about the nature of the environment.

The general tendency of observers is to perceive that other people's behaviour is internally controlled, or due to disposition, when outcomes are unfavourable. Yet, we tend to attribute our own unfavourable outcomes to the situation. In contrast, when we explain our own favourable outcomes, we are more than

---

[43] Rosabeth Moss Kanter, *Men and Women of the Corporation*, Basic Books, New York, 1977.
[44] Edward E. Jones, David E. Kanouse, Harold H. Kelley, Richard E. Nisbett, Stuart Valins, and Bernard Weiner, *Attribution: Perceiving the Causes of Behavior*, General Learning Press, Morristown, NJ, 1972.

willing to attest that they were due to our disposition. For others, however, we attribute their success to the situation.

If we assume that problem behaviour is internally controllable, we make a dispositional attribution and then focus our responses on trying to "fix" or replace the person. If, on the other hand, we assume that problem behaviour is externally caused, we make a situational attribution and then focus our responses on the organizational systems that may have contributed to the situation. Such attributions typically occur when we lack sufficient information about other people. To make more accurate attributions, managers should consider the following factors:

- *Distinctiveness*: Does the person display different behaviours in different situations? If the answer is yes, then the current behaviour is likely a result of the situation. If the answer is no, then the current behaviour is likely a result of the person's disposition.
- *Consensus*: Do other people display similar behaviours in a similar situation? If the answer is yes, then the current behaviour is likely a result of the situation. If the answer is no, then the current behaviour is likely a result of the person's disposition.
- *Consistency*: Does the same person display similar behaviours in the same or similar situations? If the answer is yes, then the current behaviour is likely a result of the person's disposition. If the answer is no, then the current behaviour is likely a result of the situation.

Managers need to understand the potential sources of differences in how individuals see, interpret, and respond to the world around them. By understanding people's personality characteristics and individual learning styles, a manager can ensure that job assignments and leadership styles are appropriate to the individual. Managers also gain by understanding how we make attributions about people's behaviours.

Diversity

The composition of Canadian organizations today is more diverse than it has been at any other time in history. Several factors have come together to produce this unprecedented diversity. First, the dramatic inflow of women into the work force in the 1960s and 1970s constitutes one of the most significant events in recent economic history. In 1951 only 10 per cent of married women worked outside the home; by 1981, 51 per cent of married women did so.[45] Second, changes in patterns of Canadian immigration have been equally dramatic. In the 1950s, 80 per cent of immigrants came from Great Britain or Europe.[46] By the 1980s, almost 85 per cent of immigrants into Canada came from developing nations, radically changing the racial and ethnic makeup of Canada's cities, as well as its organizations. By 2006, when Canada's population is slated to move over the 30 million mark, it is estimated that 18 per cent of the population will be made up of visible minorities.[47] Third, demographics have played an important role in changing the makeup of Canadian organizations. As the baby boom has moved through the work force, organizations' members have aged, on average. The median age in the Canadian population has increased by nearly 11 years since the early 1970s.[48] Finally, as the environment becomes increasingly competitive, organizations must look to traditionally underrepresented portions of the labour force, including those with disabilities. Gender, race and ethnicity, age, and disability are four important dimensions of diversity that affect relations within organizations.

---

[45] *Morley Gunderson and Craig Riddell, Labour Market Economics, McGraw-Hill Ryerson, Toronto, ON, 1988.*
[46] *Trevor Wilson, Diversity at Work.*
[47] *C. Taylor, "Building a Case for Diversity," Canadian Business Review, 22(1)(1995): 12-15.*
[48] *Ibid.*

More than ever before, it is critical that this diverse work force be managed effectively to ensure organizational success in today's highly competitive environment. Recognizing individual differences, their sources, and their likely impacts can help a manager be more effective in this regard. The purpose of this section is twofold: to outline some core dimensions of diversity and how they may affect individual behaviour in organizations and to present evidence of the implications for organizational competitiveness of managing diversity well.

Race/Ethnicity

Changing immigration patterns have had an enormous impact on the makeup of Canadian organizations. The integration of these diverse populations into the work force creates two sets of challenges for managers. The first is the challenge of integrating people who bring diverse experiences, attitudes, assumptions, and beliefs to the organization. The second is the challenge of managing and overcoming racism — whether it is overt and intentional or not. Racism discounts or prevents the contributions by organizational members who are seen to be inferior to the dominant group.

Gender

The unprecedented entry of women into the labour force over the past three decades has led to profound organizational changes. Although they now constitute nearly half the work force, women are still underrepresented in top-management positions, making up only 6 per cent of such positions in the industrialized world.[49] Recognition of this disparity is motivating many organizations to change how women are treated.

Gender role stereotypes have limited women's mobility within organizations. Attitudes about the managerial effectiveness of women may affect how women's performance is assessed. They may also influence the granting or withholding of developmental opportunities. Organizations tackling diversity issues have sought to address such stereotyping through workshops, mentoring programs, and leadership development programs especially for women.

In addition to the challenges posed by stereotypes, women face a set of constraints related to their gender. Women remain the predominant primary caregivers for children and for the elderly. These extra-organizational constraints often mean that women require additional flexibility in terms of hours, travel demands, and time off for bearing and raising children. Accommodating this set of needs requires organizational adaptation in order for an organization to access and use the talents and abilities of women to full effect. Interestingly, innovations designed mainly for women (such as the so-called Mommy Track, in which women are able to take their careers onto a slower track while in the midst of their childbearing years) have helped men too. There are increasing numbers of men who share in the care of their young children or who are raising children themselves as single parents. Both women and men benefit from such policies, as do their organizations, which gain their added attention and commitment.

---

[49] *R. J. Burke and C. A. McKeen, "Do Women at the Top Make a Difference? Gender Proportions and the Experiences of Managerial and Professional Women," Human Relations, 49(8) (1996): 1093-1104.*

Age

The demographic makeup of Canadian society is reflected inside Canadian organizations. Three major age groups are currently in the work force, and a fourth will begin to enter in the next few years. Each cohort brings distinctive interests to the workplace.[50]

The Blessed Ones, Born 1930–1945, Population 4.3 Million

People in this small cohort were born lucky; with no competition in the job market, they couldn't help but make it. The unprecedented economic boom of the 1950s and 1960s benefited this generation immeasurably.

Baby Boomers, Born 1946–1966, Population 9.8 Million

The defining demographic cohort of Canadian life, the baby boom actually has two phases:

- **The Woodstock Generation, Born 1946–1960, Population 5.6 Million**
  This group made it to the job market before Generation X, but the competition resulting from their sheer numbers forced them to embrace the world of debt.
- **Generation X, Born 1961–1966, Population 4.2 Million**
  This group was demographically cursed. With spotty employment opportunities, Gen-Xers were often found living in basement apartments well into early adulthood.

Baby Busters, Born 1967–1978, Population 5.3 Million

Born in the wake of the baby boom crest, members of this cohort like to paint themselves as disaffected. They face roomier job market opportunities as they grow older — their McJobs will eventually turn into something meatier.

Millennials / Generation Y, Born 1979–2000, Population 9.5 Million

Relatively high numbers in this group will make competition for jobs stiff. This generation tends to be tech savvy, family centric, achievement oriented, and attention craving. Although, they are perceived to be different, survey research indicates that they share similar attributes to earlier generations including viewing work as a vehicle for personal fulfillment, valuing workplace culture, and a supportive work environment with a high priority on career development and flexibility.[51]

Perhaps the critical age-related tension that faces managers is the tension between Baby Boomers and Baby Busters. The two groups often hold stereotypes of the other, leading to dysfunctional working relationships. For example, Baby Busters perceive that Baby Boomers have achieved their positions and status simply by being born at the right time. In contrast, Baby Boomers perceive Baby Busters as cocky, unwilling to pay their dues, disloyal, and uncommitted to the organization.[52]

---

[50] Elaine O'Reilly, "Making Career Sense of Labour Market Information," 2nd ed., BC WorkInfoNet, January 2001, makingcareersense.org/CHAPTER2/CHAP2-11.HTM, accessed September 14, 2003.

[51] D. Schell, F. Follero-Pugh, and D. Lloyd, "Making Career Sense of Labour Market Information," 2010 ed., www.aspect.bc.ca/userfiles/file/publicfiles/MCSLMI_2010.pdf, accessed March 31, 2015.

[52] Don Hellriegel, John W. Slocum, Jr., Richard W. Woodman, and N. Sue Bruning, Organizational Behaviour, 8th, Canadian ed., ITP Nelson, Toronto, 1998.

Disability

A final important source of diversity in the Canadian workplace is disability. Surveys by Statistics Canada[53] tell us that roughly 13 per cent of the labour force (those between the ages of 15 and 65) is disabled, with only 50 per cent of those people gainfully employed compared to 70 per cent of the labour force that is not disabled. However, over 90 per cent of those who are under 35 and disabled describe their disability as mild to moderate. Moreover, while 85 per cent of disabled people in the workforce report some level of limitation at work, less than 20 per cent report the need for accommodation in the workplace. Finally, the disabled also comprise a well educated proportion of the workforce with over half having completed a high school education and one third having completed post secondary diplomas or degrees. Going forward, employers cannot afford to ignore this underutilized segment of the Canadian workforce

Implications of Managing Diversity for Organizational Competitiveness

Taylor Cox and Stacy Blake, from the University of Michigan, have reviewed the research literature to assess the effects of successful management of diversity on organizational competitiveness. Among their findings are the following highlights. Cox and Blake cite Kanter's study, which finds that companies that have done a better job than most in eradicating sexism, racism, and classism and that have tended to employ more women and members of visible minorities are more innovative than comparable others.[54] The conclusion drawn is that minority views can stimulate alternative approaches and generate new insights in task groups. Groups exposed to minority viewpoints are more creative than are more homogeneous groups.[55]

Similar studies on groups of varying degrees of homogeneity find that more diversity (up to a point) produces decisions of better quality than more homogeneous groups. Cox and Blake summarize, "Decision quality is best when neither excessive diversity nor excessive homogeneity are present."[56] Where a minority view is present, a larger number of alternatives are considered, assumptions are more carefully scrutinized, and possible implications of various alternatives are more carefully thought out.

Finally, the effective management of diversity enhances organizational flexibility. This occurs for two reasons. First, it appears that women and racio-ethnic minorities tend to have more flexible cognitive structures than do white males. Research has indicated, for example, that women tend to have a higher tolerance for ambiguity than do men, which has been linked to factors related to flexibility, such as cognitive complexity and the ability to excel in undertaking ambiguous tasks.[57] Moreover, there is evidence that as the organization becomes more tolerant of diverse viewpoints based on age, gender, and racio-ethnic diversity, it becomes more open to new ideas in general, making it in turn more fluid and adaptable.[58]

---

[53] Source: Statistics Canada, "Health and Activity Limitation Survey, 1991," Survey of Labour and Income Dynamics (1994).
[54] Rosabeth Moss Kanter, The Change Masters, Simon & Schuster, New York, 1983.
[55] Charlene Jeanne Nemeth, "Differential Contributions of Majority and Minority Influence," Psychology Review, 93(1986): 23-32.
[56] Taylor H. Cox and Stacey Blake, "Managing Cultural Diversity: Implications for Organizational Performance," Academy of Management Executive, 5(3) (1991): 51.
[57] Naomi G. Rotter and Agnes N. O'Connell, "The Relationships Among Sex-Role Orientation Cognitive Complexity, and Tolerance for Ambiguity," Sex Roles, 8(12) (1982): 1209-20; David R. Shaffer et al., "Interactive Effects of Ambiguity Tolerance and Task Effort on Dissonance Reduction," Journal of Personality, 41, (2) (1973): 45-54.
[58] Taylor H. Cox and Stacey Blake, "Managing Cultural Diversity," 45-54.

SUMMARY

In this chapter we have introduced you to a number of theories and concepts that you will find useful in thinking about managing people in organizations. As this chapter has pointed out, the job of a manager requires knowledge not only of the structures and culture of the organization, but also of how people are motivated, led, and persuaded to work toward the goals of the organization. Moreover, as the workplace becomes more diverse and competition more intense, the job of the manager is made increasingly complex. An understanding of individual differences — both cognitive and demographic — becomes even more important in understanding how to manage people effectively. As you approach the challenge of management, we hope you will use this knowledge to think creatively about approaches to various individuals and situations and will be well equipped to manage people effectively.

Revisiting Burns and Stalker: Formal Structure and New Venture Performance in Emerging Economic Sectors
Author(s): Wesley D. Sine, Hitoshi Mitsuhashi and David A. Kirsch
Source: *The Academy of Management Journal*, Vol. 49, No. 1 (Feb., 2006), pp. 121-132
Published by: Academy of Management
Stable URL: http://www.jstor.org/stable/20159749
Accessed: 19-08-2014 20:22 UTC

© Academy of Management Journal
2006, Vol. 49, No. 1, 121–132.

REVISITING BURNS AND STALKER: FORMAL STRUCTURE AND NEW VENTURE PERFORMANCE IN EMERGING ECONOMIC SECTORS

WESLEY D. SINE
Cornell University

HITOSHI MITSUHASHI
University of Tsukuba

DAVID A. KIRSCH
University of Maryland

This study examines the effects of formal structure on the performance of new ventures in the emergent Internet sector during the years 1996–2001. Burns and Stalker (1961) argued that in dynamic economic sectors, firms with organic structures are more effective than those with more mechanistic structures. We suggest this proposition does not hold for new ventures in turbulent, emergent economic sectors. Building on Stinchcombe's (1965) arguments concerning new ventures' liability of newness, we hypothesize that new ventures with higher founding team formalization, specialization, and administrative intensity outperform those with more organic organizational structures. Results support these hypotheses.

Since the seminal work of Burns and Stalker (1961), researchers have considered the organic organizational form, characterized by a lack of formally defined tasks and an emphasis on horizontal as opposed to vertical coordination to be the exemplar structure for firms operating in turbulent environments. Although past research supports this proposition for large, established firms, is it also true for small, new organizations in turbulent, emerging economic sectors? In this study, we explore the limits of this conventional wisdom by examining how structural features influence performance during the earliest phase of organizational existence in a turbulent setting assumed to be inhospitable to mechanistic structure.

In dynamic contexts, new ventures and large,

mature organizations face fundamentally different structural challenges (Cameron & Quinn, 1983; Gilbert, 2005, 2006; Kimberly, 1979; Shane, 2003). These differences are particularly evident in emergent economic sectors, which are typically characterized by turbulence and uncertainty (Aldrich, 1999; Sine & David, 2003). As a result of embedded formalized roles and routines, functional silos, and administration by managers insulated by multiple bureaucratic layers from the changing realities of the marketplace, large, mature organizations often have difficulty responding to environmental turbulence (Mintzberg, 1978). In contrast, new ventures in emerging sectors initially lack formalized roles and routines and are small, flexible, and innovative; their employees and founding team have frequent interactions with customers. These firms are, in essence, founded as a reaction to opportunities in a changing environment. Instead of needing more flexibility, these organizations suffer from a structural "liability of newness" (Stinchcombe, 1965).

Herein lies the puzzle. On the one hand, both theorists and practitioners suggest that in turbulent environments, organizations should become more organic (Burns & Stalker, 1961). On the other hand, in his classic essay, Stinchcombe (1965) argued that one of the key reasons that new organizations in new economic sectors are at a disadvantage vis-à-vis older, established firms is their *lack* of struc-

Hitoshi Mitsuhashi and David Kirsch contributed equally to this research. Wesley Sine acknowledges support from the Robert H. Smith School of Business at the University of Maryland and the Johnson Graduate School of Management at Cornell University. Research support to Hitoshi Mitsuhashi was provided by the Japanese Ministry of Education, Culture, Sports, Science, and Technology's Grant-in-Aid for Young Scientists (A) (15683003). David Kirsch acknowledges financial support from the Robert H. Smith School of Business and the Alfred P. Sloan Foundation. We are grateful to Chris Robinson of OneSource/Corptech and to Brandon Lee for their assistance, and we thank Marshall Schminke and three anonymous reviewers for their helpful comments.

ture, which results in role ambiguity and uncertainty. High levels of uncertainty impede individual and organizational action (David & Han, 2003; O'Toole & Meier, 2003). Formalized organizational roles reduce work ambiguity, enable individual focus, learning, and decision making, decrease the cost of coordination, and increase efficiency (Perrow, 1986), all outcomes of vital importance for new ventures with meager resources. Moreover, Stinchcombe (1965) suggested that new ventures in emerging sectors not only need formalization and specialization, but also require greater managerial resources than mature firms. Whereas mature firms are often impeded by intensive administration and the structural inertia of legacy bureaucracies, new ventures need extensive managerial resources and a structural framework to reduce uncertainty and increase organizational efficiency and responsiveness.

To examine these issues, we reviewed classical and contemporary literature on organizational structure. Focusing on three fundamental structural attributes of new ventures—(1) role formalization in founding teams,[1] (2) specialization in founding teams, and (3) administrative intensity—we assessed their relative contributions to firm performance. We explored these questions using a unique sample of Internet firms, all founded in 1996, the year the Internet sector "took off." We found that where the benefits of flexibility should have been the greatest, among new ventures in a highly turbulent environment, instead embracing basic structural features was positively associated with strong performance.

By examining these questions, this study contributes to theory about organizational design and structure. Our research demonstrates that Burns and Stalker's classic structural theory is contingent on an organization's stage of development; that is, new ventures have different structural requirements than mature organizations (Cameron & Quinn, 1983). Whereas past research on established firms in dynamic contexts indicated that organizations with more organic structures outperformed those with less organic structures, we found the opposite to be true for new ventures. This research also offers entrepreneurs insight into one of their most fundamental tasks: designing organizational architecture (David & Han, 2003; Donaldson, 1995). Although founding teams are typically resource constrained, our results emphasize the importance

of dedicating precious resources to developing formal structure. Finally, this study reinvigorates work on organizational structure that has received less attention since the rise to popularity of the open-system approach to organizations in the 1980s (Scott, 1981). Our analysis suggests the continued relevance of research on organizational structure and the environment to both theorists and practitioners alike.

THEORIES OF STRUCTURE AND PERFORMANCE

Research on formal structure[2] in organizations hearkens back to the very origins of organizational theory. Weber's classic text on bureaucracy proclaimed that the bureaucratic organization, with its clear-cut division of activities, assignment of roles, and hierarchically arranged authority, is "technically superior to all other forms of organization" (1947: 196). According to Weber, the formal structures that made up the modern organization enabled greater precision, speed, task knowledge, and continuity, while reducing friction and ambiguity. Building on Merton (1949) and Durkheim (1997), Burns and Stalker (1961) proposed a contingent relationship between formal structure and organizational performance, arguing that organizations with organic structures, or loosely coupled networks of workers, are better adapted to dynamic environments. Organizations with Weberian mechanistic structure (bureaucracy), where work is "distributed among specialist roles within a clearly defined hierarchy" (Burns & Stalker, 1961: 6), were viewed as more suitable for static environments.

During the past four decades, a host of studies have examined Burns and Stalker's propositions and have generally confirmed that organizations in dynamic environments do better if their structures are more organic (e.g., Aiken, Bacharach, and French [1980]; Covin and Slevin [1989]; but see Wally and Baum [1994] for an exception). The majority of the empirical tests of this theory have used samples of mature organizations.

Despite this strong research tradition, little is known about whether or not this theory applies to newly created ventures in emerging industries.

---

[1] Founding teams are the initial teams that found and manage organizations for the first several years of operations.

[2] The structure of an organization is typically defined as "the sum total of the ways in which it divides its labor into distinct tasks and then achieves coordination among them" (Mintzberg, 1979: 2). Formal structure is "the documented, official relationships among members of the organization," and informal structure is the "unofficial relationships within the workgroup" (Mintzberg, 1979: 9–10). We focus on formal structure in this paper.

Stinchcombe (1965) suggested that the relative lack of structure that characterizes new ventures is a liability, *not* a benefit. He argued that this liability of newness is particularly difficult to overcome in emerging economic sectors that lack industry norms about work processes and organizational design. In this study, we focused on three attributes of new venture structure[3]: role formalization, specialization, and administrative intensity (Pugh, Hickson, Hinings, MacDonald, Turner, & Lupton, 1963; Stinchcombe, 1965) and their association with new venture performance.

Role Formalization in Founding Teams

Pugh and a group of colleagues from Aston University identified the formalization of organizational tasks and roles as a key attribute of modern organizational structure (Pugh et al., 1963). Roles are "standardized patterns of behavior" (Katz & Kahn, 1978: 43). Role formalization in founding teams captures "what one is asked to do" (Dalton, Todor, Spendolini, Fielding, & Porter, 1980: 58) and refers to the identification and designation of particular functional roles and their assignment to specific individuals. New ventures are initially characterized by relatively little role formalization and typically lack functional completeness at inception (Aldrich, 1999; Stinchcombe, 1965).

Burns and Stalker (1961) argued that in a dynamic environment, formalization decreases organizational adaptability to environmental changes and increases the risk of organizational failure. By contrast, the organic ideal type emphasizes role flexibility rather than "the breaking down of tasks

into specialisms" and the precise definition of the "duties and powers attached to each functional role" (Burns & Stalker, 1961: 5). Several empirical studies of mature organizations have supported the inverse correlation between formalization and firm performance in dynamic environments (Glisson & Martin, 1980; Wally & Baum, 1994).

Although it may make sense to advise established firms with rigid formal bureaucracies to become more flexible and adaptable in dynamic environments, the same advice may not necessarily be appropriate for new ventures characterized by nascent structure and uncertain roles. Rather, a lack of role formalization may lead to role ambiguity (Stinchcombe, 1965). Role ambiguity causes confusion about *who* is supposed to do particular routine tasks. In contrast, the formalization of roles and behavior enables organizations to reduce, predict, and control variability because role formalization creates a condition in which "everyone knows exactly what to do" and ultimately decreases coordination costs (Mintzberg, 1979: 83). In turbulent and changing environments, role ambiguity may also cause confusion about *what* should be done to adapt to new circumstances. When environmental change necessitates organizational adaptation, new ventures that lack clear boundaries of responsibility will be forced to rely upon decision making by consensus, thereby decreasing the speed and increasing the cost of any particular decision. Role formalization assigns decision-making authority to individuals in particular roles and thereby delineates what founding team members in those roles can and cannot decide. These boundaries empower particular individuals to make decisions on behalf of their organization and result in both decreased coordination costs and increased decision-making speed. Lower costs, which are particularly important to financially strapped new ventures, and increased decision-making speed increase firm performance in volatile environments (Eisenhardt & Schoonhoven, 1990).

Formalization may also increase a new venture's legitimacy. New ventures are often constrained by their lack of legitimacy, credibility, and acceptance from important external constituents, including providers of financial resources, external marketing partners, suppliers, and distributors (Aldrich, 1999; Stinchcombe, 1965). Past research on new ventures suggests that because their eventual success is highly uncertain, resource providers rely on symbolic signals of competence (Meyer & Rowan, 1977; Stuart, Hoang, & Hybels, 1999). Creating common formal positions such as chief financial officer and vice president of human resources signals management experience and know-how and con-

---

[3] We chose these dimensions because past research suggests they capture important aspects of both horizontal and vertical organizational structure and have special applicability to new ventures (Baron, Burton, & Hannan, 1999). Pugh et al. (1963) identified six primary dimensions of structure: specialization, standardization, formalization, centralization, configuration, and flexibility. We focused our efforts on specialization, formalization, and administrative intensity (capturing both centralization and configuration) because they were the most relevant to new ventures. We did not study standardization because it makes little sense for new ventures in new industries who are experimenting with various processes and technologies to standardize these while they are still evolving. Similarly, we did not include flexibility in this study because there was little variation among firms in this sample in terms of flexibility. Our measure of administrative intensity captures both centralization, defined as the extent to which power is centralized in a few figures or diffused among several administrators, and organizations' hierarchical configurations.

formity to accepted management structure and practices. Given that access to external resources is critical for new venture growth, the increased credibility and legitimacy associated with role formalization will likely enhance new venture performance.

Drawing on these arguments, we suggest the following hypothesis:

Hypothesis 1. Greater role formalization in founding teams increases new venture performance.

Functional Specialization in Founding Teams

The second structural attribute of new ventures that this study examined is functional specialization in founding teams, which we define as the concentration of the types of tasks assigned to any one founding team member. Role formalization and functional specialization are interrelated, as the former relates to the formal recognition and delineation of tasks within an organization and the latter captures the extent to which individual founding team members focus their efforts on narrower or broader sets of tasks. According to Burns and Stalker (1961), specialization increases coordination costs and decreases the flexibility of an organization and therefore its ability to react to environmental changes. The relationship between specialization and performance has received little attention from empirical researchers and is still undetermined (Dalton et al., 1980).

We argue that new ventures facing the highly volatile environment of an emerging sector benefit from functional specialization of founding teams. Functional specialization allows organization members to concentrate on the execution of specified and narrowly defined tasks and to accumulate task-related knowledge, and thus it enhances information-processing capabilities (Thompson, 1967). Concentration of tasks also increases the accountability of actors and facilitates monitoring. Thus,

Hypothesis 2. Greater functional specialization in founding teams increases new venture performance.

We expect the effects of founding team size and specialization to interact. It is more difficult for small founding teams to specialize than it is for large founding teams because small founding teams lack the managerial resources needed to allow founders to focus on only a few tasks and lack the financial resources necessary to outsource unassigned tasks. Thus, specializing in one function, such as finance, may lead to less attention being

paid to a function of equal importance, such as marketing. Thus, we predict that specialization will be more beneficial for larger founding teams with sufficient managerial resources to cover important functional areas.

Hypothesis 3. The positive effect of functional specialization in founding teams on new venture performance increases with the size of founding teams.

Administrative Intensity

Organic organizations have flat structures with coordination occurring via lateral "consultation rather than vertical commands" (Burns & Stalker, 1961: 121). Classical sociological studies of organizational structure have identified administrative intensity—measured by the ratio of administrators to employees—as an important feature of organizational structure (Bendix, 1956; Blau & Schoenherr, 1971; Melman, 1951). The argument in much of this literature is that this ratio reflects the degree of bureaucratization within an organization (Evers, Bohlen, & Warren, 1976; Parkinson, 1957). According to this research tradition, larger administrative ratios indicate an inefficient expansion of administrative activities in growing organizations and an inertial tendency in declining organizations (Ford, 1980; McKinley, 1987). Using samples of mature firms in established industries, researchers have observed a negative relationship between administrative intensity and organizational performance (Bidwell & Kasarda, 1975; Melman, 1951). Many practitioners and educators have also espoused the negative relationship between administrative intensity and performance, arguing that excess management often stifles innovation and may get in the way of firm productivity (Peters & Waterman, 1987; Timmons & Spinelli, 2003). Whether or not this principle of lean administrative intensity applies to new ventures is largely untested.

In the context of new ventures, we focus on the size of a founding team vis-à-vis the total number of employees in its organization as the key indicator of administrative intensity. Baron, Hannan, and Burton (1999) argued that the founding team is the most fundamental administrative component of a new venture. New ventures are typically small and rarely have middle managers (Mintzberg, 1979). The size of the founding team relative to the size of the organization plays an essential role in the development of a new venture, establishing its bureaucratic intensity. Because of the importance of the founding team, we suggest that administrative intensity in new ventures is best captured by the ratio of the number of founding team members to employees.

We argue that, unlike mature organizations in dynamic environments, in which high administrative ratios may impede the ability to adapt, new ventures benefit from high levels of administrative intensity. Stinchcombe (1965: 148) attributed the liability of newness in part to the fact that new organizations, particularly "new types of organizations," must construct and learn new roles that are temporarily filled by employees with "generalized skills" from other firms. In established firms, "former occupants of roles can teach their successors, communicating not only skills but also decision criteria, responsibilities to various people who have relations to the role occupant, . . . what sort of things can go wrong with routine procedures, and so on" (Stinchcombe, 1965: 148). In contrast, founders and employees of new organizations in nascent economic sectors are responsible for inventing new roles, a process that has a "high cost in time, worry, conflict, and temporary inefficiencies" (Stinchcombe, 1965: 148). Moreover, the deficit of knowledge about organizational activities is more difficult to overcome in new sectors, because population-level learning is unavailable (Miner & Haunschild, 1995). The iterative process of role construction requires substantial managerial interaction with employees. In emerging economic sectors, where formal training programs may be relatively unavailable and best practices have yet to be institutionalized, this process demands significant efforts by founders to mentor and train employees. Thus, we argue that new ventures benefit from a larger ratio of founding team members to employees.

New ventures also suffer from a lack of organizational routines, a critical mechanism for increasing reproducibility. The lack of accumulated operational experience and routines in new ventures substantially increases reliance upon managerial discretion to coordinate organizational activities. Higher administrative intensity also enables these administrators to allocate more time and resources to organization-building activities, such as working with employees to set up formal coordination procedures and fine-tuning information-processing systems. In new ventures, therefore, the ratio of founding team members to organization members captures the extent to which founding team members are able to provide employees with important managerial resources needed for development and coordination. We argue that new ventures with greater administrative intensity will have higher performance than their counterparts with lower administrative intensity. Thus,

Hypothesis 4. Greater administrative intensity increases new venture performance.

METHODS

Sample

We tested our hypotheses using panel data from a sample of Internet service ventures founded in 1996 and operating in the United States during the five-year period 1996–2001. We chose the Internet sector as the setting in which to test our propositions about new ventures in dynamic sectors because of the high volatility and turbulence in this market during this time period. Although the Internet (independent, packet-switched communications networks) had existed since the late 1960s, prior to the 1990s it operated largely within the confines of government research centers and nonprofit organizations like universities (Abbate, 1999). During the mid and late 1990s, reacting to a series of institutional reforms and technical changes, many new ventures were established to exploit the commercial potential of the Internet, and the sector became characterized by rapid growth and extreme environmental turbulence. Tens of millions of citizens connected to the Internet for the first time and faced bewildering choices among new, unproven technologies vying for market acceptance (Zakon, 2004). From 1994 to 1996, Internet "backbone traffic" expanded a hundredfold, and during the following five years (1996–2001), traffic increased an additional fifty-fold (Odlyzko, 2003). Many firms did not survive this turbulent period and the resulting "dot.com" crash of 2000–2001. Up to $4 trillion of paper wealth disappeared as stock prices fell (Lowenstein, 2004). Taken as a whole, the commercialization of the Internet in the late 1990s was an extreme instance of environmental dynamism, turbulence, and uncertainty. These features make it an ideal setting in which to test relationships between organizational structure and performance in new ventures.

We constructed a data set for the cohort of Internet firms founded in 1996 in the United States using data from the CorpTech database. This database tracks firms operating in various high-technology sectors and compiles self-reported data on a wide range of organizational characteristics, including organization size, revenue, and management team structure.

Several researchers (Arora & Gambardella, 1997; Stuart, Hoang, & Hybels, 1999) have used the CorpTech database as a source of data. This database was initially created as a marketing vehicle to permit vendors to reach technology-oriented firms.

CorpTech employees maintain a high degree of comprehensiveness in this data by regularly checking for newly founded firms in local telephone directories. For the sample of firms used in this study, CorpTech employees regularly contacted the firms in their database, typically interviewing one member of each management team annually. Because it is unlikely that a newly founded firm proceeds without obtaining a phone number, it was reasonable to expect that the 449 Internet firms that we identified constituted a significant fraction of the 1996 cohort. These start-ups provided Internet services ranging from basic Internet access to more complex Web design, data management, and custom software service for corporate and individual customers. Because of missing data, organizational exits, and our use of a "lead variable" for our dependent variable, our final sample consisted of 1,049 firm-year observations with complete data. The median organizational size was 6 employees, and 70 percent of the firms had 11 or fewer employees. This observation is consistent with other studies that suggest new ventures typically have fewer than 10 employees (Aldrich, 1999). Less than 5 percent of the firms in our sample received funding from venture capital firms.

We checked the accuracy of our data in several ways. First, we used the Lexis-Nexis database of business press releases and business news and also contacted the companies surviving at the time of our study directly via phone and e-mail to confirm elements of the company profile reported in the CorpTech database. However, many companies in the initial sample had since failed and were therefore unavailable for follow-up data collection. Many of these same firms did not release formal business press releases and/or were too small to have received coverage in the mainstream business press. We used the Internet Archive, a digital archive of the World Wide Web, to confirm data reported in CorpTech, to fill in gaps in the CorpTech data (i.e., the names of senior management), and to check the dates of firm entrances and exits.

Dependent Variable: Performance

With 12 exceptions, all of the firms in our sample were privately owned (the exceptions were partially or entirely owned by publicly held firms). The market-based and accounting-based performance measures that are typically used in analyzing the financial performance of publicly held firms were therefore not applicable. Further, interviews with several practitioners suggested that the independent variables of interest (see below) had a rapid impact on the revenues of the firms in this

sector, implying that the typical one-year lag between measuring these variables and revenue was too long. To alleviate this problem, we used the moving average of revenue (in millions of dollars) in years t and $t + 1$ to shorten the lag time between our independent and dependent variables. Revenue data were collected by CorpTech personnel.

Independent Variables

Role formalization. The CorpTech database tracks common functional areas, including corporate development, chief executive officer, chief financial officer, chief engineering officer, human resources, international sales, manufacturing, management and information systems, marketing, purchasing, quality control, research and development, sales, strategic planning, and technology transfers. The role formalization variable was the number of formalized functions in a new venture divided by the potential maximum number of functional roles. Our measure was adapted from Dalton et al.'s (1980) definition of role formalization.

Functional specialization. Our measure of specialization, adapted from Pugh et al.'s (1963) definition of specialization, was the average number of functional assignments per founding team member.

Administrative intensity. We measured administrative intensity as the number of executives in a founding team divided by the number of total employees. This measure was adapted from Blau and Schoenherr's (1971) administrative ratio measure.

Control Variables

We also controlled for other variables that might explain organizational revenue, such as firm size, founding team size, primary business area, product diversity, and market size. *Firm size* was the natural logarithm of the total number of organizational members, including executives and employees. *Founding team size* was the number of executives in a firm.

Because firms with only one founding team member might be fundamentally different from other firms in our sample, we controlled for these firms with the variable *single executive*, which was coded 1 if a firm had only one founder. We also controlled for founder exits because changes in a founding team could cause turbulence that might affect performance. *Founder exit* was coded as 1 for each year in which one of the founders of a firm departed. In our sample, 77 founders left during the observation period.

Past research suggests that the breadth of product offering affects performance (Carroll & Hannan,

2000). *Product diversity* measured the number of business domains (e.g., telecommunication, software, photonics, etc.) in which these firms operated. *Product line* was the number of products or services that these firms provided in the Internet business domains (e.g., Internet access, Web-page design, online shopping, etc.).

Two dummy variables indicate the areas of business in which firms primarily operated. *SIC 4813* was coded as 1 when a firm's primary business was in that category, which covers telephone communications (e.g., Internet service providers) and 0 otherwise. We also coded *SIC 7375* as 1 when a firm's main business area was in this category (e.g., information retrieval services) and 0 otherwise.

We also controlled for effects of market demand and the size of the economic sector in two ways. *Host* was the number of Internet hosts at time t, obtained from the Internet Software Consortium. *Shipment* indicated the potential number of Internet users in the United States, measured with the dollar amount of semiconductor shipments to U.S. markets at time t. We collected this statistic from the Semiconductor Industry Association.

Finally, because 131 firms in our sample eventually exited from the sector because of either merger or bankruptcy during the five-year observation period, we corrected for potential selection biases using a generalization of the Heckman selection model (Lee, 1983). In this correction, we computed the probability of firm exit, whether by bankruptcy or merger, with Cox regression models and included this generated sample correction variable, lambda, into our regression models.

Analysis

Our data set consisted of five panels. Following Baron et al. (1999), we used generalized estimating equations (GEE) with unstructured working correlation matrixes to test our hypotheses (Liang & Zeger, 1986). We preferred this estimation method to fixed-effect estimations because some of the variables had little variance over time.

Because role formalization, functional specialization, founding team size, and the interaction term between founding team size and functional specialization were highly correlated, the variance inflation factor for our regressions exceeded the threshold for multicollinearity recommended by Chatterjee and Price (1991). We reduced multicollinearity in our model by orthogonalizing formalization, functional specialization, founding team size, and the interaction of specialization and founding team size using a modified Gram-Schmidt procedure (Saville & Wood, 1991). This technique "partials out" the common variance, creating transformed variables that are uncorrelated with one another. We then tested for multicollinearity and found that variance-inflation factors in all of the models presented below were lower than 5.

RESULTS

Table 1 shows the descriptive statistics and correlations for the dependent, independent, and control variables. Table 2 presents the results of our analysis.

In Table 2, model 1 is the baseline equation con-

TABLE 1
Descriptive Statistics[a]

	Mean	s.d.	1	2	3	4	5	6	7	8	9	10	11	12	13	14
1. Performance	15.03	114.53														
2. Role formalization[b]	0.02	1.00	.30													
3. Functional specialization[b]	−0.05	0.97	.08	.04												
4. Administrative intensity	0.36	0.27	−.17	−.08	−.18											
5. Firm size[c]	0.41	1.31	.52	.50	.47	−.59										
6. Founding team size[b]	0.05	0.98	.10	.01	.04	−.10	.29									
7. Single executive	0.33	0.47	−.07	−.44	−.45	−.09	−.37	−.08								
8. Founder exit	0.03	0.16	.04	.08	.03	−.12	.16	.05	−.04							
9. Product diversity	1.25	0.62	.52	.25	.13	−.12	.34	.02	−.11	.00						
10. Product line	3.34	1.28	.38	.11	−.13	.09	.01	−.13	−.03	−.09	.46					
11. SIC 4813	0.60	0.49	−.13	−.19	−.18	.23	−.31	−.12	.09	−.06	−.23	.17				
12. SIC 7375	0.22	0.42	.02	.05	.10	−.18	.17	.05	−.02	.07	.06	−.30	−.66			
13. Host	1.86E+07	8.99E+06	.09	.09	.04	−.11	.16	.09	−.01	.17	.07	.02	.00	.00		
14. Shipment	3.76E+06	1.67E+05	−.04	−.04	−.03	.06	−.08	−.01	−.01	−.09	−.03	−.04	.00	.00	−.28	
15. Lambda	0.96	0.54	−.07	.03	.09	−.09	.08	.06	−.04	.11	.00	−.09	−.02	−.03	.71	−.26

[a] $n = 1,024$.
[b] Orthogonalized variable.
[c] Log-transformed variable.

TABLE 2
Results of Regression Analyses[a]

Variable	Model 1	Model 2	Model 3	Model 4[c]
Role formalization[a]		10.22**	9.42**	0.96***
		(3.55)	(3.62)	(0.30)
Functional specialization[a]		11.20**	8.97**	0.56*
		(3.64)	(3.80)	(0.27)
Administrative intensity		27.09**	27.90**	2.89**
		(10.56)	(10.79)	(1.07)
Role formalization × founding team size[a]			5.86*	1.66***
			(2.73)	(0.21)
Firm size[b]	20.55***	19.83***	20.21***	3.59***
	(2.59)	(2.96)	(3.02)	(0.48)
Founding team size[a]	18.92***	19.81***	17.92***	1.09***
	(2.92)	(2.89)	(3.02)	(0.21)
Single executive	1.17	18.81**	11.67[†]	0.99*
	(5.08)	(6.24)	(7.20)	(0.56)
Founder exit	−0.89	7.07	4.96	−0.44
	(7.54)	(7.31)	(7.55)	(0.99)
Product diversity	49.14***	43.57***	46.08***	−0.13
	(7.16)	(7.14)	(7.32)	(0.35)
Product line	15.48***	17.41***	16.60***	−0.15
	(3.60)	(3.60)	(3.65)	(0.15)
SIC 4813	11.32	12.83	12.92	0.03
	(11.09)	(11.04)	(11.15)	(0.45)
SIC 7375	12.61	16.83	15.36	0.07
	(11.74)	(11.57)	(11.73)	(0.52)
Host	1.76E-07	1.44E-07	2.86E-07	2.48E-08
	(7.21E-07)	(7.05E-07)	(6.86E-07)	(3.19E-08)
Shipment	1.16E-05	1.26E-05	1.42E-05	1.36E-06*
	(1.18E-05)	(1.17E-05)	(1.12E-05)	(6.72E-07)
Lambda	1.30	2.01	1.45	0.49
	(5.46)	(5.12)	(5.24)	(0.53)
Constant	−207.08***	−226.08***	−232.31***	−12.57***
	(55.32)	(54.87)	(52.76)	(3.14)
Wald chi-square	301.14***	341.19***	335.53	547.61***
Change in Wald chi-square		22.64***	4.60*	
Scale parameter	7,862.53	7,832.70	7,944.72	15.97
n	1,049	1,049	1,049	993

[a] Orthogonalized variable.

[b] Log-transformed variable.

[c] Only includes firms with fewer than 150 employees.

[†] $p < .10$

* $p < .05$

** $p < .01$

*** $p < .001$

taining the control variables, and model 2 introduces administrative intensity, role formalization, and functional specialization. Model 3 builds on the previous model by introducing the interaction term between functional specialization and founding team size. Wald joint tests for the differences between the three models were significant, demonstrating that adding the hypothesized variables from one model to the next significantly improved the model fit. Model 4 is a robustness check of model 3 and only includes observations with fewer than 150 employees.

The results of the analysis generally supported all four hypotheses, and we base the interpretation of the results on the coefficients from model 3. Of the control variables, product diversity, product line, and firm size all had a significant, positive effect on revenue. Similarly to Eisenhardt and Schoonhoven (1996) and Baron et al. (1999), we found that founding team size had a positive effect on future revenue.

Hypotheses 1 and 2 suggest positive associations between role formalization and functional specialization in founding teams and firm performance. With all other variables fixed to their means, the results indicate that an increase of one standard deviation in role formalization and functional specialization increases future revenue by 60.8 percent and 55.8 percent respectively,[4] supporting Hypotheses 1 and 2. Hypothesis 3 states that founding team size increases the impact of specialization on firm performance. The interaction term between functional specialization and founding team size is positive and significant; a one-standard-deviation increase in team size increases the effect of specialization on future revenue by 37.7 percent, supporting Hypothesis 3. Hypothesis 4 predicts a positive correlation between administrative intensity and future new venture performance. The coefficients in model 3 indicate that an increase of one standard deviation in administrative intensity increases future revenue by 47.7 percent, supporting Hypothesis 4.

We checked the robustness of these findings in the following three ways. First, we ran regression models only with firms employing fewer than 150 organizational members in order to make sure that the largest organizations in our sample did not skew our results. The results of this analysis are presented in model 4 in Table 2. In both analyses, the data suggested significant effects of the hypothesized independent variables on organizational performance. However, it is important to note that the coefficients are much larger in model 3. We tested the significance of the coefficient differences between the two models and found the differences to be significant, suggesting that the impact of the structural measures was significantly higher in larger new ventures. This distinction makes good sense because small organizations are naturally limited in their ability to specialize.

Second, we performed the regressions applying different assumptions about the relationship between panels, assuming, for instance, autocorrelation or independence. We also ran all models using the Huber-White estimator of variance, which produces valid standard errors even if the error terms are heteroskedastic or if the correlations within a group are not as hypothesized by the specified correlation structure (Allison, 1999). The results with these robustness checks remained substantively the same; the direction and significance of the variables did not change. Third, we ran fixed-effects models[5] for the analysis presented in model 3. The

fixed-effects models accounted for the unobserved heterogeneity related to firm attributes that do not change over time, such as the strengths and weaknesses of a founding team (Greene [2000]; see Bunderson and Sutcliffe [2002] for a review of important top management team attributes). The results for the hypothesized independent variables remained substantively the same in the fixed-effects regression: positive and significant at the .05 level.

DISCUSSION

Our objective in this study was to examine the relationship between the formal structure of new ventures and organizational performance in a dynamic emergent economic sector. Combining arguments based on classical organization theory and entrepreneurial research, we theorized that new ventures with greater founding team formalization, functional specialization, and administrative intensity would outperform those firms that had less of these attributes. We also posited that founding team size would moderate the impact of functional specialization on new venture performance. Results from our research support these hypotheses. Moreover, we found that the impacts of formalization, specialization, and administrative intensity were greater for larger new ventures.

These results stand in contrast to empirical research based on work by Burns and Stalker, indicating that in a dynamic industry, firms with less formal structures (more organic structures) outperform firms with more formal structures (more mechanistic). This contrast is likely a result of the fact that Burns and Stalker's *The Management of Innovation* (1961) was a case study of large, established British and Scottish firms and was never really intended to address this phenomenon in new ventures. Similarly, most of the empirical work on this topic has also used samples of *established* firms in dynamic sectors. Our results suggest a new scope condition for Burns and Stalker's structural theory—namely, that the effects of structure are contingent on an organization's and industry's stages of development. We found that structure increased performance in new ventures, even in the context of a very dynamic emergent sector, substantiating the claims of theorists who have long proclaimed the importance of formal structure to or-

---

[4] Our interpretation of the effects of role formalization, specialization, and the interaction variable are based on coefficients from the transformed variables.

[5] A weakness of fixed-effects models is that they cannot estimate effects for variables that change very little

over time, although they do control for these effects. We were therefore unable to control for team size in these models because team size did not vary substantially year to year.

ganizational performance and the liabilities associated with its absence (Mintzberg, 1979; Perrow, 1986; Stinchcombe, 1965; Thompson, 1967; Weber, 1947).

This research illustrates the intellectual risks of generalizing theories derived from and tested in samples of large, established organizations to the domain of small, new ventures. These findings also support claims put forth by organizational life cycle theorists who have argued for a more nuanced approach to studying organizations because the challenges they face change over their life courses (e.g., Cameron & Quinn, 1983). Echoing these concerns, a growing body of scholars have called for more empirical research on how extant organizational theory applies to new ventures (Aldrich, 1999; Shane, 2003). We therefore build on a recent stream of research that examines new ventures in new sectors (for example, see Eisenhardt and Schoonhoven [1990, 1996] and Sine, Haveman, & Tolbert [2005]), adding additional insight about the relationship between structure and performance.

Our results inform entrepreneurial practice regarding the impact of particular structural features upon firm performance early in the development of new ventures, providing new and important guidance for entrepreneurs forming new ventures in emergent sectors. This study suggests that entrepreneurs should pay particular attention to initial organizational structure. The construction and founding of a new venture are often chaotic events, and organizational design often takes a back seat to the exigencies of the moment (Aldrich, 1999). We argue that the creation and management of a new venture require substantial managerial resources, and our results suggest that larger founding teams are correlated with higher future revenues. Having sufficient managerial resources is particularly important for organizations with more employees, as demonstrated by the large effects of administrative intensity. Our results also demonstrate that new ventures that formalize functional assignments and assign important tasks to team members who specialize in those assignments outperform firms whose founding teams have relatively undefined roles.

Limitations

One of the strengths of this research is that it examines a unique set of firms from founding through their first five years of existence in a turbulent environment, yet using this type of sample also creates some limitations. First, because new ventures have a very high mortality rate (Aldrich, 1999), at least half of the firms in our sample no longer existed by the end of our study; we were unable to gather information that was not either archival or on the firms' Web sites. Thus, information on attributes of founders was unavailable. We did use various search engines to try to obtain data on founder experience, but these efforts inevitably fell short for our sample of firms. Second, because most of the firms in our sample were private, we were limited to data that these firms were willing to disclose, which in this case did not include common measures of profitability, such as return on investment. Moreover, exit was not a useful indicator of performance because it indicated success as well as failure, and we could not always distinguish between the two. For these two reasons, our indicator of performance was limited to revenue. Third, the Internet sector is an extreme instance of environmental dynamism, turbulence, and uncertainty. In our setting, capital barriers to entry were limited, and the new technology underlying the sector was adaptable to many existing industries and activities, resulting in very high growth. Moreover, the prospects of the sector were constantly changing and went from boom to bust within the time frame of our sample. This dynamism made the Internet sector an ideal setting in which to test relationships between new venture structure, dynamic environments, and performance. However, the extremity of the environment might reduce the generalizability of our results to other sectors. Nevertheless, we believe that the benefits of structure also accrue to new ventures in other turbulent environments, even if they are less extreme.

Conclusion

In dynamic, turbulent, and uncertain environments, new ventures and mature organizations face fundamentally different challenges requiring different approaches to organizational structure. Whereas mature organizations with well-defined structure and embedded practices typically need to become more organic and flexible in order to adapt to dynamic environments (Burns & Stalker, 1961), the opposite is true for new ventures. We argue that new ventures are already extremely flexible and attuned to their environment, but that they often lack the benefits of organizational structure, such as low role ambiguity, high levels of individual focus and discretion, low coordination costs, and generally high levels of organizational efficiency. Moreover, because new ventures in new economic sectors need to develop new roles, activities, and employees, they require greater managerial resources per employee than mature organizations. Our results demonstrate that new ventures that have greater role formalization and specialization in founding teams, as well as administrative intensity, also show better future performance. This study is only a first step in exploring how the relationship between particular types of formal structure and organizational performance is contingent on both environmental and organizational factors. Our research was limited to a population of firms in their first five years of life. Future research could build on these findings by examining the relationship between structural attributes (including those not studied here), life cycle stages, transitions between life cycle stages, and environmental stability. Understanding these relationships will delineate the environmental and life cycle contingencies that determine the relationship between particular types of organizational structure and firm performance.

REFERENCES

Abbate, J. 1999. *Inventing the Internet.* Cambridge, MA: MIT Press.

Aiken, M., Bacharach, S., & French, J. 1980. Organizational structure, work process, and proposal making in administrative bureaucracies. *Academy of Management Journal*, 23: 631–652.

Aldrich, H. 1999. *Organizations evolving.* London: Sage.

Allison, P. 1999. *Multiple regression: A primer.* Thousand Oaks, CA: Sage.

Arora, A., & Gambardella, A. 1997. Domestic markets and international competitiveness: Generic and product specific competencies in the engineering sector. *Strategic Management Journal*, 18: 53–74.

Baron, J., Hannan, M., & Burton, M. 1999. Building the iron cage: Determinants of managerial intensity in the early years of organizations. *American Sociological Review*, 64: 527–548.

Bendix, R. 1956. *Work and authority in industry.* New York: Wiley.

Bidwell, C. E., & Kasarda, J. D. 1975. School district organization and student achievement. *American Sociological Review*, 40: 55–70.

Blau, P. M., & Schoenherr, R. A. 1971. *The structure of organizations.* New York: Basic Books.

Bunderson, J. S., & Sutcliffe, K. M. 2002. Comparing alternative conceptualizations of functional diversity in management teams: Process and performance effects. *Academy of Management Journal*, 45: 875–893.

Burns, T., & Stalker, G. M. 1961. *The management of innovation.* London: Tavistock.

Cameron, K. S., & Quinn, R. E. 1983. Organizational life cycle and shifting criteria of effectiveness: Some preliminary evidence. *Management Science*, 29: 33–51.

Carroll, G. R., & Hannan, M. T. 2000. *The demography of corporations and industries.* Princeton, NJ: Princeton University Press.

Chatterjee, S., & Price, B. 1991. *Regression analysis by example.* New York: Wiley.

Covin, J., & Slevin, D. 1989. Strategic management of small firms in hostile and benign environments. *Strategic Management Journal*, 10: 75–88.

Dalton, D. R., Todor, W. D., Spendolini, M. J., Fielding, G. J., & Porter, L. W. 1980. Organization structure and performance: A critical review. *Academy of Management Review*, 5: 49–64.

David, R, & Han, S. 2003. A systematic assessment of the empirical support for transaction cost economics. *Strategic Management Journal*, 25: 39–58.

Donaldson, L. 1995. *American anti-management theories of organization: A critique of paradigm proliferation.* New York: Cambridge University Press.

Durkheim, E. 1997. *The division of labor in society* [W. D. Halls, trans.]. New York: Free Press.

Eisenhardt, K., & Schoonhoven, C. 1990. Organizational growth: Linking founding team, strategy, environment and growth among U.S. semiconductor ventures, 1978–1988. *Administrative Science Quarterly*, 35: 504–529.

Eisenhardt, K., & Schoonhoven, C. 1996. Resource-based view of strategic alliance formation: Strategic and social explanations in entrepreneurial firms. *Organizational Science*, 7: 136–150.

Evers, F., Bohlen, J., & Warren, R. 1976. The relationship of selected size and structure indicators in economic organizations. *Administrative Science Quarterly*, 21: 326–342.

Ford, J. 1980. The administrative component in growing and declining organizations: A longitudinal analysis. *Academy of Management Journal*, 23: 615–630.

Gilbert, C. 2005. Unbundling the structure of inertia: Resource versus routine rigidity. *Academy of Management Journal*, 48: 741–763.

Gilbert, C. 2006. Change in the presence of residual fit: Can competing frames coexist? *Organization Science:* In press.

Glisson, C., & Martin, P. 1980. Productivity and efficiency in human service organizations as related to structure, size and age. *Academy of Management Journal*, 23: 21–38.

Greene, W. 2000. *Econometric analysis.* Upper Saddle River, NJ: Prentice-Hall.

Katz, D. K., & Kahn, R. L. 1978. *The social psychology of organizations.* New York: Wiley.

Kimberly, J. R. 1979. Issues in the creation of organizations: initiation, innovation, and institutionalization. *Academy of Management Journal*, 22: 437–457.

Lee, L. F. 1983. Generalized econometric models with selectivity. *Econometrica*, 51: 507–512.

Liang, K., & Zeger, S. 1986. Longitudinal data analysis using generalized linear models. *Biometrika*, 73: 13–22.

Lowenstein, R. 2004. *Origins of the crash*. New York: Penguin Press.

McKinley, W. 1987. Complexity and administrative intensity: The case of declining organizations. *Administrative Science Quarterly*, 32: 87–105.

Melman, S. 1951. The rise of administrative overhead in the manufacturing industries of the United States, 1899-1947. *Oxford Economic Papers*, 3: 62–112.

Merton, R. 1949. *Social theory and social structure*. Toronto: Collier-Macmillan.

Meyer, J. W., & Rowan, B. 1977. Institutionalized organizations: Formal structure as myth and ceremony. *American Journal of Sociology*, 83: 340–363.

Miner, A. S., & Haunschild, P. R. 1995. Population level learning. In L. L. Cummings & B. M. Staw (Eds.), *Research in organizational behavior*, vol. 17: 115–166. Greenwich, CT: JAI Press.

Mintzberg, H. 1979. *The structuring of organizations*. Englewood Cliffs, NJ: Prentice-Hall.

Odlyzko, A. M. 2003. Internet traffic growth: Sources and implications. In B. B. Dingel, W. Weiershausen, A. K. Dutta, & K.-I. Sato (Eds.), *Optical transmission systems and equipment for WDM networking II, Proceedings SPIE*, 5247: 1–15.

O'Toole, L. J., & Meier, K. J. 2003. Bureaucracy and uncertainty. In B. C. Burden (Ed.), *Uncertainty in American politics*: 98–117. Cambridge, U.K.: Cambridge University Press.

Parkinson, C. N. 1957. *Parkinson's law and other studies in administration*. Boston: Houghton Mifflin.

Peters, T., & Waterman, R. 1987. *In search of excellence*. New York: Harper & Row.

Perrow, C. 1986. *Complex organizations: A critical essay* (3rd ed.). New York: Random House.

Pugh, D. S., Hickson, D. J., Hinings, C. R., MacDonald, K. M., Turner, C., & Lupton, T. 1963. A conceptual scheme for organizational analysis. *Administrative Science Quarterly*, 8: 289–315.

Saville, D. J., & Wood, G. R. 1991. *Statistical methods: The geometric approach*. New York: Springer.

Scott, W. R. 1981. *Organizations: Rational, natural, and open systems*. Englewood Cliffs, NJ: Prentice-Hall.

Shane, S. 2003. *A general theory of entrepreneurship: The individual opportunity nexus*. Northampton, MA: Edward Elgar.

Sine, W. D., & David, R. 2003. Environmental jolts, institutional change, and the creation of entrepreneurial opportunity in the U.S. electric power industry. *Research Policy*, 32: 185–207.

Sine, W. D., Haveman, H. A., & Tolbert, P. S. 2005. Risky business: Entrepreneurship in the new independent-power sector. *Administrative Science Quarterly*, 50: 200–232.

Stinchcombe, A. 1965. Social structure and organizations. In J. March (Ed.), *Handbook of organizations*: 142–193. Chicago: Rand McNally.

Stuart, T. E., Hoang, H., & Hybels, R. C. 1999. Interorganizational endorsements and the performance of entrepreneurial ventures. *Administrative Science Quarterly*, 44: 315–349.

Thompson, J. D. 1967. *Organizations in action*. New York: McGraw-Hill.

Timmons, J., & Spinelli, S. 2003. *New venture creation: Entrepreneurship for the 21st century*. New York: McGraw-Hill.

Wally, S., & Baum, J. R. 1994. Personal and structural determinants of the pace of strategic decision making. *Academy of Management Journal*, 37: 932–956.

Weber, M. 1947. *The theory of social and economic organization* [A. M. Henderson & T. Parsons, trans.]. New York: Oxford.

Zakon, R. 2004. *Hobbes' Internet timeline* (Internet Engineering Task Force [IETF] RFC 2235). http://www.zakon.org/robert/internet/timeline/.

———————————ᴧᴧ———————————

Wesley D. Sine (*wds4@cornell.edu*) is an assistant professor of management and organization at the Johnson Graduate School of Management at Cornell University. He received his Ph.D. from the School of Industrial and Labor Relations at Cornell University. His current research interests include industry and technology emergence, institutional change, and technology entrepreneurship.

Hitoshi Mitsuhashi (*hitoshi@sk.tsukuba.ac.jp*) is an assistant professor of organization and management theory in the Graduate School of Social Systems and Management at the University of Tsukuba. He received his doctorate from the School of Industrial and Labor Relations at Cornell University. His current research interests include the path dependency of organizational behavior, the evolutionary dynamics of interorganizational relationships, and the performance consequences of organizational design.

David. A. Kirsch (*dkirsch@rhsmith.umd.edu*) is an assistant professor of strategy and entrepreneurship at the Robert H. Smith School of Business at the University of Maryland, College Park. He received his doctorate from Stanford University. His research focuses on industry emergence, organizational failure, and the history of the technology, media, and telecommunications (TMT) revolution of the 1990s.

———————————ᴧᴧ———————————

CASE: OB-69
DATE: 09/01/09

NOTE ON ORGANIZATIONAL CULTURE

Many people are skeptical of the idea that organizational cultures exert any real effects on individual and organizational behavior. One reason for this suspicion is that when people use the word culture to explain why a firm behaves the way it does, they often use it as a catch-all category for "the way things are done" in that firm. But "the way things are done" can often be discussed in much more concrete terms by focusing on specific aspects of the formal organization, such as the structure of the incentive plans in place, the formal grouping and linking principles encoded in the formal organizational structure, and the established routines and operating procedures in the firm. If the organizational culture concept merely summarizes these elements, it does seem fair to ask whether the concept adds any value.

An important first step in discussing organizational culture is therefore to define it. Following Schein (1992), an organizational culture consists of a set of basic assumptions that have developed as a consequence of the organization's attempts to adapt to internal and external problems. This definition suggests that organizational culture may be shaped by senior management to align with strategic goals, but it may also evolve in an emergent fashion, without direct influence from management. Organizational culture operates at the level of basic beliefs and values that have been internalized (to a greater or lesser extent) by the organization's members.

To better understand why organizational cultures might play an important role in shaping organizational behavior, consider two generic problems that firms face. The first is the problem of exercising control while at the same time delegating decision-making authority. Managers commonly need to make decisions under conditions of uncertainty, and therefore need to assess what kinds of actions are optimal, from the firm's perspective, and implement them. If different managers within the same firm react differently to similar situations, the organization may have difficulty executing its basic strategy; in short, a lack of consensus can be a source of strategic change, both good and bad. A second, somewhat related problem faced by firms is how to ensure consistent behavior over time, particularly in the face of turnover among its employees. If we have devised a complex yet efficient means of producing our widgets, it would be nice if we

Professor Jesper B. Sørensen prepared this note as the basis for class discussion rather than to illustrate either effective or ineffective handling of an administrative situation.

could do this day in and day out, even if the particular people doing the job on Day 1 are not the same as the people doing the job on Day 100.

Both of these problems can be thought of as problems of persistence: how does a certain way of doing things get maintained, either across people or across time, or both? Organizational cultures play a central role in these situations by defining both cognitive and normative bases for decisions. An organizational culture defines a *normative order* consisting of basic assumptions about what are the "right" and "wrong" kinds of behavior. By virtue of this set of normative assumptions, organizational cultures are social control mechanisms, much like formal reporting relationships, auditing systems and incentive systems (O'Reilly and Chatman, 1996). An organizational culture also defines a *cognitive order* consisting of basic assumption about how the world works; these assumptions frame people's interpretations of organizational events and understanding of organizational processes. Schein (1991: 15) emphasizes that organizational cultures "provide group members with a way of giving meaning to their daily lives, setting guidelines and rules for how to behave, and, most important, reducing and containing the anxiety of dealing with an unpredictable and uncertain environment."

STRONG CULTURES AND PERFORMANCE

Extensive empirical research suggests that organizational cultures play a crucial role in shaping the capabilities of organizations and guiding the behavior of individuals within organizations. The most compelling evidence comes from studies of the effects of strong corporate cultures on firm performance. An organizational culture is said to be strong when the basic assumptions of the culture are widely shared and deeply held by members of the organizations. Studies show that firms with strong corporate cultures — such as Johnson & Johnson and Wal-Mart — have higher average levels of performance than firms in the same industry with weaker cultures, and that this competitive advantage is enhanced in highly competitive markets (Burt et al. 1994). More recent research shows that in most cases, firms with strong cultures not only perform at a higher level, they also do so more consistently (Sørensen 2002). The fact that their performance is generally less volatile gives strong culture firms an added competitive advantage; for example, studies in corporate finance show that firms with high cash flow volatility suffer from under-investment.

Researchers have pointed to three interrelated reasons why strong culture firms outperform weak culture firms. First, widespread consensus and endorsement of organizational values and norms facilitates social control within the firm. When everyone agrees that certain behaviors are more appropriate than others, violations of behavioral norms may be detected and corrected faster. Corrective actions are more likely to come from other employees, regardless of their place in the formal hierarchy. Informal social control is therefore likely more effective and lower cost than formal control structures (O'Reilly and Chatman, 1996). Second, strong corporate cultures enhance goal alignment. With clarity about corporate goals and practices, employees face less uncertainty about the proper course of action when faced with unexpected situations, and can react appropriately. Goal alignment also facilitates coordination, as there is less room for debate between different parties about the firm's best interests (Kreps, 1990). Finally, strong cultures can enhance employee motivation and performance due to the perception that behavior is more freely chosen (O'Reilly, 1989).

The social control and goal alignment aspects of strong organizational cultures suggest a tradeoff associated with culture strength. One simple way to think about this tradeoff is in terms of the implications of strong cultures for organizational learning, and in particular for the balance between exploration and exploitation (March, 1991). Sørensen (2002) argues that, in general, strong corporate cultures encourage exploitation, at the expense of exploratory learning. One consequence of this is that the value of a strong corporate culture is contingent on the degree of change and volatility in a firm's competitive environment. Sørensen (2002) shows that while strong corporate cultures encourage performance reliability in stable environments, strong cultures may be a liability in volatile, rapidly changing environments. In this sense, strong organizational cultures may be a liability, particularly when the basic assumptions encoded in the culture conflict with evolving strategic realities.

CREATING AND MAINTAINING STRONG CORPORATE CULTURES

The evidence of performance benefits linked to strong cultures might leave you wondering: If strong cultures are so good, why doesn't every firm have a strong culture? What are the factors that encourage the persistence of a set of basic assumptions? In general, strong corporate cultures can be arrived at through two routes: selection and socialization. In general, an exclusive reliance on selecting new employees based on cultural fit is a difficult (i.e., expensive and time-consuming) means of creating a strong culture, and is difficult to sustain with even moderate levels of employee turnover or growth. This points to the importance of socialization processes, which may vary dramatically in their level of intensity. The hazing rituals of college fraternities, in response to high, yearly turnover, are an extreme example.

It is useful to think of socialization pressures in an organization as coming from two sources: the firm's leadership and an individual's co-workers. To the extent that the leaders in a firm forcefully and consistently articulate and enact the firm's core values, socialization pressures will be higher. At the same time, such efforts by leaders may be counteracted to the extent that co-workers in the firm hold and espouse beliefs that differ from those of the leaders. Countervailing beliefs among the majority of employees can easily neutralize the best efforts of leadership; this fact points to the central importance of demographic processes (i.e., growth, turnover) in establishing and maintaining corporate culture (for an extended, sophisticated treatment of these issues, see Harrison and Carroll 2006).

A full discussion of the determinants of cultural persistence is beyond the scope of this note. Here, we will limit our attention to a factor that is particularly important when considering the relationship between organizational culture and other elements of organizational design. This factor is the importance of objective, external representations of the culture.

Consider the following insights from social psychology. In a classic experiment, Sherif (1935) exposed individuals to a so-called "autokinetic" situation. If an individual is placed in a darkened room and a stationary pinpoint of light is projected on the wall, the light will appear to move, even though it is perfectly stationary. Sherif found that people's assessments of the amount of movement were totally subjective (i.e., each person developed their own peculiar assessment) but were also very stable over repeated tests. Sherif also found that if several people were in the room at the same time, they arrived at a common assessment of the amount of movement. In fact, the experimenters could shape the group's assessment by having a confederate (someone working for them) make the first verbal assessment. This suggests that people's perceptions of objective reality are shaped through interpersonal influence processes.

But this result is not so surprising. We know from our own lives that the people around us can shape how we see the world. What is less clear is to what extent they shape our perceptions once they leave the room. In other words, is there persistence in these influence effects? One way to test this question is to run the autokinetic experiment over several "generations" of a group, where people enter and exit the group at different times. Zucker (1977) modified the Sherif experiment in this way in order to study the persistence problem. The first generation consisted of two people, one of whom worked for Zucker, who were exposed to the autokinetic situation. The confederate made the first assessment, and the second person's assessments was very close to the confederate's. The confederate then left the group and was replaced by a new person. The experiment was repeated with the new person and the veteran, with veteran making the first assessment. The veteran then left and was replaced by a new person, and so on.

Zucker varied what she told people before they entered the room. In the "personal influence condition," people were simply told that the study involved problem solving in groups, and that the person already in the room had already done the "work" before. For this group, there was little persistence: the assessments in the early generations were very weakly correlated with the assessments in the later generations. In the "organizational context condition," people were told that the study was about problem solving in *organizations*, and that they would be working with a member of the organization. In this case, the assessments of movement persisted very strongly across subsequent generations, such that the assessment of the person in the first generation was very similar to the assessment of a person from several generations later.

There are two important lessons to draw from these experiments. First, social influence processes can shape the way in which people interpret seemingly objective phenomena. This means that organizations can "define the situation" for their members, in part simply through the transmission of beliefs from existing employees to new hires. The second lesson, however, is that you cannot depend on interpersonal transmission of beliefs alone, unless turnover rates are very low. A set of cultural beliefs and perceptions are much more likely to persist if they appear objective and external to any particular individual. The simple fact the newcomer was told that the other person in the room was an organizational representative was enough to dramatically increase levels of persistence. The "organizational" assessment was treated as being much more authoritative than another person's. In a more sociological language, cultures are more likely to persist if they are *institutionalized.*

This has important implications for the relationship between strategy, culture and organizational design. Organizational cultures are much more likely to persist if the basic assumptions are expressed concretely in organizational practices, espoused values and cultural artifacts. The culture has much greater force if it is tied to visible symbols, and these symbols are used to remind people of the organizations core beliefs and values. Similarly, leaders can increase their socialization influence on subordinates through the use of signals, where signals are understood as costly actions or investments that are undertaken to be consistent with the espoused beliefs and values. This in turn means that if organizations want to foster and maintain a strong culture, they need to invest resources and awareness in symbols and signals that are consistent with the basic assumptions of the culture.

This gives us another way of thinking about the decisions involved in choosing formal elements of organizational design, like incentive systems and formal structures, as well as explicit statements of strategic intent. These formal elements are often the most visible symbols of what the organization "really means." They must therefore be carefully chosen with an eye toward whether they are consistent with the desired or established basic assumptions of the culture.

The fact that strong cultures are typically "built in" to the other elements of organization design suggests a downside of having a strong culture. In cases where the organizational culture is reinforced by such things as incentive plans, formal structure and resource allocation patterns, change can be difficult, because change in one element of the organization has implications for other parts. Strong culture organizations in particular have greater difficulty changing their basic assumptions about the world around them, even when the world has changed. One important consequence of this is that strong culture firms have difficulty adjusting to periods of fundamental change in the structure and dynamics of their environments, to the extent that the performance benefits of strong cultures disappear in volatile environments (Sørensen 2002).

References

Burt, Ronald S., Shaul M. Gabbay, Gerhard Holt, and Peter Moran. 1994. "Contingent organization as a network theory: The culture performance contingency function." *Acta Sociologica* 37: 345-370.

Harrison, J. Richard, and Glenn R. Carroll.   2006. Culture and Demography in Organizations. Princeton: Princeton University Press.

Kreps, David M. 1990. "Corporate culture and economic theory." Pp. 90-143 in J.E. Alt and K.A. Shepsle (eds.), *Perspectives on Positive Political Economy* Cambridge, England: Cambridge University Press.

O'Reilly, Charles A. 1989 "Corporations, culture and commitment: Motivation and social control in organizations." *California Management Review* 31: 9-25.

O'Reilly, Charles A. and Jennifer A. Chatman. 1996. "Culture as social control: corporations, culture and commitment." *Research in Organizational Behavior* 18: 157-200.

Schein, Edgar H. 1991. "The role of the founder in the creation of organizational culture." Pp. 14-25 in Peter J. Frost et al. (eds), *Organizational Cultures*. Beverly Hills, CA: Sage. Schein, Edgrar H. 1992 *Organizational Culture and Leadership* (2nd edition). San Francisco: Jossey-Bass.

Sherif, M. 1935. "A study of some social factors in perception." *Archives of Psychology*, No 187.

Sørensen, Jesper B. 2002. "The strength of corporate culture and the reliability of firm performance." *Administrative Science Quarterly* 47: 70-91.

Zucker, Lynne G. 1977. "The role of institutionalization in cultural persistence." *American Sociological Review* 42: 726-743.

GOING FLAT: PURSUIT OF A DEMOCRATIC ORGANIZATIONAL STRUCTURE

Bella Wilfer graduated from the Darden Graduate School of Business Administration in 2010, ready to become a principled leader in the world of practical affairs. Wilfer had pursued the consulting track while at Darden and had spent her summer internship at a large, prestigious management consulting firm. After being offered a full-time job and deciding that her summer employer was not a good fit, Wilfer had taken time in the fall of her second year to explore other options for full-time employment after graduation before accepting her offer.

In her off-grounds search, Wilfer had found Ethical Business Company (EBC) through an alumni connection and was instantly intrigued. Not only did the company consult on many of the ethical issues that were important to Wilfer, it also had a flat organizational structure. When she compared it with the other large, hierarchical organizations, she decided she would have a greater impact earlier in her career and more control over it at EBC. Although it was a riskier choice than going with a larger and more established firm, Wilfer was excited about being able to use her skills in direct interaction with clients and senior executives, rather than having them hidden beneath multiple layers of hierarchy. After long consideration, she turned down the offer from her summer employer and signed with EBC.

Company History

John Harmon, the CEO of EBC, had earned a BA in philosophy from Duke in 1986 and his MA in philosophy from Columbia in 1988. He had subsequently graduated from Yale Law School in 1991 and accepted a position at a Boston law firm. After less than a year at the firm, Harmon decided to start his own company. He wanted to help companies prevent the ethical problems that led to lawsuits, rather than having to deal with them after the fact. His firm offered training and a series of workshops to engage and educate employees on ethical issues as well as advisory services related to corporate ethics.

In 2001 and 2002, the scandals at Enron and WorldCom rocked the corporate world. The surge of interest in corporate ethics that resulted created a boom in business for EBC, particularly in advisory services, and the company's visibility increased when Harmon was interviewed for several articles on corporate ethics. By EBC's 15th anniversary, it had grown to 400 employees in four global offices and included a number of notable *Fortune* 500 companies in its client base. There were only a few small firms that dealt specifically with ethics issues, but EBC still faced competition from larger management consulting firms whose competencies included organizational behavior and change.

Then in 2008, Harmon published *Flat: A New Business Operating System*, a manifesto on the need for change in the business community to more effectively inspire principled performance. Harmon tapped into growing trends toward decentralized organizational structures inspired by an increasingly globalized and interconnected world. Companies such as Semco and Google had been successful by eliminating organizational layers, and hierarchy was declining in companies across industries. Shortly after its publication, Harmon's book was in the top 100 books bought from Amazon.com and one of the top 20 books on business and investing.

In 2009, EBC acquired a 30-person boutique consulting firm called Rokesmith and Handford, LLC, that specialized in addressing human rights issues. The same year, Harmon began restructuring the combined company based on the principles outlined in his book.

Philosophy

Harmon envisioned a business that operated as a democracy, characterized by flat governance, open communication, shared leadership, and radical transparency. In his own company, he had a specific plan to implement this vision. The existing leadership structure of the CEO and several vice presidents would become an executive committee that was aided in its decision making by four committees democratically elected by all personnel. Employees throughout the company would be encouraged to think about their roles differently. Rather than organizing the company hierarchically with titles that reflected seniority, employees would be categorized by work area. Specifically, they would be grouped into three categories of responsibility: "Support," "Seek," and "See."

EBC would make other changes to solidify the new organizational structure and get employees thinking in the new mindset. The company would move into a new office space designed to reflect the flatter organizational structure. Offices for senior-level managers would be replaced by cubicles for all levels of employees and shared office space. Performance reviews that had been based primarily on individual metrics would be replaced by more collective division and company goals.

The Office

The highlight of Wilfer's first day at ECB was her office. Harmon had designed every detail, down to the furniture and wall décor, and loved to give tours to anyone who visited the office. Harmon was clearly very passionate about his work. He struck Wilfer as a cross between a politician and a motivational speaker.

The space into which EBC had moved earlier that year was a physical representation of the flatness and transparency of the company. The office was very open and full of natural light, with a beautiful view overlooking Boston Common. The internal walls were all glass, allowing its occupants to enjoy the light and the view from anywhere in the spacious office. The cubicle walls were low and made of glass, so Wilfer could see clear across the office from where she sat. There were no closed doors, and the space conveyed openness and accessibility. Throughout the office were a variety of shared meeting spaces, all with state-of-the-art technology, as well as movable walls to allow for different types of collaboration.

In each cubicle and meeting space was a copy of the Leadership Charter, a diagram of the traits of a successful leader taken from Harmon's book. The charter not only reinforced the company's values but also supported the idea that everyone in the company was a leader. The meeting spaces were named after such core company values as integrity and trust. Even the artwork reflected the company's vision with depictions of famous philosophers and their notable quotes. Wilfer did not think any of her fellow b-school graduates walked past pictures of Confucius, Gandhi, and Adam Smith on a daily basis.

Settling In

In her first week, Wilfer went through training with four other new employees. Many names were mentioned during the training, and one of Wilfer's fellow hires had asked to see an organizational chart in order to put names with faces. The response: There was no organizational chart because EBC was a flat company. As Wilfer was introduced to new people, she found it confusing not to know where they fit in the company hierarchy. Who were her colleagues? Who would she be managing? Who would be managing her? As part of adjusting to the company culture, she figured she would have to get over her impulse to categorize people hierarchically.

By noon on her second day, Wilfer had been given her laptop and her e-mail had been set up, so she read her first messages. One e-mail introduced five new employees with a brief paragraph about each of their backgrounds. She glanced through the e-mail and noticed that she was not referred to as an associate but as a person who operated with a "Support mindset." She looked at the two other employees hired right out of b-school. One was also listed as "Support," but the other was listed as "See."

During a break in afternoon training, Wilfer asked her cohort what was meant by a mindset. One person had mentioned that "Seek" referred to more senior people who were involved in engaging new clients, "See" referred to those people who were working to find solutions for those clients, and "Support" referred to people who were involved in activities such as HR that enabled other employees. Someone else asked about the categories and got these responses: "See" stood for the more senior people who set company vision and strategy, "Support" stood for people who supported that vision in their daily work with clients, and "Seek" stood for HR because it sought out new talent. But when Wilfer asked another employee to clarify further, he merely shrugged and said the definitions were not firm.

At the end of her second day, Wilfer looked through a stack of papers from that day's training and found a to-do list for new hires. Working her way down the list, she looked for something quick she could finish before she left. Because ordering business cards seemed straightforward, she went to the website and began filling out the form until she came to the place for her title. She was stuck. Should she put associate? Could she hand a client a business card that said "Support mindset"? Since EBC had done away with titles, what other option did she have? With a sigh, she realized she would have to ask someone, although she didn't know who to ask.

Coffee Chat

As she walked to work on Monday morning her second week of work, Wilfer was excited to be done with training and ready for her first project. She was assigned to help a major electric utility conduct an assessment of its internal transparency and recommend ways to improve communication across the company. At least on the project, it was clear who the manager was. After chatting with her teammates, she was able to figure out who had MBAs versus who had college degrees and how long everyone had been at the company. Wilfer was more comfortable once she had worked out the seniority on her own.

On Tuesday morning, the project manager asked Wilfer to put some survey results into PowerPoint by the end of the day. Looking at her schedule, Wilfer thought she would have plenty of time to complete the task and agreed to do it. The only thing she had on her calendar in the afternoon was a coffee chat with John Harmon. She had scheduled an hour and a half for that, and she assumed it was a social meet and greet to give everyone a chance to talk informally with the CEO. She had hoped to be able to talk more to the charismatic leader of the company.

As an Outlook reminder popped up on her screen to remind her of the coffee chat, she was surprised when everyone started moving toward the lobby. When she made a comment about this to a colleague named Eugene Wrayburn, he said, "Oh, coffee chats are mandatory." Wilfer found this odd but was still looking forward to it. When she reached the crowded lobby, she was surprised when John Harmon began addressing the entire group. Harmon announced that he was aware of the concerns regarding his recent post on his business blog and launched into a speech.

Wilfer was confused as to what this was all about, but she began to understand as she listened to Harmon's speech and was helped by a few whispered comments from Wrayburn. Harmon's blog post had focused on EBC's journey to becoming a flat organization. In the article, he had referenced the company's four democratically elected committees. In reality, the committees had not been elected democratically: Following an initial nomination process for committee members that was open to all employees, Harmon had added more criteria for nomination including number of years at the company and alignment with EBC values. This change in the process effectively narrowed the pool of nominees to members of the senior leadership who had managed the company before its restructuring.

One specific grievance concerned an employee named Jenny Wren. Wren had been nominated by a number of people for the employee excellence committee, which handled EBC's HR functions. Before coming to work at EBC, Wren had spent several years as a human capital consultant. For this reason, her co-workers thought she would be a valuable asset to the committee. But Wren had only a college degree and just two years of work experience at EBC, so her name was removed from the ballot before the election. Many employees believed this action was contrary to the idea of democratic governance. Wilfer agreed.

The larger issue, however, was not the election itself, but how Harmon had portrayed it publicly. Given that one of EBC's service offerings was implementing organizational change, employees thought it was misleading to gloss over the company's own implementation process. Employees argued that although most companies might not be so open and transparent about their internal struggles, EBC was not most companies. EBC claimed to hold itself to a higher standard. Harmon apologized for the article, saying it was an error in wording that should have been caught before publication. He also stated that the elections were part of an ongoing process on EBC's journey toward democratic leadership.

Wilfer left the coffee break concerned about the election and the blog and disappointed in Harmon's response. When she got back to her desk, she was shocked to see that the coffee break had taken two hours. As she scrambled to finish her work before the end of the day, she kept thinking about the coffee break. Her concern was not only about the content of the meeting, but also how many working hours across the organization had been devoted to it.

Leadership Charter

As the week continued, Wilfer was preoccupied with getting up to speed on her project, which had already started. Later in the week, she headed to a conference room for a team meeting. When she arrived, she learned that the project manager was running late and the other recent MBA grad would be calling in from another location. For the moment, she was accompanied only by the more junior employees or, as they called themselves, "the employees formerly known as analysts." While they waited, she became distracted by the conversation going on around her.

The conversation was about the Leadership Charter that took up a large part of one wall of the conference room. The "analysts" were making jokes about the language in the charter, which contrasted the traits of a poor leader with those of a good leader. One example was, "Watches the clock" versus "Time has no meaning," which prompted one person to remark about working in the Twilight Zone, and someone else to comment that some part describing the trait did not even make grammatical sense. Another pairing, "Stops at the minimum" versus "Never stops" had inspired one employee to sketch on the board an Energizer Bunny leading lemmings off a cliff.

Wilfer was not sure how to react. Although she agreed that some of the language in the Leadership Charter was over the top, she felt uncomfortable openly mocking the core principles of the company. But she did not want to say anything because she did not think it was her job to try and instill respect for the charter in her fellow employees. That raised the question of whose job it was, but before she had time to think about that, she saw the project manager headed toward the conference room. The sketch had disappeared, and everyone had their laptops up and ready by the time the manager arrived.

Passion

At the end of the meeting, the project manager asked Wilfer to book a conference room for three hours on the following Monday. Wilfer pulled up Outlook immediately to book the room, but she was not yet familiar with the names and capacities of all of the rooms, so Eugene Wrayburn stayed to help. As she studied the meeting planner, Wilfer realized it was going to be hard to find a room available for three hours. Almost all of those with enough room for their entire team did not show any three-hour gaps. Only the "Passion" room looked available.

"Looks like we can't schedule it on Monday," Wrayburn said. When Wilfer responded that Passion was open, Wrayburn said, "Passion is never available." Not sure what to make of his comment, Wilfer booked Passion for a three-hour block on Monday. Then, heeding Wrayburn's warning, she also booked the "Trust" room for Tuesday just in case. Immediately, she received two automated responses: One confirmed "Trust" for Tuesday, and the other notified her that "Passion" was unavailable. "What's up with 'Passion'?," Wilfer asked.

Wrayburn responded that it was Harmon's office. But Wilfer already thought she knew from the tour where Harmon's cubicle was. Wrayburn explained that, although Harmon had a cubicle, everyone knew that the "Passion" conference room, located directly behind his cubicle, was reserved for his use at all times. Wrayburn said that, in addition to the conference table, it even had a large desk and with pictures of Harmon's family. Wilfer did not have any problem with Harmon having an office like other CEOs did. She just thought it weird that he pretended not to have one. The situation reminded her of a quote in George Orwell's *Animal Farm* in which the animals' new society was created on the principle that "all animals are equal," before the pigs added, "but some animals are more equal than others."

Town Hall Meeting

By Friday, Wilfer was frustrated. She noticed an hour blocked off on her calendar for a town hall meeting in the afternoon. She had other meetings scheduled for client work and other internal projects and was worried about finding time to get it all done. When she asked Wrayburn what a town hall meeting was, he replied that it was a forum for Harmon to respond to employee concerns. "How is it different from a coffee chat?" Wilfer asked. "It isn't," he replied.

The concerns raised at the town hall meeting had to do with the division that had been Rokesmith and Handford, LLC, before its acquisition the previous year. The complaints were focused on goals and hiring. Earlier in the week, Harmon had announced the goals for EBC's upcoming fiscal year, and he had said that no one would be eligible for a bonus unless his or her division met its goal. Overall, the company's goal was to grow by 10%. But that growth was very unevenly distributed. The division that had been Rokesmith and Handford was required to double that growth, whereas the rest of the company's requirement was less than 2%. The employees of the Rokesmith and Handford division wanted an explanation as to why their growth targets were so much higher, particularly given that the division was not scheduled for a proportionally high staff increase.

In addition, all employees were concerned that it was taking too long to hire new staff. Wilfer had been hired before the council structure had been implemented. Since that time, the hiring process had slowed, and it was now taking more than six months to get people on board. The company had three positions still unfilled since January, and it was now July. Several people had interviewed for each position, and the employee excellence committee had repeatedly said it was in the final stages of the hiring process but gave no further details.

Harmon responded with metaphorical answers to employees' straightforward operational questions. When asked how goals were determined, Harmon talked about the vision of a horizontal organization and then explained how the root of "horizontal" was the word "horizon." He claimed that the horizon was as far as the eye could see and indicated unlimited, unknown possibilities. As Harmon orated, Wilfer realized he was not going to answer the question, and she noticed most of her colleagues in the room had tuned him out.

The Exodus

On Thursday of her third week, Wilfer once again headed to the lobby for an "all hands" meeting. This time, Wilfer was expecting more employee complaints, so she was not prepared for what happened. At the front of the lobby with Harmon were four of the most senior employees at the company. Then, one at a time, all four announced that they were leaving and gave their reasons for departure: "I'm taking some time off to travel," "I've never stayed with any company longer than five years and feel it's time to move on," "After so many years as a consultant, I need to work in industry to gain experience in implementation," and "I'd like to spend more time with my family." The reasons were transparent, and the overall message was clear: Four high-level people were jumping ship.

That afternoon, employees in the Rokesmith and Handford division worried about how they were going to meet their aggressive targets without two of their senior leaders. Everyone worried about how long it was going to take to replace four senior-level people, given the existing hiring backlog. There was speculation as to why the employees were really leaving and worry that qualified people would not want to work at EBC for the same reasons. Some said it was because the flatter organizational structure involved a flatter compensation plan, which was no longer competitive in the industry. Others added that, because collective goals had replaced individual metrics, the bonus plan was also not competitive. And some even said that Harmon was forcing out anyone who did not buy into the restructuring and the ideas in his manifesto.

The next day, Wilfer sat in a meeting with all the project managers, those who represented the next layer of management under the four people who had announced their departures. These managers were worried about how the company was going to attract the new clients necessary for them to meet their performance goals. Everyone contributed to the list of what needed to be done, but no one offered to do anything. Wilfer was surprised that in a room of people with MBAs and years of experience at the firm, most of them concentrated on the problems instead of the solutions. Top people had just stepped down, but no one stepped up. She had thought the problem was that Harmon was not ready to let go of the reins, but maybe the problem was that no one was ready to pick them up. After years of being insulated within a hierarchy, her co-workers were not going to stick their necks out and take on a bigger role in managing the company.

The Dilemma

Wilfer reflected on everything that had happened during her three weeks at EBC. She agreed with the idea of a flat, democratic organization, but now she was not sure just how to achieve it. She wondered if a flat structure was right for all companies and all employees or if there were certain companies and people who fit better in the hierarchy more than others. She tried to decide what she would have done differently if she had been John Harmon. Most of all, Wilfer worried about what she should do about her current situation at EBC.

Harvard Business Review

www.hbrreprints.org

Leaders who successfully transform businesses do eight things right (and they do them in the right order).

Leading Change
Why Transformation Efforts Fail

by John P. Kotter

Included with this full-text *Harvard Business Review* article:

Reprint R0701J

Leading Change
Why Transformation Efforts Fail

The Idea in Brief

Most major change initiatives—whether intended to boost quality, improve culture, or reverse a corporate death spiral—generate only lukewarm results. Many fail miserably.

Why? Kotter maintains that too many managers don't realize transformation is a *process*, not an event. It advances through stages that build on each other. And it takes years. Pressured to accelerate the process, managers skip stages. But shortcuts never work.

Equally troubling, even highly capable managers make critical mistakes—such as declaring victory too soon. Result? Loss of momentum, reversal of hard-won gains, and devastation of the entire transformation effort.

By understanding the stages of change—and the pitfalls unique to each stage—you boost your chances of a successful transformation. The payoff? Your organization flexes with tectonic shifts in competitors, markets, and technologies—leaving rivals far behind.

The Idea in Practice

To give your transformation effort the best chance of succeeding, take the right actions at each stage—and avoid common pitfalls.

Stage	Actions Needed	Pitfalls
Establish a sense of urgency	• Examine market and competitive realities for potential crises and untapped opportunities. • Convince at least 75% of your managers that the status quo is more dangerous than the unknown.	• Underestimating the difficulty of driving people from their comfort zones • Becoming paralyzed by risks
Form a powerful guiding coalition	• Assemble a group with shared commitment and enough power to lead the change effort. • Encourage them to work as a team outside the normal hierarchy.	• No prior experience in teamwork at the top • Relegating team leadership to an HR, quality, or strategic-planning executive rather than a senior line manager
Create a vision	• Create a vision to direct the change effort. • Develop strategies for realizing that vision.	• Presenting a vision that's too complicated or vague to be communicated in five minutes
Communicate the vision	• Use every vehicle possible to communicate the new vision and strategies for achieving it. • Teach new behaviors by the example of the guiding coalition.	• Undercommunicating the vision • Behaving in ways antithetical to the vision
Empower others to act on the vision	• Remove or alter systems or structures undermining the vision. • Encourage risk taking and nontraditional ideas, activities, and actions.	• Failing to remove powerful individuals who resist the change effort
Plan for and create short-term wins	• Define and engineer visible performance improvements. • Recognize and reward employees contributing to those improvements.	• Leaving short-term successes up to chance • Failing to score successes early enough (12-24 months into the change effort)
Consolidate improvements and produce more change	• Use increased credibility from early wins to change systems, structures, and policies undermining the vision. • Hire, promote, and develop employees who can implement the vision. • Reinvigorate the change process with new projects and change agents.	• Declaring victory too soon—with the first performance improvement • Allowing resistors to convince "troops" that the war has been won
Institutionalize new approaches	• Articulate connections between new behaviors and corporate success. • Create leadership development and succession plans consistent with the new approach.	• Not creating new social norms and shared values consistent with changes • Promoting people into leadership positions who don't personify the new approach

Leaders who successfully transform businesses do eight things right (and they do them in the right order).

Leading Change
Why Transformation Efforts Fail

by John P. Kotter

Editor's Note: Guiding change may be the ultimate test of a leader—no business survives over the long term if it can't reinvent itself. But, human nature being what it is, fundamental change is often resisted mightily by the people it most affects: those in the trenches of the business. Thus, leading change is both absolutely essential and incredibly difficult.

Perhaps nobody understands the anatomy of organizational change better than retired Harvard Business School professor John P. Kotter. This article, originally published in the spring of 1995, previewed Kotter's 1996 book *Leading Change*. It outlines eight critical success factors—from establishing a sense of extraordinary urgency, to creating short-term wins, to changing the culture ("the way we do things around here"). It will feel familiar when you read it, in part because Kotter's vocabulary has entered the lexicon and in part because it contains the kind of home truths that we recognize, immediately, as if we'd always known them. A decade later, his work on leading change remains definitive.

Over the past decade, I have watched more than 100 companies try to remake themselves into significantly better competitors. They have included large organizations (Ford) and small ones (Landmark Communications), companies based in the United States (General Motors) and elsewhere (British Airways), corporations that were on their knees (Eastern Airlines), and companies that were earning good money (Bristol-Myers Squibb). These efforts have gone under many banners: total quality management, reengineering, rightsizing, restructuring, cultural change, and turnaround. But, in almost every case, the basic goal has been the same: to make fundamental changes in how business is conducted in order to help cope with a new, more challenging market environment.

A few of these corporate change efforts have been very successful. A few have been utter failures. Most fall somewhere in between, with a distinct tilt toward the lower end of the scale. The lessons that can be drawn are interesting and will probably be relevant to even more organizations in the increasingly competitive business environment of the coming decade.

The most general lesson to be learned from the more successful cases is that the change process goes through a series of phases that, in total, usually require a considerable length of time. Skipping steps creates only the illusion of speed and never produces a satisfying result. A second very general lesson is that critical mistakes in any of the phases can have a devastating impact, slowing momentum and negating hard-won gains. Perhaps because we have relatively little experience in renewing organizations, even very capable people often make at least one big error.

Error 1: Not Establishing a Great Enough Sense of Urgency

Most successful change efforts begin when some individuals or some groups start to look hard at a company's competitive situation, market position, technological trends, and financial performance. They focus on the potential revenue drop when an important patent expires, the five-year trend in declining margins in a core business, or an emerging market that everyone seems to be ignoring. They then find ways to communicate this information broadly and dramatically, especially with respect to crises, potential crises, or great opportunities that are very timely. This first step is essential because just getting a transformation program started requires the aggressive cooperation of many individuals. Without motivation, people won't help, and the effort goes nowhere.

Compared with other steps in the change process, phase one can sound easy. It is not. Well over 50% of the companies I have watched fail in this first phase. What are the reasons for that failure? Sometimes executives underestimate how hard it can be to drive people out of their comfort zones. Sometimes they grossly overestimate how successful they have already been in increasing urgency. Sometimes they lack patience: "Enough with the preliminaries; let's get on with it." In many cases, executives become paralyzed by the downside possibilities. They worry that employees with seniority will become defensive, that morale will drop, that events will spin out of control, that short-term business results will be jeopardized, that the stock will sink, and that they will be blamed for creating a crisis.

A paralyzed senior management often comes from having too many managers and not enough leaders. Management's mandate is to minimize risk and to keep the current system operating. Change, by definition, requires creating a new system, which in turn always demands leadership. Phase one in a renewal process typically goes nowhere until enough real leaders are promoted or hired into senior-level jobs.

Transformations often begin, and begin well, when an organization has a new head who is a good leader and who sees the need for a major change. If the renewal target is the entire company, the CEO is key. If change is needed in a division, the division general manager is key. When these individuals are not new leaders, great leaders, or change champions, phase one can be a huge challenge.

Bad business results are both a blessing and a curse in the first phase. On the positive side, losing money does catch people's attention. But it also gives less maneuvering room. With good business results, the opposite is true: Convincing people of the need for change is much harder, but you have more resources to help make changes.

But whether the starting point is good performance or bad, in the more successful cases I have witnessed, an individual or a group always facilitates a frank discussion of potentially unpleasant facts about new competition, shrinking margins, decreasing market share, flat earnings, a lack of revenue growth, or other relevant indices of a declining competitive position. Because there seems to be an almost universal human tendency to shoot the bearer of bad news, especially if the head of the organization is not a change champion, executives in these companies often rely on outsiders to bring unwanted information. Wall Street analysts, customers, and consultants can all be helpful in this regard. The purpose of all this activity, in the words of one former CEO of a large European company, is "to make the status quo seem more dangerous than launching into the unknown."

In a few of the most successful cases, a group has manufactured a crisis. One CEO deliberately engineered the largest accounting loss in the company's history, creating huge pressures from Wall Street in the process. One division president commissioned first-ever customer satisfaction surveys, knowing full well that the

Now retired, **John P. Kotter** was the Konosuke Matsushita Professor of Leadership at Harvard Business School in Boston.

results would be terrible. He then made these findings public. On the surface, such moves can look unduly risky. But there is also risk in playing it too safe: When the urgency rate is not pumped up enough, the transformation process cannot succeed, and the long-term future of the organization is put in jeopardy.

When is the urgency rate high enough? From what I have seen, the answer is when about 75% of a company's management is honestly convinced that business as usual is totally unacceptable. Anything less can produce very serious problems later on in the process.

Error 2: Not Creating a Powerful Enough Guiding Coalition

Major renewal programs often start with just one or two people. In cases of successful transformation efforts, the leadership coalition grows and grows over time. But whenever some minimum mass is not achieved early in the effort, nothing much worthwhile happens.

It is often said that major change is impossible unless the head of the organization is an active supporter. What I am talking about goes far beyond that. In successful transformations, the chairman or president or division general manager, plus another five or 15 or 50 people, come together and develop a shared commitment to excellent performance through renewal. In my experience, this group never includes all of the company's most senior executives because some people just won't buy in, at least not at first. But in the most successful cases, the coalition is always pretty powerful—in terms of titles,

EIGHT STEPS TO TRANSFORMING YOUR ORGANIZATION

1 Establishing a Sense of Urgency
- Examining market and competitive realities
- Identifying and discussing crises, potential crises, or major opportunities

2 Forming a Powerful Guiding Coalition
- Assembling a group with enough power to lead the change effort
- Encouraging the group to work together as a team

3 Creating a Vision
- Creating a vision to help direct the change effort
- Developing strategies for achieving that vision

4 Communicating the Vision
- Using every vehicle possible to communicate the new vision and strategies
- Teaching new behaviors by the example of the guiding coalition

5 Empowering Others to Act on the Vision
- Getting rid of obstacles to change
- Changing systems or structures that seriously undermine the vision
- Encouraging risk taking and nontraditional ideas, activities, and actions

6 Planning for and Creating Short-Term Wins
- Planning for visible performance improvements
- Creating those improvements
- Recognizing and rewarding employees involved in the improvements

7 Consolidating Improvements and Producing Still More Change
- Using increased credibility to change systems, structures, and policies that don't fit the vision
- Hiring, promoting, and developing employees who can implement the vision
- Reinvigorating the process with new projects, themes, and change agents

8 Institutionalizing New Approaches
- Articulating the connections between the new behaviors and corporate success
- Developing the means to ensure leadership development and succession

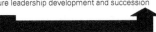

If you can't communicate the vision to someone in five minutes or less and get a reaction that signifies both understanding and interest, you are not done.

information and expertise, reputations, and relationships.

In both small and large organizations, a successful guiding team may consist of only three to five people during the first year of a renewal effort. But in big companies, the coalition needs to grow to the 20 to 50 range before much progress can be made in phase three and beyond. Senior managers always form the core of the group. But sometimes you find board members, a representative from a key customer, or even a powerful union leader.

Because the guiding coalition includes members who are not part of senior management, it tends to operate outside of the normal hierarchy by definition. This can be awkward, but it is clearly necessary. If the existing hierarchy were working well, there would be no need for a major transformation. But since the current system is not working, reform generally demands activity outside of formal boundaries, expectations, and protocol.

A high sense of urgency within the managerial ranks helps enormously in putting a guiding coalition together. But more is usually required. Someone needs to get these people together, help them develop a shared assessment of their company's problems and opportunities, and create a minimum level of trust and communication. Off-site retreats, for two or three days, are one popular vehicle for accomplishing this task. I have seen many groups of five to 35 executives attend a series of these retreats over a period of months.

Companies that fail in phase two usually underestimate the difficulties of producing change and thus the importance of a powerful guiding coalition. Sometimes they have no history of teamwork at the top and therefore undervalue the importance of this type of coalition. Sometimes they expect the team to be led by a staff executive from human resources, quality, or strategic planning instead of a key line manager. No matter how capable or dedicated the staff head, groups without strong line leadership never achieve the power that is required.

Efforts that don't have a powerful enough guiding coalition can make apparent progress for a while. But, sooner or later, the opposition gathers itself together and stops the change.

Error 3: Lacking a Vision
In every successful transformation effort that I have seen, the guiding coalition develops a picture of the future that is relatively easy to communicate and appeals to customers, stockholders, and employees. A vision always goes beyond the numbers that are typically found in five-year plans. A vision says something that helps clarify the direction in which an organization needs to move. Sometimes the first draft comes mostly from a single individual. It is usually a bit blurry, at least initially. But after the coalition works at it for three or five or even 12 months, something much better emerges through their tough analytical thinking and a little dreaming. Eventually, a strategy for achieving that vision is also developed.

In one midsize European company, the first pass at a vision contained two-thirds of the basic ideas that were in the final product. The concept of global reach was in the initial version from the beginning. So was the idea of becoming preeminent in certain businesses. But one central idea in the final version—getting out of low value-added activities—came only after a series of discussions over a period of several months.

Without a sensible vision, a transformation effort can easily dissolve into a list of confusing and incompatible projects that can take the organization in the wrong direction or nowhere at all. Without a sound vision, the reengineering project in the accounting department, the new 360-degree performance appraisal from the human resources department, the plant's quality program, the cultural change project in the sales force will not add up in a meaningful way.

In failed transformations, you often find plenty of plans, directives, and programs but no vision. In one case, a company gave out four-inch-thick notebooks describing its change effort. In mind-numbing detail, the books spelled out procedures, goals, methods, and deadlines. But nowhere was there a clear and compelling statement of where all this was leading. Not surprisingly, most of the employees with whom I talked were either confused or alienated. The big, thick books did not rally them together or inspire change. In fact, they probably had just the opposite effect.

In a few of the less successful cases that I have seen, management had a sense of direction, but it was too complicated or blurry to be useful. Recently, I asked an executive in a midsize company to describe his vision and received in return a barely comprehensible 30-

minute lecture. Buried in his answer were the basic elements of a sound vision. But they were buried—deeply.

A useful rule of thumb: If you can't communicate the vision to someone in five minutes or less and get a reaction that signifies both understanding and interest, you are not yet done with this phase of the transformation process.

Error 4: Undercommunicating the Vision by a Factor of Ten

I've seen three patterns with respect to communication, all very common. In the first, a group actually does develop a pretty good transformation vision and then proceeds to communicate it by holding a single meeting or sending out a single communication. Having used about 0.0001% of the yearly intracompany communication, the group is startled when few people seem to understand the new approach. In the second pattern, the head of the organization spends a considerable amount of time making speeches to employee groups, but most people still don't get it (not surprising, since vision captures only 0.0005% of the total yearly communication). In the third pattern, much more effort goes into newsletters and speeches, but some very visible senior executives still behave in ways that are antithetical to the vision. The net result is that cynicism among the troops goes up, while belief in the communication goes down.

Transformation is impossible unless hundreds or thousands of people are willing to help, often to the point of making short-term sacrifices. Employees will not make sacrifices, even if they are unhappy with the status quo, unless they believe that useful change is possible. Without credible communication, and a lot of it, the hearts and minds of the troops are never captured.

This fourth phase is particularly challenging if the short-term sacrifices include job losses. Gaining understanding and support is tough when downsizing is a part of the vision. For this reason, successful visions usually include new growth possibilities and the commitment to treat fairly anyone who is laid off.

Executives who communicate well incorporate messages into their hour-by-hour activities. In a routine discussion about a business problem, they talk about how proposed solutions fit (or don't fit) into the bigger picture. In a regular performance appraisal, they talk

about how the employee's behavior helps or undermines the vision. In a review of a division's quarterly performance, they talk not only about the numbers but also about how the division's executives are contributing to the transformation. In a routine Q&A with employees at a company facility, they tie their answers back to renewal goals.

In more successful transformation efforts, executives use all existing communication channels to broadcast the vision. They turn boring, unread company newsletters into lively articles about the vision. They take ritualistic, tedious quarterly management meetings and turn them into exciting discussions of the transformation. They throw out much of the company's generic management education and replace it with courses that focus on business problems and the new vision. The guiding principle is simple: Use every possible channel, especially those that are being wasted on nonessential information.

Perhaps even more important, most of the executives I have known in successful cases of major change learn to "walk the talk." They consciously attempt to become a living symbol of the new corporate culture. This is often not easy. A 60-year-old plant manager who has spent precious little time over 40 years thinking about customers will not suddenly behave in a customer-oriented way. But I have witnessed just such a person change, and change a great deal. In that case, a high level of urgency helped. The fact that the man was a part of the guiding coalition and the vision-creation team also helped. So did all the communication, which kept reminding him of the desired behavior, and all the feedback from his peers and subordinates, which helped him see when he was not engaging in that behavior.

Communication comes in both words and deeds, and the latter are often the most powerful form. Nothing undermines change more than behavior by important individuals that is inconsistent with their words.

Error 5: Not Removing Obstacles to the New Vision

Successful transformations begin to involve large numbers of people as the process progresses. Employees are emboldened to try new approaches, to develop new ideas, and to provide leadership. The only constraint is that the actions fit within the broad parameters of the overall vision. The more people involved, the better the outcome.

To some degree, a guiding coalition empowers others to take action simply by successfully communicating the new direction. But communication is never sufficient by itself. Renewal also requires the removal of obstacles. Too often, an employee understands the new vision and wants to help make it happen, but an elephant appears to be blocking the path. In some cases, the elephant is in the person's head, and the challenge is to convince the individual that no external obstacle exists. But in most cases, the blockers are very real.

Sometimes the obstacle is the organizational structure: Narrow job categories can seriously undermine efforts to increase productivity or make it very difficult even to think about customers. Sometimes compensation or performance-appraisal systems make people choose between the new vision and their own self-interest. Perhaps worst of all are bosses who refuse to change and who make demands that are inconsistent with the overall effort.

One company began its transformation process with much publicity and actually made good progress through the fourth phase. Then the change effort ground to a halt because the officer in charge of the company's largest division was allowed to undermine most of the new initiatives. He paid lip service to the process but did not change his behavior or encourage his managers to change. He did not reward the unconventional ideas called for in the vision. He allowed human resource systems to remain intact even when they were clearly inconsistent with the new ideals. I think the officer's motives were complex. To some degree, he did not believe the company needed major change. To some degree, he felt personally threatened by all the change. To some degree, he was afraid that he could not produce both change and the expected operating profit. But despite the fact that they backed the renewal effort, the other officers did virtually nothing to stop the one blocker. Again, the reasons were complex. The company had no history of confronting problems like this. Some people were afraid of the officer. The CEO was concerned that he might lose a talented executive. The net result was disastrous. Lower-level managers concluded that senior management had lied to them about their commitment to renewal, cynicism grew, and the whole effort collapsed.

In the first half of a transformation, no organization has the momentum, power, or time to get rid of all obstacles. But the big ones must be confronted and removed. If the blocker is a person, it is important that he or she be treated fairly and in a way that is consistent with the new vision. Action is essential, both to empower others and to maintain the credibility of the change effort as a whole.

Error 6: Not Systematically Planning for, and Creating, Short-Term Wins

Real transformation takes time, and a renewal effort risks losing momentum if there are no short-term goals to meet and celebrate. Most people won't go on the long march unless they see compelling evidence in 12 to 24 months that the journey is producing expected results. Without short-term wins, too many people give up or actively join the ranks of those people who have been resisting change.

One to two years into a successful transformation effort, you find quality beginning to go up on certain indices or the decline in net income stopping. You find some successful new product introductions or an upward shift in market share. You find an impressive productivity improvement or a statistically higher customer satisfaction rating. But whatever the case, the win is unambiguous. The result is not just a judgment call that can be discounted by those opposing change.

Creating short-term wins is different from hoping for short-term wins. The latter is passive, the former active. In a successful transformation, managers actively look for ways to obtain clear performance improvements, establish goals in the yearly planning system, achieve the objectives, and reward the people involved with recognition, promotions, and even money. For example, the guiding coalition at a U.S. manufacturing company produced a highly visible and successful new product introduction about 20 months after the start of its renewal effort. The new product was selected about six months into the effort because it met multiple criteria: It could be designed and launched in a relatively short period, it could be handled by a small team of people who were devoted to the new vision, it had upside potential, and the new product-development team could operate outside the established departmental structure without practical problems. Little was left to chance, and the win boosted the credibility of the renewal process.

Managers often complain about being forced to produce short-term wins, but I've found that pressure can be a useful element in a change effort. When it becomes clear to people that major change will take a long time, urgency levels can drop. Commitments to produce short-term wins help keep the urgency level up and force detailed analytical thinking that can clarify or revise visions.

Error 7: Declaring Victory Too Soon

After a few years of hard work, managers may be tempted to declare victory with the first clear performance improvement. While celebrating a win is fine, declaring the war won can be catastrophic. Until changes sink deeply into a company's culture, a process that can take five to ten years, new approaches are fragile and subject to regression.

In the recent past, I have watched a dozen change efforts operate under the reengineering theme. In all but two cases, victory was declared and the expensive consultants were paid and thanked when the first major project was completed after two to three years. Within two more years, the useful changes that had been introduced slowly disappeared. In two of the ten cases, it's hard to find any trace of the reengineering work today.

Over the past 20 years, I've seen the same sort of thing happen to huge quality projects, organizational development efforts, and more. Typically, the problems start early in the process: The urgency level is not intense enough, the guiding coalition is not powerful enough, and the vision is not clear enough. But it is the premature victory celebration that kills momentum. And then the powerful forces associated with tradition take over.

Ironically, it is often a combination of change initiators and change resistors that creates the premature victory celebration. In their enthusiasm over a clear sign of progress, the initiators go overboard. They are then joined by resistors, who are quick to spot any opportunity to stop change. After the celebration is over, the resistors point to the victory as a sign that the war has been won and the troops should be sent home. Weary troops allow themselves to be convinced that they won. Once home, the foot soldiers are reluctant to climb back on the ships. Soon thereafter, change comes to a halt, and tradition creeps back in.

Instead of declaring victory, leaders of successful efforts use the credibility afforded by short-term wins to tackle even bigger problems. They go after systems and structures that are not consistent with the transformation vision and have not been confronted before. They pay great attention to who is promoted, who is hired, and how people are developed. They include new reengineering projects that are even bigger in scope than the initial ones. They understand that renewal efforts take not months but years. In fact, in one of the most successful transformations that I have ever seen, we quantified the amount of change that occurred each year over a seven-year period. On a scale of one (low) to ten (high), year one received a two, year two a four, year three a three, year four a seven, year five an eight, year six a four, and year seven a two. The peak came in year five, fully 36 months after the first set of visible wins.

Error 8: Not Anchoring Changes in the Corporation's Culture

In the final analysis, change sticks when it becomes "the way we do things around here," when it seeps into the bloodstream of the corporate body. Until new behaviors are rooted in social norms and shared values, they are subject to degradation as soon as the pressure for change is removed.

Two factors are particularly important in institutionalizing change in corporate culture. The first is a conscious attempt to show people how the new approaches, behaviors, and attitudes have helped improve performance. When people are left on their own to make the connections, they sometimes create very inaccurate links. For example, because results improved while charismatic Harry was boss, the troops link his mostly idiosyncratic style with those results instead of seeing how their own improved customer service and productivity were instrumental. Helping people see the right connections requires communication. Indeed, one company was relentless, and it paid off enormously. Time was spent at every major management meeting to discuss why performance was increasing. The company newspaper ran article after article showing how changes had boosted earnings.

The second factor is taking sufficient time to make sure that the next generation of top management really does personify the new

After a few years of hard work, managers may be tempted to declare victory with the first clear performance improvement. While celebrating a win is fine, declaring the war won can be catastrophic.

approach. If the requirements for promotion don't change, renewal rarely lasts. One bad succession decision at the top of an organization can undermine a decade of hard work. Poor succession decisions are possible when boards of directors are not an integral part of the renewal effort. In at least three instances I have seen, the champion for change was the retiring executive, and although his successor was not a resistor, he was not a change champion. Because the boards did not understand the transformations in any detail, they could not see that their choices were not good fits. The retiring executive in one case tried unsuccessfully to talk his board into a less seasoned candidate who better personified the transformation. In the other two cases, the CEOs did not resist the boards' choices, because they felt the transformation could not be undone by their successors. They were wrong. Within two years, signs of renewal began to disappear at both companies.

• • •

There are still more mistakes that people make, but these eight are the big ones. I realize that in a short article everything is made to sound a bit too simplistic. In reality, even successful change efforts are messy and full of surprises. But just as a relatively simple vision is needed to guide people through a major change, so a vision of the change process can reduce the error rate. And fewer errors can spell the difference between success and failure.

Reprint R0701J
To order, see the next page
or call 800-988-0886 or 617-783-7500
or go to www.hbrreprints.org

Leading Change

Why Transformation Efforts Fail

Further Reading

ARTICLES

Building Your Company's Vision
by James C. Collins and Jerry I. Porras
Harvard Business Review
September–October 1996
Product no. 96501

Collins and Porras describe the glue that holds a change effort together. Great companies have a clear sense of why they exist—their core ideology—and where they want to go—their envisioned future. The mechanism for getting there is a BHAG (Big, Hairy, Audacious Goal), which typically takes 10 to 30 years to accomplish. The company's business, strategies, and even its culture may change, but its core ideology remains unchanged. At every step in this long process, the leader's key task is to create alignment with the vision of the company's future, so that regardless of the twists and turns in the journey, the organizational commitment to the goal remains strong.

Successful Change Programs Begin with Results
by Robert H. Schaffer and Harvey A. Thomson
Harvard Business Review
January–February 1992
Product no. 92108

Although a change initiative is a process, that doesn't mean process issues should be the primary concern. Most corporate change programs have a negligible impact on operational and financial performance because management focuses on the activities, not the results. By contrast, results-driven improvement programs seek to achieve specific, measurable improvements within a few months.

BOOKS

The Heart of Change: Real-Life Stories of How People Change Their Organizations
by John P. Kotter and Dan S. Cohen
Harvard Business School Press
2002
Product no. 2549

This book is organized around Kotter's eight-stage change process, and reveals the results of his research in over 100 organizations in the midst of large-scale change. Although most organizations believe that change happens by making people think differently, the authors say that the key lies more in making them feel differently. They introduce a new dynamic—"see-feel-change"—that sparks and fuels action by showing people potent reasons for change that charge their emotions. The book offers tips and tools to you apply to your own organization.

Leading Change
by John P. Kotter
Harvard Business School Press
1996
Product no. 7471

This book expands upon the article about why transformation efforts fail. Kotter addresses each of eight major stages of a change initiative in sequence, highlighting the key activities in each, and providing object lessons about where companies often go astray.

Harvard Business Review 🛡

To Order

For *Harvard Business Review* reprints and subscriptions, call 800-988-0886 or 617-783-7500. Go to www.hbrreprints.org

For customized and quantity orders of *Harvard Business Review* article reprints, call 617-783-7626, or e-mail customizations@hbsp.harvard.edu

Harvard Business Review ⚜

www.hbrreprints.org

U.S. and Canada
800-988-0886
617-783-7500
617-783-7555 fax

The McKinsey *Quarterly*

Organization Practice

The **irrational side** of change management

Most change programs fail, but the odds of success can be greatly improved by taking into account these counterintuitive insights about how employees interpret their environment and choose to act.

**Carolyn Aiken and
Scott Keller**

In 1996, John Kotter published *Leading Change*. Considered by many to be the seminal work in the field of change management, Kotter's research revealed that only 30 percent of change programs succeed. Since the book's release, literally thousands of books and journal articles have been published on the topic, and courses dedicated to managing change are now part of many major MBA programs. Yet in 2008, a McKinsey survey of 3,199 executives around the world found, as Kotter did, that only one transformation in three succeeds. Other studies over the past ten years reveal remarkably similar results. It seems that, despite prolific output, the field of change management hasn't led to more successful change programs.

It also hasn't helped that most academics and practitioners now agree on the building blocks for influencing employee attitudes and management behavior. McKinsey's Emily Lawson and Colin Price provided a holistic perspective in "The psychology of change management,"[1] which suggests that four basic conditions are necessary before employees will change their behavior: a) *a compelling story*, because employees must see the point of the change and agree with it; b) *role modeling*, because they must also see the CEO and colleagues they admire behaving in the new way; c) *reinforcing mechanisms*, because systems, processes, and incentives must be in line with the new behavior; and d) *capability building*, because employees must have the skills required to make the desired changes.

[1] Colin Price and Emily Lawson, "The psychology of change management," mckinseyquarterly.com, June 2003.

Neil Webb

This prescription is well grounded in the field of psychology and is entirely rational. One of its merits is its intuitive appeal: many managers feel that, once revealed, it is simply good common sense. And this, we believe, is precisely where things go wrong. The prescription is right, but rational managers who attempt to put the four conditions in place by applying "common sense" typically misdirect time and energy, create messages that miss the mark, and experience frustrating unintended consequences from their efforts to influence change. Why? Because when they implement the prescription, they disregard certain, sometimes irrational—but predictable—elements of human nature.

In our research and by working with companies attempting change, we have identified nine insights into how human nature gets in the way of successfully applying the four conditions required for behavioral change. As we describe these insights, we'll show how various companies have, either by conscious awareness or simple luck, overcome or leveraged counterintuitive sides of human behavior in making change happen.

Creating a compelling story

Change-management thinking extols the virtues of creating a compelling change story, communicating it to employees, and following it up with ongoing communications and involvement. This is good advice, but in practice there are three pitfalls to achieving the desired impact.

1. What motivates you doesn't motivate most of your employees. We see two types of change stories consistently told in organizations. The first is the "good to great" story: something along the lines of, "Our historical advantage has been eroded by intense competition and changing customer needs; if we change, we can regain our leadership position." The second is the turnaround story: "We're performing below industry standard and must change dramatically to survive. We can become a top-quartile performer in our industry by exploiting our current assets and earning the right to grow."

These stories both seem intuitively rational, yet they too often fail to have the impact that change leaders desire. Research by a number of leading thinkers in the social sciences, such as Danah Zohar, has shown that when managers and employees are asked what motivates them the most in their work they are equally split among five forms of impact—impact on society (for instance, building the community and stewarding resources), impact on the customer (for example, providing superior service), impact on the company and its shareholders, impact on the working team (for example, creating a caring environment), and impact on "me" personally (my development, paycheck, and bonus).

This finding has profound implications for leaders. What the leader cares about (and typically bases at least 80 percent of his or her message to others on) does not tap into roughly 80 percent of the workforce's primary motivators for putting extra energy into the change program. Change leaders need to be able to tell a change story that covers all five things that motivate employees. In doing so, they can unleash tremendous amounts of energy that would otherwise remain latent in the organization.

Consider a cost reduction program at a large US financial-services company. The program started with a change story that ticked the conventional boxes related to the company's competitive position and future. Three months into the program, management was frustrated with employee resistance. The change team worked together to recast the story to include an element related to society (to deliver affordable housing, for example), customers (fewer errors, more competitive prices), the company (expenses are growing faster than revenues, which is not sustainable), working teams (less duplication, more delegation), and individuals (more attractive jobs).

This relatively simple shift in approach lifted employee motivation measures from 35.4 percent to 57.1 percent in a month, and the program went on to achieve 10 percent efficiency improvements in the first year—a run rate far above initial expectations.

2. You're better off letting them write their own story. Well-intentioned leaders invest significant time in communicating their change story. Road shows, town halls, and Web sites are but a few of the many approaches typically used. Certainly the story (told in five ways) needs to get out there, but the insight we are offering is that much of the energy invested in communicating it would be better spent listening, not telling.

In a famous behavioral experiment, half the participants are randomly assigned a lottery ticket number while the others are asked to write down any number they would like on a blank ticket. Just before drawing the winning number, the researchers offer to buy back the tickets from their holders. The result: no matter what geography or demographic environment the experiment has taken place in, researchers have always found that they have to pay at least five times more to those who came up with their own number.

This reveals something about human nature: when we choose for ourselves, we are far more committed to the outcome (almost by a factor of five to one). Conventional approaches to change management underestimate this impact. The rational thinker sees it as a waste of time to let others discover for themselves what he or she already knows—why not just tell them and be done with it? Unfortunately this approach steals from others the energy needed to drive change that comes through a sense of ownership of the answer.

At BP, to develop a comprehensive training program for frontline leaders, a decision was made to involve every key constituency in the design of the program, giving them a sense of "writing their own lottery ticket." It took a year and a half to complete the design using this model but was well worth it: now in implementation, the program is the highest rated of its kind at BP. More than 250 active senior managers from across the business willingly teach the course, and, most important, managers who have been through the training program are consistently ranked higher in performance than those who haven't, both by their bosses and by the employees who report to them.

3. It takes a story with both + and − to create real energy. The "deficit based" approach—which identifies the problem, analyzes what's wrong and how to fix it, plans, and then takes action—has become the model predominantly taught in business schools and is presumably the default change model in most organizations. Research has shown, however, that a story focused on what's wrong invokes blame and creates fatigue and resistance, doing little to engage people's passion and experience.

This has led to the rise of the "constructionist based" approach to change, where the change process is based on *discovery* (discovering the best of what is), *dreaming* (imagining what might be), *designing* (talking about what should be), and *destiny* (creating what will be). The problem with this approach is that an overemphasis on the positive can lead to watered-down aspirations and impact. The reason is that, as humans, we are more willing

*The fact is that human beings consistently think they are better than they are— a phenomenon referred to in psychology as a **self-serving bias***

to take risks to avoid losing what we've got than we are to gain something more. Some anxiety is useful when it comes to spurring behavioral change.

We believe the field of change management has drawn an artificial divide between deficit-based and constructionist-based approaches and stories. While it is impossible to prescribe generally how the divide should be split between positive and negative messages (as it will be specific to the context of any given change program), we strongly advise managers not to swing the pendulum too far in one direction or another. Consider Jack Welch, former CEO at GE, who took questions of "what's wrong here?" (poorly performing businesses, silo-driven behavior, and so forth) head-on, as well as "imagining what might be" (number one or two in every business, openness, and accountability).

Role modeling

Conventional change management suggests leaders should take actions that role model the desired change and mobilize a group of influence leaders to drive change deep into the organization. Unfortunately, this does not necessarily deliver the desired impact.

4. Leaders believe mistakenly that they already "are the change." Most senior executives understand and generally buy into Gandhi's famous aphorism, "Be the change you want to see in the world." They commit themselves to personally role modeling the desired behaviors. And then, in practice, nothing significant changes.

The reason for this is that most executives don't count themselves among the ones who need to change. How many executives when asked privately will say no to the question, "Are you customer focused?" and yes to the question "Are you a bureaucrat?" Of course, none. The fact is that human beings consistently think they are better than they are—a phenomenon referred to in psychology as a self-serving bias. Consider that 94 percent of men rank themselves in the top half according to male athletic ability. Whereas conventional change-management approaches surmise that top team role modeling is a matter of will or skill, the truth is that the real bottleneck to role modeling is knowing what to change at a personal level.

Typically, insight into what to change can be created by concrete 360-degree feedback techniques, either via surveys, conversations, or both. Look at Amgen CEO Kevin Sharer's approach of asking each of his top 75, "What should I do differently?" and then sharing his development needs and commitment publicly with them. Consider the top team of a national insurance company who routinely employed what they called the circle of fire during their change program: every participant receives feedback live—directly from their colleagues—in relation to being the change, such as "What makes you great?" and "What holds you back?"

5. "Influence leaders" aren't a panacea for making change happen. Almost all change-management literature places importance on identifying and mobilizing those in the organization who either by role or personality (or both) have disproportionate influence over how others think and behave. We believe this is sound and timeless advice. However, we have observed that the role of influence leaders has gradually shifted—from being perceived as a helpful element of a broader set of interventions, to a panacea for making change happen.

Our experiences working with change programs suggest that success depends less on how persuasive a few selected leaders are and more on how receptive the "society" is to the idea. In practice it is often unexpected members of the rank and file who feel compelled to step up and make a difference in driving change. That's why we warn against overinvesting in influence leaders and advocate that change leaders' attention should be balanced across the right application of all four conditions for change, to ensure they reinforce each other in ways that maximize the probability of the change spark taking off like wildfire across the organization.

Reinforcing mechanisms

Conventional change management emphasizes the importance of reinforcing and embedding desired changes in structures, processes, systems, target setting, and incentives. We agree. To be effective, however, these mechanisms must take into account that people don't always behave rationally.

6. Money is the most expensive way to motivate people. Companies that try to link the objectives of change programs to the compensation of staff find that it rarely enhances their motivation for change to the extent desired. The reason for this is as practical as it is psychological in nature. The reality is that in the vast majority of companies, it is exceedingly difficult to incorporate a meaningful link to the change program within compensation systems that are based on a vast array of metrics. Moreover, many studies have found that for human beings satisfaction equals perception minus expectation (an equation often accompanied by the commentary, "reality has nothing to do with it").

The beauty of this equation for change managers is that small, unexpected rewards can have disproportionate effects on employees' satisfaction with a change program. Gordon M. Bethune, while turning around Continental Airlines, sent an unexpected $65 check to every employee when Continental made it to the top five for on-time airlines. John McFarlane, former CEO of ANZ Bank, sent a bottle of champagne to every employee for Christmas with a card thanking them for their work on the company's "Perform, Grow, and Break-out" change program. Most change managers would refer to these as merely token gestures and argue that their impact is limited and short-lived. Employees on the receiving end beg to differ. Indeed, they consistently report back that the rewards have a disproportionately positive impact on change motivation that lasts for months, if not years.

7. The process and the outcome have got to be fair. Employees will go against their own self-interest if the situation violates other notions they have about fairness and justice. Consider a bank, which, as part of a major change program, created new risk-adjusted return on capital (RAROC) models and

delivered the resulting new pricing schedules to the front line along with new and appropriate sales incentives. The result: customer attrition (not only of the unprofitable ones) and price overrides went through the roof and significant value was destroyed by the effort. What went wrong? Because the frontline bankers perceived the changes as unfair to the customer, a significant number of them vocally bad-mouthed the bank's policies to customers and used price overrides to show their good faith, even though it meant they were less likely to achieve individual sales goals.

In making any changes to company structures, processes, systems, and incentives, change managers should pay what might strike them as an

Recommended reading

John P. Kotter, *Leading Change*, Boston: Harvard Business Press, 1996.

Danah Zohar, *Rewiring the Corporate Brain: Using the New Science to Rethink How We Structure and Lead Organizations*, San Francisco: Berrett-Koehler, 1997.

Richard Barrett, *Liberating the Corporate Soul: Building a Visionary Organization*, Woburn, MA: Butterworth-Heinemann, 1998.

Don Edward Beck and Christopher C. Cowan, *Spiral Dynamics: Mastering Values, Leadership, and Change*, Oxford, UK: Blackwell Publishing, 1996.

Ellen J. Langer, "The illusion of control," in *Judgment under Uncertainty: Heuristics and Biases*, eds. Daniel Kahneman, Paul Slovic, and Amos Tversky, Cambridge, UK: Cambridge University Press, 1982. This chapter describes the lottery ticket study mentioned on page 103.

Andreas Priestland and Robert Hanig, "Developing first-level leaders," *Harvard Business Review*, 2005, Volume 83, Number 6, pp. 112–20.

Bernard J. Mohr and Jane Magruder Watkins, *The Essentials of Appreciative Inquiry: A Roadmap for Creating Positive Futures*, Waltham, MA: Pegasus, 2002. The juxtaposition of the deficit-based and constructionist-based approaches to change is described in this work.

Daniel Kahneman and Amos Tversky, "Choices, values, and frames," *American Psychologist*, 1984, Volume 39, Number 4, pp. 341–50. In this article, Kahneman and Tversky propose evidence that humans are "irrational" loss avoiders.

Brad M. Barber and Terrance Odean, "Boys will be boys: Gender, overconfidence, and common stock investment," *Quarterly Journal of Economics*, 2001, Volume 116, Number 1, pp. 261–92.

Michael Ross and Fiore Sicoly, "Egocentric biases and availability and attribution," *Journal of Personality and Social Psychology*, 1979, Volume 37, pp. 322–36.

Dan Ariely, *Predictably Irrational: The Hidden Forces that Shape Our Decisions*, New York: Harper Collins, 2008.

Fred Nickols, "Change management books," home.att.net/~nickols/change_biblio.pdf, April 2, 2006. This list, compiled by Nickols, aggregates highly recommended books on change management.

unreasonable amount of attention to employees' sense of the fairness of the change process and its intended outcome. Particular care should be taken where changes affect how employees interact with one another (such as head count reductions and talent-management processes) and with customers (sales stimulation programs, call center redesigns, and pricing). Ironically, in the pricing example described above, the outcome was inherently fair (customers are being asked to pay commensurate to the risk the bank is taking on), and therefore the downward spiral described could have been avoided (and has been by other banks adopting RAROC-based pricing) by carefully tending to employees' perceptions of fairness in the communications and training surrounding the changes.

Capability building

Change-management literature emphasizes the importance of building the skills and talent needed for the desired change. Though hard to argue with, in practice there are two insights that demand attention in order to succeed.

8. Employees are what they think, feel, and believe in. As managers attempt to drive performance by changing the way employees behave, they all too often neglect the thoughts, feelings, and beliefs that, in turn, drive behavior. Consider a bank that through a benchmarking exercise discovered that its sales per banker were lagging behind those of the competition. After finding that bankers spent too little time with customers and too much time on paperwork, the bank set about reengineering the loan-origination process in order to maximize customer-facing time. Unfortunately, six months later, the levels of improvement were far lower than envisioned.

Related articles on mckinseyquarterly.com

The psychology of change management

Driving radical change

Creating organizational transformations: McKinsey Global Survey Results

A further investigation, with an eye to the bankers' mind-sets rather than their behaviors, revealed that they simply found customer interactions uncomfortable and therefore preferred paperwork. This feeling was driven by a combination of introverted personalities, poor interpersonal skills, and a feeling of inferiority when dealing with customers who (by and large) have more money and education than the bankers do. Finally, most bankers were loath to think of themselves as salespeople—a notion they perceived as better suited to employees on used-car lots than in bank branches.

Armed with these root-cause insights, training for bankers was expanded to include elements related to personality types, emotional intelligence, and vocational identity (recasting "sales" as the more noble pursuit of "helping customers discover and fulfill their unarticulated needs"). This enhancement not only put the program back on track within six months but also ultimately delivered sustainable sales lifts in excess of original targets.

9. Good intentions aren't enough. Good skill-building programs usually take into account that people learn better by doing than by listening. These programs are replete with interactive simulations and role plays, and commitments are made by participants regarding what they will "practice" back in the workplace. But come Monday morning, very few keep their commitments.

This lack of follow-through is usually not due to ill intent: it is because nothing formal has been done to lower the barriers to practicing new skills. The time and energy required to do something additional, or even to do something in a new way, simply don't exist in the busy day-to-day schedules of most employees. This failure to create the space for practice back in the workplace dooms most training programs to deliver returns that are far below their potential.

We advocate a number of enhancements to traditional training approaches in order to hardwire day-to-day practice into capability-building processes. First, training should not be a one-off event. Instead, a "field and forum" approach should be taken, in which classroom training is spread over a series of learning forums and fieldwork is assigned in between. Second, we suggest creating fieldwork assignments that link directly to the day jobs of participants, requiring them to put into practice new mind-sets and skills in ways that are hardwired into their responsibilities. These assignments should have quantifiable, outcome-based measures that indicate levels of competence gained and certification that recognizes and rewards the skills attained.

In the same way that the field of economics has been transformed by an understanding of uniquely human social, cognitive, and emotional biases, so too is the practice of change management in need of a transformation through an improved understanding of how humans interpret their environment and choose to act. While sustained impact can be measured only over numbers of years, our early results when applying these insights give us the confidence to broadly share our thinking. Q

Carolyn Aiken is a principal in McKinsey's Toronto office, and Scott Keller is a principal in the Chicago office. Copyright © 2009 McKinsey & Company. All rights reserved.

We welcome your comments on this article.
Please send them to quarterly_comments@mckinsey.com.

Journal of Management Studies 41:6 September 2004
0022-2380

Kurt Lewin and the Planned Approach to Change: A Re-appraisal

Bernard Burnes

Manchester School of Management

ABSTRACT   The work of Kurt Lewin dominated the theory and practice of change management for over 40 years. However, in the past 20 years, Lewin's approach to change, particularly the 3-Step model, has attracted major criticisms. The key ones are that his work: assumed organizations operate in a stable state; was only suitable for small-scale change projects; ignored organizational power and politics; and was top-down and management-driven. This article seeks to re-appraise Lewin's work and challenge the validity of these views. It begins by describing Lewin's background and beliefs, especially his commitment to resolving social conflict. The article then moves on to examine the main elements of his Planned approach to change: Field Theory; Group Dynamics; Action Research; and the 3-Step model. This is followed by a brief summary of the major developments in the field of organizational change since Lewin's death which, in turn, leads to an examination of the main criticisms levelled at Lewin's work. The article concludes by arguing that rather than being outdated or redundant, Lewin's approach is still relevant to the modern world.

INTRODUCTION

> Freud the clinician and Lewin the experimentalist – these are the two men whose names will stand out before all others in the history of our psychological era.

The above quotation is taken from Edward C Tolman's memorial address for Kurt Lewin delivered at the 1947 Convention of the American Psychological Association (quoted in Marrow, 1969, p. ix). To many people today it will seem strange that Lewin should have been given equal status with Freud. Some 50 years after his death, Lewin is now mainly remembered as the originator of the 3-Step model of change (Cummings and Huse, 1989; Schein, 1988), and this tends often to be

Address for reprints: Bernard Burnes, Manchester School of Management, UMIST, Manchester M60 1QD, UK (Bernard.Burnes@umist.ac.uk).

dismissed as outdated (Burnes, 2000; Dawson, 1994; Dent and Goldberg, 1999; Hatch, 1997; Kanter et al., 1992; Marshak, 1993). Yet, as this article will argue, his contribution to our understanding of individual and group behaviour and the role these play in organizations and society was enormous and is still relevant.

In today's turbulent and changing world, one might expect Lewin's pioneering work on change to be seized upon with gratitude, especially given the high failure rate of many change programmes (Huczynski and Buchanan, 2001; Kearney, 1989; Kotter, 1996; Stickland, 1998; Waclawski, 2002; Wastell et al., 1994; Watcher, 1993; Whyte and Watcher, 1992; Zairi et al., 1994). Unfortunately, his commitment to extending democratic values in society and his work on Field Theory, Group Dynamics and Action Research which, together with his 3-Step model, formed an inter-linked, elaborate and robust approach to Planned change, have received less and less attention (Ash, 1992; Bargal et al., 1992; Cooke, 1999). Indeed, from the 1980s, even Lewin's work on change was increasingly criticized as relevant only to small-scale changes in stable conditions, and for ignoring issues such as organizational politics and conflict. In its place, writers sought to promote a view of change as being constant, and as a political process within organizations (Dawson, 1994; Pettigrew et al., 1992; Wilson, 1992).

The purpose of this article is to re-appraise Lewin and his work.. The article begins by describing Lewin's background, especially the origins of his commitment to resolving social conflict. It then moves on to examine the main elements of his Planned approach to change. This is followed by a description of developments in the field of organizational change since Lewin's death, and an evaluation of the criticisms levelled against his work. The article concludes by arguing that rather than being outdated, Lewin's Planned approach is still very relevant to the needs of the modern world.

LEWIN'S BACKGROUND

Few social scientists can have received the level of praise and admiration that has been heaped upon Kurt Lewin (Ash, 1992; Bargal et al., 1992; Dent and Goldberg, 1999; Dickens and Watkins, 1999; Tobach, 1994). As Edgar Schein (1988, p. 239) enthusiastically commented:

> There is little question that the intellectual father of contemporary theories of applied behavioural science, action research and planned change is Kurt Lewin. His seminal work on leadership style and the experiments on planned change which took place in World War II in an effort to change consumer behaviour launched a whole generation of research in group dynamics and the implementation of change programs.

For most of his life, Lewin's main preoccupation was the resolution of social conflict and, in particular, the problems of minority or disadvantaged groups. Underpinning this preoccupation was a strong belief that only the permeation of democratic values into all facets of society could prevent the worst extremes of social conflict. As his wife wrote in the Preface to a volume of his collected work published after his death:

> Kurt Lewin was so constantly and predominantly preoccupied with the task of advancing the conceptual representation of the social-psychological world, and at the same time he was so filled with the urgent desire to use his theoretical insight for the building of a better world, that it is difficult to decide which of these two sources of motivation flowed with greater energy or vigour. (Lewin, 1948b)

To a large extent, his interests and beliefs stemmed from his background as a German Jew. Lewin was born in 1890 and, for a Jew growing up in Germany, at this time, officially-approved anti-Semitism was a fact of life. Few Jews could expect to achieve a responsible post in the civil service or universities. Despite this, Lewin was awarded a doctorate at the University of Berlin in 1916 and went on to teach there. Though he was never awarded tenured status, Lewin achieved a growing international reputation in the 1920s as a leader in his field (Lewin, 1992). However, with the rise of the Nazi Party, Lewin recognized that the position of Jews in Germany was increasingly threatened. The election of Hitler as Chancellor in 1933 was the final straw for him; he resigned from the University and moved to America (Marrow, 1969).

In America, Lewin found a job first as a 'refugee scholar' at Cornell University and then, from 1935 to 1945, at the University of Iowa. Here he was to embark on an ambitious programme of research which covered topics such as child-parent relations, conflict in marriage, styles of leadership, worker motivation and performance, conflict in industry, group problem-solving, communication and attitude change, racism, anti-Semitism, anti-racism, discrimination and prejudice, integration-segregation, peace, war and poverty (Bargal et al., 1992; Cartwright, 1952; Lewin, 1948a). As Cooke (1999) notes, given the prevalence of racism and anti-Semitism in America at the time, much of this work, especially his increasingly public advocacy in support of disadvantaged groups, put Lewin on the political left.

During the years of the Second World War, Lewin did much work for the American war effort. This included studies of the morale of front-line troops and psychological warfare, and his famous study aimed at persuading American housewives to buy cheaper cuts of meat (Lewin, 1943a; Marrow, 1969). He was also much in demand as a speaker on minority and inter-group relations

(Smith, 2001). These activities chimed with one of his central preoccupations, which was how Germany's authoritarian and racist culture could be replaced with one imbued with democratic values. He saw democracy, and the spread of democratic values throughout society, as the central bastion against authoritarianism and despotism. That he viewed the establishment of democracy as a major task, and avoided simplistic and structural recipes, can be gleaned from the following extracts from his article on 'The special case of Germany' (Lewin, 1943b):

> . . . Nazi culture . . . is deeply rooted, particularly in the youth on whom the future depends. It is a culture which is centred around power as the supreme value and which denounces justice and equality . . . (p. 43)

> To be stable, a cultural change has to penetrate all aspects of a nation's life. The change must, in short, be a change in the 'cultural atmosphere,' not merely a change of a single item. (p. 46)

> Change in culture requires the change of leadership forms in every walk of life. At the start, particularly important is leadership in those social areas which are fundamental from the point of view of power. (p. 55)

With the end of the War, Lewin established the Research Center for Group Dynamics at the Massachusetts Institute of Technology. The aim of the Center was to investigate all aspects of group behaviour, especially how it could be changed. At the same time, he was also chief architect of the Commission on Community Interrelations (CCI). Founded and funded by the American Jewish Congress, its aim was the eradication of discrimination against all minority groups. As Lewin wrote at the time, 'We Jews will have to fight for ourselves and we will do so strongly and with good conscience. We also know that the fight of the Jews is part of the fight of all minorities for democratic equality of rights and opportunities . . .' (quoted in Marrow, 1969, p. 175). In pursuing this objective, Lewin believed that his work on Group Dynamics and Action Research would provide the key tools for the CCI.

Lewin was also influential in establishing the Tavistock Institute in the UK and its Journal, *Human Relations* (Jaques, 1998; Marrow, 1969). In addition, in 1946, the Connecticut State Inter-Racial Commission asked Lewin to help train leaders and conduct research on the most effective means of combating racial and religious prejudice in communities. This led to the development of sensitivity training and the creation, in 1947, of the now famous National Training Laboratories. However, his huge workload took its toll on his health, and on 11 February 1947 he died of a heart attack (Lewin, 1992).

LEWIN'S WORK

Lewin was a humanitarian who believed that only by resolving social conflict, whether it be religious, racial, marital or industrial, could the human condition be improved. Lewin believed that the key to resolving social conflict was to facilitate learning and so enable individuals to understand and restructure their perceptions of the world around them. In this he was much influenced by the Gestalt psychologists he had worked with in Berlin (Smith, 2001). A unifying theme of much of his work is the view that '. . . the group to which an individual belongs is the ground for his perceptions, his feelings and his actions' (Allport, 1948, p. vii). Though Field Theory, Group Dynamics, Action Research and the 3-Step model of change are often treated as separate themes of his work, Lewin saw them as a unified whole with each element supporting and reinforcing the others and all of them necessary to understand and bring about Planned change, whether it be at the level of the individual, group, organization or even society (Bargal and Bar, 1992; Kippenberger, 1998a, 1998b; Smith, 2001). As Allport (1948, p. ix) states: 'All of his concepts, whatever root-metaphor they employ, comprise a single well-integrated system'. This can be seen from examining these four aspects of his work in turn.

Field Theory

This is an approach to understanding group behaviour by trying to map out the totality and complexity of the field in which the behaviour takes place (Back, 1992). Lewin maintained that to understand any situation it was necessary that: 'One should view the present situation – the *status quo* – as being maintained by certain conditions or forces' (Lewin, 1943a, p. 172). Lewin (1947b) postulated that group behaviour is an intricate set of symbolic interactions and forces that not only affect group structures, but also modify individual behaviour. Therefore, individual behaviour is a function of the group environment or 'field', as he termed it. Consequently, any changes in behaviour stem from changes, be they small or large, in the forces within the field (Lewin, 1947a). Lewin defined a field as 'a totality of coexisting facts which are conceived of as mutually interdependent . . .' (Lewin, 1946, p. 240). Lewin believed that a field was in a continuous state of adaptation and that 'Change and constancy are relative concepts; group life is never without change, merely differences in the amount and type of change exist' (Lewin, 1947a, p. 199). This is why Lewin used the term 'quasi-stationary equilibrium' to indicate that whilst there might be a rhythm and pattern to the behaviour and processes of a group, these tended to fluctuate constantly owing to changes in the forces or circumstances that impinge on the group.

Lewin's view was that if one could identify, plot and establish the potency of these forces, then it would be possible not only to understand why individuals, groups and organizations act as they do, but also what forces would need to be diminished or strengthened in order to bring about change. In the main, Lewin saw behavioural change as a slow process; however, he did recognize that under certain circumstances, such as a personal, organizational or societal crisis, the various forces in the field can shift quickly and radically. In such situations, established routines and behaviours break down and the status quo is no longer viable; new patterns of activity can rapidly emerge and a new equilibrium (or quasi-stationary equilibrium) is formed (Kippenberger, 1998a; Lewin, 1947a).

Despite its obvious value as a vehicle for understanding and changing group behaviour, with Lewin's death, the general interest in Field Theory waned (Back, 1992; Gold, 1992; Hendry, 1996). However, in recent years, with the work of Argyris (1990) and Hirschhorn (1988) on understanding and overcoming resistance to change, Lewin's work on Field Theory has once again begun to attract interest. According to Hendry (1996), even critics of Lewin's work have drawn on Field Theory to develop their own models of change (see Pettigrew et al., 1989, 1992). Indeed, parallels have even been drawn between Lewin's work and the work of complexity theorists (Kippenberger, 1998a). Back (1992), for example, argued that the formulation and behaviour of complex systems as described by Chaos and Catastrophe theorists bear striking similarities to Lewin's conceptualization of Field Theory. Nevertheless, Field Theory is now probably the least understood element of Lewin's work, yet, because of its potential to map the forces impinging on an individual, group or organization, it underpinned the other elements of his work.

Group Dynamics

> . . . the word 'dynamics' . . . comes from a Greek word meaning force . . . 'group dynamics' refers to the forces operating in groups . . . it is a study of these forces: what gives rise to them, what conditions modify them, what consequences they have, etc. (Cartwright, 1951, p. 382)

Lewin was the first psychologist to write about 'group dynamics' and the importance of the group in shaping the behaviour of its members (Allport, 1948; Bargal et al., 1992). Indeed, Lewin's (1939, p. 165) definition of a 'group' is still generally accepted: '. . . it is not the similarity or dissimilarity of individuals that constitutes a group, but interdependence of fate'. As Kippenberger (1998a) notes, Lewin was addressing two questions: What is it about the nature and characteristics of a particular group which causes it to respond (behave) as it does to the forces which impinge on it, and how can these forces be changed in order to elicit a more desirable form of behaviour? It was to address these questions that Lewin began to develop the concept of Group Dynamics.

Group Dynamics stresses that group behaviour, rather than that of individuals, should be the main focus of change (Bernstein, 1968; Dent and Goldberg, 1999). Lewin (1947b) maintained that it is fruitless to concentrate on changing the behaviour of individuals because the individual in isolation is constrained by group pressures to conform. Consequently, the focus of change must be at the group level and should concentrate on factors such as group norms, roles, interactions and socialization processes to create 'disequilibrium' and change (Schein, 1988).

Lewin's pioneering work on Group Dynamics not only laid the foundations for our understanding of groups (Cooke, 1999; Dent and Goldberg, 1999; French and Bell, 1984; Marrow, 1969; Schein, 1988) but has also been linked to complexity theories by researchers examining self-organizing theory and non-linear systems (Tschacher and Brunner, 1995). However, understanding the internal dynamics of a group is not sufficient by itself to bring about change. Lewin also recognized the need to provide a process whereby the members could be engaged in and committed to changing their behaviour. This led Lewin to develop Action Research and the 3-Step model of change.

Action Research

This term was coined by Lewin (1946) in an article entitled 'Action research and minority problems'. Lewin stated in the article:

> In the last year and a half I have had occasion to have contact with a great variety of organizations, institutions, and individuals who came for help in the field of group relations. (Lewin, 1946, p. 201)

However, though these people exhibited . . .

> . . . a great amount of good-will, of readiness to face the problem squarely and really do something about it . . . These eager people feel themselves to be in a fog. They feel in a fog on three counts: 1. What is the present situation? 2. What are the dangers? 3. And most importantly of all, what shall we do? (Lewin, 1946, p. 201)

Lewin conceived of Action Research as a two-pronged process which would allow groups to address these three questions. Firstly, it emphasizes that change requires action, and is directed at achieving this. Secondly, it recognizes that successful action is based on analysing the situation correctly, identifying all the possible alternative solutions and choosing the one most appropriate to the situation at hand (Bennett, 1983). To be successful, though, there has also to be a 'felt-need'. Felt-need is an individual's inner realization that change is necessary. If felt-need is low in the group or organization, introducing change becomes problematic. The theoretical foundations of Action Research lie in Gestalt psychology, which stresses that change can only successfully be achieved by helping individuals to reflect on and gain new insights into the totality of their situation. Lewin (1946, p. 206) stated that Action Research '. . . proceeds in a spiral of steps each of which is composed of a circle of planning, action, and fact-finding about the results of the action.' It is an iterative process whereby research leads to action and action leads to evaluation and further research. As Schein (1996, p. 64) comments, it was Lewin's view that '. . . one cannot understand an organization without trying to change it . . .' Indeed, Lewin's view was very much that the understanding and learning which this process produces for the individuals and groups concerned, which then feeds into changed behaviour, is more important than any resulting change as such (Lewin, 1946).

To this end, Action Research draws on Lewin's work on Field Theory to identify the forces that focus on the group to which the individual belongs. It also draws on Group Dynamics to understand why group members behave in the way they do when subjected to these forces. Lewin stressed that the routines and patterns of behaviour in a group are more than just the outcome of opposing forces in a forcefield. They have a value in themselves and have a positive role to play in enforcing group norms (Lewin, 1947a). Action Research stresses that for change to be effective, it must take place at the group level, and must be a participative and collaborative process which involves all of those concerned (Allport, 1948; Bargal et al., 1992; French and Bell, 1984; Lewin, 1947b).

Lewin's first Action Research project was to investigate and reduce violence between Catholic and Jewish teenage gangs. This was quickly followed by a project to integrate black and white sales staff in New York department stores (Marrow, 1969). However, Action Research was also adopted by the Tavistock Institute in Britain, and used to improve managerial competence and efficiency in the newly-nationalized coal industry. Since then it has acquired strong adherents throughout the world (Dickens and Watkins, 1999; Eden and Huxham, 1996; Elden and Chisholm, 1993). However, Lewin (1947a, p. 228) was concerned that:

A change towards a higher level of group performance is frequently short lived; after a 'shot in the arm,' group life soon returns to the previous level. This indicates that it does not suffice to define the objective of a planned change in group performance as the reaching of a different level. Permanency at the new level, or permanency for a desired period, should be included in the objective.

It was for this reason that he developed his 3-Step model of change.

3-Step Model

This is often cited as Lewin's key contribution to organizational change. However, it needs to be recognized that when he developed his 3-Step model Lewin was not thinking only of organizational issues. Nor did he intend it to be seen separately from the other three elements which comprise his Planned approach to change (i.e. Field Theory, Group Dynamics and Action Research). Rather Lewin saw the four concepts as forming an integrated approach to analysing, understanding and bringing about change at the group, organizational and societal levels.

A successful change project, Lewin (1947a) argued, involved three steps:

- *Step 1: Unfreezing*. Lewin believed that the stability of human behaviour was based on a quasi-stationary equilibrium supported by a complex field of driving and restraining forces. He argued that the equilibrium needs to be destabilized (unfrozen) before old behaviour can be discarded (unlearnt) and new behaviour successfully adopted. Given the type of issues that Lewin was addressing, as one would expect, he did not believe that change would be easy or that the same approach could be applied in all situations:

  > The 'unfreezing of the present level may involve quite different problems in different cases. Allport . . . has described the 'catharsis' which seems necessary before prejudice can be removed. To break open the shell of complacency and self-righteousness it is sometimes necessary to bring about an emotional stir up. (Lewin, 1947a, p. 229)

  Enlarging on Lewin's ideas, Schein (1996, p. 27) comments that the key to unfreezing '. . . was to recognise that change, whether at the individual or group level, was a profound psychological dynamic process'. Schein (1996) identifies three processes necessary to achieve unfreezing: disconfirmation of the validity of the status quo, the induction of guilt or survival anxiety, and creating psychological safety. He argued that: '. . . unless sufficient psychological safety is created, the disconfirming information will be denied or in other ways defended against, no survival anxiety will be felt. and consequently, no change will take place' (Schein, 1996, p. 61). In other words, those concerned have to feel safe from loss and humiliation before they can accept the new information and reject old behaviours.

- *Step 2: Moving*. As Schein (1996, p. 62) notes, unfreezing is not an end in itself; it '. . . creates motivation to learn but does not necessarily control or predict the direction'. This echoes Lewin's view that any attempt to predict or identify a specific outcome from Planned change is very difficult because of the complexity of the forces concerned. Instead, one should seek to take into account all the forces at work and identify and evaluate, on a trial and error basis, all the available options (Lewin, 1947a). This is, of course, the learning approach promoted by Action Research. It is this iterative approach of research, action and more research which enables groups and individuals to move from a less acceptable to a more acceptable set of behaviours. However, as noted above, Lewin (1947a) recognized that, without reinforcement, change could be short-lived.

- *Step 3: Refreezing.* This is the final step in the 3-Step model. Refreezing seeks to stabilize the group at a new quasi-stationary equilibrium in order to ensure that the new behaviours are relatively safe from regression. The main point about refreezing is that new behaviour must be, to some degree, congruent with the rest of the behaviour, personality and environment of the learner or it will simply lead to a new round of disconfirmation (Schein, 1996). This is why Lewin saw successful change as a group activity, because unless group norms and routines are also transformed, changes to individual behaviour will not be sustained. In organizational terms, refreezing often requires changes to organizational culture, norms, policies and practices (Cummings and Huse, 1989).

Like other aspects of Lewin's work, his 3-Step model of change has become unfashionable in the last two decades (Dawson, 1994; Hatch, 1997; Kanter et al., 1992). Nevertheless, such is its continuing influence that, as Hendry (1996, p. 624) commented:

Scratch any account of creating and managing change and the idea that change is a three-stage process which necessarily begins with a process of unfreezing will not be far below the surface.

LEWIN AND CHANGE: A SUMMARY

Lewin was primarily interested in resolving social conflict through behavioural change, whether this be within organizations or in the wider society. He identified two requirements for success:

(1) To analyse and understand how social groupings were formed, motivated and maintained. To do this, he developed both Field Theory and Group Dynamics.
(2) To change the behaviour of social groups. The primary methods he developed for achieving this were Action Research and the 3-Step model of change.

Underpinning Lewin's work was a strong moral and ethical belief in the importance of democratic institutions and democratic values in society. Lewin believed that only by strengthening democratic participation in all aspects of life and being able to resolve social conflicts could the scourge of despotism, authoritarianism and racism be effectively countered. Since his death, Lewin's wider social agenda has been mainly pursued under the umbrella of Action Research (Dickens and Watkins, 1999). This is also the area where Lewin's Planned approach has been most closely followed. For example, Bargal and Bar (1992) described how, over a number of years, they used Lewin's approach to address the conflict between Arab-Palestinian and Jewish youths in Israel through the development of inter-group workshops. The workshops were developed around six principles based on Lewin's work:

(a) a recursive process of data collection to determine goals, action to implement goals and assessment of the action; (b) feedback of research results to trainers; (c) cooperation between researchers and practitioners; (d) research based on the laws of the group's social life, on three stages of change – 'unfreezing,' 'moving,' and 'refreezing' – and on the principles of group decision making; (e) consideration of the values, goals and power structures of change agents and clients; and (f) use of research to create knowledge and/or solve problems. (Bargal and Bar, 1992, p. 146)

In terms of organizational change, Lewin and his associates had a long and fruitful relationship with the Harwood Manufacturing Corporation, where his approach to change was developed, applied and refined (Marrow, 1969). Coch and French (1948, p. 512) observed that, at Harwood: 'From the point of view of factory management, there were two purposes to the research: (1) Why do people resist change so strongly? and (2) What can be done to overcome this resistance?' Therefore, in both his wider social agenda and his narrower organizational agenda, Lewin sought to address similar issues and apply similar concepts. Since his death, it is the organizational side of his work which has been given greater prominence by his followers and successors, mainly through the creation of the Organization Development (OD) movement (Cummings and Worley, 1997; French and Bell, 1995).

OD has become the standard-bearer for Kurt Lewin's pioneering work on behavioural science in general, and approach to Planned change in particular (Cummings and Worley, 1997). Up to the 1970s, OD tended to focus on group issues in organizations, and sought to promote Lewin's humanistic and democratic approach to change in the values it espoused (Conner, 1977; Gellerman et al., 1990; Warwick and Thompson, 1980). However, as French and Bell (1995) noted, since the late 1970s, in order to keep pace with the perceived needs of organizations, there has been a major broadening of scope within the OD field. It has moved away from its focus on groups and towards more organization-wide issues, such as Socio-Technical Systems, organizational culture, organizational learning and radical transformational change. Nevertheless, despite OD's attempts to modernize itself, in the last 20 years Lewin's legacy has met with increasing competition.

NEWER PERSPECTIVES ON CHANGE

By the early 1980s, with the oil shocks of the 1970s, the rise of corporate Japan and severe economic downturn in the West, it was clear that many organizations needed to transform themselves rapidly and often brutally if they were to survive (Burnes, 2000). Given its group-based, consensual and relatively slow nature, Lewin's Planned approach began to attract criticism as to its appropriateness and efficacy, especially from the Culture-Excellence school, the postmodernists and the processualists.

The Culture-Excellence approach to organizations, as promoted by Peters and Waterman (1982) and Kanter (1989), has had an unprecedented impact on the management of organizations by equating organizational success with the possession of a strong, appropriate organizational culture (Collins, 1998; Watson, 1997; Wilson, 1992). Peters and Waterman (1982) argued that Western organizations were losing their competitive edge because they were too bureaucratic, inflexible, and slow to change. Instead of the traditional top-down, command-and-control style of management which tended to segment organizations into small rule-driven units, proponents of Culture-Excellence stressed the integrated nature of organizations, both internally and within their environments (Kanter, 1983; Watson, 1997). To survive, it was argued, organizations needed to reconfigure themselves to build internal and external synergies, and managers needed to encourage a spirit of innovation, experimentation and entrepreneurship through the creation of strong, appropriate organizational cultures (Collins, 1998; Kanter, 1983; Peters and Waterman, 1982; Wilson, 1992).

For proponents of Culture-Excellence, the world is essentially an ambiguous place where detailed plans are not possible and flexibility is essential. Instead of close supervision and strict rules, organizational objectives need to be promoted by loose controls, based on shared values and culture, and pursued through empowered employees using their own initiative (Watson, 1997). They argue that change cannot be driven from the top but must emerge in an organic, bottom-up fashion from the day-to-day actions of all in the organization (Collins, 1998; Hatch, 1997). Proponents of Culture-Excellence reject as antithetical the Planned approach to change, sometimes quite scathingly, as the following quotation from Kanter et al.'s (1992, p. 10) shows:

Lewin's model was a simple one, with organizational change involving three stages; unfreezing, changing and refreezing . . . This quaintly linear and static conception – the organization as an ice cube – is so wildly inappropriate that it is difficult to see why it has not only survived but prospered . . . Suffice it to say here, first, that organizations are never frozen, much less refrozen, but are fluid entities with many 'personalities'. Second, to the extent that there are stages, they overlap and interpenetrate one another in important ways.

At the same time that the Culture-Excellence school were criticizing Planned change, others, notably Pfeffer (1981, 1992), were claiming that the objectives, and outcomes, of change programmes were more likely to be determined by power struggles than by any process of consensus-building or rational decision-making. For the postmodernists, power is also a central feature of organizational change, but it arises from the socially-constructed nature of organizational life:

> In a socially-constructed world, responsibility for environmental conditions lies with those who do the constructing . . . This suggests at least two competing scenarios for organizational change. First, organization change can be a vehicle of domination for those who conspire to enact the world for others . . . An alternative use of social constructionism is to create a democracy of enactment in which the process is made open and available to all . . . such that we create opportunities for freedom and innovation rather than simply for further domination. (Hatch, 1997, pp. 367–8)

The other important perspective on organizational change which emerged in the 1980s was the processual approach, which derives from the work of Andrew Pettigrew (1973, 1979, 1985, 1990a, 1990b, 1997). Processualists reject prescriptive, recipe-driven approaches to change and are suspicious of single causes or simple explanations of events. Instead, when studying change, they focus on the inter-relatedness of individuals, groups, organizations and society (Dawson, 1994; Pettigrew and Whipp, 1993; Wilson, 1992). In particular, they claim that the process of change is a complex and untidy cocktail of rational decision processes, individual perceptions, political struggles and coalition-building (Huczynski and Buchanan, 2001). Pettigrew (1990a, 1990b) maintains that the Planned approach is too prescriptive and does not pay enough attention to the need to analyse and conceptualize organizational change. He argues that change needs to be studied across different levels of analysis and different time periods, and that it cuts across functions, spans hierarchical divisions, and has no neat starting or finishing point; instead it is a 'complex analytical, political, and cultural process of challenging and changing the core beliefs, structure and strategy of the firm' (Pettigrew, 1987, p. 650).

Looking at Planned change versus a processual approach, Dawson (1994, pp. 3–4) comments that:

990   B. Burnes

Although this [Lewin's] theory has proved useful in understanding planned change under relatively stable conditions, with the continuing and dynamic nature of change in today's business world, it no longer makes sense to implement a planned process for 'freezing' changed behaviours . . . The processual framework . . . adopts the view that change is a complex and dynamic process which should not be solidified or treated as a series of linear events . . . central to the development of a processual approach is the need to incorporate an analysis of the politics of managing change.

Also taking a processualist perspective, Buchanan and Storey's (1997, p. 127) main criticism of those who advocate Planned change is:

. . . their attempt to impose an order and a linear sequence to processes that are in reality messy and untidy, and which unfold in an iterative fashion with much backtracking and omission.

Though there are distinct differences between these newer approaches to change, not least the prescriptive focus of the Culture-Excellence approach versus the analytical orientation of the processualists, there are also some striking similarities which they claim strongly challenge the validity of the Planned approach to change. The newer approaches tend to take a holistic/contextual view of organizations and their environments; they challenge the notion of change as an ordered, rational and linear process; and there is an emphasis on change as a continuous process which is heavily influenced by culture, power and politics (Buchanan and Storey, 1997; Burnes, 2000; Dawson, 1994; Kanter et al., 1992; Pettigrew, 1997). Accompanying and offering support to these new approaches to change were new perspectives on the nature of change in organizations. Up to the late 1970s, the incremental model of change dominated. Advocates of this view see change as being a process whereby individual parts of an organization deal incrementally and separately with one problem and one goal at a time. By managers responding to pressures in their local internal and external environments in this way, over time, their organizations become transformed (Cyert and March, 1963; Hedberg et al., 1976; Lindblom, 1959; Quinn, 1980, 1982).

In the 1980s, two new perspectives on change emerged: the punctuated equilibrium model and the continuous transformation model. The former approach to change:

. . . depicts organizations as evolving through relatively long periods of stability (equilibrium periods) in their basic patterns of activity that are punctuated by relatively short bursts of fundamental change (revolutionary periods). Revolutionary periods substantively disrupt established activity patterns and install the basis for new equilibrium periods. (Romanelli and Tushman, 1994, p. 1141)

The inspiration for this model arises from two sources: firstly, from the challenge to Darwin's gradualist model of evolution in the natural sciences (Gould, 1989); secondly, from research showing that whilst organizations do appear to fit the incrementalist model of change for a period of time, there does come a point when they go through a period of rapid and fundamental change (Gersick, 1991).

Proponents of the continuous transformation model reject both the incrementalist and punctuated equilibrium models. They argue that, in order to survive, organizations must develop the ability to change themselves continuously in a fundamental manner. This is particularly the case in fast-moving sectors such as retail (Greenwald, 1996). Brown and Eisenhardt (1997, p. 29) draw on the work of complexity theorists to support their claim for continuous change:

> Like organizations, complex systems have large numbers of independent yet interacting actors. Rather than ever reaching a stable equilibrium, the most adaptive of these complex systems (e.g., intertidal zones) keep changing continuously by remaining at the poetically termed 'edge of chaos' that exists between order and disorder. By staying in this intermediate zone, these systems never quite settle into a stable equilibrium but never quite fall apart. Rather, these systems, which stay constantly poised between order and disorder, exhibit the most prolific, complex and continuous change . . .

Complexity theories are increasingly being used by organization theorists and practitioners as a way of understanding and changing organizations (Bechtold, 1997; Black, 2000; Boje, 2000; Choi et al., 2001; Gilchrist, 2000; Lewis, 1994; Macbeth, 2002; Shelton and Darling, 2001; Stacey et al., 2002; Tetenbaum, 1998). Complexity theories come from the natural sciences, where they have shown that disequilibrium is a necessary condition for the growth of dynamic systems (Prigogine and Stengers, 1984). Under this view, organizations, like complex systems in nature, are seen as dynamic non-linear systems. The outcome of their actions is unpredictable but, like turbulence in gases and liquids, it is governed by a set of simple order-generating rules (Brown and Eisenhardt, 1997; Lewis, 1994; Lorenz, 1993; Mintzberg et al., 1998; Stacey et al., 2002; Tetenbaum, 1998; Wheatley, 1992). For organizations, as for natural systems, the key to survival is to develop rules which are capable of keeping an organization operating 'on the edge of chaos' (Stacey et al., 2002). If organizations are too stable, nothing changes and the system dies; if too chaotic, the system will be overwhelmed by change. In both situations, radical change is necessary in order to create a new set of order-generating rules which allow the organization to prosper and survive (MacIntosh and MacLean, 2001).

As can be seen, the newer approaches to change and the newer perspectives on the nature of change have much in common. One of the problems with all three perspectives on change – incrementalism, punctuated equilibrium and continuous change – is that all three are present in organizational life and none appear dominant. Indeed, Burnes (2000) even questions whether these are separate and competing theories, or merely different ways of looking at the same phenomenon: change. He points out that sectoral, temporal and organizational life cycle differences can account for whether organizations experience incremental, punctuated equilibrium or continuous change (Kimberley and Miles, 1980). He also draws on the natural sciences, in the form of population ecology, to argue that in any given population of organizations one would expect to see all three types of change (Hannan and Freeman, 1988). Therefore, rather like the Jungian concept of the light and dark, these various perspectives on change may be shadow images of each other, none of which by themselves capable of portraying the whole (Matthews, 2002).

LEWIN'S WORK: CRITICISMS AND RESPONSES

From the 1980s onwards, as newer perspectives on organizational life and change have emerged, Lewin's Planned approach has faced increasing levels of criticisms. This section summarizes the main criticisms and responds to them.

Criticism 1

Many have is argued that Lewin's Planned approach is too simplistic and mechanistic for a world where organizational change is a continuous and open-endèd process (Dawson, 1994; Garvin, 1993; Kanter et al., 1992; Nonaka, 1988; Pettigrew, 1990a, 1990b; Pettigrew et al., 1989; Stacey, 1993; Wilson, 1992).

Response 1. These criticisms appear to stem from a misreading of how Lewin perceived stability and change. He stated:

> One should view the present situation – the *status quo* – as being maintained by certain conditions or forces. A culture – for instance, the food habits of a certain group at a given time – is not a static affair but a live process like a river which moves but still keeps to a recognizable form . . . Food habits do not occur in empty space. They are part and parcel of the daily rhythm of being awake and asleep; of being alone and in a group; of earning a living and playing; of being a member of a town, a family, a social class, a religious group . . . in a district with good groceries and restaurants or in an area of poor and irregular food supply. Somehow all these factors affect food habits at any given time. They determine the food habits of a group every day anew just as the amount of water supply and the nature of the river bed determine the flow of the river, its constancy or change. (Lewin, 1943a, pp. 172–3)

Far from viewing social or organizational groups as fixed and stable, or viewing change as linear and uni-dimensional, it is clear that he understood the limits of stability at least as well as his critics. He argued that social settings are in a state of constant change but that, just like a river, the rate varies depending on the environment. He viewed change not as a predictable and planned move from one stable state to another, but as a complex and iterative learning process where the journey was more important than the destination, where stability was at best quasi-stationary and always fluid, and where, given the complex forces involved, outcomes cannot be predicted but emerge on a trial and error basis (Kippenberger, 1998a; Lewin, 1947a). Therefore, rather than being prescriptive, Lewin recognized the unpredictable (non-linear) nature of change and, as Hendry (1996) notes, he adopted the same 'contextualist' and learning approach favoured by many of his critics. Indeed, as outlined earlier, some argue that Lewin's conception of stability and change is very similar to that of many complexity theorists (Back, 1992; Elrod and Tippett, 2002; Kippenberger, 1998a; MacIntosh and MacLean, 2001; Tschacher and Brunner, 1995).

We should also note that when Lewin wrote of 'refreezing', he referred to preventing individuals and groups from regressing to their old behaviours. In this respect, Lewin's view seems to be similar to that of his critics. For example, the last stage in Kanter et al.'s (1992, p. 384) model of change is to 'Reinforce and institutionalize the change'. More telling, though, is that when Elrod and Tippett (2002) compared a wide range of change models, they found that most approaches to organizational change were strikingly similar to Lewin's 3-Step model. When they extended their research to other forms of human and organizational change, they also found that 'Models of the change process, as perceived by diverse and seemingly unrelated disciplines [such as bereavement theory, personal transition theory, creative processes, cultural revolutions and scientific revolutions] . . . follow Lewin's . . . three-phase model of change . . .' (Elrod and Tippett, 2002, p. 273).

Criticism 2

Lewin's work is only relevant to incremental and isolated change projects and is not able to incorporate radical, transformational change (Dawson, 1994; Dunphy and Stace, 1992, 1993; Harris, 1985; Miller and Friesen, 1984; Pettigrew, 1990a, 1990b).

Response 2. This criticism appears to relate to the speed rather than the magnitude of change because, as Quinn (1980, 1982) pointed out, over time, incremental change can lead to radical transformations. It is also necessary to recognize that Lewin was concerned with behavioural change at the individual, group, organizational and societal levels (Dickens and Watkins, 1999), whereas rapid transformational change is seen as only being applicable to situations requiring major structural change (Allaire and Firsirotu, 1984; Beer and Nohria, 2000; Burnes, 2000; Cummings and Worley, 1997). Even in such situations, as Kanter et al. (1992) maintain, these 'Bold Strokes' often need to be followed by a whole series of incremental changes (a 'Long March') in order to align an organization's culture and behaviours with the new structure. Lewin did recognize that radical behavioural or cultural change could take place rapidly in times of crisis (Kippenberger, 1998a; Lewin, 1947a). Such crises may require directive change; again, this may be successful in terms of structural change but research by Lewin and others has shown that it rarely works in cases where behavioural change is required (Lewin, 1947b; Kanter et al., 1992; Schein, 1996; Stace and Dunphy, 2001).

Criticism 3

Lewin's stands accused of ignoring the role of power and politics in organizations and the conflictual nature of much of organizational life (Dawson, 1994; Hatch, 1997; Pettigrew, 1980; Pfeffer, 1992; Wilson, 1992).

Response 3. Given the issues that Lewin was addressing, this seems a strange criticism. Anyone seriously addressing racism and religious intolerance, as Lewin was, could not ignore these issues. As Bargal et al. (1992, p. 8) note, Lewin's approach to change required '. . . the taking into account differences in value systems and power structures of all the parties involved . . .' This is clear from the following quotation (Lewin, 1946, p. 203):

> An attempt to improve inter-group relations has to face a wide variety of tasks. It deals with problems of attitude and stereotypes in regard to other groups and one's own group, with problems of development of attitudes and conduct during childhood and adolescence, with problems of housing, and the change of the legal structure of the community; it deals with problems of status and caste, with problems of economic discrimination, with political leadership, and with leadership in many aspects of community life. It deals with the small social body of the family, a club or a friendship group, with the larger social body of a school or school system, with neighborhoods and with social bodies of the size of a community, of the state and with international problems.
>
> We are beginning to see that it is hopeless to attack any one of these aspects of inter-group relations without considering the others.

One also needs to be aware that French and Raven's Power/Interaction Model (French and Raven, 1959; Raven, 1965), on which much of the literature on power and politics is based, owes much to Lewin's work (Raven, 1993). French was a long-time collaborator of Lewin and Raven studied at the Research Center for Group

Dynamics in the 1950s. Both have acknowledged the importance and influence of his work on their perspective on power (House, 1993; Raven, 1993, 1999).

Criticism 4

Lewin is seen as advocating a top-down, management-driven approach to change and ignoring situations requiring bottom-up change (Dawson, 1994; Kanter et al., 1992; Wilson, 1992).

Response 4. Lewin was approached for help by a wide range of groups and organizations:

> They included representatives of communities, school systems, single schools, minority organizations of a variety of backgrounds and objectives; they included labor and management representatives, departments of the national and state governments, and so on. (Lewin, 1946, p. 201)

He clearly recognized that the pressure for change comes from many quarters, not just managers and leaders, and sought to provide an approach which could accommodate this. However, regardless of who identified the need to change, Lewin argued that effective change could not take place unless there was a 'felt need' by all those concerned; he did not see one group or individual as driving or dominating the change process but saw everyone as playing a full and equal part (Lewin, 1947b). He believed that only by gaining the commitment of all those concerned, through their full involvement in the change process, would change be successful (Bargal et al., 1992; Dickens and Watkins, 1999; French and Bell, 1984). Consequently, rather than arguing that Lewin saw behavioural change as a top-down process, it would be more accurate to say that Lewin recognized that it could be initiated from the top, bottom or middle but that it could not be successful without the active, willing and equal participation of all.

CONCLUSION

Lewin undoubtedly had an enormous impact on the field of change. In re-appraising Lewin's Planned approach to change, this article seeks to address three issues: the nature of his contribution; the validity of the criticisms levelled against him; and the relevance of his work for contemporary social and organizational change.

Looking at Lewin's contribution to change theory and practice, there are three key points to note. The first is that Lewin's work stemmed from his concern to find an effective approach to resolving social conflict through changing group behaviour (whether these conflicts be at the group, organizational or societal level). The second point is to recognize that Lewin promoted an ethical and humanist approach to change, that saw learning and involvement as being the key processes for achieving behavioural change. This was for two reasons: (a) he saw this approach as helping to develop and strengthen democratic values in society as whole and thus acting as a buffer against the racism and totalitarianism which so dominated events in his lifetime; (b) based on his background in Gestalt psychology and his own research, he saw this approach as being the most effective in bringing about sustained behavioural change. The last point concerns the nature of Lewin's work. Lewin's Planned approach to change is based on four mutually-reinforcing concepts, namely Field Theory, Group Dynamics, Action Research and the 3-Step model, which are used in combination to bring about effective change. His critics, though, tend to treat these as separate and independent elements of Lewin's work and, in the main, concentrate on his 3-Step model of change. When seen in isolation, the 3-Step model can be portrayed as simplistic. When seen alongside the other elements of Lewin's Planned approach, it becomes a much more robust approach to change.

We can now examine the criticisms made of Lewin's Planned approach to change. The main criticisms levelled at Lewin are that: (1) his view of stability and change in organizations was at best no longer applicable and at worst 'wildly inappropriate' (Kanter et al., 1992, p. 10); (2) his approach to change is only suitable for isolated and incremental change situations; (3) he ignored power and politics; and (4) he adopted a top-down, management-driven approach to change. These criticisms were addressed above, but to recap:

(1) There is substantial evidence that Lewin (1947a, p. 199) recognized that: 'Change and constancy are relative concepts; group life is never without change, merely differences in the amount and type of change exist'. There is also a substantial body of evidence in the social, and even physical sciences, to support Lewin's 3-Step perspective on to change (Elrod and Tippett, 2002; Hendry, 1996).

(2) As Dickens and Watkins (1999, p. 127) observed: Lewin's approach is '. . . intended to foster change on the group, organizational and even societal levels'. In the main, he saw change as a slow process of working with and through groups to achieve behavioural and cultural change. However, writers as diverse as Quinn (1980, 1982) and Kanter et al. (1992) have recognized that an incremental approach can achieve organizational transformation. Lewin also recognized that, under certain crisis conditions, organizational transformations can be achieved rapidly (Kippenberger, 1998a; Lewin, 1947a). Nevertheless, in the main, even amongst Lewin's critics, the general view is that only structural and technical change can be achieved relatively speedily (Dawson, 1994; Kanter et al., 1992; Pettigrew et al., 1989, 1992; Wilson, 1992).

(3) Given Lewin's concern with issues such as racial and religious conflict, the accusation that he ignored the role of power and politics is difficult to sustain. One of the main strengths of Field Theory and Group Dynamics is that they identify the forces within and between groups and show how individuals behave in response to these. In addition, the iterative, investigative and learning approaches which lie at the heart of Action Research and the 3-Step model are also designed to reveal and address such issues (Bargal and Bar, 1992).

(4) The issues Lewin sought to tackle were many and varied (Cartwright, 1952; Lewin, 1948a). Lewin's sympathies were clearly with the underdog, the disadvantaged and the discriminated against (Cooke, 1999; Marrow, 1969). His assistance was sought by a wide range of parties including national and local government, religious and racial groups, and employers and unions; his response emphasized learning and participation by all concerned (Lewin, 1946). In the face of this, the charge that he saw change as only being top-down or management-driven is difficult to sustain.

Lewin's critics have sought to show that his Planned approach to change was simplistic and outmoded. By rejecting these criticisms, and by revealing the nature of his approach, this article has also shown the continuing relevance of Lewin's work, whether in organizations or society at large. The need to resolve social conflict has certainly not diminished since Lewin's day. Nor can one say that Lewin's approach seems dated, based as it is on building understanding, generating learning, gaining new insights, and identifying and testing (and retesting) solutions (Bargal and Bar, 1992; Darwin et al., 2002). Certainly, there seems little evidence that one can achieve peace, reconciliation, co-operation or trust by force (Olsen, 2002). Likewise, in organizations, issues of group effectiveness, behaviour and change have not diminished in the half century since Lewin's death, though they may often now be labelled differently. However, as in Lewin's day, there are no quick or easy ways of achieving such changes, and Lewin's approach is clearly still valuable and influential in these areas (Cummings and Worley, 1997). This can be seen from the enormous emphasis that continues to be placed on the importance of group behaviour, involvement, empowerment (Argyris, 1992; Handy, 1994; Hannagan, 2002; Huczynski and Buchanan, 2001; Kanter, 1989; Mullins, 2002; Peters, 1993; Schein, 1988; Senge, 1990; Wilson, 1992). Indeed, the advent of the complexity perspective appears to be leading to a renewed interest in Lewin's work (Back, 1992; Kippenberger, 1998a; MacIntosh and MacLean, 2001; Tschacher and Brunner, 1995).

In conclusion, therefore, though Lewin's contribution to organizational change has come under increasing criticism since the 1980s, much of this appears to be unfounded and/or based on a narrow interpretation of his work. In contrast, the last decade has also seen a renewed interest in understanding and applying his approach to change (Bargal and Bar, 1992; Elrod and Tippett, 2002; Hendry, 1996; Kippenberger, 1998a; MacIntosh and MacLean, 2001; Wooten and White, 1999). In many respects, this should not come as a surprise given the tributes and acknowledgments paid to him by major figures such as Chris Argyris (Argyris et al., 1985) and Edgar Schein (1988). Above all, though, it is a recognition of the rigour of Lewin's work, based as it was on a virtuous circle of theory, experimentation and practice, and which is best expressed by his famous dictum that '. . . there is nothing so practical as a good theory' (Lewin, 1943–44, p. 169).

REFERENCES

Allaire, Y. and Firsirotu, M. E. (1984). 'Theories of organizational culture'. *Organization Studies*, **5**, 3, 193–226.

Allport, G. W. (1948). 'Foreword'. In Lewin, G. W. (Ed.), *Resolving Social Conflict*. London: Harper & Row.

Argyris, C. (1990). *Overcoming Organizational Defenses*. Boston, MA: Allen and Bacon.

Argyris, C. (1992). *On Organizational Learning*. Oxford: Blackwell.

Argyris, C., Putnam, R. and McLain-Smith, D. (1985). *Action Science: Concepts, Methods and Skills for Research and Intervention*. San Francisco, CA: Jossey Bass.

Ash, M. G. (1992). 'Cultural contexts and scientific change in psychology – Lewin, Kurt in Iowa'. *American Psychologist*, **47**, 2, 198–207.

Back, K. W. (1992). 'This business of topology'. *Journal of Social Issues*, **48**, 2, 51–66.

Bargal, D. and Bar, H. (1992). 'A Lewinian approach to intergroup workshops for Arab-Palestinian and Jewish Youth'. *Journal of Social Issues*, **48**, 2, 139–54.

Bargal, D., Gold, M. and Lewin, M. (1992). 'The heritage of Kurt Lewin – Introduction'. *Journal of Social Issues*, **48**, 2, 3–13.

Bechtold, B. L. (1997). 'Chaos theory as a model for strategy development'. *Empowerment in Organizations*, **5**, 4, 193–202.

Beer, M. and Nohria, N. (2000). 'Cracking the code of change'. *Harvard Business Review*, May–June, 133–41.

Bennett, R. (1983). *Management Research*. Management Development Series, 20. Geneva: International Labour Office.

Bernstein, L. (1968). *Management Development*. London: Business Books.

Black, J. (2000). 'Fermenting change: capitalizing on the inherent change found in dynamic non-linear (or complex) systems'. *Journal of Organizational Change Management*, **13**, 6, 520–25.

Boje, D. M. (2000). 'Phenomenal complexity theory and change at Disney: response to Letiche'. *Journal of Organizational Change Management*, **13**, 6, 558–66.

Brown, S. L. and Eisenhardt, K. M. (1997). 'The art of continuous change: linking complexity theory and time-paced evolution in relentlessly shifting organizations'. *Administrative Science Quarterly*, **42**, March, 1–34.

Buchanan, D. A. and Storey, J. (1997). 'Role-taking and role-switching in organizational change: the four pluralities'. In McLoughlin, I. and Harris, M. (Eds), *Innovation, Organizational Change and Technology*. London: International Thompson.

Burnes, B. (2000). *Managing Change*, 3rd edition. Harlow: FT/Pearson Educational

Cartwright, D (1951). 'Achieving change in people: some applications of group dynamics theory'. *Human Relations*, **6**, 4, 381–92.

Cartwright, D. (Ed.) (1952). *Field Theory in Social Science*. London: Social Science Paperbacks.

Choi, T. Y., Dooley, K. J. and Rungtusanatham, M. (2001). 'Supply networks and complex adaptive systems: control versus emergence'. *Journal of Operations Management*, **19**, 3, 351–66.

Coch, L. and French, J. R. P. Jr (1948). 'Overcoming resistance to change'. *Human Relations*, **1**, 4, 512–32.

Collins, D. (1998). *Organizational Change*. London: Routledge.

Conner, P. E. (1977). 'A critical enquiry into some assumptions and values characterizing OD'. *Academy of Management Review*, **2**, 1, 635–44.

Cooke, B. (1999). 'Writing the left out of management theory: the historiography of the management of change'. *Organization*, **6**, 1, 81–105.

Cummings, T. G. and Huse, E. F. (1989). *Organization Development and Change*, 4th edition. St Paul, MN: West Publishing.

Cummings, T. G. and Worley, C. G. (1997). *Organization Development and Change*, 6th edition. Cincinnati, OH: South-Western College Publishing.

Cyert, R. M. and March, J. G. (1963). *A Behavioral Theory of the Firm*. Englewood Cliffs, NJ: Prentice Hall.

Darwin, J., Johnson, P. and McAuley, J. (2002). *Developing Strategies for Change*. Harlow: FT/Prentice Hall.

Dawson, P. (1994). *Organizational Change: A Processual Approach*. London: Paul Chapman Publishing.

Dent, E. B. and Goldberg, S. G. (1999). 'Challenging resistance to change'. *Journal of Applied Behavioral Science*, **35**, 1, 25–41.

Dickens, L. and Watkins, K. (1999). 'Action research: rethinking Lewin'. *Management Learning*, **30**, 2, 127–40.

Dunphy, D. D. and Stace, D. A. (1992). *Under New Management*. Sydney: McGraw-Hill.

Dunphy, D. D. and Stace, D. A. (1993). 'The strategic management of corporate change'. *Human Relations*, **46**, 8, 905–18.

Eden, C. and Huxham, C. (1996). 'Action research for the study of organizations'. In Clegg, S. R., Hardy, C. and Nord, W. R. (Eds), *Handbook of Organization Studies*. London: Sage.

Elden, M. and Chisholm, R. F. (1993). 'Emerging varieties of action research: Introduction to the Special Issue'. *Human Relations*, **46**, 2, 121–42.

Elrod P. D. II and Tippett, D. D. (2002). 'The "Death Valley" of change'. *Journal of Organizational Change Management*, **15**, 3, 273–91.

French, W. L. and Bell, C. H. (1984). *Organization Development*, 4th edition. Englewood Cliffs, NJ: Prentice-Hall.

French, W. L. and Bell, C. H. (1995). *Organization Development*, 5th edition. Englewood Cliffs, NJ: Prentice-Hall.

French, J. R. P. Jr and Raven, B. H. (1959). 'The bases of social power'. In Cartwright, D. (Ed.), *Studies in Social Power*. Ann Harbor, MI: Institute for Social Research.

Garvin, D. A. (1993). 'Building a learning organization'. *Harvard Business Review*, July–August, 78–91.

Gellerman, W., Frankel, M. S. and Ladenson, R. F. (1990). *Values and Ethics in Organizational and Human Systems Development: Responding to Dilemmas in Professional Life*. San Francisco, CA: Jossey Bass.

Gersick, C. J. G. (1991). 'Revolutionary change theories: a multilevel exploration of the punctuated equilibrium paradigm'. *Academy of Management Review*, **16**, 1, 10–36.

Gilchrist, A. (2000). 'The well-connected community: networking to the edge of chaos'. *Community Development Journal*, **3**, 3, 264–75.

Gold, M. (1992). 'Metatheory and field theory in social psychology: relevance or elegance?' *Journal of Social Issues*, **48**, 2, 67–78.

Gould, S. J. (1989). 'Punctuated equilibrium in fact and theory'. *Journal of Social Biological Structure*, **12**, 117–36.

Greenwald, J. (1996). 'Reinventing Sears'. *Time*, 23 December, 53–5.

Handy, C. (1994). *The Empty Raincoat*. London: Hutchinson.

Hannagan, T. (2002). *Management: Concepts and Practices*, 3rd edition. Harlow: FT/Pearson.

Hannan, M. T. and Freeman, J. (1988). *Organizational Ecology*. Cambridge, MA: Harvard University Press.

Harris, P. R. (1985). *Management in Transition*. San Francisco, CA: Jossey Bass.

Hatch, M. J. (1997). *Organization Theory: Modern, Symbolic and Postmodern Perspectives*. Oxford: Oxford University Press.

Hedberg, B., Nystrom, P. and Starbuck, W. (1976). 'Camping on seesaws: prescriptions for a self-designing organization'. *Administrative Science Quarterly*, **17**, 371–81.

Hendry, C. (1996). 'Understanding and creating whole organizational change through learning theory'. *Human Relations*, **48**, 5, 621–41.

Hirschhorn, L. (1988). *The Workplace Within*. Cambridge, MA: MIT Press.

House, J. S. (1993). 'John R French, Jr: A Lewinian's Lewinian'. *Journal of Social Issues*, **49**, 4, 221–6.

Huczynski, A. and Buchanan, D. (2001). *Organizational Behaviour*, 4th edition. Harlow: FT/Prentice Hall.

Jaques, E. (1998). 'On leaving the Tavistock Institute'. *Human Relations*, **51**, 3, 251–7.

Kanter, R. M. (1983). *The Change Masters*. New York: Simon & Schuster.

Kanter, R. M. (1989). *When Giants Learn to Dance: Mastering the Challenges of Strategy, Management, and Careers in the 1990s*. London: Unwin.

Kanter, R. M., Stein, B. A. and Jick, T. D. (1992). *The Challenge of Organizational Change*. New York: Free Press.

Kearney, A. T. (1989). *Computer Integrated Manufacturing: Competitive Advantage or Technological Dead End?* London: Kearney.

Kimberley, J. and Miles, R. (Eds) (1980). *The Organizational Life Cycle*. San Francisco, CA: Jossey Bass.

Kippenberger, T. (1998a). 'Planned change: Kurt Lewin's legacy'. *The Antidote*, **14**, 10–12.

Kippenberger, T. (1998b). 'Managed learning: elaborating on Lewin's model'. *The Antidote*, **14**, 13.

Kotter, J. P. (1996). *Leading Change*. Boston, MA: Harvard Business School Press.

Lewin, K. (1939). 'When facing danger'. In Lewin, G. W. (Ed.), *Resolving Social Conflict*. London: Harper & Row.

Lewin, K. (1943a). 'Psychological ecology'. In Cartwright, D. (Ed.), *Field Theory in Social Science*. London: Social Science Paperbacks.

Lewin, K. (1943b). 'The special case of Germany'. In Lewin, G. W. (Ed.), *Resolving Social Conflict*. London: Harper & Row.

Lewin, K. (1943–44). 'Problems of research in social psychology'. In Cartwright, D. (Ed.), *Field Theory in Social Science*. London: Social Science Paperbacks.

Lewin, K. (1946). 'Action research and minority problems'. In Lewin, G. W. (Ed.), *Resolving Social Conflict*. London: Harper & Row.

Lewin, K. (1947a). 'Frontiers in group dynamics'. In Cartwright, D. (Ed.), *Field Theory in Social Science*. London: Social Science Paperbacks.

Lewin, K. (1947b). 'Group decisions and social change'. In Newcomb, T. M. and Hartley, E. L. (Eds), *Readings in Social Psychology*. New York: Henry Holt.

Lewin, G. W. (Ed.) (1948a). *Resolving Social Conflict*. London: Harper & Row.

Lewin, G. W. (1948b). 'Preface'. In Lewin, G. W. (Ed.), *Resolving Social Conflict*. London: Harper & Row.

Lewin, M. (1992). 'The impact of Kurt Lewin's life on the place of social issues in his work'. *Journal of Social Issues*, **48**, 2, 15–29.

Lewis, R. (1994). 'From chaos to complexity: implications for organizations'. *Executive Development*, **7**, 4, 16–17.

Lindblom, C. E. (1959). 'The science of muddling through'. *Public Administration Review*, **19**, Spring, 79–88.

Lorenz, E. (1993). *The Essence of Chaos*. London: UCL Press.

Macbeth, D. K. (2002). 'Emergent strategy in managing cooperative supply chain change'. *International Journal of Operations and Production Management*, **22**, 7, 728–40.

MacIntosh, R. and MacLean, D. (2001). 'Conditioned emergence: researching change and changing research'. *International Journal of Operations and Production Management*, **21**, 10, 1343–57.

Marrow, A. J. (1957). *Making Management Human*. New York: McGraw-Hill.

Marrow, A. J. (1969). *The Practical Theorist: The Life and Work of Kurt Lewin*. New York: Teachers College Press.

Marshak, R. J. (1993). 'Lewin meets Confucius: a re-view of the OD model of change'. *The Journal of Applied Behavioral Science*, **29**, 4, 393–415.

Matthews, R. (2002). 'Competition, archetypes and creative imagination'. *Journal of Organizational Change Management*, **15**, 5, 461–76.

Miller, D. and Friesen, P. H. (1984). *Organizations: A Quantum View*. Englewood Cliffs, NJ: Prentice Hall.

Mintzberg, H., Ahlstrand, B. and Lampel, J. (1998). *Strategy Safari*. Hemel Hempstead: Prentice Hall.

Mullins, L. (2002). *Management and Organisational Behaviour*, 6th edition. Harlow: FT/Pearson.

Nonaka, I. (1988). 'Creating organizational order out of chaos: self-renewal in Japanese firms'. *Harvard Business Review*, November–December, 96–104.

Olsen, B. D. (2002). 'Applied social and community interventions for crisis in times of national and international conflict'. *Analyses of Social Issues and Public Policy*, **2**, 1, 119–29.

Peters, T. (1993). *Liberation Management*. London: Pan.

Peters, T. and Waterman, R. H. (1982). *In Search of Excellence: Lessons from America's Best-Run Companies*. London: Harper and Row.

Pettigrew, A. M. (1973). *The Politics of Organisational Decision Making*. Tavistock: London.

Pettigrew, A. M. (1979). 'On studying organizational culture'. *Administrative Science Quarterly*, **24**, 4, 570–81.

Pettigrew, A. M. (1980). 'The politics of organisational change'. In Anderson, N. B. (Ed.), *The Human Side of Information Processing*. Amsterdam: North Holland.

Pettigrew, A. M. (1985). *The Awakening Giant: Continuity and Change in ICI*. Oxford: Blackwell.

Pettigrew, A. M. (1987). 'Context and action in the transformation of the firm'. *Journal of Management Sciences*, **24**, 6, 649–70.

Pettigrew, A. M. (1990a). 'Longitudinal field research on change: theory and practice'. *Organizational Science*, **3**, 1, 267–92.

Pettigrew, A. M. (1990b). 'Studying strategic choice and strategic change'. *Organizational Studies*, **11**, 1, 6–11.

Pettigrew, A. M. (1997). 'What is a processual analysis?' *Scandinavian Journal of Management*, **13**, 40, 337–48.

Pettigrew, A. M. and Whipp, R. (1993). 'Understanding the environment'. In Mabey, C. and Mayon-White, B. (Eds), *Managing Change*, 2nd edition. London: The Open University/Paul Chapman Publishing.

Pettigrew, A. M., Hendry, C. N. and Sparrow, P. (1989). *Training in Britain: Employers' Perspectives on Human Resources*. London: HMSO.

Pettigrew, A. M., Ferlie, E. and McKee, L. (1992). *Shaping Strategic Change*. London: Sage.

Pfeffer, J. (1981). *Power in Organizations*. Cambridge, MA: Pitman.

Pfeffer, J. (1992). *Managing with Power: Politics and Influence in Organizations*. Boston, MA: Harvard Business School Press.

Prigogine, I. and Stengers, I. (1984). *Order Out of Chaos: Man's New Dialogue with Nature*. New York: Bantam Books.

Quinn, J. B. (1980). *Strategies for Change: Logical Incrementalism*. Homewood, IL: Irwin.

Quinn, J. B. (1982). 'Managing strategies incrementally'. *Omega*, **10**, 6, 613–27.

Raven, B. H. (1965). 'Social influence and power'. In Steiner, I. D. and Fishbein, M. (Eds), *Current Studies in Social Psychology*. New York: Holt, Rinehart, Winston.

Raven, B. H. (1993). 'The bases of power – origins and recent developments'. *Journal of Social Issues*, **49**, 4, 227–51.

Raven, B. H. (1999). 'Kurt Lewin Address: Influence, power, religion, and the mechanisms of social control'. *Journal of Social Issues*, **55**, 1, 161–89.

Romanelli, E. and Tushman, M. L. (1994). 'Organizational transformation as punctuated equilibrium: an empirical test'. *Academy of Management Journal*, **37**, 5, 1141–66.

Schein, E. H. (1988). *Organizational Psychology*, 3rd edition. London: Prentice Hall.

Schein, E. H. (1996). 'Kurt Lewin's change theory in the field and in the classroom: notes towards a model of management learning'. *Systems Practice*, **9**, 1, 27–47.

Senge, P. M. (1990). *The Fifth Discipline: The Art and Practice of the Learning Organization*. London: Century Business.

Shelton, C. K. and Darling, J. R. (2001). 'The quantum skills model in management: a new paradigm to enhance effective leadership'. *Leadership and Organization Development Journal*, **22**, 6, 264–73.

Smith, M. K. (2001). 'Kurt Lewin: groups, experiential learning and action research'. *The Encyclopedia of Informal Education*. http://www.infed.org/thinkers/et-lewin.htm, 1–15.

Stace, D. and Dunphy, D. (2001). *Beyond the Boundaries: Leading and Re-creating the Successful Enterprise*, 2nd edition. Sydney: McGraw-Hill.

Stacey, R. D. (1993). *Strategic Management and Organisational Dynamics*. London: Pitman.

Stacey, R. D., Griffin, D. and Shaw, P. (2002). *Complexity and Management: Fad or Radical Challenge to Systems Thinking?* London: Routledge.

Stickland, F. (1998). *The Dynamics of Change: Insights into Organisational Transition from the Natural World*. London: Routledge.

Tetenbaum, T. J. (1998). 'Shifting paradigms: from Newton to chaos'. *Organizational Dynamics*, **26**, 4, 21–32.

Tobach, E. (1994). 'Personal is political is personal is political'. *Journal of Social Issues*, **50**, 1, 221–44.

Tschacher, W. and Brunner, E. J. (1995). 'Empirical-studies of group-dynamics from the point-of-view of self-organization theory'. *Zeitschrift fur Sozialpsychologie*, **26**, 2, 78–91.

Waclawski, J. (2002). 'Large-scale organizational change and performance: an empirical examination'. *Human Resource Development Quarterly*, **13**, 3, 289–305.

Warwick, D. P. and Thompson, J. T. (1980). 'Still crazy after all these years'. *Training and Development Journal*, **34**, 2, 16–22.

Wastell, D. G., White, P. and Kawalek, P. (1994). 'A methodology for business process redesign: experience and issues'. *Journal of Strategic Information Systems*, **3**, 1, 23–40.

Watcher, B. (1993). *The Adoption of Total Quality Management in Scotland*. Durham: Durham University Business School.

Watson, T. J. (1997). *In Search of Management*. London: Thompson International.

Wheatley, M. J. (1992). *Leadership and the New Science: Learning About Organization from an Orderly Universe*. San Francisco, CA: Berrett-Koehler.

Whyte, J. and Watcher, B. (1992). *The Adoption of Total Quality Management in Northern England*. Durham: Durham University Business School.

Wilson, D. C. (1992). *A Strategy of Change*. London: Routledge.

Wooten, K. C. and White, L. P. (1999). 'Linking OD's philosophy with justice theory: postmodern implications'. *Journal of Organizational Change Management*, **12**, 1, 7–20.

Zairi, M., Letza, S. and Oakland, J. (1994). 'Does TQM impact on bottom line results?' *TQM Magazine*, **6**, 1, 38–43.

From Programmed Change to Self Design: Learning How to Change Organizations

Thomas G. Cummings
University of Southern California

Cummings, T. (1995). From programmed change to self design: Learning how to transform organizations. *Organization Development Journal*, 13, 20-31

Abstract

This article addresses a significant problem facing organizations today--how to implement innovations requiring fundamental and continuous organizational changes. Organizations have difficulty changing themselves because they apply a programmed change strategy that is ill-suited to fundamental and continuous change. The article describes a more promising approach to organizational change called self design. This strategy is flexible and empowering, and provides organizations with the capability to design and implement organizational changes continuously.

2

Today's organizations are facing enormous pressures to change themselves. They are experiencing competitive demands to perform more quickly and efficiently at lower cost and higher quality. They are increasingly forced to adapt to turbulent environments where technological, economic, and cultural forces are changing rapidly and unpredictably.

In order to compete or even to survive in this organizational whitewater, organizations must be flexible and agile performers with rapid response times and adaptive capabilities (Vaill, 1989; Galbraith, 1995). This requires fundamental changes in how organizations traditionally structure and manage themselves and in how they perform, compete, and relate to customers. Moreover, these new structures and practices themselves require continual modification and change as environmental turbulence is likely to persist or even increase for the foreseeable future (D'Aveni, 1994). Consequently, organizations must not only be able to design and implement fundamental changes but they must be capable of redesigning and renewing themselves continually in the face of incessant and unpredictable change. They must learn how to "camp on seesaws" (Starbuck, 1985) rather than how to erect permanent structures on solid ground.

Unfortunately, most organizations face tremendous barriers to undertaking such dramatic and continual change successfully (Katz and Kahn, 1978; Hall, 1987). There are strong pressures to preserve the status quo, such as entrenched interests, liability of newness, and structural inertia. Organizational members may have limited skills or experience to manage change. They may not understand nor agree with the need for change and may fear letting go of the known and moving toward the unknown. Slack resources and time to innovate may be scarce. The organization's culture may be control oriented and not support the organizational learning required to manage change.

Although these barriers present formidable obstacles to organization change, a more subtle and perhaps more pernicious deterrent derives from the very methods and approaches that organizations use to manage innovation and change. This paper first argues that organizations traditionally apply a programmed strategy for designing and implementing change; this approach has inherent limitations that prevent organizations from undertaking the kinds of fundamental and continuous changes that are needed in today's environment. Next, an alternative strategy for organizational change is presented that is more suited to these situations. Called "self design", this approach provides organizations with the capacity to design and implement their own improvements. It enables organizations to learn how to change and improve themselves continually in a valued direction.

Programmed Change

Organizations traditionally undertake innovation and change from a programmed perspective (Beer, Eisenstat, and Spector, 1990). This approach is well learned and widely accepted in most organizations, and thus is the predominate mode for addressing organizational improvement. It includes a number of features that are aimed at rationalizing the change process and affording organizations control over it.

Features of Programmed Change

Programmed change resembles a rational problem-solving process. It is typically directed at solving specific organizational problems such as poor customer service, excessive costs, and employee absenteeism; or it may address more general issues such as finding better ways of organizing and performing. Those problems that reach sufficient thresholds of recognition and of felt need for change become the focus and motivation for organizational improvement.

3

Programmed change is led by managers or administrators who have responsibility for solving problems and improving the organization. Because they are held accountable for the consequences of change, mangers seek to maximize control over the change process. They apply formal methods to analyze problems and to select relevant solutions. They rely heavily on staff and external experts to design innovations that are rationally defensible. Managers seek to gain compliance with the changes through formal structures and mechanisms including the managerial hierarchy, information and control systems, and reward practices.

The rationality and control inherent in programmed change result in innovations that are well defined with clear costs and expected results. The changes tend to be packaged into a discrete change program that is maximally specified with a specific beginning and end to implementation. Such packaged change programs are often given names or slogans signifying the focus of change; they also include schedules and guides for implementation along with explicit communication and training materials. In order to assure consistency of application, the changes are generally rolled out in the organization along formal lines of authority with limited opportunities for adjustments or modifications.

Problems with Programmed Change

Programmed change is the predominate method for innovation and improvement in contemporary organizations. It is seen as affording managers high levels of rationality and control over the change process and thus is well learned and taken for granted in most organizations. Programmed change has a mixed record of success, however. It is particularly relevant to solving problems that are limited in scope and require minimal amounts of organizational change. When applied to the kinds of fundamental and continuous organizational changes addressed in this paper, programmed change has a number of inherent problems and limitations (Beer, Eisenstat, and Spector, 1990).

Programmed change is unlikely to lead to high levels of commitment to change. It is fundamentally a problem-solving process with limited stakeholder involvement. Programmed change is controlled by managers, designed by experts, and rolled out to lower-level employees who are the primary targets of change. Because employees and other relevant stakeholders, such as customers and suppliers, are not actively involved in the analysis and design phases of the change process, the changes may not take into account their needs and interests. Consequently, these stakeholders may not support the changes and may even resist or sabotage them.

Programmed change frequently results in conflict between the designers and implementers of change. This can lead to change programs that are well designed yet not implemented successfully. Programmed change involves a division of labor where staff experts or consultants design the change program, and managers and employees implement it. This division can lead to differences in design criteria and change orientation between the two sides. Design experts tend to favor change programs that are maximally specified with explicit schedules, guidelines, and change activities. Moreover, they seek innovations with proven records of success, and consequently rely on change programs that have worked well in other settings and that can be readily packaged and adopted by the existing organization. These features are intended to assure designers that their expertise will be recognized and valued in the organization and that the integrity of their designs will persist. Implementers, on the other hand, tend to prefer change programs that are minimally specified and that afford them maximum freedom to modify and adjust the changes to fit their specific situations. They seek flexibility and local control over changes.

4

These fundamental differences often lead to conflicts and disagreements between designers and implementers that can have disastrous consequences for change programs. Implementers often complain that change programs are too rigid and non-adaptive to their situation. Designers argue that allowing implementers to modify the change program can negatively impact the very things that make it successful and can lead to inconsistencies and confusion across the organization. Such conflict can lead to a vicious cycle where the more designers seek to defend and to gain compliance with the change program, the more implementers try to change or resist it. Eventually, the change process can become mired in an escalating game of blaming each other for program failure. Such distrust and animosity often taint future attempts at organizational change and improvement.

The most troublesome limitation of programmed change is that it does little to improve the organization's ability to manage future changes. Programmed change is aimed at solving particular organizational problems, not at providing managers and employees with the skills and knowledge necessary to analyze and solve future problems. Because the expertise to design innovations resides in staff experts and consultants, managers and employees tend to become dependent on them and see little need to gain such skills themselves. Moreover, programmed change treats organizational innovation as a singular event with a specific beginning and end; changes are seen as discrete entities that can be adopted or implemented within a particular time period. Thus, once the changes are implemented and the problem is resolved, there is little need for further problem solving and change, at least until the next problem arises and gains sufficient attention to initiate action. Because managers and employees tend to view change as a discrete problem-solving event rather than as a continuous process of organizational improvement, there is little motivation to gain the skills and knowledge needed to design and implement innovations.

When taken together, these problems with programmed change explain why this approach to organizational improvement does not fit well with the kinds of fundamental and continuous organizational changes needed to compete in today's turbulent environments. Organizations are increasingly having to transform themselves into leaner, more flexible structures where employees are empowered to make relevant decisions and changes. They are seeking to improve themselves continuously as they adapt to competitive conditions that are changing rapidly and unpredictably. These organizational innovations require a change strategy that enables organizations to make significant and often radical transformations in how they are structured and how they operate (Nadler, Shaw, and Walton, 1995). Transformational change needs considerable support and commitment from all relevant stakeholders including top executives, middle and first-line managers, employees, and staff experts. They must be actively involved in analyzing the organization and its environment, designing appropriate innovations, and implementing them. Programmed change fails to achieve extensive involvement and commitment. It involves limited stakeholders in the change process, and thus is unlikely to achieve the broad support and high levels of commitment needed for transformational change.

Today's organizational innovations also require a change strategy that enables organizations to change continuously in response to emerging conditions. Continuous change needs to be highly flexible and treated as a verb or on-going process not as a noun or discrete entity (Drucker, 1995). The capacity to change and to improve continually must be built into the organization and become part of its normal functioning. All members--managers, staff experts, and employees alike--must have the skills and knowledge necessary to design their own innovations and to manage their own change processes. Programmed change is ill-suited to

5

achieving such widespread expertise. It is highly dependent on staff experts and consultants to design innovations and change processes. It treats organizational innovation as a discrete entity with a specified beginning and end. Both of these features reduce mangers' and employees' motivation to gain the skills and knowledge necessary to design and implement organizational changes.

Self-Designed Change

Given the inherent limitations of programmed change, organizations are increasingly seeking alternative change strategies that are more attuned to the dynamics of fundamental and continuous organizational change. They are exploring change processes that emphasize extensive member involvement and widespread application of change skills and knowledge within the organization. These new change strategies are being developed in a myriad of organizational contexts and are referred to variously as "appreciative inquiry" (Cooperrider and Srivastva, 1987), "participatory action research" (Elden, 1983), "organizational learning" (Senge, 1990), "action inquiry" (Fisher and Torbert, 1995), and "self-designing organizations" (Mohrman and Cummings, 1989). Regardless of the name or specific action steps, these approaches all treat organizational change as an on-going process of continuous improvement and innovation. They involve multiple stakeholders in the change process and empower them to participate actively in all phases of innovation, from diagnosis and design to implementation and assessment. The strategies treat organizational change as a learning process where participants learn through their actions how to improve the organization and the learning process itself.

The following pages describe in more detail one of these new change strategies called "self design" (Mohrman & Cummings, 1989). It will serve to illustrate how these approaches are applied and will provide more concrete understanding of what this kind of organizational change entails.

Like the name implies, self design is aimed at involving organizational members in the design and implementation of their own improvements. It was initially developed during the early 1980s by members from the Center for Effective Organizations at the University of Southern California. These action researchers worked collaboratively with a variety of organizations undergoing significant and continuous change. The change efforts were intended to make the organizations more flexible and lean and more responsive to customers and competitive conditions. They resulted in high-involvement designs emphasizing employee empowerment, self-managed teams, skill-based pay and gainsharing, flat hierarchies, and team-based selection practices.

The participants--managers, employees, staff experts, and researchers--jointly learned that implementing high-involvement designs requires a change strategy that is also high involvement. Because such designs require members to learn new work behaviors and ways of relating to each other, the change process itself must facilitate and support behavioral change. Unfortunately, behavioral change cannot be learned abstractly or passively by reading a book or listening to an expert. It must be learned in situ through direct involvement in trying new behaviors, assessing the results, making necessary adjustments, and so on. Moreover, behavioral change is extremely difficult for most people, and consequently requires a good deal of personal understanding and commitment to change. Involvement in designing the changes increases the likelihood that they will be understood and accepted.

Self design evolved as a strategy for getting members involved in designing and implementing organizational changes. It can be applied to a variety of organizational settings and

6

can include the entire organization, a particular operating unit or functional area, or some combination of subunits. Self design is structured differently depending on the size of the focal organization. When applied to the total organization or a large subunit, it typically involves cross-functional and cross-level design teams that carry out design tasks for the rest of the organization. All organizational members provide input to the design teams, discuss their proposals, and subsequently implement them in their respective units. They refine and tailor the designs to fit their particular situations and continually improve them. When applied to smaller organizational settings such as a work team or start-up business, self design generally involves all members directly in the design and implementation activities.

Self design requires strong leadership that is usually provided by those responsible for the organization or unit undergoing change. In large-scale change efforts, this leadership function may reside in a steering committee composed of representatives of key stakeholders, such as senior executives, staff administrators, and union officers. In smaller settings, leadership is typically provided by the top manager of the unit. Regardless of who performs the leadership role, leaders of self design must provide a clear vision of the change process as well as guidance and support as members learn how to change themselves and improve the organization. Leaders must model the learning behaviors needed to implement change and provide the protection and encouragement that members need if they are to try new things and learn from their mistakes. Leaders must aggressively promote self design while showing patience and empathy for the personal difficulties inherent in trying to change the organization fundamentally and continuously.

The self-design strategy is explained more fully below. It involves a number of interrelated actives that overlap and mutually influence each other. The activities comprise a cycle of events emphasizing that self design is an iterative learning process. As members cycle through these activities, they learn how to change and improve the organization including their own work behaviors and interactions. This learning feeds into the next cycle of self design and so on. Thus, over time, members' capacity to change and to learn how to change are enhanced and refined.

Laying the Foundation

Self design requires an initial foundation of knowledge and expertise if organizational members are to become responsible and effective partners in change. They must have rudimentary understanding of how organizations function, how specific innovations can improve performance, and how self design can be applied. They must also clarify the underlying values or standards that will guide the change process and assess how well the organization is doing on them.

In laying the foundation for self design, organizations make an initial investment in time and resources that will have longer-term payoffs as members learn to improve the organization. Moreover, this preliminary knowledge and expertise are enhanced as members cycle through self-design activities and gain new skills and understanding.

Unfortunately, organizations often question the need for these upfront investments. There is a strong tendency to seek quick fixes and to move quickly and prematurely to the design and implementation phases of change. In the absence of a strong foundation for self design, organizational changes are likely to be superficial and incomplete. They are unlikely to result in significant behavioral changes or improvements in performance.

7

Laying the foundation consists of three related activities: (1) acquiring knowledge, (2) valuing, and (3) diagnosing. These are described below.

Acquiring knowledge. Organizational members need to gain conceptual and practical knowledge to guide their self-design efforts. Conceptually, they need to be familiar with broad systems models of organizations describing different design components and how they fit together to promote high performance. These frameworks explain: how organizational designs integrate with business strategies and objectives; how the success of the designs is contingent on such factors as technology, personal characteristics, and task environment; how changes in specific design components require congruent changes in other design elements. Members may also review information about different innovations that are currently making organizations more competitive and adaptive to change, such as self-managed work teams, gainsharing, employee empowerment, flexible benefits, and horizontal structures.

This conceptual learning can be supplemented with more practical understanding of how self design works and how innovations are applied in specific organizations. Members can take advantage of a plethora of opportunities for learning about the pragmatics of change. They can visit the many firms that welcome visitors and that show and explain to them how organizational transformation and continuous improvement are achieved in their settings; they can attend numerous conferences and workshops where practitioners share practical knowledge; they can read or view the growing list of books, magazines, and videos that are devoted to concrete descriptions of organizational innovation and change.

Valuing. Probably the most important task in laying the foundation for self design is clarifying the organizational values that will guide the change process. Values are enduring beliefs about what behaviors or outcomes are personally and socially desirable. They tend to be deep-seated and taken for granted, and have a powerful impact on how we behave and make judgments.

Organizational values are shared by members and influence their work behaviors and decision making. They affect design choices and determine which innovations and changes are seen as good or bad. Because organizational values are understood tacitly, they are rarely questioned or challenged. Thus, members' design choices tend to perpetuate the status quo. This can be disastrous if changes in competitive conditions or business strategy require entirely new ways of organizing and working.

A key task of laying the foundation for self design is to make explicit the organization's current values and to judge their relevance to competitive conditions. This may result in replacing certain values; or in the case of a new start-up organization, it may lead to an entirely new set of values. Moreover, because multiple stakeholders, often with diverse interests, are involved in self design, this valuing process should seek to uncover underlying value conflicts among the different participants. Such conflicts need to be identified and resolved early in the change process so they do not adversely affect subsequent design and implementation activities. Unless organizational changes take into account the interests of the different stakeholders, there is likely to be differential support and commitment for them. Addressing value conflicts may require various conflict resolution methods including collaborating, compromising, and negotiating. The key objective is to achieve sufficient value agreement among the stakeholders so they can proceed with self design in a shared and committed direction.

A common outcome of valuing activities is a value or vision statement. This clearly explicates the values that will guide self design including valued human and performance

8

outcomes and valued organizational conditions for achieving them. The vision statement may also include a brief introductory explanation of the mission or business purpose of the organization or subunit. Although valuing occurs early in self design, members may periodically reassess and modify the values as they continually cycle through self design activities. Thus, the vision statement is a living document that is open to modification and refinement.

    Diagnosing. This phase of laying the foundation for self design involves assessing the organization or subunit against the values. This can reveal value gaps where the organization is not functioning or performing consistent with the values. Such inconsistencies direct subsequent self-design activities toward designing and implementing innovations to close the gaps. In essence, self design is aimed at continually assessing and improving the organization in a valued direction.

    Diagnosing involves collecting and analyzing information about the organization to identify value gaps and to determine their underlying causes. Fortunately, there are numerous diagnostic frameworks and methods to guide these efforts, and members can gain familiarity with them as part of acquiring knowledge for self design. For example, diagnosis may proceed from a relatively broad systems model of organizations which assesses the organization's strategy and competitive environment, how well the current design fits with them, and the level of human and performance outcomes. Diagnosis may also focus on particular organizational design components, such as reward systems, work designs, or structures; it may address particular work flows such as developing new products or filling customer orders. Whatever the particular orientation, diagnosis results in a clearer understanding of value gaps and informs members where their subsequent designing activities need to be directed.

Designing

    Based on the results of laying the foundation for self design, designing involves developing specific organizational changes to reduce value gaps and to move the organization in a valued direction. Members apply knowledge of organizational innovations to the diagnostic information to create changes consistent with their values. They may determine that only limited change from the status quo is necessary and existing conditions need to be fine tuned; or that more extensive change is needed requiring innovations that imitate what other organizations are doing or that are entirely new and original.

    Designing is a creative process involving considerable discovery and ingenuity. Members explore new ways for organizing and working and generally develop an array of possible innovations. Although the changes must be responsive to personal, task, and competitive conditions, members are encouraged to confront imagined or real constraints and to design with as much freedom as possible. They learn that organizational designing is not deterministic but that there is choice in developing appropriate innovations. Members also gain a clearer understanding of the design implications of their values as they iterate back and forth between the values which serve as design guides and the designs themselves.

    The designing phase of self design results in innovations that are minimally specified and sufficiently flexible to permit adjustment and modification during implementation. Such flexibility is necessary because organizational designs are not mechanical objects that can be maximally specified and implemented in one step from design to operation. Rather, they are like metaphors offering members general prescriptions for how they should work and interrelate. Thus, organization designs require considerable development and innovation in situ as members learn behaviorally how to enact them. Moreover, organizational designs need to be minimally

9

specified so they can be tailored to fit local situations and changing conditions. They must have sufficient flexibility to permit members to learn how to change and improve them as the circumstances demand.

Implementing and Assessing

In this phase of self design, members take action to implement and assess organizational innovations. This involves action learning. They learn through their behavior how to enact the changes and how to refine and improve them continuously.

Action learning involves an on-going cycle of implementing and assessing activities. Members take action to implement or modify innovations. They then collect relevant data to assess whether the innovations and implementation process are progressing as intended, and if not, make plans to modify them. The core of this feedback-adjustment process is behavioral change. Members learn from their behaviors how to change them. They try out new work behaviors, examine their consequences, and attempt to change them if necessary. Such action learning continues indefinitely as members learn the work behaviors inherent in the innovations and seek to improve the performance of those behaviors continuously.

In self design, implementing and assessing activities are directed at three levels of action learning. At the most basic level which is referred to as "single-loop learning", members focus on getting the innovations implemented in accordance with the values. They seek to reduce deviations from the innovations' underlying values. This level of learning is the most prevalent in self design and occurs when values are responsive to competitive conditions and there is strong agreement on them among the different stakeholders.

The next higher level of action learning is called "double-loop learning" and involves changing the values themselves. Members learn how to confront value inconsistencies and conflicts and modify values accordingly; they learn how to change values that may no longer support the organization's strategy and competitive situation. This level of action learning occurs periodically in self design and generally requires members to return to the valuing and designing phases. They may learn that the values set initially in self design need to be modified and that renewed designing, implementing, and assessing activities need to occur. Because double-loop learning involves value change, it is likely to alter more radically the status quo than single-loop learning.

The highest level of learning is named "deutero learning" and concerns learning how to learn. This is the most difficult form of action learning and is the most important for self design. Because organizational learning processes tend to be tacit and taken for granted, members are not accustomed to examining or questioning them. This can lead to repetition of leaning mistakes and disorders. Deutero learning involves self-design activities aimed at the learning process itself. Members examine values, organizational conditions, and behaviors that inhibit single- and double-loop learning; they try to design more effective learning processes. Members then engage in implementing and assessing activities aimed at learning how to enact the new learning behaviors. Over time, deutero learning enables members to enhance their capacity to learn, and thus become better at implementing organizational innovations and improving them.

Summary and Conclusions

We live in an era of unprecedented change. Organizations are undergoing dramatic changes as they seek to transform themselves from slow-moving bureaucracies to lean and flexible structures capable of quick responses. Competitive environments are changing rapidly and unpredictably placing heavy demands on organizations' adaptive capabilities. These pressures to

10

change are unlikely to abate in the foreseeable future, and some argue that they may even get worse. If so, the ability to change fundamentally and continuously may become organizations' core competence (Prahalad and Hamel, 1990).

A major barrier to achieving such capability is the way that organizations traditionally approach innovation and change. They seek the control and certainty inherent in programmed change which is led by managers, designed by experts, and rolled out to employees who are the targets of change. This approach is well learned and taken for granted in most organizations, and thus is rarely questioned or examined. Although programmed change may solve specific problems, it fails to provide the high levels of commitment and learning needed to transform organizations and to improve them continually. Programmed change makes managers and employees dependent on experts for organizational improvement, and consequently they fail to gain the expertise and experience to design and implement their own innovations.

A more promising approach to the kinds of fundamental and continuous change needed in today's organizations is self-designed change. This strategy seeks to include all relevant stakeholders in the change process and to provide them with the knowledge and skills to design and implement organizational changes. Self design treats organizational change as an action-learning process where participants learn through their behaviors how to enact the changes and how to improve the organization continuously.

As we approach the start of the twenty-first century, organizations are facing difficult choices about managing change. Most know that significant organizational change is necessary; most have clear conceptions of what it should look like; yet few understand how to implement it.

In the face of ambiguity about implementation, there is a strong tendency to retreat to the well-learned habit of programmed change and the control and certainty that it traditionally affords. Unfortunately, the more that programmed change is applied to the kinds of changes needed in today's organizations, the less controllable and certain they become. In these situations, the rational features of programmed change produce seemingly irrational behavior. There is lack of commitment and support for the changes; there is conflict between the designers and the implementers of change; there is little motivation to gain the skills and knowledge needed for fundamental and continuous change.

Self-designed change is more suited to these change situations. It produces almost the opposite behaviors of programmed change. Yet for those inexperienced with self design, it appears less controllable and certain than programmed change. It requires more upfront investment and is more flexible and empowering than programmed change; it appears more messy and risky than programmed change.

For organizations questioning about whether to proceed with self design, there are no definitive nor easy responses to these concerns. There is no precise calculus for predicting its costs and benefits; there are no simple recipes for how it should unfold. Some would even say that it takes a leap of faith to set out into this relatively uncharted territory. Those organizations that pioneered self design started the exploration with little more than a strong conviction that programmed change was not working and that a more involving and adaptable alternative was needed. Hopefully, this paper will make the journey a bit less daunting for future explorers.

11

References

Beer, M., Eisenstat, R., & Spector, B. (1990)."Why change programs don't produce change." *Harvard Business Review* 33 (2): 158-166.

Cooperrider, D., & Srivastva, S. (1987). "Appreciative inquiry in organizational life," in Woodman, R., & Pasmore, W. (Eds.). Research in Organizational Change and Development, Vol. 1:129-169. Greenwich, CT: JAI Press.

D'Aveni, R. (1994). *Hypercompetition: Managing the Dynamics of Strategic Maneuvering*. New York: The Free Press.

Drucker, P. (1995). *Managing in a Time of Great Change*. New York: Penguin USA.

Elden, J.M. (1983). "Democratization and participatory research in developing local theory," Journal of Occupational Behavior 4 (1): 21-34.

Fisher, D., & Torbert, W. (1995). *Personal and Organizational Transformations: The True Challenge of Continual Quality Improvement*. New York: McGraw-Hill.

Galbraith, J. (1995*). Designing Organizations: An Executive Briefing on Strategy, Structure, and Process*. San Francisco: Jossey-Bass Publishers.

Katz, D., & Kahn, R. (1978). *The Social Psychology of Organizations*, 2nd Edition. New York: John Wiley & Sons.

McGrath, J. (1984). *Groups: Interaction and Performance*. Englewood Cliffs, NJ: Prentice Hall.

Mohrman, S., & Cummings, T. (1989). *Self-Designing Organizations: Learning How to Create High Performance*. Reading, MA: Addison-Wesley.

Nadler, D., Shaw, R., & Walton, A.E. (1995*). Discontinuous Change: Leading Organizational Transformation*. San Francisco: Jossey-Bass.

Prahalad, C.K., & Hamel, G. (1990). "Core competence of the corporation," *Harvard Business Review* 68 (3): 79-91.

Senge, P. (1990). *The Fifth Discipline*. New York: Doubleday Currency.

Starbuck, W. (1985). "Camping on seesaws," *Administrative Science Quarterly* 30 (3): 224-236.

Vaill, P. (1989). *Managing as a Performing Art: New Ideas for a World of Chaotic Change*. San Francisco: Jossey-Bass.

12

C E ⬤

Center for
Effective
Organizations

BUILDING A CHANGE CAPABILITY AT
CAPITAL ONE FINANCIAL

CEO PUBLICATION
G 08-09 (545)

CHRISTOPHER G. WORLEY, PH.D.
Center for Effective Organizations
Marshall School of Business
University of Southern California

EDWARD E. LAWLER III, PH.D.
Center for Effective Organizations
Marshall School of Business
University of Southern California

May 2008

Center for Effective Organizations - Marshall School of Business
University of Southern California - Los Angeles, CA 90089–0871
(213)740-9814   FAX (213) 740-4354
http://ceo.usc.edu

Building a Change Capability at Capital One Financial

Christopher G. Worley, Ph.D.

Research Scientist

Center for Effective Organizations

Marshall School of Business

University of Southern California

3415 South Figueroa Street, DCC 200

Los Angeles, CA 90089-0871

213-740-9814

cworley@marshall.usc.edu

Edward E. Lawler III, Ph.D.

Director

Center for Effective Organizations

Marshall School of Business

University of Southern California

3415 South Figueroa Street, DCC 200

Los Angeles, CA 90089-0871

213-740-9814

elawler@marshall.usc.edu

May, 2008

This article was published in Organizational Dynamics, Vol. 38, No. 4, pp. 245-251, 2009
www.elsevier.com/locate/orgdyn

Executive Summary

This article describes the development of an enterprise-wide change capability at Capital One Financial. Despite the rhetoric that organizations need to be more flexible and adaptable to meet the demands of change, globalization, competition, and innovation, few organizations have been able to implement the organization designs necessary to support flexibility or the orchestration capabilities to ensure that change can be routine. Capital One has met both of those criteria and we describe their journey toward adaptability.

For organizations seeking to develop a change capability, the Capital One case yields three practical learnings. First, organizations must consciously decide to increase the amount of change-related skills and knowledge in the organization. Second, they must implement supporting organizational systems and structures, and third, they must engage in and learn from change. Only by embracing change as a normal part of organizational functioning can they build the social capital necessary to make change a competitive advantage.

Building a Change Capability at Capital One Financial

In an era when environments are changing faster and faster, the rhetoric on organizational effectiveness is clear: successful organizations must be more agile and adaptable. Redesigning work processes, integrating acquired businesses, implementing large-scale information technology (IT) systems, and entering foreign markets are a few of the challenging changes companies are implementing. Any one of them can prove very difficult to accomplish - most estimates put the success rate for a large-scale organization change at about 25-30 percent. Successfully implementing several of them in a short time period is virtually impossible.

Capital One, the very successful financial services company, has built an organization that loves to change. It does not "manage change" as if it were some unwanted intruder; it does not view change management as an afterthought to improve the chances of getting some key resistors to "buy into" a new initiative. Change is integrated into the way Capital One formulates strategy, structures itself, and measures and rewards performance.

Capital One created an enterprise-wide change capability to give it the ability to orchestrate a variety of changes. Matt Schuyler, the chief human resources officer, said: "We purposefully set out to create an organization change capability that would allow us to execute changes, both large and small, faster and more efficiently while minimizing the effect on our associates. We wanted to make change management a core competency at Capital One, one that enables and supports our business strategy."

CAPITAL ONE FINANCIAL AS A BUILT-TO-CHANGE ORGANIZATION

Capital One's founder and chief executive officer (CEO), Rich Fairbank, was the first to see and believe in the power of marrying information technology and rigorous analytic programs to uncover market opportunities. When he joined Signet Bank, he got a chance to pilot his information-based approach. In 1993, Signet tested the assumption that people were dissatisfied with carrying high interest credit card debt. Signet offered a targeted group of customers the opportunity to transfer their credit card balances to a Signet credit card at lower interest rates. The enormous success of this campaign and the promise of the information-based approach encouraged Fairbank to lead Capital One's spin off from Signet.

In mid-2008, the organization's return on investment is over 1368% since its founding, it employed more than 31,800 people, and had revenues over $15 billion.

Capital One's organizational approach puts change at the core of its identity. Research suggests that "built-to-change" organizations have a strong focus on the future, use a robust strategy to generate a series of momentary competitive advantages, and leverage flexible organization features (Table 1). They also build in the capability to implement and orchestrate major changes.

TABLE 1	ELEMENTS OF A BUILT TO CHANGE ORGANIZATION.	
BUILT TO CHANGE FEATURE	DEFINITION	CAPITAL ONE DIMENSIONS
Strong future focus	Spend more time thinking about the future - give possible future scenarios more weight in current strategic decision-making	Dedicate a large percentage of analysts' time to thinking about future trends and their implications on a line of business
Robust strategy and momentary advantages	A recurring metaphor that explains a series of advantages over time	"Test and learn" strategy generates opportunities for new revenue streams
Flexible organization design	Create empowered organizations, flat structures, flexible performance management systems	Few tiers of jobs, pay for results and competencies related to changing, reorganize frequently
Orchestration capability	The ability to change routinely	Building a Change Capability Project

Strong Future Focus

Capital One is obsessed with the future. Each business line has its own analysts – as high as 20 percent of FTEs in some cases – who are skilled at exploring future trends. Instead of focusing solely on a current large customer or a set of existing strengths and weaknesses, Capital One's businesses focus on what might happen in the future and the skills and knowledge that will be needed to be successful. Fairbank has said, "80 percent of strategy is figuring out where the world is going, and 20percent is figuring out what you are going to do in response. If you can figure out where the world is going, what you need to do usually becomes obvious."

According to Mike McDermott, former Director of Organization Effectiveness, "Strategic thinking goes pretty deep on two levels. On one level, the strategic planning organization runs a variety of scenarios that look several years out. On another level, the executive committee meets regularly to discuss and debate a set of annual 'imperatives' or bold challenges. The imperatives are just that…they are things that *must* be done if we are to achieve our long-term vision. The imperatives are also a good tool because they can morph and change over time— they reinforce the importance of change management." Some of the more important corporate imperatives to come out over the last several years include diversification, customer experience, and several relate to human capital management.

Robust Strategies and Momentary Advantages

The information-based approach Fairbank created thrives on data, experiments, and analysis. One manager joked, "We count everything here. There's probably a spreadsheet somewhere describing the ratio of tables to chairs in the cafeteria." It results in a robust "test and learn" strategy, and it works like this. Terabytes of consumer data are analyzed statistically to generate potential risk profiles. For example, someone who responds to an invitation is a lesser credit risk than someone who calls up on the phone and asks for credit. Combined with guesses about how the environment is changing, a profile or hypothesis can be tested with an offer – interest rate, payment options, perquisites, or rewards – for credit services. Over the course of a year, Capital One's managers can conduct over 50,000 of these "tests."

When an identified risk profile and its associated offer get a response rate greater than some threshold amount, a potential momentary competitive advantage exists. The offer is broadened based on this information; as new accounts are generated, managers must rearrange the human capital, resources, systems, and structures necessary to monetize the advantage. However, because consumer profiles, competitor behaviors, and other market forces change, any current advantage is fleeting and new ones must be identified to grow revenues. Constant change, or moving from one competitive advantage to the next, is at the core of Capital One's strategy and identity.

Flexible Organization

An agile organization is necessary to adapt quickly to new competitive advantages. Capital One's approach to creating a flexible organization begins with a hiring process that selects for people who like change. As part of the rigorous interviewing process, candidates are asked about their leadership of and learning from change. The interviewers also focus on identifying people who have a passion for excellence and collaborate well with others.

Complimenting the hiring process is an organization structure that is decentralized and fluid. Capital One managers like to say, "what gets resourced, gets done," and so the organization has traditionally relied on a few tiers of responsibility instead of multiple layers of management. This has pushed decision-making down into the organization and allowed people to take on a variety of tasks without having to worry about job descriptions and pay grades.

For example, associates can have three or four bosses in a year. Suzanne Newton, an HR (human resources) client consultant, described her first year experiences, "All the change does take some getting used to, you really learn to develop your own ability to change. As an intern, I facilitated organization change projects and worked on the Building Change Capability project. Shortly after I became fulltime, I was asked to join the cultural integration team to support our bank acquisition. It was tough to have to refocus on a narrower set of tasks and to figure out how a new boss preferred working. When Katrina hit, a whole new, but temporary team, was assembled with new leadership to help in disaster relief. It was dizzying at first, but it really helped me to understand that every shift, every change was made to align resources to the highest priority work...there's always a line of sight."

An adaptable performance management system completes Capital One's flexible design. It keeps managers and associates focused on current performance as well as change. Carol Anderson leads the performance management process and notes, "One overlay to the whole performance management strategy is that the actual philosophy and core infrastructure of the program has not changed. We've always had a system that included 360-degree feedback and well-grounded compensation models. And importantly, there's always been an equal emphasis on rewarding current results as well as developing and demonstrating competencies we think are important for the future." This ongoing balance of rewarding results *and* the development of competencies allow Capital One to adjust the criteria for current performance, but also encourage associates and managers to learn new skills for future success.

However, Capital One's agile design was not complete. What is not apparent in the above description is the way Capital One was able to transition from one advantage to another. That is, while the test-and-learn strategy identified the advantages, and the flexible organization features allowed reconfiguration of the resources and systems to support the advantages, the strategy and design could not, by themselves, orchestrate the transitions from one advantage to another. The missing built-to-change ingredient – what Capital One's organization effectiveness group saw and created – was an enterprise-wide change capability that gave the organization the ability to reconfigure itself over and over again.

DEVELOPING THE CHANGE CAPABILITY AT CAPITAL ONE

Events between 2000 and 2002 led to a general awareness and acceptance within Capital One that change was going to be a constant companion. In July 2000, for example, regulators imposed a memorandum of understanding requesting that Capital One increase its reserve requirements and tighten up internal control systems. The test-and-learn strategy was a novel business model, and regulators who understood (and probably preferred) more conservative approaches to financial management judged the strategy too risky. Although the strategy was centrally concerned with determining risk, it was the informal decision-making process, symbolized by impromptu meetings between Fairbank and co-founder Nigel Morris, that made regulators uncomfortable. The unexpected regulator announcement sent a temporary shock through the market, and Capital One's stock dropped 40 percent in one day.

Within days, the organization increased reserves, tightened controls, and created a more formal executive committee to review data and decisions. Although the stock price rebounded quickly, the increased cost of borrowing resulting from its damaged reputation pointed to an important strategic weakness—Capital One was too dependent on a narrow range of institutional investors. Its increasing size and related growth goals strongly suggested that the organization broaden its source of funds.

Shortly thereafter, Capital One announced its diversification imperative and, between 2001 and 2003, broadened its product lines to include auto, home, and healthcare financing. The success of the diversification imperative led to explorations of entry into traditional consumer banking-eventually leading to the acquisition of Hibernia Bank in 2005, and North Fork Bank in 2006.

Designing a Change Management Architecture

However, aggressive growth and diversification by Capital One often left associates feeling overwhelmed by the rapidly changing product/service offerings. Frequent updates in the knowledge base required of associates, reorganizations that tested an associate's ability to remain flexible, and changes in work processes added to the stress. The organization needed tools, methods, and processes to help make change more comfortable and even routine.

Initial attempts to be more change-ready followed the conventional wisdom of the day. In early 2001, McDermott asked the University of Southern California's (USC) Center for

Effective Organizations to deliver a leadership development course in change management and organization design to 20 high potential human resource generalists. Using principles from the courses, participants conducted eight action-learning projects to demonstrate the value of a disciplined approach to change. The visible and dramatic success of these change projects created the support needed to continue the effort.

After the training, McDermott considered how to deploy this new resource. Neither of the two most common architectures – creating a center of excellence that managers could draw on, or assigning the resources to business units – felt quite right.

McDermott, and an informal group of HR associates and line managers convened to debate the approaches, worried that neither of these architectures guaranteed an enterprise-wide capability. First, if the resources were deployed to the line, there was a strong likelihood that they would "go native" and a variety of customized change processes would develop. Any accumulated knowledge and skills were unlikely to scale up to an organization-wide capability. Moreover, leveraging the assets across the corporation would still require the creation of a corporate program management office. Second, the center of excellence approach meant that change resources would be out of sight (and probably out of mind as well). Instead of building change into managers' thinking about strategy and organization, the organization would increase line manager's dependency on the HR function. They would be rewarding managers for "calling for help" and reacting to the need for change.

A new view. An alternative change capability approach emerged from brainstorming meetings and debates within McDermott's team: an "embedded architecture," where line managers possessed sufficient knowledge and skills to lead most organizational change. This approach deviated from both the deployed resource and center of excellence approaches. Instead of generalist or specialist, it needed "versatilist" managers that excelled at a particular blend of skills. Versatilist managers could shorten change cycle times because they did not need to ask for help-they already possessed the information and skills needed to carry out most changes on their own.

Tasking managers with change management responsibilities raised important questions about the role of a manager. In fast-changing environments, the ability to understand customers, markets, people, and technologies was not enough. Managers needed to be able to combine their business expertise with knowledge about change-so that as new momentary advantages appeared, the organization could shift quickly.

The embedded change architecture approach requires a simple, standardized change methodology. As with a single, shared information system architecture, there is a great deal of efficiency in shared models, language, and mindsets. For any large-scale change that requires the cooperation of, say, the credit card business, IT services, regulatory compliance, and HR, all parties need to be familiar and comfortable with the same change model. If every business unit has a different change management model and tools, coordinating large-scale change efforts is bound to be expensive and time consuming.

Selecting a model. The grassroots group created an internal website to display and compare the different change models and tools in use. The first surprise was that Capital One was using over 17 different change models, including General Electric Co.'s (GE) change acceleration process, Kotter's 8-step change model, Lewin's change process, and a variety of action research models. In addition, there were more than 160 different change navigation

tools, including numerous variations of stakeholder mapping processes, change readiness

surveys, project planning guides, and vision development protocols.

As the grassroots group had feared, the absence of a coordinated change strategy had

resulted in a broad range of change perspectives. Each practitioner defended his/her model and

tools as "best practice." During one video conference call to discuss the models, the group

struggled with the criteria for an acceptable model. An internal consultant presented a "best

practice" change model to the group noting that it had worked for several years within the

Capital One organization. The group began to ask questions to support the best practice claim.

"In what other organizations has this model been applied successfully?" (Answer: none) "What

studies have been done or articles have been written documenting its effectiveness?" (Answer:

none)

Two events pushed the group toward consensus. The first was the identification of a

change methodology that no one in the organization was using. In her Internet searches, Teresa

Spinicci, a member of the group, discovered the change management model developed by

Prosci's Change Management Learning Center. The ADKAR model suggested that successful

individual and organization change followed a process of (1) creating *awareness*, (2) having the

desire, (3) possessing the *knowledge*, (4) having the *ability*, and (5) being *reinforced* for change.

The methodology was simple, easy to understand, had a case database to support claims of

"best practice," and supported the principles from the USC training. This event helped to

overcome the win/lose dynamics of picking one person's favorite model over another.

The second event was more a function of serendipity than conscious planning. Steve Arneson, a human resources senior vice president (VP), was leading the Achieving Competitive Economics (ACE) process to understand the requirements of being a world-class financial services organization. He went to the group's website to find the HR-related change initiatives expected to come out of the ACE process. What he found was lots of tools but no help. The site, reflecting the state of the group's progress, was full of change management models and tools with no taxonomy to sort them out. Arneson saw clearly the need for a single, organization-wide change model, and he encouraged the grassroots group to identify it.

Implementing the BCC

During the 2005 planning cycle, the Building a Change Capability (BCC) project was formally endorsed as an HR imperative. This legitimacy provided the project with the management attention and resources required for implementation.

Spread the word. A key feature of the implementation process was two change courses offered through Capital One's corporate university. The two-day certification course – attended by both managers and staff – went deep into the change methodology. A key feature of the course was the opportunity to apply and use the model on real-life change projects brought by class participants. This helped to teach the concepts, gave the participants practice with the model, and actually drove change in the organization.

The second course was a one-day program specifically designed for line managers. It provided an overview of the methodology. It also linked change management behaviors, such as "describes and explains change clearly and constructively," in the organization's competency models to the organization's values of "communication." This helped managers see the connection between the BCC project and the performance management system. By leveraging the existing resources and capabilities of Capital One's corporate university, it was possible to quickly build common change-related skills and knowledge.

A major makeover of the grassroots group's original website also helped spread the word about change in the organization. The new change management portal featured best practice case studies and research findings; assessment tools to diagnose organizational features, resistance, or training needs; and templates to help managers develop change and communication plans. It also contained a variety of Capital One generated PowerPoint presentations that provided an overview of the ADKAR methodology, why it was important, and how to use it.

Transfer knowledge and skill. The BCC project set the goal of *eliminating* all full-time equivalents (FTEs) in the HR organization committed exclusively to change management. This confirmed that the BCC effort was clearly focused on distributing the capability throughout the organization, and *not* on providing change management resources to projects. Exemplifying the managerial attitude the embedded architecture was hoping for, Judy Pahren, an operations vice president in the card business and one of the first managers to go through the training said, "People know I know this stuff and I'm always getting calls from other line managers to think through a change issue. I consider it part of my job."

The BCC project targeted several visible, large-scale change demonstration projects and created an internal "buzz" for the methodology. It supported the change initiatives coming out of the ACE, a large-scale systems conversion project, an HR reengineering effort, and a workplace redesign process called the Future of Work. In general, they targeted projects where a "don't teach it, use it" approach could be applied.

For example, the Future of Work project involved shifting the physical workplace from "cube farms" to "neighborhoods" and to virtual work approaches. Members of McDermott's team deliberately guided managers through the change methodology to implement flexible work schedules, telecommuting, and virtual meetings using mobile personal productivity technologies, such as laptops, personal digital assistants (PDAs), and instant messaging. Leading the process through hands-on application embedded the change management capability in the manager's skill set and set the norm that successful change depended on a manager's active support and sponsorship.

Adjust and align the systems. The BCC project worked with Carol Anderson's performance management team to measure and reward competencies related to change management. At the time that the BCC was gaining critical mass, Anderson's team was working to revise the rating process as well as updating the competencies. Local champions, in the form of senior VPs who represented their line of business, were made a part of the performance management design team. The design team increased the number of change-related behaviors in the competencies and highlighted them in the training on the change methodology as described above. This sent a clear message about the importance of these behaviors for the future. The champions were able to reinforce the importance of the new behaviors in the implementation of the performance management process and provided important synergies for the BCC implementation.

Today, Capital One managers believe that meeting aggressive but achievable goals - which accounts for 50 percent of their appraisal score- requires them to lead change and build new operational capabilities. Reflecting this, one manager remarked, "If I lead change in the group but leave my people behind, I'm not doing my job and my bonus is at risk." The other 50 percent of the appraisal score is on the extent to which associates and managers are demonstrating the values and competencies of the corporation. The performance management system's consistent balancing of current results and competency demonstration is critical. It reinforces the belief that results cannot be achieved without change.

FROM CAPABILITY TO ADVANTAGE

In building an enterprise-wide change capability, Capital One used specific change projects to create an integrated, embedded capability that complements Capital One's organization design and strategy. Capital One's change capability marries a business leaders' intimate knowledge of technology, markets, and customers with the processes of change. The specifics of the business and the resources that leverage a momentary competitive advantage are what drive the capability. When the process of change is integrated with the content of the business, it creates an organization that delivers both current performance and future results. It creates an organization that loves to change. When we look back at the development of a change capability at Capital One, three important lessons emerge about how to turn a change capability into a competitive advantage.

Change-related Human Capital

If an organization wants to develop a change capability, it must signal that commitment by increasing the level of change-related skills and knowledge in the organization. It needs to measure and reward skill acquisition and provide learning opportunities.

Creating a Change Architecture

Capabilities are supported by organization design elements – structures, policies, and systems – that provide an architecture within which to operate. Capital One's embedded model ("versatilist" managers and common change framework) allowed change agents, change leaders, and change participants to share a common language and learn similar skills. It increased communication efficiency, the speed of change, and organizational integration. The embedded architecture was directly related to implementation success and the ease with which the organization built its change-related human capital.

Experience Builds Social Capital

Organizational capabilities, and especially change capabilities, do not come fully developed and ready to go, nor do they exist in a vacuum. Organizations must have experience with behaviors to build up the deep and often tacit knowledge that underlies a capability. If the organization has no conscious experience with change, then it cannot have a change capability.

Early on in the change capability effort, there was a focus on small but visible change projects. Using the "don't teach it, use it" approach, and in the classic tradition of organization development efforts, the early efforts transferred knowledge and skill to the line managers and built capacity for change. In addition, the lessons learned from the change efforts, were carried forward into subsequent change efforts through postings on the change management portal, learning events among managers and change consultants, and perhaps most important, conversations among the managers who worked with each other to solve change problems.

CONCLUSION

Like a muscle that gets better with exercise, Capital One's change capability got more sophisticated as it was applied to more and more issues. Organizations that are good at change, not surprisingly, engage in lots of change. At Capital One, the implementation and success of its change capability has left it with the feeling that "we can take on more change because with this new muscle, it doesn't seem like we are changing all that much. It feels like we are changing less because we are capable of handling more change than most organizations."

Organizations must carefully think through the calculus of investing in a change capability *versus* buying the capability when it is needed for episodic change. For some organizations, the investment may not be worth it. But in fast-changing industries, the shift in economic logic – from execution and stability to changeability – may provide the impetus, as it did for Capital One, to see an internal change capability as the "missing ingredient" in organizational effectiveness.

SELECTED BIBLIOGRAPHY

For more information about our thinking about agile, flexible organizations, please see E. Lawler and C. Worley, *Built to Change* (San Francisco: Jossey-Bass, 2006). Other books that have addressed this issue include S. Haeckel, *Adaptive Enterprise* (Boston: Harvard Business School Press, 1999) and H. Volberda, *Building the Flexible Firm* (New York: Oxford University Press, 1999).

For those looking for a general overview on the field of change, the leading textbook in the field of organization development is T. Cummings and C. Worley, *Organization Development and Change*, 9th ed. (Mason, OH: Cengage, 2008).

Built-to-change organizations are based on a variety of organization design principles. Jay Galbraith's *Designing Organizations* (San Francisco: Jossey-Bass, 2002) is one of the most popular overviews of the field. In addition, other articles and books contribute more specialized knowledge about certain features in organizations. For example, Ed Lawler's *Talent* (San Francisco: Jossey-Bass, 2008) speaks directly to the issue of managing people and building a flexible workforce. Mary Jo Hatch has done great work on integrating organizational culture with brand, image, and reputation to describe organizational identity (M. Hatch and M. Schultz, "The Dynamics of Organizational Identity," *Human Relations* 2002, 55, 989-1018). Finally, we were very interested in how Tom Friedman (T. Friedman, *The World is Flat* (New York: Farrar, Straus and Giroux, 2006) picked up on the idea of a versatilist in the second half of his book on globalization.

The work of Andy Pettigrew is also worth noting here. The results of his large-scale research program on innovation and complimentarity among organizational systems provides empirical support for the hypothesis that organizations that move to more flexible forms enjoy

important performance advantages: A. Pettigrew and E. Fenton, *The Innovative Organization*

(Newbury Park, CA: Sage Publications, 2000).

Chris Worley (Ph.D., University of Southern California) is a research scientist at USC's Center for Effective Organizations and an associate professor of management at Pepperdine University. Worley is coauthor of *Built to Change, Integrated Strategic Change, and Organization Development and Change*, the leading textbook on organization development. He lives in San Juan Capistrano with his wife and three children.

Edward E. Lawler III is director of the Center for Effective Organizations at the University of Southern California. He is the author of over 350 articles and 43 books. His most recent books include *Built to Change* (2006) and *Talent: Making People Your Competitive Advantage* (2008). For more information, visit http://www.edwardlawler.com.

BRIEF CASES

9-913-527
AUGUST 24, 2012

JOHN J. GABARRO

COLLEEN KAFTAN

Jess Westerly at Kauflauf GmbH

On November 21, 2011, after months of explaining, defending, and reshaping her stalled change initiative for sales call patterns at Kauflauf GmbH, Jess Westerly finally got approval from the director of sales, Klaus Kristoff, to try again. Westerly was the assistant product owner of CRM (customer relationship management) applications for computer and office supply wholesalers and retailers at Kauflauf, a fast-growing provider of subscription enterprise software headquartered in Heidelberg, Germany. As assistant product owner, she was responsible for positioning her group's product lines to optimize design, sales, and profitability. The job was similar to that of a product manager in other companies, and it required working with the designers, the global sales force, and her fellow assistant product owners to build an effective overall marketing strategy.

Founded in early 2002 as one of the first European organizations to offer "software as a service," the company had reached significant annual subscription sales by the time Westerly joined in March of 2011. CRM software services accounted for more than two-thirds of Kauflauf's overall revenues, and the computer and office supplies customer segment represented 30% of those sales in 2010. The company had grown quickly by targeting mid-sized and top-tier smaller firms that could benefit from cloud-based subscription software and by its differentiated approach to serving this market with highly qualified sales representatives who offered consultant-like services to clients.

Several weeks after completing the extensive Kauflauf orientation program, Westerly had circulated an email in June 2011, asking her colleagues in sales to redirect call patterns toward greater coverage of larger, more established potential purchasers of CRM software services in the computer and office supply business. Approved by her boss, Tim Roeder, who was product owner for all CRM services, her memo outlined her directive, explained the reasons behind it, and stated that she would be happy to answer questions for anyone who contacted her. (**Exhibit 1** reproduces Westerly's email.)

Robert Lin, the regional sales director (RSD) for Asia-Pacific, had reported almost immediately that his field reps (called "field consultants") were offended by the memo's implied infringement on their decisions about how to spend their time and its apparent insensitivity to the relationship-oriented nature of developing business in Asia. Westerly responded by carefully explaining to Lin her research methods, her data, and the long-run implications about the greater profitability of larger

---

clients. The RSDs of the two other regions received equally negative reactions from their field consultants, although the range of complaints was greater. The RSD for Europe/Middle East and Africa confided in Roeder that a number of his field consultants had not even bothered to respond to Westerly's email because they thought her recommendations were so uninformed as to be irrelevant. Roeder reported this to Westerly, saying that their dismissing her email out of hand troubled him even more than the loud complaints that Lin had reported and the reactions Westerly herself had received (see **Exhibit 2** for selected excerpts). It was clear, Roeder added, that Westerly should have done much more "pre-work with the RSDs and field consultants." In the meantime, he suggested that she "stay cool and wait to see what happens."

By late August, however, no discernible changes in call patterns had occurred anywhere. Westerly felt at that point that her efforts had amounted to a failed and feeble attempt at change that had cost her heavily in terms of credibility within the organization and with the RSDs and field consultants in particular.

Jess Westerly

An American who had lived with her family in Germany as a child, Westerly had a longstanding love of the country and a respectable degree of fluency in the language. She used her time in the Kauflauf orientation program to polish her language skills by developing informal relationships with colleagues, even though the program itself took place in English. Perhaps because of this effort, she felt warmly accepted at headquarters despite her double minority status as a non-German woman.

Before joining Kauflauf, Westerly had held a similar position with a rapidly growing CRM software service provider in the United States, where she had demonstrated great success in growing market share. It was because of these highly visible results that she was recruited by Kauflauf. Tim Roeder was especially impressed with her analytical capabilities and her keen grasp of market evolution. Her background included a bachelor's degree in computer science, a joint master's degree in systems design and marketing, and two years' experience with Microsoft before graduate school. She was drawn to the opportunity at Kauflauf because it seemed to combine her interests in computers, management, and international business. She turned 29 in February 2011 and moved to Heidelberg in March to begin her career at Kauflauf.

Westerly joined the other new managerial hires in a rigorous two-month orientation program at Kauflauf's Heidelberg headquarters, followed by several weeks visiting RSDs in the field. During this time she gained a sense of the corporate culture, which was deeply imprinted despite the relatively short time since Kauflauf's founding. In addition to spending their first two months at headquarters, all management-level employees returned there for annual conferences and other events.

Westerly was struck by how solution-oriented and relationship-driven the organization was and the extent to which its culture emphasized norms of collaboration, technical excellence, and mutual respect. She had also never been in an organization that was as nonhierarchical or in which informal networks were so key to getting things done across divisions. Colleagues repeatedly described the Kauflauf culture as unique and pervasive. Many joked that "no matter where in the world you live, if you work for Kauflauf you live in Heidelberg." Most considered this attachment to a common culture a source of pride; others occasionally found it frustrating. But the best-performing people in all parts of the company were seen as masters of developing informal relationships with colleagues in Heidelberg and in the regional offices.

Westerly learned a lot about such attitudes during her time in field training. She also noticed that Kauflauf's field consultants were spending a large portion of their time on relatively small accounts. Her detailed calculations showed that shifting toward larger customers with larger user groups would eventually yield higher profit margins for Kauflauf. (Each individual user increased the revenue stream from a subscription client, but required only minuscule additional development and/or storage costs.)

Eager to test her findings, she started working on a proposal during her orientation. She gathered extensive data to support her idea, and validated it by talking with several people inside the company as well as with classmates and former colleagues on the outside. By early June, she had officially assumed her position as assistant product owner for CRM applications in the computer and office supplies group. Shortly thereafter she sent out her ill-fated memo to the field sales force.

Kauflauf GmbH

The subscription software-as-a-service model was in its infancy when Kauflauf's founders left SAP to start the new company in 2002. SAP was a top-tier global provider of turnkey hardware and software solutions for customers seeking the most up-to-date enterprise management systems. In contrast, subscription software, like Kauflauf's, ran on clients' existing hardware and Internet connections, using cloud-based software and data storage facilities. This required a much smaller initial investment by the customer and all but eliminated internal software maintenance expense, which was covered in monthly subscription fees. Additionally, the subscription model promised continuous software updates to meet customers' emerging needs.

The founders positioned Kauflauf to disrupt established firms like SAP and Oracle, beginning with CRM applications created largely for German auto parts manufacturers. They set up shop in Heidelberg, a university town north of SAP's headquarters in Walldorf, and before long began expanding to other industries and companies operating across the globe. The venture offered a broad range of CRM and ERP (enterprise resource planning) products to a customer list that ranged from auto parts manufacturers and distributors to providers of computer and office products and, more recently, suppliers of medical devices. Kauflauf's open platforms allowed existing customers and new adopters to develop their own applications alongside the company's regular releases.

The earliest developers and sales specialists were a small group of former SAP employees and computer engineering graduates—almost all of them German men. Together they created a culture characterized by small-company friendliness and deep pride in superior software engineering. Kauflauf emulated the youth-oriented, anti-hierarchical ethos of many successful Silicon Valley start-ups. Most employees considered the resulting work atmosphere an important part of their professional image and experience.

Nevertheless, over time, the company's private investors began to insist on more structure and stricter controls. As a result, after about two years, a few "grown-ups," including Kristoff and van Hoorn, were brought in to build a sales and marketing capacity as powerful as the product development team. The two also served in the office of the CEO along with the Director of Development/Customer Support and the two founders, who were now respectively CEO and Managing Director.

Strong incumbents such as SAP and Oracle represented the early competition for Kauflauf's disruptive software solutions. As it made inroads into these companies' traditional markets, Kauflauf began to compete more directly with subscription software competitors located mainly in Silicon

Valley and Bangalore. In the universe of global online connections, however, physical location had little impact on a competitor's chances of success. Far more important were the software products' capabilities, the pace and quality of updates, and the availability of technical support from sales representatives and development engineers. The hands-on consulting and support provided by Kauflauf's field consultants, backed up by their ties to Kauflauf's development group, provided Kauflauf with a strong competitive advantage. This was especially the case with middle-market and small, but high-end customers.

Kauflauf grew much more quickly than its founders had imagined. By the time Jess Westerly arrived, more than half of its employees worked in product development and support services. Management believed that Kauflauf's rapid growth and strong financial performance reflected its success in both products and markets. The company enjoyed the greatest year-on-year revenue growth, greatest return on equity, and highest EBITDA (earnings before interest, taxes, debt, and amortization) of all its competitors, regardless of size.

Early Success

Kauflauf's founders attributed much of the start-up's success to its choice of target market and its differentiated approach to sales, in which highly qualified field reps offered consultant-like services to the *Mittelstand,* or middle market and top-tier smaller customers. (Kauflauf currently defined middle-market customers as having revenues between €100 million and €1 billion.) Kauflauf's sales force used a combination of client education, hand-holding, and customization to win customer accounts and loyalty. Thus, while SAP and other large competitors focused on larger clients and contracts, Kauflauf gained a top market position with the vast but underserved universe of small to mid-sized companies. The middle-market segment, particularly in Germany, comprised one of the largest markets for CRM and ERP products. This was also the case in several other Eurozone and Asian markets, and Kauflauf was beginning to make inroads in U.S. markets as well.

Kauflauf's customization process required input from its software development engineers to support the sales force's requests. But while the development group remained in Germany, the sales function was eventually reorganized into three regions to cover global sales. As part of this expansion, Kauflauf adopted English as the official corporate language in 2005. The original and most profitable product line, renamed "Parts Tracker," allowed middle-market distributors from all over the world to manage their own and their customers' inventory with a few easy strokes on a web-enabled keyboard.

The strategy proved so successful with auto parts manufacturers and distributors that Kauflauf expanded by modifying Parts Tracker and other CRM and ERP products to serve computer and office supplies wholesalers and retailers, and, later, providers of medical devices. At the same time, Kauflauf added a layer of product owners to shepherd each product line's development. Product owners worked with the design team and the regional sales divisions to prioritize new features and direct salespeople toward the most profitable customers in each sales region. **Exhibit 3** diagrams the relevant parts of the corporate organization.

The Marketing-Sales Organization

Kauflauf's marketing and sales organizations reported directly to the office of the CEO, as did the development/support services group (see **Exhibit 3**). Westerly's boss, Tim Roeder, served as product owner for all CRM products and reported to Director of Marketing Heinz van Hoorn. Westerly had counterparts with similar responsibilities in the original CRM product group, auto parts, and in the newer one—medical devices. The ERP products division was similarly designed, but the ERP assistant product owners' positions for office supplies and medical devices remained vacant until sales growth would warrant filling them. For the moment, Westerly and her fellow CRM assistant product managers consulted with their ERP colleague in auto parts whenever necessary.

Director of Sales Klaus Kristoff managed global sales through three geographic divisions: Europe/Middle East/Africa; Americas; and Asia-Pacific. In each region, a regional sales director (RSD) supervised a number of strategically located field consultants, so called because of the heavy advisory component of their work with middle-market customers. In addition, there was a global "inside" sales force, consisting of six representatives at headquarters and two in each of the three regions. Their job was to identify and cold-call potential customers to secure opportunities for the field consultants to demonstrate Kauflauf's cloud-based software products and services.

The Regional Sales Director and Field Consultant Roles

All three of the RSDs had worked at headquarters before relocating to develop business in their respective regions. They all had extensive experience in sales before being promoted to their RSD positions. The field consultants were a blend of local and international hires, all recruited centrally by the human resources (HR) staff in Heidelberg. HR culled the most promising applicants from long lists of qualified university graduates in engineering, computer science, or management information systems. All field consultants went through initial orientation; most returned at least annually to headquarters for further training. In the process, they tended to develop close business relationships and friendships with their peers at headquarters and in the field.

Field consultants lived and worked in assigned territories based on potential sales volume and proximity, to reduce necessary travel time. In general, they visited clients four days a week (often staying overnight in the field) and worked at home or in the regional offices on the fifth day. They were in frequent contact with RSDs throughout the week. Occasionally, a field consultant might call a friend in product development or customer support to ensure the feasibility of a promise made to a customer. These were strictly informal conversations, however, since the decisions about product features and updates remained with the product owners.

Kauflauf's sales organization stood in stark contrast to that of most competitors, which used dedicated sales teams and development teams that focused only on large accounts. Some also had dedicated teams for mid-market customers while others did not. Kauflauf management believed that its highly skilled and agile field sales force had been essential to its success in the middle market.

The field consultants prided themselves on being able to deliver technical assistance, cutting edge products, and superior service to clients while maintaining friendly professional relationships. They were paid on a straight salary basis, with total remuneration (including travel and other expenses) in line with comparable sales representatives from other companies.

The RSDs gave the field consultants broad responsibility for planning their own activities. As one RSD put it, "These are highly trained and highly motivated professionals. We respect that and see ourselves more as their mentors than as their supervisors." Another RSD explained:

It's not exactly the sort of industrial democracy or self-management we learned about at University, but there are certain similarities. Our consultants are proud of their expertise, and they learn to find their own way in our organization. They have no real authority over the development and customer support people in Heidelberg, so they have to build relationships with the people who will help them deliver for their customers. They need to persuade the product owners that their customers' needs are important enough to have priority in the pipeline of software releases.

I think of the successful field consultant as a three-legged stool that the customer can rely on. The three legs are understanding client needs (sometimes before the client recognizes them), understanding current and future product capabilities, and understanding how to get our organization to deliver the right programs, features, and upgrades in a timely fashion.

My role as RSD is to guide and motivate my field consultants to perform at their best in these three jobs so the customer has a sturdy stool to sit on. My prior experience in sales is very helpful when I think about what a field consultant needs from a manager. I know exactly what it's like to help a customer build a system that works for his business, and I also understand the pleasure of making that happen.

An internal survey of field consultants' attitudes revealed that they experienced the highest level of satisfaction from completing a successful sale. Nearly all respondents also offered stories of solving customers' problems as the next most important motivator. All claimed that monetary rewards were lowest on the scale of personal incentives. In fact, the RSDs had the right to award cash bonuses for outstanding sales performance, but to date two out of three RSDs had never made such an award. The remaining RSD questioned whether his bonuses had really served any purpose in motivating star performers and had stopped using them.

Reshaping the CRM Product Line for Office Equipment/Supplies

Westerly's responsibilities as assistant product owner included understanding markets and customers and establishing product development priorities to serve both existing and future customer needs. She interacted with RSDs and field consultants, on the one hand, to learn about and evaluate customer requests. On the other hand, she relied on her contacts in the development/support group to gauge the feasibility and likely time frame for meeting the sales group's requests. Finally, she attended trade shows and maintained contacts with outside sources to help establish a road map for improving Kauflauf's value proposition and profitability within her product group.

With guidance from Westerly and her fellow product owners, the developers coded, debugged, and delivered customized apps and upgrades throughout the year. Major new-feature releases took place annually or slightly more often, depending on the product group.

For example, before Westerly's arrival, Tim Roeder had mapped out the plan for translating "Parts Tracker" and other CRM applications into product families that could perform similar functions for the computer and office products market. The resulting software (including "Supplies Tracker" and "Equipment Tracker") allowed the sales group to describe "user stories" to help customers picture the advantages of partnering with Kauflauf. User stories expressed the capabilities that could enhance any manufacturer's, distributor's, or retailer's value proposition for its own customers, such as:

- I [computer or office supplies manufacturer, wholesaler, or retailer] can track my customers' sales and inventory as well as or better than they can.
- I can spot or predict gaps in my customers' inventory or product lines.

- I can suggest less-expensive or generic products to substitute for higher-priced branded lines.
- I can offer automatic ordering for standard, high-volume product lines.
- I can offer just-in-time delivery.

A recent, widely recounted user story concerned the adoption of Kauflauf's CRM product by Dart, one of the world's largest suppliers of computer parts, supplies, and equipment. Although the Dart purchase predated Westerly's arrival, she thought that it strongly supported her proposal to redirect call patterns toward larger accounts. The original contact with Dart had come through one of its small U.S. distributors, already a satisfied user of Kauflauf's CRM product. As a result of the distributor's introduction, the field consultant began to work with Dart's North American operations, which also subsequently adopted a version of the product. The application's immediate success led to a further adoption of a tailored version by Dart's Asian operations and, finally, its adoption globally. With these transactions Kauflauf had displaced three of its major competitors. From Westerly's perspective, Kauflauf's success with the client had resulted from a steady migration of sales calls from smaller to larger accounts, although in this case they were all within the same client firm.

Westerly planned to keep adding sophisticated user stories for office products CRM, while customizing and refining the existing software to serve larger customers. She expected to get feedback from the RSDs and field consultants on the kinds of user stories that would attract the largest customers in each of the regional sales divisions. Although she lacked formal authority over either the development engineers or the sales force, she assumed that her analysis and explanations would persuade them that her plan was the best one to pursue.

Redeploying Field Consultants' Time

In Westerly's opinion, Kauflauf's software products, its features development pipeline, and its web-based storage capacities were all robust enough to guarantee "dial tone reliability"(an industry term denoting perfect, non-stop connectivity)—the performance standard all major customers demanded before consigning their CRM and ERP data to the Web. Moving toward larger customers would entail mostly modest tweaking and customization by the product development engineers. Support services, and especially customer training, would benefit greatly from the expanded user base each large new customer would enroll.

Westerly respected the RSDs and field consultants and had started building relationships with several of them during orientation. She realized that working with smaller and medium-sized customers was often quite satisfying for the sales force. Yet all of her data indicated that Kauflauf was losing significant sales opportunities with its current customer call patterns. In developing her plan, she had first analyzed sales figures against the field consultants' time allocation reports. This calculation revealed that only 35% of the consultants' time went to customers who produced 85% of revenues. The remaining time was spent with smaller, less-profitable accounts. Recognizing the imbalance, Westerly sorted customers into six categories based on annual sales volume, as follows:

Sales Class	1	2	3	4	5	6
Annual Sales Volume (in €)	Over 3 million	1 million to 3 million	500,000 to 999,999	250,000 to 499,999	100,000 to 249,999	Under 100,000

Using these categories, she ran a series of simulations and found that regardless of assumptions, the model could never justify allocating field consultants' time to customers in class 6. Likewise, time invested with class 5 customers would yield suboptimal returns. If she reduced the amount of field consultants' time spent with these two customer classes by just 20% and reallocated it to customers in classes 1-3, the model showed a minimum 30% increase in overall annual revenues. She concluded that the field consultants should redirect at least 30% of the time they allocated to class 6 customers and redeploy it toward the other sales classes.

Westerly had shared these results with Tim Roeder back in early May. Roeder was intrigued enough to ask her for further analysis using a variety of additional assumptions. Each new simulation reinforced the previous findings. She explained the implications in terms of the field consultants' activities:

> If we ask a field consultant to triple the time spent on certain accounts, we're not requesting three times as many calls, or three times as many hours of customer contact. Rather, we're talking about tripling the overall time and effort spent on the account. This can include consulting with software engineers in Heidelberg, helping to develop meaningful user-training programs, offering tours of our facilities, or setting up meetings with other satisfied customers. Whatever the field consultant needs to do—both within Kauflauf and using outside resources—to anticipate needs and deliver value for that customer, we consider a valid allocation of time.

Westerly and Roeder agreed that the best field consultants already allocated their time in such a way. Those with good relationships at headquarters could get advice from developers almost immediately; others needed more time to obtain the help they needed. Roeder also believed that the newer, less-experienced and less-connected field consultants were the ones least likely to aim for larger accounts because they did not yet have the credibility or relationships needed to garner the necessary product development support from Heidelberg.

In terms of user stories, Roeder observed that consultants often complained about delays in getting their requests for new or customized features into the development pipeline: for every sale that failed to materialize, they claimed that a critical missing app was to blame.

Sometimes, in the heat of negotiations, a field consultant promised functionality that was not yet available or demanded a new app for a customer who later decided not to buy it. In such cases, the field consultant's credibility with developers and product owners tended to suffer lasting damage—especially for newer field consultants.

Field consultants who disagreed with the product owners' development priorities could escalate their complaints through the sales hierarchy. If the case for changing the priorities was compelling enough, Director of Sales Klaus Kristoff would discuss it with Director of Marketing Heinz van Hoorn, and occasionally the two would agree to revise the development pipeline. On the rare occasions when this happened, the request was invariably for a large, profitable customer account.

The June Memo to the Sales force

With Roeder's blessing, Westerly had sent out her memo in mid-June (see **Exhibit 1**). The memo included a brief description of her rationale for redeploying the field consultants' time. It was soon thereafter that she received the call from Robert Lin, the RSD for Asia-Pacific: His best field consultants thought she was being arbitrary and didn't understand their markets. There were rumblings from the other regions as well. Westerly contacted all three RSDs to explain that while the sales organization as a whole should spend less time with smaller customers, she respected the individual consultants' decisions about where to focus their efforts. She offered the same explanation to the field consultants who responded directly to her email.

Westerly had argued that it was really a matter of moving to a new stage of growth for the computer and office supplies product group. The RSDs countered that many small and mid-sized customers had become big customers over the years, and that consultants had much easier access to the decision makers in mid-sized and smaller firms. In contrast, for large customers they had to navigate a much larger and more complex client bureaucracy as well as Kauflauf's own marketing and development organizations, resulting in fewer and less frequent opportunities for closing sales. But even when Westerly's simulations had taken into account all of these arguments, the outcomes remained the same.

With data and logic seemingly on her side, Westerly had been disappointed by the lack of progress toward her goals over the summer. The inside sales group had found many potential larger customers for the field consultants to visit for initial demos, but in general the consultants seemed too busy to follow up. Clearly, her call pattern change attempt had failed.

Trying Again

Frustrated and embarrassed, Westerly revisited her plan in September. With further analysis she developed a new, more robust proposal. This time, she took pains to obtain approval one senior manager at a time. Tim Roeder had been enthusiastic about Westerly's ideas all along, and had supported her first attempt to implement them. Indeed, he had hired Westerly specifically to achieve higher sales volume and greater penetration in the global CRM subscription software market for the computer and office supply industry.

Roeder asked for support from his own boss, Director of Marketing Heinz van Hoorn. Impressed with Westerly's preparation and with the logic of her proposal, van Hoorn set up a meeting with Director of Sales Klaus Kristoff in November. Kristoff was skeptical, but eventually agreed to give Westerly's new plan another try for CRM sales and for global cross-selling of ERP subscription software as well. Kristoff's main concern was that Westerly's shift in call patterns might distract from Kauflauf's highly successful focus on middle market and top-tier smaller companies. By the end of the meeting, however, all three executives had concluded that the marginal changes in call patterns recommended by Westerly would not endanger Kauflauf's strong position in the middle market but could have a significant impact on both margins and revenues. As a result, the three agreed to endorse her new recommendations and gave Westerly a mandate to devise an implementation proposal by December 20. She could then start executing it immediately after the holidays. That gave her a month to come up with a comprehensive plan.

Westerly recognized that her June analysis had been stronger than her attempt at implementation and that it had cost her credibility and strained her relationships with the RSDs. Now van Hoorn and Kristoff were endorsing her proposal, but they wanted her to map out an equally effective execution program. She already had their support for her analytic conclusions; now she vowed to earn their respect for her ability to manage the change process as well. She planned to start by figuring out why her earlier initiative hadn't yielded the results she expected. Should she have suggested changes to the compensation system, or found other ways to elicit the field consultants' cooperation? Should she now plan a rollout meeting in Heidelberg for the RSDs and the best consultants? Should she include the entire sales organization in her plan? Should she enlist the designers' support as well? Who else should be involved? This time she was determined to succeed.

Exhibit 1   Jess Westerly's Email to the Sales Force

Date: 14 June 2011
From: Jess Westerly, CRM Product Owner for office equipment and supplies
To: Field consultants distribution list
cc: T.Roeder, RSDs

Subject: Redeploying your field consulting efforts

Greetings to my new sales colleagues at Kauflauf GmbH. I have met several of you already and hope to meet all in the near future. After weeks of market study and analysis, I have learned a great deal about market segments and potential profitability per segment. As a result, Tim Roeder has asked me to forward the following new guidelines for allocating your time with clients and new prospects.

Attachment 1* (Market Segments Analysis) shows that we have been focusing on small-to-medium size customers in the office supplies and computer equipment sector for CRM sales (classes 5 and 6) instead of on bigger companies in classes 1-3, much as we did with auto parts distributors in the early days of Kauflauf's existence.

Attachment 2* (Simulation Model) describes the basis of my analysis concerning potential profitability by size (class) of customer.

Attachment 3* (Simulation Results) confirms that by redirecting your sales efforts (i.e., call patterns and developmental work) away from classes 5 and 6 and toward classes 1, 2, and 3, you will find your sales and profitability performance improving dramatically. As you can see, I have run the simulation under multiple economic scenarios and assumptions, and the results support the above conclusions every time. Indeed, the research shows that if you reduce by just 20% the time spent on customer classes 5 and 6, and reallocate that time to customers in classes 1-3, you should increase your annual revenues by a minimum of 30%.

Therefore, to begin the shift toward more profitable clients, we request that you shift 30% of the time you normally spend with class 6 customers and reallocate that time to classes 1-3. The inside sales force will begin identifying call opportunities with these larger clients in your territory next week, and you can expect to begin receiving their leads by July 1.

It goes without saying that I am available to answer any questions and provide further details. Please email or call me at any time if you wish to discuss this revised time allocation for your sales calls.

*[Casewriter's note: Selected content from the attachments appears in the text of this case.]

Source: Casewriter records.

Exhibit 2   Sample of Responses to Jess Westerly's Email of 14 June, 2011 (Excerpts)

- (From a 4th year Argentine field consultant [FC] serving South American clients, based in Miami) …Good idea for people whose territory includes a lot of larger accounts. Unfortunately that is not true of my market…

- (From a 5th year FC based in the United Kingdom) … I left [a large competitor] to join Kauflauf because I no longer wanted to be part of a three to four person team selling cookie-cutter solutions to large accounts, and spending half my time with bureaucrats. Please check my record. You will see that I have been very successful serving as a sales solutions consultant with both mid-size and smaller clients, and I have no interest whatsoever in changing that pattern…

- (From a relatively new FC in the United States) …Not a good idea for Kauflauf. We are geared up to do custom work here — it's our competitive advantage. [Westerly's former employer] uses sales teams and development teams but they do not offer the quality solutions that we provide…

- (From a 3rd year FC located in Lyons, France, sent to the RSD with cc to Jess Westerly)…Who does this American take herself for, trying to change our way of doing business? She appears to have no idea of my client base. If she doesn't understand my territory, I doubt she understands that of anyone else…

- (From a 42-year old University of Heidleberg graduate, who joined Kauflauf in 2002) …More than half of my revenues come from class 1 and 2 accounts. Your idea is good, as long as we don't stray too far from our sweet spot: the middle market. My major concern is that Kauflauf does not presently have enough development capacity to support more class 1 and 2 sales.

- (From another FC with a large percentage of class 1 and 2 accounts)…Your proposal is unrealistic at the present moment. To sell and service [class 1 and 2 accounts] requires a lot of support which we now get on a one-off basis. Kauflauf does not have either the infrastructure or the capacity to handle a major increase in class 1 and 2 work.

- (From a 2nd year Chinese-American FC based in Shanghai)…No offense, but you might try spending some time accompanying FCs as they make customer calls before you start changing call patterns.

- (From a very senior and successful Netherlands-based FC)…The whole proposal is not only unworkable, it is counter-strategic to the middle market emphasis that has made us successful from the beginning. We are four times as large as your former employer and are growing faster than they are. Your great ideas might have worked for them but are inappropriate for us…

Source: Casewriter records.

Exhibit 3   Kauflauf Organization Chart

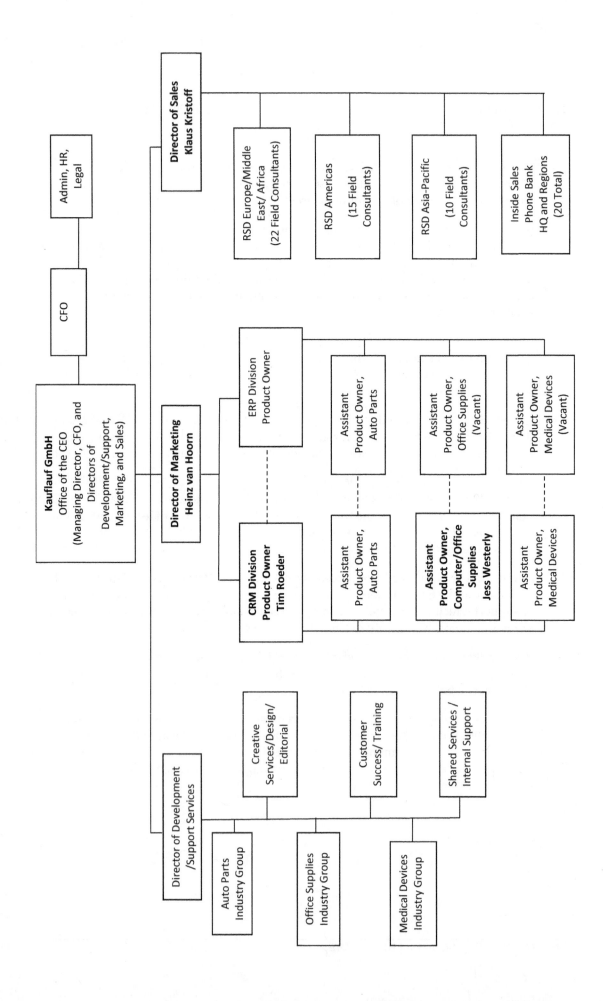

Copyright Acknowledgments

Index